PENAL REFORM *in* OVERCROWDED TIMES

Edited by

Michael Tonry

OXFORD

UNIVERSITY PRESS

2001

OXFORD
UNIVERSITY PRESS

Oxford   New York
Athens   Auckland   Bangkok   Bogotá   Buenos Aires   Cape Town
Chennai   Dar es Salaam   Delhi   Florence   Hong Kong   Istanbul   Karachi
Kolkata   Kuala Lumpur   Madrid   Melbourne   Mexico City   Mumbai   Nairobi
Paris   São Paulo   Shanghai   Singapore   Taipei   Tokyo   Toronto   Warsaw

and associated companies in
Berlin   Ibadan

Library of Congress Cataloging-in-Publication Data
Penal reform in overcrowded times / edited by Michael Tonry.
    p.   cm.
Includes bibliographical references.
ISBN 0–19–514124–5; ISBN 0–19–514125–3 (pbk.)
1. Sentences (Criminal procedure) 2. Corrections.
I. Tonry, Michael H.   II. Overcrowded times.
K5121 .P46 2001
364.6 — dc21   00–065232

9 8 7 6 5 4 3 2 1

Printed in the United States of America
on acid-free paper

Preface

Most Western countries are in the throes of something loosely and misleadingly known as penal reform. The usage is loose because it encompasses everything from diversionary alternatives to prosecution to expedited appeal of death penalty decisions, and it is misleading because one person's salutary innovation is another's disastrous mistake. Even wanted changes often produce unforeseen and unwanted effects. Norval Morris often quotes a possibly apocryphal Victorian administrator's observation, "Reform, reform, don't speak to me of reform. Things are bad enough as it is," and it is as apt now as it was then.

"Penal reform" is used somewhat more narrowly in this volume to refer to changes in laws, policies, and practices that govern judges' sentencing decisions and the operation of sanctioning programs from probation to prison. Sometimes these changes are aimed at making punishments harsher or more humane, but more often they have sought to reduce costs, increase efficiency, or make decisions in individual cases more consistent, accountable, or transparent.

This is the third *Overcrowded Times* volume. The first, *Intermediate Sanctions in Overcrowded Times* (Northeastern University Press 1995), had the emphasis its title suggests. The second, *Sentencing Reform in Overcrowded Times* (Oxford University Press 1997), like this volume, covered developments in selected U.S. states and selected countries. The goal of each volume is to document changes in what various jurisdictions do with persons convicted of crime, and what differences those changes make. For reasons I don't understand, there have never been robust scholarly or professional literatures on these matters. That seems odd, since the defendant standing in the dock is the quintessential instance of the conflict between the interests of the individual and the state. It would not be unreasonable to suppose that scholars and public officials would share and act on an abiding interest in understanding how such conflicts are resolved, and with what effects. In the United States, however, to use a parochial example, there have been but three short bursts of relevant research triggered by the fleeting availability of federal research funds—on sentencing guidelines and determinate sentencing in the late 1970s, on intermediate sanctions in the late 1980s, and on federally encouraged sentence-toughening laws in the late 1990s. Otherwise, the literatures are thin, fugitive, and occasional, and even the three bursts produced little of lasting value.

The bimonthly journal *Overcrowded Times* sought to document major penal policy changes in states and countries by commissioning series of short, nontechnical articles on particular jurisdictions in the hope that cumulatively over time they would offer something akin to policy histories. No doubt the articles are idiosyncratic and incomplete, but for most jurisdictions they have no rivals. *Sentencing Reform in Overcrowded Times* contains such series of articles on the U.S. states that undertook the most ambitious sentencing changes—Minnesota, North Carolina, Pennsylvania, Oregon, and Washington—and on a number of countries (particularly Australia, England and Wales, and Germany). A rationale for that policy history focus, at least for U.S. jurisdictions, is that new ideas and policies were being tested in the 1980s and early 1990s, and documenting their origins, development, and effects would help others later on understand what happened and why.

Most of what was purportedly new in the United States in the late 1990s, however, was emulation, not innovation. Accordingly, the focus of *Overcrowded Times* and of this volume changed from cumulative policy histories to documentation of penal policy processes in a wider set of countries and to generalization about penal policy processes and effects. For good or ill, English is the global language of scholarship and policy studies. More than ever before, we can look across traditional linguistic boundaries to see how other countries do things and, at least occasionally, try to learn from other countries' experiences. In recent years, therefore, *Overcrowded Times* set as its primary purpose the publication of informed accounts of penal policies in a wide range of Western countries and in Japan.

Overcrowded Times, which was published for the ten years from 1990 to 1999, was created to serve as an intramural newsletter for the State-Centered Program, a penal reform initiative of the Edna McConnell Clark Foundation in Alabama, Delaware, and Pennsylvania. The newsletter's scope and focus quickly changed in the directions described, but the foundation nonetheless continued its financial support for eight years. Kate Blake, Stan C. Proband, and I were the principal staff throughout and are grateful to Peter Bell, at the outset the foundation's president, and to Ken Schoen, head of its Justice Program, for their support. Kate Blake, the newsletter's associate editor and coeditor of *Intermediate Sanctions in Overcrowded Times* and *Sentencing Reform in Overcrowed Times*, did much of the work in preparing this volume. Like *Overcrowded Times* itself, it would not exist without her energy and talent.

Cambridge, England   M. T.
March 2001

Contents

Contributors

Marcelo F. Aebi is professor of criminology at the School of Forensic Science and Criminology, University of Lausanne, Switzerland.

Hans-Jörg Albrecht is director of the Max Planck Institute for International and Comparative Penal Law in Freiburg, Germany.

Andrew Ashworth is Vinerian Professor of English Law, All Souls College, Oxford, England.

Katherine Beckett is associate professor of criminal justice at the University of Washington, Seattle.

Anthony N. Doob is professor of criminology at the University of Toronto, Ontario, Canada.

Arie Freiberg is professor of criminology at the University of Melbourne, Victoria, Australia.

Koichi Hamai is senior research officer, Research and Training Institute, Ministry of Justice, Japan.

Michael Hough is professor of social policy at South Bank University, London.

Nils Jareborg is professor of law at Uppsala University, Uppsala, Sweden.

Josine Junger-Tas is visiting professor of criminology at the University of Lausanne, Switzerland, and visiting research fellow at the University of Leyden, the Netherlands.

Cynthia Kempinen is senior associate director of the Pennsylvania Commission on Sentencing.

Annie Kensey is a sociologist and specializes in correctional demography at the French Prison Administration.

Martin Killias is professor of criminology at the University of Lausanne, Switzerland.

André Kuhn is professor of criminology and criminal law at the University of Lausanne, Switzerland.

Britta Kyvsgaard is a research specialist at the Ministry of Justice in Denmark.

Tapio Lappi-Seppälä is director of the National Research Institute of Legal Policy in Helsinki, Finland.

Paul Larsson is senior research associate, Department of Criminology, University of Oslo, Norway.

Robin L. Lubitz is senior deputy director of the North Carolina Administrative Office of the Courts.

Rod Morgan is professor of criminology in the Faculty of Law of the University of Bristol, England.

Ian O'Donnell is deputy director of the Institute of Criminology, University of Dublin, Dublin, Ireland.

Fritz Rauschenberg is deputy director of the Ohio Criminal Sentencing Commission, Columbus.

Kevin R. Reitz is professor of law at the University of Colorado at Boulder School of Law.

Julian V. Roberts is professor of criminology in the Department of Criminology, University of Ottawa.

Simone Rônez is a statistician at the Office fédéral de la statistique, Bern, Switzerland.

Gerrit Schurer is the manager of Giant-Soft Company, Leeuwarden, the Netherlands.

Jane B. Sprott is an assistant professor at the University of Guelph, Ontario.

Peter J. P. Tak is professor of law at the Catholic University of Nijmegen, the Netherlands.

Michael Tonry is director of the Institute of Criminology and professor of law and public policy, Cambridge University, Cambridge, England, and Sonosky Professor of Law and Public Policy, University of Minnesota.

Patrik Törnudd was formerly director of the National Research Institute of Legal Policy in Helsinki, Finland.

Pierre Tournier is senior research officer at the Centre de Recherches Sociologiques sur le Droit et les Institutions Pénales (CESDIP, Ministry of Justice, Paris) and teaches at the University of Paris I Panthéon Sorbonne.

Anton M. van Kalmthout is professor of law at the Catholic University of Brabant, the Netherlands.

Reinier van Loon is a staff member at the Parket-Generaal of the Public Prosecutors Service, The Hague, the Netherlands.

Richard D. Van Wagenen is criminal justice policy adviser to the governor of Washington. Previously, he was executive officer of the Washington State Sentencing Guidelines Commission.

Bruce Western is assistant professor in the department of sociology and faculty associate at the Office of Population Research at Princeton University.

Ronald F. Wright is professor of law at the Wake Forest University School of Law, Winston-Salem, North Carolina.

PENAL REFORM *in* OVERCROWDED TIMES

Introduction:
Penal Policies at the
Beginning of the
Twenty-First Century

Penal reform is or recently has been on the policy agenda of every Western jurisdiction. The details vary, but everywhere change is under way or under consideration. Scandinavian countries have recast their sentencing laws and created new sanctions. Other Western European countries have adopted new systems of prosecutorial guidelines, plea bargaining, day fines, electronic monitoring, and community service. Most U.S. jurisdictions have comprehensively overhauled their sentencing laws and policies, usually to reduce officials' discretion and to make penalties harsher. England and Wales and several Australian states have followed the U.S. lead and adopted similar policies in diluted forms. Sometimes, in some countries, notably Sweden (Jareborg 1995) and Finland (Lappi-Seppälä 2001), changes have been premised on human rights considerations. In a number of countries, changes have resulted from political and popular pressures that Anthony Bottoms famously called "populist punitiveness" (Bottoms 1995).

And these are overcrowded times in the prisons of many countries. The more than 2 million people behind bars in U.S. jails and prisons constitute 700 of every 100,000 residents. If children and those over 65 are dropped from the denominator, between one and two of every 100 adult Americans is locked up. Those rates are five times higher than at any time in the twentieth century prior to 1973, when they began their unprecedented climb.

But the United States is not alone. Imprisonment rates have increased and sentences become harsher in many countries. In Holland (Tak 2001; Junger-Tas, in this volume), England (Ashworth 2001), Italy (Kuhn, in this volume), Portugal (Kuhn, in this volume), and some Australian states (Freiberg 2001), imprisonment rates are higher than at any time in the twentieth century. In France, the numbers of people sentenced to imprisonment and average sentence lengths have increased, and American-style population increases have been avoided largely by serendipitous use of broad-based amnesties and commutations (Kensey and Tournier, in this volume). Elsewhere, for example, in Germany (Weigend 2001), imprisonment

3

use and rates have increased moderately or fluctuated. Only in a few countries, most notably Japan (Hamai, in this volume) and Finland (Lappi-Seppälä 2001), did incarceration rates decline substantially in recent decades.

The articles in this volume describe and assess penal policy trends in many countries and in selected U.S. states. The articles stand alone and speak for themselves, so I see no point in summarizing them here. Instead, this introduction tries to set a stage by discussing why penal policy is important, why it is at the center of political contention in many places, and why it is important that countries attempt to learn from one another's experiences.

The Importance of Penal Policy

Penal policy encompasses the fundamental values of freedom from fear and harm and the right to be let alone. Whether directly through deterrence, incapacitation, and rehabilitation; indirectly through community, developmental, and situational crime prevention; or diffusely through norm-reinforcement, socialization, and moral-educative effects, criminal justice systems influence levels and patterns of crime. And the state's authority to take power over citizens in the name of law enforcement or crime prevention impinges on and often diminishes the autonomy and liberty of citizens.

It is not easy to get the balance right. Too little security, and the state fails to satisfy an irreducible core obligation. Too much, and it intrudes unduly and un-justly on citizens' liberty. Herbert Packer (1968) encapsulated these competing interests in the terms "the crime control model" and "the due process model." The first gives primacy to protecting citizens from disorder and insecurity, the second to protecting citizens from unwarranted intrusions. Neither can be realized without sacrifice, and pursuing one singlemindedly necessarily incurs sacrifices to the other.

How societies balance these competing interests varies over time. I use the contemporary United States as a frame of reference because I know it best and because in penal policy terms it is on most issues the extreme case. U.S. courts and legislators gave relatively greater weight to due process values in the 1960s, and accordingly less to crime control values, than they have since. In 2001, pol-icymakers, and, implicitly, citizens, in a state like California, which enacted broadly defined three-strikes and sexual psychopath laws, give less weight to due process values than do policymakers and citizens in a state like Washington, which enacted such laws narrowly, or in Maine, which did not enact such laws at all.

The balance also varies across space. While it was conventional to argue that U.S. law in the 1950s through the 1970s gave greater weight to due process values than did the inquisitory processes of Western Europe, at the beginning of the twenty-first century that is no longer true. As U.S. enthusiasm has waned, Euro-pean enthusiasm, under the influence of the European Human Rights Convention (Kurki 2001; Morgan 2001), has waxed. Professor Hans-Heinrich Jeschek, found-ing and long-time director of the Max Planck Institute for International and Com-parative Penal Law in Freiburg, Germany, has told me of his dismay that U.S.

courts and lawmakers in the 1980s and 1990s so extensively repudiated values that post–World War II German policymakers and scholars greatly admired and sought to emulate and entrench in the German constitution and legal system.

Examples can be given of changes and differences in the balance of influence of crime control and due process values. These include capital punishment, incarceration, defendants' procedural protections, and acceptance of international human rights standards. By all those criteria, the United States is a country committed more to crime control and less to due process values in 2001 than any Western European or other major English-speaking country, or than it itself was in 1970.

Concerning capital punishment, for example, there was a de facto moratorium in 1970 and a widespread belief that the Supreme Court would soon declare the death penalty unconstitutional. In 1999, capital punishment was authorized in 38 states and the federal system, 98 people were executed, and at year's end 3,625 were on death row (Death Penalty Information Center 2000). No Western European country, or Australia, Canada, England, or New Zealand, allows capital punishment. Courts in South Africa and Hungary declared their countries' capital punishment laws unconstitutional, and the dozens of Eastern and Southern European countries that joined the Council of Europe agreed to forgo capital punishment as a condition of membership.

Concerning incarceration, the U.S. rate of 700 per 100,000 population in 1999 was almost five times the 1970 U.S. rate of 150 per 100,000 (Maguire and Pastore 2000). It was also five times the rates in 2000 of Portugal, New Zealand, and England, the Western countries that confine the next largest fractions of their residents. Similarly, in 1970, U.S. mandatory minimum sentences were modest in scope and severity, there were no meaningful three-strikes or sexual-psychopath laws, and few prisoners were sentenced to terms of life without possibility of parole or to nonparolable terms measured in decades. All of those sentences, including lengthy mandatory minimums, are commonplace in America in 2001 and rare or nonexistent elsewhere.

Concerning defendants' procedural protections, the names of the Warren Court compared with the Burger and Rehnquist Courts have come in the United States to symbolize courts that are and are not deeply concerned with ensuring that defendants are fairly treated. By contrast, in Europe, the influences of the European Human Rights Court and Convention have steadily increased, and constitutional courts of individual countries have become more protective of defendants' interests. Even in England, committed for centuries to the constitutional principle of parliamentary supremacy and the related idea that there can be no written constitution, the provisions of the European Convention of Human Rights became enforceable in courts in fall 2000. Thus, the European Court's more protective approach to criminal procedure became part of English law.

Finally, concerning international human rights norms, the United States is notorious in the international community for its unwillingness to subject itself to the jurisdiction of international human rights treaties or institutions. When it appears to do so, it does so only sophistically by adopting ratification qualifications that provisions are adopted only insofar as they are consistent with the holdings of U.S. courts as they construe parallel provisions of the U.S. Constitution (Albrecht 2001; Kurki 2001).

My guess is that most informed Western observers outside the United States (e.g., Pfeiffer 1996; Windlesham 1998) would say that contemporary U.S. penal policies get the balance between crime control and due process wrong. An extreme example is the retention of capital punishment generally and particularly recent placement of Supreme Court imprimaturs on the execution of mentally retarded people and people who were 16 or 17 years old when they committed their crimes. Another is real-offense sentencing in the federal courts—the practice of sentencing offenders for all crimes the judge by a civil law standard of proof finds they committed, even if charges for some of those offenses were never filed, were dismissed, or resulted in a jury acquittal (Tonry 1999c). A third is the California three-strikes statute requiring a mandatory 25-year or sometimes life-without-possibility-of-parole sentence for some offenders sentenced for a third felony, no matter how trivial. Notorious examples include such third felonies as taking two pieces of pizza and selling a few grams of marijuana (Zimring, Hawkins, and Kamin 2000).

Much more important though than characterization of contemporary U.S. practices is recognition that penal policy raises issues at the core of democratic values. The United States may or may not have gotten the balance between security and liberty grievously wrong, but setting that balance is a centrally important issue for democratic countries. For the past quarter century in the United States and the past decade in England, governments in power have treated penal policy as if it were not a centrally important subject but something subsidiary to electoral politics and as if only crime control values need be acknowledged. Although all Western countries have felt the pressures of populist punitivism, as many articles in this volume explain, most have continued to give substantial weight to due process values and human rights concerns.

The Determinants of Penal Policy

The extraordinary increase in the severity of U.S. sentencing laws and in the number of prison inmates, and the lesser but recently rapid increases in England, have precipitated a fledgling literature on the determinants of penal policy (e.g., Zimring and Hawkins 1993; Young and Brown 1993; Bottoms 1995; Tonry 1999b: Caplow and Simon 1999; Garland 2001). Many of the central arguments are plausible enough, but they raise more and deeper questions than they answer. Not surprisingly, perhaps, since the harshest polices have been adopted in England and in the United States, most of the writers (but not all; see, e.g., Wacquant 2001) are from and the writing is about those countries. Hans-Jörg Albrecht has pointed out that the English-language literature is a bit ethnocentric in its tendency to assume that the developments it explains occurred in England or the United States "and elsewhere," when often they have not (Albrecht 2001, p. 294). The phenomenon of harsher public attitudes toward crime and criminals, however, exists or is believed to exist in most Western countries, as many articles in this volume attest.

Most explanations for the harsher public attitudes in England and the United States are curiously parochial and invoke causal explanations that, if valid, should apply to many countries. For example, if the four forces of rising crime rates, economic and social disruption, postmodernist angst, and populist punitivism caused the modern shifts in U.S. and English penal policies (and Australia; see Freiberg 2001), why didn't they have the same effects in other Western countries that experienced the same things? Finnish policies have become less harsh and imprisonment rates have declined since the early 1970s and those in Sweden, Norway, and Denmark have remained broadly stable; yet the same four forces were not absent. Nor were they absent from Germany, where policies became milder and imprisonment rates fell in the 1970s and have fluctuated within a narrow band since; from France, where imprisonment rates seesawed for two decades; or from Canada, which retains in 2001 penal and sentencing policies not greatly different from those it had in 1965.

The four destabilizing forces affected all Western countries (but not Japan, which at least avoided rising crime rates). In most countries, both official crime data and, where available, victim survey findings showed substantial increases in criminal activity from the early 1970s through the early to mid-1990s. It is not implausible to hypothesize that increased victimization would anger and frighten citizens, that they would demand harsher policies, and that punishments would become severer and prison populations rise as a result. The evidence, however, doesn't support the hypothesis. In only two countries, the Netherlands and the United States, did incarceration rates rise more or less continuously after 1975, and in Holland the rise was not attributable primarily to the enactment of harsher laws.

Nor, relatedly, is it implausible to assume that crime and punishment trends would move in parallel: increased crime rates would produce more arrests, convictions, and sentences, and prison use would increase accordingly. Something like this seems to have happened in Holland (Junger-Tas, in this volume), where rising prison admissions and harsher sentences imposed by judges are the primary explanations for rising prison populations, but crime rates increased in most Western countries and no other except the United States and Holland experienced continuously rising prison populations.

The other three destabilizing forces—economic and social disruption, postmodernist angst, and populist punitivism—I discuss together for the reason that they were ubiquitous. What we see is as affected by when we look as by where we stand, and so it is hard to know whether the past quarter-century has experienced more and more profound disruption than any other. Whether or not recent decades have been more disrupted than others, no one can disagree that there have been major social, political, and technological changes. These include the economic restructuring and destabilization of work associated with the global economy, changes in social norms and institutions associated with the civil, gay, and women's rights movements, global population movements and the increasing heterogeneity of most countries, the end of the Cold War and the collapse of the Soviet Union, and the advent of the internet, e-mail, and e-commerce.

One linking of these three forces goes like this: massive social and economic changes have disrupted most people's lives, often traumatically and repeatedly; there is widespread resulting insecurity, unease, and instability that might be called postmodernist angst; when people are unhappy they look for scapegoats, and criminals, immigrants, and welfare recipients are easy and vulnerable targets. Crime rates have risen, and the mass media have amplified people's awareness of crime; ergo, populist punitivism, a mass phenomenon superficially about crime and criminals but really a displacement onto vulnerable targets of angers and fears associated with much larger, incomprehensible, and seemingly invulnerable social forces.

Lack of convincing answers to two questions seriously undermines this composite disruption/angst/punitivism argument. First, if it explains U.S. and English crime politics and policies, why have not the same forces produced similar politics and policies in Scandinavia, Germany, and Canada? Relatedly, why did these factors produce such policies in England only in the 1990s, at the end of two decades of crime-rate increases and in a decade when crime rates for at least several years fell?

Second, and more fundamental, are there valid bases for believing that the disruptions and insecurities of the past quarter century are worse or more important than those of any other period? Explanations built on postmodernist platforms take it as given that recent decades have witnessed social changes of unprecedented disruption, but is that true? The past century experienced, before 1975, numerous garden-variety economic recessions, Prohibition, the Great Depression, the Roaring Twenties, decolonization of much of Asia and Africa, the first and second world wars, numerous colonial wars for independence, many civil wars, the Korean War, the Vietnam War, and the Cold War, not to mention technological advances from the automobile to the computer to nuclear weapons. The direct and indirect effects of these events on individuals' lives and social norms, practices, and institutions were not small. In every era, I suspect, people attribute much that they dislike or disapprove to the seemingly unprecedented changes of their times and, with the benefit of imperfect memory and good-old-days nostalgia, believe these changes are more consequential than those of other times.

For these reasons, I don't believe that explanations of the centrality of crime as a contentious public issue based on the four destabilizing forces are persuasive.

There are, however, at least three plausible causal explanations for U.S. crime policy developments, but they suffer the limitation that they don't seem generalizable to other countries. First, Ted Caplow and Jonathan Simon have argued that elected U.S. officials have adopted a "governing through crime" strategy for winning elections (Caplow and Simon 1999). They argue that the breakdown of broad-based political parties and geographical political stabilities (e.g., Democrats in the South, Republicans in the West), the rise of single-issue interest groups, and Americans' lack of confidence in government have made it difficult for politicians to win elections by relying on broad positive appeals. Issues must be found that do not alienate important interest groups and that have comparatively broad appeal. Such issues tend to be negative: no important constituency is offended when campaigns are launched against welfare recipients, immigrants, or criminals, and criminals least of all (or, formerly, communism or the Soviet Union, but that negative appeal is no longer galvanizing). As a result, in order to win elections and thereby to govern, politicians have addressed crime issues in polemical and stereotyped ways. Because it is difficult to oppose polemical claims about emotional subjects with reasoned arguments, American politicians compete to show who is tougher.

Former president Bill Clinton is often said to have taken the crime issue away from the Republicans by deciding never to let the Republicans get to his right (similar claims are made in England about Tony Blair and his Home Secretary, Jack Straw, in relation to the Tories). It does seem to be true that crime has received less attention in U.S. elections since 1992, perhaps because the parties are now stalemated on the issue. Unfortunately, that means there can be no significant changes in U.S. penal (including drug) policy until elected officials are willing to risk being accused of softness. Most politicians' risk aversiveness makes that unlikely anytime soon.

The governing-through-crime argument is coherent and plausible. However, the U.S. background story doesn't apply to England, where a similar crime policy stalemate is in place. England still has two dominant political parties with strong traditions of party discipline, so the need to appeal to a fractured electorate seems less intense there than in the United States. Yet political risk aversion concerning crime policy seems as present in England as in the United States.

Conversely, the governing-through-crime analysis prima facie might be more applicable to European countries like Holland, Belgium, Germany, and Italy that have many well-established political parties and a tradition of coalition governments. However, no continental European country has adopted U.S.-style rhetoric or policy, and none but Holland has had a dramatic, long-term run-up in incarceration rates.

The second plausible U.S. account concerns race. Southern Republicans, and conservatives more generally, it is said (Edsall and Edsall 1991), appealed to the anxieties and biases of working-class whites by focusing on welfare and crime, two issues that are in the abstract racially neutral but that in media imagery have black faces. Voting for candidates who were tough on crime or welfare was a respectable way for whites to express latent or unexpressed racist sentiments. No one can credibly deny that blacks in the 1970s and 1980s were overrepresented among recipients of Aid to Families with Dependent Children, the principal U.S. income support program for the poor, or among people arrested for serious crimes (Tonry 1995, chap. 1). This provided support for the political stereotypes. Nor can anyone credibly deny that crime and drug policies from 1985 to 2000 greatly worsened the disproportionate presence of blacks in jails and prisons and on death rows. Whether conservatives cynically adopted policies that would simultaneously elicit white support and damage black interests or whether they adopted crime and drug policies in good faith is a matter on which no uncontroversial judgment is ever likely to be possible. Nor is there any way to prove or disprove Löic Wacquant's hypothesis that modern imprisonment policies operate functionally to preserve the dominance of whites over blacks that slavery and Jim Crow no longer provide (Wacquant 2001). It is at very least not unlikely that such policies would have been changed had their disproportionate effects burdened middle-class whites rather than poor blacks and Hispanics (Blumstein 1993*b*).

I believe the racial influence arguments have considerable weight in explaining U.S. policies in the late twentieth century: conservatives did play the race card, many were motivated by or at least indifferent to the disparate effects of crime control policies on blacks, and many were less impelled to change policies that adversely affected blacks than they would have been had those policies adversely affected whites (Tonry 1995). However, the racial politics argument doesn't seem to have much weight elsewhere.

In England, for example, Afro-Caribbeans are imprisoned at rates even more out of proportion to their share of the overall population than are blacks in the United States, but this group has never been a potent political force in England or made up more than 2 percent of the population. Moreover, no one argues that any British party has played the race card for short-term political advantage as it was played in the United States, or that stereotyped racial politics have had or could have the galvanizing effects they had in the United States (I refer to antiblack appeals; many observers accuse both major parties of xenophobic politics in relation to immigrants generally). That racial disparities affecting blacks in England are worse than those in the United States seriously undermines any claim that racial politics have motivated penal policy changes and prison population increases in Western countries generally. This is confirmed by data showing that ethnic and national minorities, their identities varying widely with time and place, are as overrepresented in the prisons of every Western country as are blacks in America (Tonry 1997).

The third explanation is that contemporary U.S. crime and drug policies are the product of an interaction between long-term patterns of tolerance and intolerance of deviance, a series of late-twentieth-century moral panics, and the ubiquity and sensationalism of mass-media crime coverage (Tonry 1999*c*). The argument is based on historical works that show how long-term cycles of tolerance and intolerance concerning drug use, religious belief, sexual practice, and artistic expression predict popular beliefs and public policies. At times of declining drug use, for example, popular attitudes toward drugs become more rigid, moralistic, and unforgiving, laws harsher, and law enforcement more zealous. During moral panics, people tend to exaggerate the dangers and scale of things they fear, to overreact, and to adopt policies and to do things they will later regret. The argument, by analogy to drug tolerance cycles, is that as U.S. crime rates have fallen since the early 1980s, attitudes have hardened, voices that would have been raised against draconian policies in earlier times have been stilled, and severe policies and overcrowded prisons have resulted. Moral panics about crack cocaine, youth violence, and street gangs made it worse.

There is a ring of truth in this hypothesis as it pertains to the United States, but it doesn't offer much for other countries. English crime rates steadily rose through the mid-1990s, but imprisonment rates didn't. Most Western countries' crime rates rose steadily through the 1970s and 1980s, but their incarceration rates varied widely (Kuhn, in this volume). Crime rates in many countries began to fall in the early or mid-1990s, but there was no converse general pattern of an increase in incarceration.

Populist punitivism is a recognizable phenomenon in many Western countries. However, its origins are unclear and its effects widely diverse. Most systematic efforts to explain national differences in penal policies or punitiveness offer a few tentative hypotheses (e.g., Zimring and Hawkins 1993; Young and Brown 1993), as I have, and conclude that the explanations are most likely to be found in distinctive differences in national history and culture, as I do.

The Transferability of Penal Policy

Countries and their subdivisions can learn from other jurisdictions' penal policy experiences and ought to be better able to do so in our time than in earlier times. The widespread use of English and the speed of modern communication ensure that little goes on anywhere that cannot be learned about elsewhere. Processes of adoption and adaptation, however, are not easy or straightforward, and any hope that the simple attractiveness or effectiveness of an innovation in one place will lead to its emulation elsewhere is Pollyannaish. Human resistance to change, even concerning seemingly objective scientific developments (Kuhn 1996), often requires that there be shifts in paradigms before new ways seem imaginable. Mundanely, for example, parole and sentencing guidelines were nearly unimaginable in the United States until the indeterminate sentencing paradigm began to break down. Similarly, the political science literature on innovation instructs that policy-making is serendipitous and that better knowledge seldom leads directly to better policies (e.g., Lynn 1978). That transfers of policies and practices are not simple does not mean that they do not happen. At least three different kinds of stories can be told.

First are dispersion stories about innovations that seem to satisfy important needs better than previous practices. The gradual spread of day fines, community service, and prosecutorial fines offers examples (Albrecht 2001). Day fines can be scaled to offenders' means (prototypically, a day's net income) and the seriousness of the crime (with the number of day fines rising with the seriousness of the offense). Thus, they provide a punitive sentencing option that can plausibly substitute for imprisonment and be calibrated to ensure proportionality of punishment. They can spare offenders the pains and the state the costs of imprisonment. Day fines began in Scandinavia, spread to Germany in the 1970s and to Portugal and Austria a little later, and were adopted for some crimes in other European countries (Albrecht 2001). In the United States, where there were federally funded pilot projects in the 1980s and 1990s, and in England, where they were authorized by statute but abandoned less than a year after taking effect, they failed. In Australia, Canada, and New Zealand, they were not attempted. The day fine thus appears to be a sanction that appeals to the sensibilities of Western European civil law countries but not to those of English-speaking common law countries.

Community service — performing a specified number of hours of unpaid work for public benefit — began as an institutionalized sanction in California in the

1960s and spread to England in the 1970s, Scotland in the 1980s, and the Netherlands in the 1990s (Tonry 1999d). In the last three instances, community service was conceived as an alternative to incarceration, and the early evaluations suggested that it was used that way half the time. In the Netherlands, particularly, its use grew rapidly in the 1990s (Tak 2001). Community service has now been adopted in some form in most Western countries. It is seldom used as an alternative to confinement or as a punishment in its own right in the United States. Instead, generally it is ordered as one among many conditions to probation sentences.

Prosecutorial fines, also called conditional dismissals, began in the 1970s with German efforts to reduce case-processing costs and to find alternatives for short prison sentences. The German innovation began when prosecutors were given authority to offer a charge dismissal to offenders charged with designated offenses if they would agree to accept the penalty, nearly always a fine, that would have been imposed had they been convicted (Weigend 2001). The dismissal was conditioned on the offender's not committing other crimes. Over the years, the scope of conditional dismissal in Germany has expanded, and in 2001 it extends to very serious offenses and large penalties. Austria and Portugal soon emulated the German practice. So did the Netherlands, where the transaction, as it is called, constitutes a large fraction of case dispositions (Tak 2001). Belgium soon adopted the Dutch practice, and transactions there too make up a large share of dispositions. Conditional dismissal, like the day fine, has not been adopted in common law countries, though it has several times been considered by the English Home Office.

The second kind of story concerns innovations that serve important purposes but appeal to policymakers only in particular regions or countries. The day-fine and conditional-dismissal stories could be told this way, as examples of sanctions that seem to hold great appeal only to Western European policymakers. From a U.S. perspective, numerical sentencing guidelines are the preeminent example. Their demonstrated ability to reduce sentencing disparities, implement changes in sentencing policy, and tie sentencing policy to correctional resources led to their serious consideration or adoption in many states—initially in bellwether Minnesota, Pennsylvania, and Washington, then in a handful of other states, and eventually in more than half of all states (Frase 2000; Reitz 2001). No other country has followed suit, though English academics have flirted with the idea and law reform commissions in Canada and Australia have proposed its adoption (Morris and Tonry 1990, chap. 2). Holland in 1999 adopted numerical prosecution guidelines, but they are successors to earlier Dutch guidelines and were not much influenced by U.S. developments.

The third kind of story concerns symbolic innovations that serve primarily ideological ends. Most of these originate in the United States and elicit significant interest only in other English-speaking countries. "Boot camps," institutions patterned on military basic training, are an example. Whatever the good faith may have been of officials in Georgia and other pioneering states that established the first boot camps, evaluations soon showed that they were often used by judges as probation, not as prison, alternatives, that they cost, not saved, public monies, and that they had no effects on recidivism rates or offenders' postrelease self-esteem. Nonetheless, for a decade after these findings became well known, U.S. politicians from President Clinton down found the image of vigorous physical discipline appealing and actively promoted the creation and use of boot camps for nonviolent juvenile first offenders. This last shows the hypocrisy of the promotion of boot camps, since most members of this group are not likely to be sent to prison, making prison diversion and related cost savings rationales not credible. Many juvenile offenders are likely to age out of offending in any case but to be at increased risk of socialization into deviant values if placed in any correctional institution. Thus, the research evidence by 1992 fundamentally undermined the instrumental case for boot camps. Nonetheless, camps were eventually established in more than two-thirds of the states, primarily to demonstrate their proponents' toughness.

The only countries that I have been able to learn about that created boot camps are England, Australia, and Canada, and the first two quickly abandoned them. In England, the Conservative home secretary Michael Howard, generally characterized as the political figure who more than any other brought American-style law and order politics to England, saw the symbolic value of boot camps and sought their establishment in England. Prison Service and other Home Office civil servants were doubtful, and the institutions when established reflected some learning from the U.S. evaluation literature. Entry was controlled by prison officials, not judges, thereby avoiding the net-widening problem, and the institutions were enriched by various treatment programs (U.S. research had shown that the only boot camps that showed glimmers of positive treatment effects were those that were rich in treatment resources). The English boot camps were abandoned soon after the Labour government of Tony Blair took office. The Australian story is similar.

American-style sentencing changes, such as three-strikes rules, lengthy mandatory minimum sentences, and "truth in sentencing" (elimination of good time/remission, parole release, or both), are other instances of U.S. innovations that seem to have appeal only in common law jurisdictions. There are technocratic literatures on all of them. For three-strikes and for mandatory-minimum laws, the weight of the evidence is clear: in some cases they result in unduly harsh sentences, they foster circumvention and nullification by practitioners who want to avoid injustice, and they produce stark disparities in sentences of like-situated offenders. The evidence on truth in sentencing is more ambiguous, but, at very least, since neither parole nor prisons officials can influence release dates, it increases the dangers of judicial idiosyncrasies.

Despite evidence of the instrumental failings of these U.S. laws, they swept the United States, and milder versions have been adopted in England (Ashworth 2001) and most Australian states (Freiberg 2001). Parole release elimination also occurred in Holland, but the rationale was a civil liberties concern about disparities in parole practices that led to the automatic parole release of all prisoners at the first eligibility date, thereby retaining the name but ending the practice (Tak 2001).

The Spread of Innovation

It is inevitable that legal systems will converge and that countries will change institutions or practices to incorporate what look like good ideas developed elsewhere. New technologies spread across the developed world in months or years, and technology transfers are in principle no different in the justice system than elsewhere. For hardware like electronic monitoring equipment, prison security equipment, and credit/debit/smart card technology, the markets are already global. Human institutions and processes are slower to change, but the pressures of international human rights standards, common information sources, and internationalized professional communities will provide unceasing pressures in particular directions.

There is as yet no meaningfully comparative literature on penal reform. An internationally accessible literature on developments in individual jurisdictions is accumulating, however, and we can look across national boundaries in search of generalizations. Several emerge from the articles in this volume. First, the United States is no longer the only country in which politicians' short-term self-interest and punitive popular attitudes regularly trump human rights, effectiveness, or cost-effectiveness considerations. No one could expect that legal institutions or practices would be immune from popular attitudes or changes in prevailing norms and values, but in most countries elites at least long believed that legal decisions that affect individuals' liberty and property interests should be insulated from short-term popular passions and public opinion. That began changing in the United States in the 1970s. As such examples as boot camps, three-strikes rules, overbroad sexual psychopath laws, and mandatory minimum laws demonstrate, U.S. policy-making on penal subjects has for a quarter century been more symbolic than substantive. This has meant that evidence about the dangers of individual injustices or about the instrumental effectiveness of particular programs has often been ignored. Until the 1990s, the United States was the only Western country in which penal policies had been heavily politicized, but England and Australia have started down that path. So far, most continental European countries have not, but the growing influence of nativist and xenophobic social movements and political parties is likely to create pressures for the politicization of crime. Criminals are even easier to scapegoat than foreigners.

Second, continental Europe appears more receptive to rationalistic technology transfers than do the English-speaking countries. The acceptance of European Human Rights Convention obligations and the rapid dispersion of day fines, conditional dismissal policies, and community service are examples. The English have only grudgingly, after decades of foot dragging, accepted the Convention into English law, and the United States has refused to accept the application of any external human rights standards. Day fines and conditional dismissal have not been accepted.

Why civil law countries are more receptive to outside influence is unclear. Perhaps it is a by-product of the movement embodied in the European Union and many treaties toward a federal Europe. Perhaps European etatist political traditions compared with common law democratic traditions have left European countries more comfortable with the idea that elites and experts, not public opinion, should decide penal policy issues. Perhaps the typically stronger and more extensive social welfare systems of Europe have fostered value systems in which crime control policy is seen as raising more complex social issues than politicians in moralistic America believe or will admit.

Third, there remain strong cultural differences among countries that affect penal policy. Populist punitivism may exist everywhere, but its influences are widely divergent. The Swedes and the Finns continue to subscribe to a combination of humane and moralistic ideas that require punishments that respect proportionality ideas but involve modest penalties. The Americans and lately the English subscribe to moralistic ideas and accept the legitimacy of political expediency as a determinant of penal policy. This shapes the limits of the politically feasible and the practically possible. Penal values no doubt vary among Western European countries. Some, for example Holland and Germany, still seem to incorporate strong social welfare values. Prevailing penal values, whatever they are, necessarily shape and constrain penal reform.

Fourth, active humane penal reform movements exist in every country, including the United States and England. Attitudes toward crime and criminals, like attitudes toward most everything, move in cycles. When the next shift toward more humane values and greater acceptance of human weaknesses occurs, there will be people inside the bureaucracies and outside who will push for change. Maybe books like this one will help provide some of the information they need to make good decisions.

Penal Developments
in America

If American penal policy is likened to a rain forest, the canopy of sentencing statutes and guidelines overhead looks stable, but there is a profusion of new growth on the ground. Some of it, such as developments in restorative and community justice, initiatives linked to therapeutic jurisprudence, and renewed interest in rehabilitative programs, may break through the canopy and change it. Or they may grow so far and no further, or they may wither and die.

The Punitiveness Story

Three interweaving stories can be told about American penal policy over the past quarter century. The first is about punitiveness and imprisonment. The number of jail and prison inmates grew from 270,000 in 1975 to nearly 2 million in 2000, and the incarceration rate per 100,000 U.S. residents grew from 155 to nearly 700. The relevant scholarly literatures describe the changes in criminal justice policy and practice that led to the increases, the social and political developments that produced those changes, and the consequences for offenders and the general public of such vastly increased use of imprisonment.

There is little disagreement among researchers or policy analysts about the causes of increased imprisonment. Although crime rates increased sharply throughout the 1970s and during the late 1980s, use of imprisonment increased as a result of deliberate decisions to make sentencing policies harsher and sentences longer. The policy changes were exacerbated by countless decisions by prosecutors to be more aggressive, by judges to be more severe, and by parole boards to be more restrictive. Policymakers and practitioners chose to be tougher, and they were, and the prisons filled as a result.

There is also little disagreement about the mechanics of the increase. During the 1970s, increased rates of violent and property crime were a significant cause of increased imprisonment. Many more suspects were arrested, and caseloads went up from pretrial detention through parole as the increased numbers of offenders worked their way through the system. In addition, sentence lengths increased, and larger proportions of convicted felons received prison sentences. During the 1980s and early 1990s, the principal causes of prison population increases were the emphasis, as part of the war on drugs, on imprisonment of street-level drug dealers and, for other offenders, across-the-board increases in the likelihood that prison sentences would be imposed. Thereafter, prison admissions following convictions declined, but average lengths of sentences increased.

If there is broad agreement on the policy background to increased imprisonment and on what particular sentencing changes drove the increases in different periods, there is no agreement on why those policy changes were adopted. One explanation is that public fear of crime worsened and attitudes toward criminals became harsher, and both policymakers and practitioners attempted to respond to public opinion and became harsher as a result. Another is that Republican politicians, emboldened by the civil rights movement's fracturing of Democratic party domination of the South, cynically used crime (and welfare reform) as antiblack code words to attract white support. Another part of that indictment is that Republicans and conservatives more generally harped on crime issues in order to exacerbate citizens' fears and then promised and enacted tough policies to ameliorate those fears.

Other explanations are more structural and focus on changes in the U.S. electorate, on the pace and uncertainty of social change, and on long-term trends in tolerance and intolerance of deviance. The politics explanation, most commonly associated with Jonathan Simon, is sometimes referred to as "governing through crime." He suggested that Americans have lost confidence in the ability of government to do good, so broad positive social programs cannot win mass support. Politicians must find issues that can galvanize broad support without offending important single-issue interest groups, such as those for or against abortion or gun control. Emotional and stereotyped negative campaigns against criminals, welfare recipients, and foreigners satisfy those conditions, and politicians in the 1980s and 1990s used them. In order to be able to govern, politicians have to get elected, and in order to be elected they have to make demagogic appeals to crime.

David Garland and Anthony Bottoms have separately linked policy changes to changes in public attitudes, and the attitude changes to the increased uncertainties of modern life (for Bottoms, "late modernity"). Since the 1970s, residents of Western countries have experienced a massive transformation of the economy; repeated recessions; the feminist, civil rights, and gay rights movements; greater population diversity; and unprecedented technological change. Buffeted and unsettled by change and uncertainty in their private lives, and by the broader social trends to which they are witnesses, ordinary citizens are vulnerable to appeals to their baser natures. Blame for postmodernist angst and personal insecurity can be displaced onto criminals, the poor, and foreigners. And so, when politicians make those appeals, the electorate responds.

The tolerance/intolerance argument derives from work by historians on cycles of tolerance and intolerance in relation to the arts, religion, sexuality, and drug use. David Musto has several times described cycles of tolerance and intolerance of drug use and the ways policy and practice interact with the cycles. In times of rising drug use, law enforcement becomes laxer, few new antidrug laws are passed, and drug use is widely seen as a matter of personal choice. After drug use has peaked and begun to decline, law enforcement becomes more vigorous, harsher laws are passed, punishments become more severe, and drug use is seen by many as profoundly immoral. Wars on drugs, in their very nature, are seldom declared until after they have been won. Analogized to crime, the argument is that crime rates peaked in the United States in the early 1980s, and that, paralleling the drug experience, public attitudes only then hardened and policies toughened.

The Sentencing Story

Another traditional way to discuss penal policies of the past quarter century is to focus on sentencing. The indeterminate sentencing paradigm began to break down in the 1970s under pressure from declining confidence in the effectiveness of rehabilitative programs, attacks from liberals on disparities, discrimination, and arbitrariness in sentencing, and attacks from conservatives on "undue leniency." Upheavals in U.S. sentencing laws and institutions then followed for 20 years. States variously abolished parole; enacted determinate sentencing, three-strikes, and mandatory minimum laws; promulgated parole or sentencing guidelines; or did several of these at once or serially.

A variety of efforts were made to evaluate and document the avalanche of change. We learned a number of things:

Voluntary sentencing guidelines (many states) generally have little or no effect on judges' sentencing decisions.

Presumptive sentencing guidelines (Minnesota, Washington, Oregon) can affect judges' sentencing decisions, reduce disparities, and effectuate policies aimed at tying sentencing patterns to correctional resources.

Mandatory sentencing guidelines (North Carolina, the federal system) can affect judges' sentencing decisions but also shift power from judges to prosecutors and often produce unjustly severe sentences in individual cases, willful circumvention to avoid injustices, or both.

Mandatory minimum and three-strikes laws (most states) share all the unhappy consequences of mandatory guidelines, only worse.

Determinate sentencing laws (eight states in the late 1970s and early 1980s) can influence judges' sentencing decisions and sentencing patterns but, having been adopted by legislatures far removed from day-to-day court operations, are a clumsy and ineffective policy tool.

Parole guidelines (about twenty states) can make release decisions predictable and reduce disparities in prison sentence lengths.

The steam has leeched from the sentencing reform movement, and there is little vitality in the related research community. Most of the findings just summarized come from work in the 1980s. More recent research has confirmed but seldom moved beyond them. The last great burst of state legislative activity occurred in the early and mid-1990s, when about 30 states adopted three-strikes laws and a smaller number adopted truth-in-sentencing laws requiring some offenders to serve 85 percent of their announced prison terms. The last were adopted in order to qualify for federal subsidies for prison building.

The Fragmentation Story

The statutory sentencing frameworks in most U.S. states are an amalgam of institutions left over from the indeterminate sentencing systems that were ubiquitous from 1930 to 1975 and of accretions from the post-1975 sentencing reform movement. Some states, for example, have combined indeterminate sentencing's parole release and broad judicial discretion for most cases with presumptive sentencing guidelines for some cases and mandatory minimums and a three-strikes law for a few. These frameworks make up the rain forest canopies described in the opening paragraph.

The undergrowth is a congeries of programs premised on community, restorative, and therapeutic ideas. Many are in their early days, and few have been rigorously evaluated, but they are likely to presage the major developments to come. In practice, many programs reflect a combination of ideas. Sentencing circles and family group conferencing, for example (described later), might be said to incorporate restorative, community, and therapeutic elements.

Community justice is as yet more a rubric than a theme. Programs range from community corrections programs of state or county corrections departments that are so called only because they supervise offenders in the community to radically decentralized grassroots initiatives that try to "retain the conflict" and keep all state systems at arm's length. In between are many community policing initiatives, some community prosecution programs, a few community courts, and many community crime prevention efforts.

Restorative justice is more fully developed conceptually and programmatically than community justice. Though there are nuanced differences of view among proponents and popularizers, there is broad agreement that traditional criminal justice systems are ineffective and destructive and that organized responses to crime should aim to heal relationships among offenders, victims, and communities. Programs exist in most Western countries.

Restorative justice proponents claim that most premodern societies, and some traditional societies today, handle crimes and other serious conflicts much as restorative justice programs might. The first major modern development was a flowering of mediation programs and victim-offender restitution programs for young offenders in the United States in the 1970s, often under the auspices of religious groups. From there, central ideas dispersed around the globe, and activists began to reexamine customary dispute settlements of traditional peoples such as the Maori and the North American Inuit peoples.

Restorative justice programs are proliferating. Among English-speaking countries, New Zealand and Australia have taken the lead. In New Zealand, family group conferencing has become a central component of the juvenile justice system. Conferences include, besides a facilitator, the victim and offender, members of their families or close friends, and sometimes a social worker or policeman; the terms of any disposition must be unanimously agreed upon. In Australia, conferencing programs exist in most states, and the world's most publicized and carefully monitored pilot projects are under way in Canberra. In England, most programs involve mediation and restitution, are for juveniles only, and are controlled by officials. In the United States, the most common programs are mediation and restitution programs for juvenile offenders, but some programs for adults exist in the community and occasionally in prisons. Small-scale group conferencing exists in many jurisdictions, and sentencing circles in some. Circles derive from Native American traditions in which disputants, family members, and elders meet to discuss and resolve a problem. Prototypically, a stone or other object is passed around the circle, and whoever holds it speaks in turn. The circle continues until unanimity on a resolution is achieved and no one wants to say anything else.

Therapeutic jurisprudence is an offshoot of the "law and mental health" movement in the United States and focuses on the therapeutic effects of official processes for offenders and also for officials. The movement does not have a high profile in penal policy, with the important Trojan horse exception of drug courts. Drug courts are premised on the notions that drug dependence is a chronic relapsing condition and that reductions in drug use will yield reductions in crime. Drug courts, presided over by judges, oversee treatment success and failure. They provide firm but moderate and graduated sanctions for failure and support and rewards (mostly symbolic, including graduation ceremonies) for success. Drug courts have swept the United States and in 2000 existed in 700 sites. Their success has led to proposals and pilot programs for similar specialized courts to deal with sex offenders, family violence, and mental health problems. Many judges know and cite the therapeutic jurisprudence literature as rationale for the new courts. From a distance, it is hard to distinguish the drug court's therapeutic jurisprudence from indeterminate sentencing's rehabilitative ideal.

Beneath the canopy, then, lots is happening. So far, restorative justice, community justice, and therapeutic jurisprudence have produced innumerable local programs but no systemwide transformations. But they could.

The United States

U.S. Sentencing Systems Fragmenting (August 1999)
Michael Tonry

There is no longer anything that can be called "the American system" of sentencing. As recently as 1975, there was. It was usually called indeterminate sentencing, and it had changed little in the preceding 50 years. Its core features were broad authorized sentencing ranges, parole release, and case-by-case decision making. Its governing premises were that public safety and rehabilitation of offenders are primary goals, that decisions that affect individuals should be individualized, and that judges and corrections officials have special expertise for making those decisions.

Those features and premises have been under attack in most jurisdictions. Some states and the federal government abolished their parole boards, and some jurisdictions established comprehensive, detailed guidelines for sentencing. Every jurisdiction adopted one or more of mandatory minimum sentences, three-strikes laws, or truth-in-sentencing laws requiring some offenders to serve at least 85 percent of announced prison sentences.

There are now many U.S. approaches. Some states have guidelines with parole release, and some without. Some three-strikes states have adopted truth-in-sentencing; some have not. Some states have adopted mandatory minimum sentences for a few offenders, and some for many. And so on, through the litany of sentencing and corrections changes of recent decades.

At the same time, restorative justice and community justice initiatives have taken root and begun to spread. These developments start from different premises than do the sentencing law changes. One is the desirability of individualized, case-by-case responses to crimes. Most modern sentencing law changes prescribe sentences for particular crimes, and proponents invoke slogans like "do the crime, do the time" and "like punishments for like-situated offenders." Most restorative programs, by contrast, delegate to the victim, the offender, and others the decision how best to respond to the particular facts of particular cases. Many community justice programs are as concerned with solving problems related to crime as they are to prosecution and punishment of individual offenders.

Sentencing in 2001

Three conclusions emerge when sentencing policies in the 1990s are examined. First, there is no longer anything that can be characterized as *the* American way to organize sentencing and corrections. Thirty years ago there was. Every state, the federal government, and the District of Columbia had an indeterminate sentencing system in which legislatures set maximum authorized sentences (and occasionally, but seldom, minimum sentences), judges chose among imprisonment, probation, and fines and set maximum sentences, corrections officials had broad powers over good time and furloughs, parole boards set release dates, and virtually all these decisions were immune from review by appellate courts. The details varied (e.g., how much good time to allow, what was the minimum period before parole eligibility), but the broad outlines were everywhere the same.

In 2001, there is no standard approach. Some states retain parole; some have abolished it. Most states retain good time, but of lesser scope. Eight or nine states operate "presumptive" sentencing guidelines systems, another eight to 10 have "voluntary" guidelines, and one state and the federal system have "mandatory" guidelines; numbers are imprecise because systems differ so greatly that reasonable people can disagree over which adjective best characterizes a particular system. Five states have statutory determinate sentencing systems, and more than 30 retain some form of indeterminate sentencing. Nearly all are affected in diverse ways by recently enacted three-strikes, mandatory minimum, and truth-in-sentencing laws.

Second, sentencing and corrections policies are fractured and fracturing in most jurisdictions. What look like nearly monolithic tough-on-crime policies in many jurisdictions are being undermined from within. Many people, asked to characterize American crime policies, might describe the unprecedented and continuing expansion of jail and prison populations, the widespread movement to lengthen sentences for violent offenders, the federally encouraged truth-in-sentencing movement, the initiatives to limit prisoners' opportunities and to worsen their living conditions, and the reluctance of elected officials to advance policies that an opponent might characterize as soft. From this might be inferred unremitting toughness and widespread commitment to policies primarily premised on retributive notions of deserved and required harsh punishments.

While there is no doubt widespread support for such policies, that's neither the whole nor a consistent story. The burgeoning drug court movement, for example, is creating new diversion opportunities for many thousands of offenders, and in some jurisdictions eligibility is being extended to more and more serious offenses and offenders; increasing numbers of offenders who face mandatory sentences if convicted find themselves being diverted from prosecution altogether. Similarly, though these have advanced less far, restorative and community-oriented programs are moving toward dealing with increasingly serious crimes and offenders.

Third, not surprisingly, creative and ambitious people in many places are trying new things. Drug courts are one example. Efforts to incorporate broad-based community participation in corrections programs and policy setting are another. Efforts to incorporate restorative and community elements in individual programs or on departmentwide, countywide, or statewide bases are another. In many places, developments of the past decade are being extended: structured sentencing, recognition of victims' interests, expansion of community and intermediate punishments.

The Decline of Indeterminate Sentencing

If a group of corrections officials, judges, and academics from the mid-1950s were to be brought by time machine to our time, they would likely be astonished by the confusions, complexities, and inconsistencies of policies and practices in the 1990s. They would be surprised by the lack of broad agreement about the purposes of the criminal justice system and the goals of sentencing and corrections.

In the mid-1950s, indeterminate sentencing was in its golden age. Mainstream people, from members of the Supreme Court to professional corrections leaders and leading academics, agreed that the goals of sentencing were utilitarian, with particular emphasis given to rehabilitation and incapacitation. No one argued that "giving offenders their just deserts" or "the principle of proportionality" or "truth-in-sentencing" or "reflecting public sentiment" were overridingly important considerations. The closest the American Law Institute, in drafting the *Model Penal Code* (American Law Institute 1962), got to acknowledging punitive considerations and the role of public views about punishment was to provide that punishments should not be so slight as to "unduly depreciate the seriousness of the crime."

It wasn't so much that, after spirited debates, proponents of rehabilitative or individualized corrections policies persuaded others to their views but that, in the policy climate of the time, that's what most informed people believed. Law professor Albert Alschuler expressed this in 1978, commenting, on the early shifts away from indeterminate sentencing, "That I and many other academics [and corrections officials and judges] adhered in large part to this reformative viewpoint only a decade or so ago seems almost incredible to most of us today" (1978, p. 552).

When indeterminate sentencing lost credibility in the 1970s, nothing that followed commanded equally widespread support. Law and order sentiments have generated widespread support among elected politicians for parole abolition, harsher penalties, and reduced discretion, but many veteran judges and corrections officials have continued to believe, and newer ones have come to believe, in individualized decision making and in the importance of rehabilitative programs. Although for a time many people involved in formulating sentencing policy came to believe that just deserts, proportionality, and accountability were the predominant values to be pursued, that never-quite-consensus view is breaking down. As a result, there is no broadly shared agreement about the goals of sentencing and the values that should animate policy and practice. That lack of consensus has liberated practitioners and others to think new thoughts, pursue new goals, and devise new strategies.

Four Different Conceptions

Four competing conceptions of sentencing and corrections — indeterminate sentencing, structured sentencing, community/restorative sentencing, and risk-based sentencing — exist in the United States in the late 1990s. Indeterminate sentencing, which remains a reasonably apt description of a majority of states' systems, is obviously one (Tonry 1999a). Comprehensive structured sentencing is another; a number of states have promulgated guidelines for felonies and misdemeanors and for sentences to confinement, intermediate punishments, and community penalties (Tonry 1999a). What, for lack of a better or more widely used term, might be called community/restorative sentencing is a third; a fully elaborated system exists nowhere, but there is a remarkable amount of activity in many states, and such programs are beginning to deal with more serious crimes and criminals and to operate at every stage of the justice system, including within prisons (Kurki 1999). The fourth, which might be called "risk-based sentencing," starts from the premise that public safety is the overriding goal and individualized risk management the most promising strategy (Smith and Dickey 1999). The Wisconsin Governor's Task Force on Sentencing and Corrections (1996) proposed a fully elaborated system, and many features of Delaware's SENTAC system, including notably its five-level continuum of sanctions, are consistent with it (Gebelein 1996).

A number of things are striking about the four conceptions. First, and not unimportantly, they are conceptions of sentencing *and corrections*, and not only of sentencing. Each encompasses all the key decisions that determine the nature, severity, duration, or termination of dispositions of criminal offenders. This is important because it is inconsistent with much of the determinate sentencing movement, which saw the broad discretions of indeterminate sentencing as the problem, tight standards for judges' sentencing decisions and abolition of parole as the solutions, and corrections managers primarily as implementers of judicially ordered and statutorily prescribed sentences. This necessarily implied a limited vision of judges' and corrections managers' roles.

Second, although most states' current practices and laws include elements of each conception, in principle they are in some ways irreconcilable. Structured sentencing, for example, typically attaches high importance to treating like cases alike. Indeterminate sentencing attaches little importance to that value, and neither do community/restorative or risk-based sentencing.

Third, however, many corrections programs could be encompassed within all or several of them. Drug courts, for example, are probably compatible with all four but with somewhat different scope in each.

INDETERMINATE SENTENCING   These systems are the most familiar, in that they are still the most common, but they have received little recent attention. They are characterized by multiple overlapping discretions of prosecutors, judges, corrections officials, and parole boards and are premised on the need to make individualized decisions about individual offenders subject to legitimate sentencing and corrections goals that vary from case to case. Because the newer sentencing laws receive more attention from elected officials, national government agencies, and scholars, it is easy to forget that a majority of American jurisdictions continue to operate indeterminate sentencing systems not fundamentally different from those of half a century ago. Mandatory minimum, three-strikes, and "truth-in-sentencing" laws have nibbled at the edges of these systems, but they continue to handle the vast majority of cases in states (e.g., New York and Texas) that have them.

COMPREHENSIVE STRUCTURED SENTENCING   These systems have evolved from use of simple sentencing guidelines for prison terms in Minnesota, Pennsylvania, and Washington to much more comprehensive guidelines that incorporate intermediate and community punishments and related mechanisms for funding county-level programs. North Carolina offers the best-known example, but Pennsylvania and Ohio have also taken this path, and such systems are under development in a number of states. What makes these systems distinctive is that they set standards for felonies and misdemeanors and for prison, jail, intermediate, and community punishments. They also include mechanisms for tying sentencing policy to correctional capacity and for distributing state funds to stimulate and support local corrections programs.

There is a common tendency to refer to "guidelines states" or "structured sentencing" as if they were all variations on a standard type. While this was true of indeterminate sentencing jurisdictions between 1930 and 1975, it is not true of determinate/guidelines/structured sentencing today. Some determinate sentencing states have abolished parole release but have no guidelines, ranging from Maine, which has no sentencing standards at all, to Illinois and a few other states that set out broad general standards in their criminal codes. Among guidelines jurisdictions, some have "voluntary," some have "presumptive," and North Carolina and the federal system have "mandatory" guidelines. Some co-exist with parole release, and some do not. Some deal with all crimes and others only with felonies. Some set very narrow sentencing ranges, and some set broad ones. Some address sentences of all types, and some address only state prison sentences.

COMMUNITY/RESTORATIVE JUSTICE "Restorative" and "community" approaches need not necessarily be linked. A few programs considered restorative by their organizers operate within prison walls, and a few community-based corrections programs are based on restorative premises. In practice, however, most restorative programs are community based, and for convenience they are discussed together.

The "community/restorative" conception is at a much earlier developmental stage than is comprehensive structured sentencing, but it is spreading rapidly and into applications that a decade ago would have seemed visionary. These include various forms of community involvement and emphasize offender accountability, victim participation, and reconciliation, restoration, and healing as goals (though which of these goals and with what respective weights varies widely). The ideas of "community" and "community based" encompass a multitude of possible initiatives, ranging from the prosaic understanding of community corrections as anything not managed by state officials to the views of radical decentralization to neighborhood levels put forward by people who want to abolish the criminal justice system altogether.

Part of restorative justice's appeal, and one of its challenges, is that it attracts support from across ideological and political spectrums, ranging from the social gospel emphasis on reconciliation and healing to victims groups' emphases on victim empowerment, vindication, and restitution. This bears some resemblance to the early days of the determinate sentencing movement, when due-process liberals and prisoners' rights groups joined law-and-order conservatives and law enforcement groups in calling for replacement of indeterminate sentencing. In retrospect, shared views on procedural and process issues camouflaged stark differences on the substance of sentencing and corrections policies. Similar fundamental normative differences may exist among proponents of community and restorative programs.

A wide variety of initiatives fall under this heading: Vermont's statewide experiment with reparative probation boards; Deschutes County, Oregon's countywide commitment to community justice; Travis County, Texas's broad array of community participation initiatives; many jurisdictions' victim-offender mediation programs; and a diverse array of new approaches featuring sentencing circles, group conferencing, and related programs. Within the criminal justice system, some community police, prosecution, and court programs to varying degrees reflect restorative and community justice values. Related ideas are winning favor in many other countries, including notably, Australia, Austria, Belgium, and New Zealand (Kurki 2000).

COMPREHENSIVE RISK-BASED SYSTEMS Risk assessment exemplified by widespread use of empirically informed prediction and classification procedures has long been a feature of corrections management. What is distinctive about this conception is that risk management serves not only as a management tool but also as an overriding premise and objective. This conception aims at reducing risk to the community by specifying the purposes of sentences in relation not only to offenders' personal characteristics but also to particular times and places and tailoring sentencing and correctional measures accordingly. There is emphasis on community supervision — in particular, closely supervised programs with graduated and individualized responses to offenders' lapses and failures — and on using correctional resources to address conditions that give rise to local crime problems.

Risk-based sentencing is in some ways a reconceptualization of indeterminate sentencing, but with the important difference that individualized assessments of risk are seen as being a means more for achieving public safety than for facilitating offender rehabilitation. Conditions imposed on offenders, and enforced, are often related to minimizing the particular risk an offender presents to a particular community. The emphasis is thus as much on reducing crime risks in particular places as on reducing recidivism probabilities of particular offenders.

Like community/restorative sentencing, risk-based sentencing is largely inconsistent with recent initiatives to reduce or eliminate discretion and to link sanctions primarily to the crime, rather than to the criminal. Individual offenders present particular kinds of risks in particular places, and only sometimes are these closely tied to the offense that put the offender under justice system supervision. Operating such a system requires that officials be given substantial discretion to establish individualized conditions and controls and to enforce them through a flexible and efficient set of graduated sanctions.

Such a system was proposed for Wisconsin in 1997 by the Governor's Task Force on Sentencing and Corrections, and pilot projects are under way in two Wisconsin counties. This conception, like community/restorative sentencing, is less fully elaborated and less widely implemented than indeterminate or comprehensive structured sentencing and so far is not the subject of as extensive experimentation as community/restorative sentencing. However, it shares problem-solving and community-orientation elements with modern police and prosecution developments and is likely to receive increasing attention.

Similarities and Differences

Each of the four conceptions carries with it a distinct set of implicit premises, principles, and purposes concerning the aims of the justice system, the requirements of justice, and the relations between the citizen and the state. Of course, no one is surprised if in life principles sometimes conflict or if policies or programs sometimes seem self-contradictory or ad hoc. Table 1.1 sets out a preliminary effort to array the four conceptions along a number of dimensions.

Table 1.1 crudely characterizes the four conceptions as high, moderate, low, or unclear ("—") in terms of how likely they are to further or protect various possible goals or values of a sentencing and corrections system. The aim isn't to be definitive but to focus attention on what's potentially valuable, reassuring, or disturbing.

Table 1.1 identifies five kinds of values, goals, and interests and for some of these breaks them down in various ways. The five are equality, autonomy, participation, transparency, and legitimacy.

Table 1.1. Values Expressed or Served in Sentencing/Corrections Models

	Indeterminate	Structured	Community/ Restorative	Risk-Based
A. Equality				
Individualization	High	Low	High	High
Disparity risk	High	Moderate	High	High
Official discretion	High	Low	—	High
Risk of bias	High	Moderate	—	High
Desert	Low	High	Low	—
Proportionality	Low	High	Low	Low
B. Autonomy				
Paternalism	High	Low		High
Public safety	Moderate	—	—	High
C. Participation				
Victims	Low	Low	High	Low
Communities	Low	Low	High	—
Offenders	Low	Low	Moderate	Low
D. Transparency	Low	High	Low	Moderate
E. Legitimacy	—	—	High	Moderate

EQUALITY   The axiom that "like cases should be treated alike and different cases differently" commands wide support. The claim that indeterminate sentencing often results in disparities (like cases being treated differently) is a recurring criticism. Reduction of sentencing disparities is a major goal of many determinate sentencing laws and structured sentencing systems. The ideas that people should be treated fairly, especially by the state, and that fairness includes equal treatment, are widely shared, and present challenges for indeterminate, community/restorative, and risk-based sentencing.

In our time, the influence of retributive ideas makes people think of "like-situated" in terms primarily of crimes and criminal histories. Thus, when two people convicted or accused of the same crime are handled in substantially different ways under an indeterminate, a community/restorative, or a risk-based sentencing system, it is natural to see the contrast as an instance of "disparity."

That's the result of a particular way of thinking about "like-situated," and it is open to proponents of other conceptions to argue that two offenders who have committed the same crimes are nonetheless differently situated in terms of "rehabilitative need," "community connectedness," or "risk profile."

Proponents of community/restorative sentencing, for example, might argue that seemingly similar crimes can have very different effects on different victims and that traditional equality-in-punishment approaches ignore those differences, while community/restorative approaches do not. They might also argue that equal treatment concerns are less important when the goal of the process is primarily constructive, not primarily punitive, and when the offender must agree to any final disposition.

A focus on equality also raises concerns about administration. If officials who administer punishment or processes that affect punishment are not constrained by strong policies, the likelihood of arbitrary, idiosyncratic, invidious, and stereotype-influenced decisions is greater. Thus, another part of the attack on indeterminate sentencing is a set of arguments that officials cannot be trusted to resist temptations to be willful or to be influenced by personal biases and unconscious stereotypes. Because dispositions in community-restorative programs must be accepted by the offender, these risks may be reduced.

AUTONOMY   The "right to be let alone" is another core idea in American political culture that underlay the 1970s challenges to indeterminate sentencing. Libertarian ideas wax and wane, and individuals' insulation from government in the 1990s bears little resemblance to romantic images of frontier days, but the idea that moral autonomy and personal responsibility are important values continues influential. To many people, criminals deserve to be punished because they are autonomous actors who are morally responsible for their actions. To others, social disadvantage, disrupted childhoods, and limited opportunities make some offenders less morally culpable than others. To many, criminals have a right not to be punished more severely than they deserve. To many, the state has no business intervening in people's private lives and paternalistically making choices for them.

PARTICIPATION   The third important value, participation, was not explicitly part of the attack on indeterminate sentencing, though it may have been an unarticulated source of dissatisfaction. Pressure for wider participation is part of the criminal justice context in the 1990s. From the victims' movement have come calls for victim notification, participation, consultation, restitution, and vindication. From the community and restorative justice movements have come claims that victims, family members, and members of larger communities are potentially important participants in deciding how to respond to crimes.

There is some irony in modern pressures for broader participation in decision making about dispositions in individual cases. Most histories of the criminal law describe the removal of responses to crime from the community to the state as something to be celebrated. Having the state take custody of the offender's body and take responsibility for responding to his crime was a way to prevent vigilantism, retaliation, and other forms of self-help by the victim and the victim's family or friends. Likewise, the community as a place where passions and emotions get out of hand is often contrasted with the legal system in which formal processes and dispassionate officials protect offenders from unrestrained community pressures. Indeterminate sentencing in particular was commonly seen as a way to professionalize public responses to crime. Community/restorative programs, by contrast, often attempt to deprofessionalize reactions to crime.

TRANSPARENCY   The fourth value, transparency, is another low-visibility component of the attack on indeterminate sentencing that has become more explicit. The word "transparency" is often used to describe processes whose workings are observable, in contrast with processes that take place behind closed doors or opaque windows. During the 1970s, indeterminate sentencing was disparaged as "bark-and-bite" sentencing: the judge's bark often was much fiercer than the corrections system's bite. The "truth-in-sentencing" movement is premised on the notion that the public is entitled to know that offenders will suffer the punishments that judges order. This is a reversal of the indeterminate sentencing idea that important decisions should be made by dispassionate professionals in low-visibility settings.

Proponents of community/restorative sentencing might argue that the systems they propose are more transparent than any system in which responses to crime are solely within control of public officials. The transparency that truth in sentencing offers, they would argue, is theoretical. While citizens might know, in the abstract, that offenders will serve the punishment imposed, few citizens have personal knowledge of the handling of any particular case, or of cases in general. Community and restorative programs, by contrast, have a quality of "community connectedness" that offers a different and arguably more important kind of transparency. By including victims and offenders, their families, community members, and others (employers, neighbors, friends, teachers, social workers, depending on the circumstances) in the process, community/restorative programs are more likely to be known and understood in the community most affected by a crime than are traditional programs.

LEGITIMACY   The fifth value, legitimacy, may also have been implicit in the attack on indeterminate sentencing, but it has become better understood in recent years. People resent being treated unfairly, and ideas about unfairness underlay objections to sentencing disparities and calls for sentencing rules and officials' accountability. Work on "procedural justice" most famously associated with the psychologist Tom Tyler (1990), and recently extended to matters of prison administration by Anthony Bottoms and colleagues in England (Sparks, Bottoms, and Hay 1996), has shown that people's reactions and behaviors are strongly influenced by whether they believe their interests have received fair consideration and whether procedures that led to decisions that affected their interests were fairly administered.

This notion of legitimacy is somewhat different from traditional notions of due process. The latter are based on a substantive notion that people should be treated fairly. The former is based on empirical findings that people react better to decisions against their interests when they believe they have been treated fairly. It's a happy coincidence when doing what's right (treating people fairly) is more effective in instrumental terms than doing what's wrong (treating people unfairly).

"Legitimacy" in this sense is a major component of community/restorative sentencing, which is predicated on the importance of victim, offender, and, often, community participation in the process and satisfaction with the outcome. Risk-based sentencing, by tailoring dispositions to offenders' and communities' needs, and by providing certain but graduated responses to offenders' failures to comply with conditions, treats offenders as individuals. Indeterminate and comprehensive structured sentencing, by contrast, make little effort to elicit offenders' participation or agreement or to include victims or community members in the process.

These are all complex concepts about which reasonable people differ. In table 1.1, "proportionality," "desert," and "disparity" are listed under "equality." For people who see the sentencing and corrections systems as primarily retributive in purpose and primarily concerned in practice with ordering and implementing deserved punishments, proportionality and desert are positive values and "disparity" is an evil to be avoided. For people who see the sentencing and corrections system as primarily preventive or restorative in purpose, individualization is an important value, and desert, proportionality, and disparity are at most constraints. And so on.

Compared with the 1950s and 1960s, when indeterminate sentencing was the only conception in use or under consideration, and the 1970s and 1980s, when "desert-based" guidelines for prison terms competed with indeterminate sentencing, the four conceptions permit an exploration of sentencing and corrections issues that may lead to richer understanding and to better policies.

NOTE

An earlier version of this article was published in 1999 by the National Institute of Justice as "The Fragmentation of Sentencing and Corrections in America."

The Status of Sentencing Guideline Reforms in the United States
(December 1999)
Kevin R. Reitz

The "sentencing reform movement," begun in the 1970s, aimed toward the creation of sentencing commissions and sentencing guidelines in jurisdictions across the United States. In the past three decades, the new commission-based guideline structures have emerged as the principal alternative to traditional practices of "indeterminate sentencing," under which judges and parole boards hold unguided and unreviewable discretion within broad ranges of statutorily authorized penalties.

The idea of a "commission on sentencing" can be traced to Marvin Frankel's influential writings of the early 1970s (Frankel 1973). Frankel wanted to replace what he saw as the "lawless" processes of indeterminacy with an alternative model that would promote legal regularity. His chosen vehicles were chiefly *procedural* innovations, and it is possible to speak in terms of three fundamental procedural goals: first, creation of a permanent, expert commission on sentencing in every jurisdiction, with both research and rule-making capacities; second, articulation of broad policies and more specific regulations (later called guidelines) by legislatures and sentencing commissions, to have binding legal authority on case-by-case sentencing decisions made by trial judges; and third, creation of meaningful appellate review of the appropriateness of individual sentences so that a jurisprudence of sentencing could develop through the accumulation of case decisions.

Along with these procedural elements, Frankel advocated two major *substantive* goals: first, greater uniformity in punishments imposed on similarly situated offenders, with a concomitant reduction in inexplicable disparities, including racial disparities in punishment and widely varying sentences based simply on the predilections of individual judges; and, second, substantial reduction in the overall severity of punishments imposed by the courts of the United States in the early 1970s, including a general shortening of terms of incarceration, and the expanded use of "alternatives to prison"—what are now called intermediate punishments (Frankel 1973, pp. 58–59).

We may now fast-forward nearly 30 years to ask, in broad terms: what has become of Frankel's plan? To keep things in focus, for purposes of this short article, I offer an evaluation of the progress of the new sentencing commissions against the procedural and substantive goals Frankel originally set for them.

Frankel's suggestion that U.S. jurisdictions should create permanent sentencing commissions, which in turn should author sentencing guidelines, have been enormously productive of institutional changes across the country. In the early 1970s, commissions and guidelines were wholly new ideas and existed nowhere. As of mid-year 1999, as shown in table 1.2, 16 American jurisdictions were operating with some form of sentencing guidelines. In four additional states, fully developed guideline proposals were under consideration by the legislatures, and at least four more jurisdictions were in the early stages of deliberations that might eventually lead to commission-based sentencing reform. In a 25- to 30-year span of time since Frankel's seminal writings, this is a remarkable record indeed, unrivaled by any other work of criminal-law-related scholarship over the same period.

Attending closely to all three of Frankel's procedural goals for a sentencing system, however, the number of fully realized Frankelian reforms is smaller than first appears. Of the 16 up-and-running guideline systems, seven employ "voluntary" or "advisory" guidelines that are not legally binding upon the sentencing judge. Instead of Frankel's positive law of sentencing, these states have substituted hopeful recommendations. The remaining nine guideline jurisdictions, more consistent with Frankel's approach, have given various degrees of legal force to their guidelines. In virtually all of these systems, trial judges are required to follow the "presumptive" guideline sentences unless legally adequate reasons can be cited to do otherwise. In some jurisdictions (as in the federal system), the guidelines are tightly confining of judicial sentencing discretion, and it has often proven difficult for judges to find legally supportable reasons to depart from the guidelines. In other jurisdictions (such as Minnesota and Washington), although the state guidelines have force of law, the appellate courts have in general been deferential to sentencing judges' rulings that deviate from the letter of the guidelines (see Reitz 1997).

None of the seven "voluntary" guidelines jurisdictions has established meaningful appellate review of sentencing decisions—yet another failing under the Frankel model. And, among the nine presumptive guideline systems, only seven have authorized meaningful substantive appellate review of sentencing decisions. (An eighth state might be added here in an "honorable mention" category: Alaska has established a vigorous tradition of appellate sentence review, but one based on judicially created sentencing "benchmarks" rather than commission-created guidelines.) Thus, only seven existing guideline systems are currently operating with institutional structures true to Frankel's original reform model—and, indeed, the list may be shorter still. The Tennessee legislature discontinued that state's sentencing commission in 1995, although the commission's guidelines remain in effect. Permanent commission oversight of guidelines, which was so much a feature of Frankel's vision, is no longer in use in Tennessee, and one suspects that

Table 1.2. American Sentencing Guidelines Systems in 1999

Jurisdiction	Effective Date	Features
Minnesota	May 1980	Presumptive guidelines for felonies; moderate appellate review; parole abolished; no guidelines for intermediate sanctions
Pennsylvania	July 1982	Voluntary guidelines for felonies and misdemeanors; minimal appellate review; parole retained; guidelines incorporate intermediate sanctions
Maryland	July 1983	Voluntary guidelines for felonies; no appellate review; parole retained; no guidelines for intermediate sanctions; legislature created permanent sentencing commission in 1998
Florida	October 1983	Guidelines repealed in 1997 and replaced with statutory presumptions for minimum sentences for felonies; appellate review for mitigated departures; parole abolished; no guidance re: intermediate sanctions; sentencing commission abolished effective 1998
Washington	July 1984	Presumptive guidelines for felonies; moderate appellate review; parole abolished; no guidelines for intermediate sanctions; juvenile guidelines in use
Delaware	October 1987	Voluntary guidelines for felonies and misdemeanors; no appellate review; parole abolished in 1990; guidelines incorporate intermediate sanctions
Federal Courts	November 1987	Presumptive guidelines for felonies and misdemeanors; intensive appellate review; parole abolished; no guidelines for intermediate sanctions
Oregon	November 1989	Presumptive guidelines for felonies; moderate appellate review; parole abolished; guidelines incorporate intermediate sanctions
Tennessee	November 1989	Presumptive guidelines for felonies; moderate appellate review; parole retained; no guidelines for intermediate sanctions; sentencing commission abolished effective 1995
Kansas	July 1993	Presumptive guidelines for felonies; moderate appellate review; parole abolished; no guidelines for intermediate sanctions
Arkansas	January 1994	Voluntary guidelines for felonies; no appellate review; parole retained; guidelines incorporate intermediate sanctions; preliminary discussion of guidelines for juvenile cases
North Carolina	October 1994	Presumptive guidelines for felonies and misdemeanors; minimal appellate review; parole abolished; guidelines incorporate intermediate sanctions; dispositional grid for juvenile offenders in preparation
Virginia	January 1995	Voluntary guidelines for felonies; no appellate review; parole abolished; no guidelines for intermediate sanctions; study of juvenile sentencing under way
Ohio	July 1996	Presumptive narrative guidelines (no grid) for felonies; limited appellate review; parole abolished and replaced with judicial release mechanism; no guidelines for intermediate sanctions; structured sentencing for juveniles under consideration by legislature
Missouri	March 1997	Voluntary guidelines for felonies; no appellate review; parole retained; guidelines incorporate intermediate sanctions
Utah	October 1998	Voluntary guidelines for felonies and selected misdemeanors (sex offenses); no appellate review; parole retained; no guidelines for intermediate sanctions; voluntary juvenile guidelines in use

(*continued*)

Table 1.2. (*continued*)

Jurisdiction	Effective Date	Features
Michigan	January 1999	Presumptive guidelines for felonies; appellate review authorized; parole restricted; guidelines incorporate intermediate sanctions
Alaska	Early 1980s	Judicially created "benchmark" guidelines for felonies; moderate appellate review; parole abolished for most felonies (retained for about one-third of all felonies); benchmarks do not address intermediate sanctions; no active sentencing commission
Massachusetts	Proposal pending	Presumptive guidelines for felonies and misdemeanors; appellate review contemplated; parole to be retained; guidelines would incorporate intermediate sanctions
Oklahoma	Proposal pending	Presumptive guidelines for felonies; appellate review contemplated; parole to be limited; guidelines would not incorporate intermediate sanctions
South Carolina	Proposal pending	Voluntary guidelines for felonies and misdemeanors with potential sentence of one year or more; no appellate review contemplated; parole to be abolished for all felonies; guidelines would incorporate intermediate sanctions
Wisconsin	Proposal	Voluntary guidelines for felonies; no appellate review contemplated; pending parole to be eliminated; guidelines would not incorporate intermediate sanctions; new permanent sentencing commission to be created
Washington, D.C.	Under study	Temporary sentencing commission, currently scheduled to report to City Council in April 2000
Iowa	Under study	Legislative commission to study sentencing reform, currently scheduled to report in January 2000
Alabama	Under study	Study committee has requested that Alabama Judicial Study Commission create a permanent sentencing commission in 2000
Georgia	Under study	Governor's commission charged with producing a sentencing guideline proposal by December 1999

guidelines without an institutional home will eventually become moribund. In Michigan, where the state's guidelines are so new that we cannot yet warrant how they will be applied by trial and appellate courts, the legislature has recently cut back the sentencing commission to a minimal staff. Again, this does not augur well for the future operation of a new system.

Stepping outside Frankel's model, however, it should be noted that a number of existing guideline systems have effected significant changes in their states' sentencing practices without legally binding guidelines, or without appellate sentence review. For example, Delaware, Pennsylvania, and Virginia are three jurisdictions now operating with "voluntary" or "advisory" guidelines, yet all three systems report high compliance rates by sentencing judges despite the absence of legal mechanisms for guideline enforcement. Under the auspices of guidelines, the Delaware and Pennsylvania sentencing commissions have done pioneering work in incorporating recommendations for the use of intermediate sanctions into their guideline provisions—and in convincing their state legislatures to increase funding levels for such sanctions to meet projected needs. The Virginia commission, to give a different illustration, has so far succeeded, using only "voluntary" guidelines, in its efforts to control the growth of state prison populations—and the Pennsylvania commission has recently embarked upon a similar mission.

North Carolina is an example of a state that has not followed Frankel's recommendation concerning appellate sentence review, yet it has accomplished many other goals of the 1970s reform program. In five years under guidelines, the North Carolina commission has brought the state's prison populations under control, shifted the use of prison bed-space toward violent offenders and away from property offenders, incorporated a range of intermediate sanctions into guideline provisions, lobbied successfully for increased funding for intermediate sanctions, and established political credibility within the state legislature and the state as a whole. Indeed, some observers now hold out the North Carolina scheme as the leading example of guideline reform in America today—despite one element of glaring deviation from Frankel's procedural recommendations. When it comes to sentencing reform—by its nature an incremental process—perfection in theory is not always the best gauge of whether *some* forward progress has occurred.

Turning now to Frankel's substantive criteria for commission-based guideline reforms, it is probably fair to say that "uniformity in sentencing" has proven to be a more elusive commodity than most people foresaw in the 1970s. For one thing, the past few decades have not yielded a consensus on what *counts* as uniformity. Nearly all guideline systems report that, in the majority of cases, trial judges follow the applicable guidelines when imposing sentences—which some people (and I include myself in this category) accept as evidence of a better pattern of sentencing uniformity than exists within indeterminate systems.

Critics, of the federal guidelines in particular, argue that high rates of guideline compliance show nothing more than false uniformity in sentencing. Such claims, in part, go to the very definition of uniformity: if one believes that federal guidelines mandate lock-step punishments that exclude consideration of important offender characteristics, then the federal guidelines will appear to demand rigidly disparate sentences (e.g., the person who committed crime x for reasons of economic deprivation gets the same sentence as the person who committed crime x out of pure avarice). However, if one believes that most personal characteristics of defendants should be removed from the sentencing calculus, then current federal sentences tend to look both more appropriate and more uniform. Uniformity (relative to what criteria) tends to be in the eye of the beholder.

Aside from such fundamental disagreements, which do not promise to dissipate any time soon, evaluators of existing guideline systems have discovered, or at least strongly suspected, that the plea-bargaining process can work to undermine the goal of sentencing uniformity. One sophisticated study of the federal guidelines in operation in three cities found that the parties were "circumventing" the guidelines as often as 35 percent of the time through plea negotiations (Nagel and Schulhofer 1992). At the state level, Professor Frase's assessment concluded that plea bargaining remained a major force in sentencing outcomes after Minnesota's guidelines were implemented—although perhaps no more so than before the guidelines (Frase 1993). Again, there are different ways to assess the evidence in hand. It seems likely that the plea negotiation process is channeled by the parties' expectations of what the ultimate sentences in their cases *would be* under guidelines and that negotiated resolutions thus treat the guidelines as a meaningful point of departure (cf. Scott and Stuntz 1992). I believe that this must in fact happen, but the empirical evidence is still far too slight to permit anyone to prove it. Pending further study, the controversy remains.

On the issue of racial disproportionalities in sentencing, observers of guideline reforms have so far rendered a mixed verdict. For the nation as a whole, including guideline and nonguideline jurisdictions, racial disparities in incarceration have become more pronounced since the early 1980s (see Tonry 1995). Forceful charges have been leveled that the federal guidelines, particularly for drug offenses and in conjunction with mandatory penalties for drug crimes enacted by Congress, have exacerbated preexisting racial disparities in sentencing (Tonry 1995). Among state guideline systems, the evaluation literature is scanty on this issue, but most commissions have reported a modest reduction in racially disparate sentencing following the enactment of guidelines (see Tonry 1996, chap. 2). No guideline jurisdiction claims to have made major headway on the problem of racial disproportionalities in punishment. So far, even under the best-case scenario that can be supported from available evidence, it appears that sentencing commissions and guidelines can achieve modest advances in problems of racial disparity, but commissions and guidelines (as in the federal example) can also act to make such problems worse. No one, in other words, should support guideline reform in the belief that racial equity in sentencing will automatically follow.

Finally, Marvin Frankel hoped that the rationalizing process of commission-based sentencing reform would ultimately lead to what he viewed as more humane sentencing outcomes overall: a reduced reliance on incarceration and increased creativity in the use of intermediate punishments. Writing in the early 1970s, Frankel could hardly have predicted that prison and jail confinement rates in America would in fact increase by more than a factor of four in the next 25 years, with most of the confinement explosion occurring after 1980. This certainly is not what he had in mind for the nation as a whole—but we must ask how much of the incarceration boom has been attributable to the advent of sentencing guidelines.

Some of it clearly has been. In the federal system, where our knowledge base is the deepest, federal district court judges complain regularly that the guidelines (or Congress's mandatory minimums, or both) force them to impose heavier sentences than they would otherwise have chosen. These claims are consistent with the original legislative and commission intents in promulgating the federal guidelines: There was widespread political sentiment during the Reagan administration that federal judges had been meting out sentences of undue leniency for many crimes, and the guideline reform was directed in large part to prevent that from happening by curtailing the judges' discretion (see Stith and Cabranes 1998).

Raw statistics suggest that the designers of the federal system got what they wanted—although it is far from what Marvin Frankel would have wished. In the first 10 years under the new federal guidelines, from 1987 to 1997, the federal imprisonment rate increased by 119 percent. This growth surge was 25 percent greater than the average increase in imprisonment rates for the nation as a whole during the same period (Maguire and Pastore 1998, p. 491, table 6.36). In contrast, in the decade prior to the advent of the guidelines, the federal prison system had been expanding at a much slower pace (23 percent growth in imprisonment rates from 1977 to 1987), far below the national average (77 percent growth). There is good reason to conclude that the federal sentencing guidelines, in combination with congressional mandatory penalties, ushered in an era of deliberately engineered increases in punitive severity and shifted gears in federal imprisonment from a slow-growth pace to a fast-growth pace virtually overnight.

At the state level, the relationship between guideline reform and sentence severity has been mixed but more consistent with Frankel's substantive vision than the federal system. A number of state legislatures and commissions have created guideline structures with the express purpose of containing prison growth. Minnesota was the first jurisdiction to try this, beginning in 1980, crafting guidelines with the aid of a computer simulation model to forecast future sentencing patterns (see Hunt 1998). Over the first 10 years under the state's guidelines, imprisonment rates in Minnesota did incline upward, but only by 47 percent—in a period when the nationwide imprisonment rate more than doubled (plus 110 percent) (Maguire and Pastore 1998, p. 491, table 6.36.) This pattern of *some* incarceration growth, but slower than the national average, was also seen during the first 10 years of the Washington and Oregon guidelines, respectively: Washington's imprisonment rate increased by 29 percent from 1984 to 1994 (the first 10 years under guidelines), while the national rate increased by 107 percent. Oregon's imprisonment rate rose by only 11 percent from 1989 to 1998 (data from only nine years are available), while the national rate went up 70 percent (Id.; Bureau of Justice Statistics 1999*b*, p. 3, table 3.) In a study of sentencing commissions operative in the 1980s, Thomas Marvell identified six state commissions that were instructed to consider prison capacity when promulgating guidelines. In all six jurisdictions, Marvell found "comparatively slow prison population growth," prompting him to write that "These findings are a refreshing departure from the usual negative results when evaluating criminal justice reforms" (Marvell 1995, p. 707).

In the 1990s, newer commissions in Virginia and North Carolina have also had notable success in restraining the incarceration explosion. The Virginia guidelines were created early in the administration of a new governor who had promised to crack down on violent crime and to abolish parole. While allowing the governor to keep his campaign commitments, the new Virginia guidelines have coincided with a 3 percent *decrease* in the state's imprisonment rate from 1995 to 1998 (a period in which national rates climbed by 12 percent) (Maguire and Pastore 1998, p. 491, table 6.36; Bureau of Justice Statistics 1999*b*, p. 3, table 3).

In North Carolina, the state's imprisonment rate grew at a fast (19 percent) pace during the first year of the new guidelines, from year-end 1994 to year-end 1995. This can largely be attributed to sentences still being handed down under preguidelines law, however, and the temporary growth surge was predicted by the state's sentencing commission. In the three successive calendar years of 1996 through 1998, as guideline cases entered the system in greater numbers, North Carolina's imprisonment rates fell every year (Maguire and Pastore 1998, p. 491, table 6.36; Bureau of Justice Statistics 1999b, p. 3, table 3). Perhaps just as significantly, the state's guidelines have ushered in deliberate changes in the proportionate share of convicted felons sent to prison and those routed to intermediate punishments. In the first three years under guidelines, the total confinement rate for felony offenders fell from 48 to 34 percent, reflecting the state's policy judgment that an increased share of nonviolent felons should be sentenced to intermediate punishments (Wright 1998). In order to accommodate this change, the commission successfully lobbied the state legislature to provide increased funding for intermediate-punishment programming. At the same time, however, North Carolina's guidelines substantially increased the use of prison bed-space for violent offenders. In the state's political arena, the North Carolina commission won widespread support for its tripartite agenda of severe punishment for violent criminals, expanded use of intermediate punishments for less serious offenses, and introduction of planned "resource management" of prison growth.

Slow-growth policy has not been the whole story under state guidelines, however. Like the federal commission, the Pennsylvania sentencing commission was instructed by its legislature to write guidelines that would toughen prison sentences as compared with prior judicial practice—and Pennsylvania's prisons have grown steadily under the guidelines regime. Between 1982 and 1998 (the guidelines era), Pennsylvania's imprisonment rate increased by 244 percent, while the national rate increased by "only" 171 percent (Maguire and Pastore 1998, p. 491, table 6.36; Bureau of Justice Statistics 1999b, p. 3, table 3). Even in the pioneering states of Minnesota, Washington, and Oregon, the state legislatures (and sometimes the voters, through the initiative process) have acted to toughen the sentencing guidelines and other sentencing provisions. In the late 1980s, the Minnesota legislature ordered the state sentencing commission to retool its guidelines to provide harsher sentences for violent crimes, beginning a period of planned prison growth (Frase 1993). Accordingly, during the 1990s, Minnesota's prisons grew slightly faster than the national average. Washington and Oregon steered similar courses in the late 1980s and the early 1990s, when the fear of crime was high on the list of political priorities nationwide.

Two conclusions on guidelines and prison growth emerge. First, guidelines and computer simulations are surprisingly effective technologies for the deliberate management of incarcerated populations—but they are tools that may be used with equal facility to push sentencing severity up or down. As Michael Tonry noted several years ago, virtually all sentencing guideline systems have been "successful" on this score, if we measure success against what the commission and legislature were trying to achieve (Tonry 1993). Second, the overall experience of guidelines to date has been that they have been used sometimes to retard prison growth (measured against national trends) and sometimes to parallel or exceed the course of prison expansion observable in nonguideline jurisdictions. We cannot attribute independent causal significance to guidelines as a driving force of the prison boom in the past quarter century. In a number of instances, and whenever called on to do so, guidelines have been an effective force in the opposite direction.

The project of developing guidelines for the selection among intermediate punishments, and guidelines that can encourage the use of such sanctions, has lagged
far behind the project of writing guidelines to regulate the numbers and durations
of prison sentences (Tonry 1998). Ideally, as now being attempted in North Carolina, guidelines will eventually serve a broad "resource management" function —
setting priorities for the use of scarce prison bed spaces and for scarce program
slots among the community sanctions (see American Bar Association 1994, pp. 85–
94). Our experience base is simply too thin — despite the early promising returns
from North Carolina — to proclaim that this aspect of Marvin Frankel's agenda has
been realized in an enduring fashion through guidelines, or in a way that can be
replicated across jurisdictions.

Marvin Frankel told a reporter years ago that sentencing reform is "not for the
short-winded." We now have 19 years of experience with sentencing guidelines,
in a variety of incarnations and across a plurality of the American states. Still, from
the historical perspective, commissions and guidelines are legal institutions in a
period of relative infancy. (Indeterminate sentencing, in contrast, has roots that
reach back more than a full century.) This should make us all hesitant to an-
nounce definitive conclusions about the future course of the new structures.

It is likely that the proven ability of sentencing guidelines (plus computer projections) to manage the growth of correctional populations will induce a steadily
increasing number of jurisdictions to invest in some version of guideline reform.
But the future of guidelines will also depend heavily on demonstrable improve-
ments in existing guideline technology along a number of dimensions: system
designers will have to solve the problem of finding the right balance between the
legal enforceability of guidelines and the role for judicial discretion in sentencing
determinations. Guideline drafters must also continue their experiments with incorporating consequential purposes of punishment into sentencing systems, if the
policy community is to become convinced that guidelines can do more than in-
stantiate a "one-note" just deserts program. Guideline designers will also continue
to be faced with the unsolved riddle of addressing the array of intermediate punishments with guideline prescriptions — building upon a small store of promising
initiatives from the late 1990s. Sentencing commissions will also be crucial forums
for the ongoing struggle to combat racial disproportionalities in criminal punishment — although these efforts are likely to reinforce our understanding that the
sentencing process is only one part of a much larger problem. Finally, the next
generation of guideline evolution will depend on far better assessment research
than has yet been performed so that we may better approach such conundrums
as the dynamics of charging and plea bargaining within guideline systems, the
degree to which guidelines provide room for values of both uniformity and discretion, and the successes or failures of guidelines in furthering their underlying
policy objectives. All of these issues, and others, will play out in numerous jurisdictions and in varying permutations in the coming years. Those interested in
sentencing guidelines, their established viability, and their potential must of ne-
cessity become "comparativists" — with curiosity and knowledge extending outward
across multiple systems.

Political Preoccupation with Crime Leads, Not Follows,
Public Opinion (October 1997)
Katherine Beckett

Politicians who propose harsh anticrime and antidrug policies typically claim to be carrying out the public's wishes. The irony, however, is that public opinion about crime, drugs, and punishment is profoundly shaped by the way in which politicians frame these issues in political discourse. My research shows that, during times when Americans tell pollsters that crime or drugs is America's most pressing problem, public officials and the media have previously tried to draw Americans' attention to the subject. (The full analysis appears in my *Making Crime Pay: Law and Order in Contemporary American Politics*, published in 1997 by Oxford University Press.)

Indeed, crime and punishment have taken a front-row seat in the theater of American political discourse. Over the past three decades, politicians have called attention to crime-related problems and struggled to position themselves as "tougher" than their competitors. Public concern reached record levels during this period, and members of the public became more likely to express support for punitive policies such as the death penalty and "three-strikes" sentencing laws.

Not surprisingly, these ideological shifts have been accompanied by a dramatic expansion of the criminal justice system. Between 1965 and 1993, crime control expenditures jumped from 4.6 billion to 100 billion (nominal) dollars, and the rate of incarceration in the United States became one of the highest in the world. Increasingly, "get-tough" policies such as aggressive policing, mandatory minimum sentencing laws, and capital punishment are seen as the best solutions to crime and drug problems.

The widespread adoption of "get-tough" policies has befuddled many academics and professionals who are all too aware of their dangers and limitations. In this context, some have suggested that the origins of the wars on crime and on drugs lie in the public's preference for "cracking down on criminals." According to this "democracy-at-work" thesis,[1] the increased use of the death penalty, the adoption of three-strikes laws, and other tough anticrime measures are politicians' responses to widespread popular punitiveness.

While it is certainly the case that segments of the public have become more punitive in recent years, the situation is more complicated than the democracy-at-work thesis allows. In the first place, support for punitive anticrime policies is fluid and ambiguous, rather than fixed and monolithic. Enthusiasm for the death penalty, for example, varies tremendously, weakens considerably in the presence of alternatives, and coexists uneasily with support for rehabilitative ideals (McGarrell and Sandys 1996). When given a choice, most Americans still believe that spending money on educational and job training programs is a more effective crime-fighting measure than building prisons (Cullen et al. 1990). Although punitive attitudes have become more widespread, popular beliefs about crime and punishment are complex, equivocal, and contradictory, even after decades of political initiative on these subjects (Roberts 1992).

Furthermore, it is not clear in these accounts why public support for punitive anticrime and drug policies (ambivalent as it is) has become more pronounced in recent years. Some attribute it to unusually high or increasing crime rates, although this argument has become more difficult to sustain in the face of significant decreases in rates of crime and of drug use. The argument that unusually high crime rates in the United States have produced distinctively high rates of incarceration is also difficult to sustain. According to international crime survey data, only rates of lethal assault are exceptionally high in the United States (Mayhew and van Dijk 1997*b*). Because persons convicted of homicide constitute a tiny fraction of those sentenced to prison, it appears instead that policies associated with the wars on crime and drugs—including the intensified criminalization of drug offenses, more aggressive policing and prosecution of suspected criminals, and more punitive sentencing practices—have led to the unprecedented growth of the U.S. prison and jail populations.

Other versions of the "democracy-at-work" thesis emphasize that the war on crime of the 1960s and early 1970s was accompanied by increases in the official rate of crime and that the war on drugs of the 1980s took place at a time when drug (especially cocaine) use appeared to be a growing problem. However, more careful analysis casts doubt on this argument.

The regression analysis summarized in tables 1.3 and 1.4 assesses the extent to which media coverage, political initiatives, and the reported incidence of crime and drug use are associated with the propensity of members of the public to identify crime or drugs as the nation's most important problem. The results show that the association between the reported incidence of crime and drugs and public concern about these social problems is quite weak but that the extent to which politicians focus on these issues has a significant effect on levels of public concern.

Tables 1.3 and 1.4 report regression coefficients for each of the explanatory variables. These coefficients measure the extent to which each variable is associated with public concern about crime and drugs; the asterisks placed next to them reflect the strength of each of the relationships measured. As table 1.3 shows, both

Table 1.3. Impact of the Crime Rate, Media Coverage, and Political Initiatives on Public Concern about Crime, 1964–1974

Explanatory Variables	Lag = 0 (3–5 months)	Lag = 1 (6–10 months)	Lag = 2 (9–15 months)
Crime Rate	−.0077	−.0067	−.005
	(.011)	(.013)	(.022)
Media Initiative	1.2504*	1.3103**	1.2107*
	(.5547)	(.497)	(.5372)
Political Initiative	1.3711**	1.3511**	1.2721**
	(.3509)	(.3364)	(.3409)
Adjusted R^2	.5649	.5866	.5712

Notes: Asterisks reflect the strength of each of the relationships measured: *$p < .05$; ** $p < .01$. The number in parentheses is the standard error.

Table 1.4. Impact of Rates of Drug Use, Media Coverage, and Political Initiatives on Public Concern about Drugs, 1985–1992

Explanatory Variables	Lag = 0 (3–5 months)	Lag = 1 (6–10 months)	Lag = 2 (9–15 months)
Drug Use	.0096	.0082	.014
	(.2178)	(.1917)	(.2077)
Media Initiative	.0594	.0781	.0999
	(.7459)	(.699)	(.6781)
Political Initiative	1.8393***	1.762***	1.1221**
	(.4551)	(.446)	(.4997)
Adjusted R^2	.6337	.6291	.6009

Notes: Asterisks reflect the strength of each of the relationships measured: ** $p < .01$; *** $p < .001$. The number in parentheses is the standard error.

media coverage of and political initiatives on the crime issue were significantly associated with subsequent levels of public concern about crime, but the reported incidence of crime was not. Similarly, the results presented in table 1.4 indicate that political initiatives on the drug issue had a significant effect on levels of public concern about drugs, but the reported rate of drug use did not. Together, these results suggest that the extent to which political actors paid attention to the crime and drug problems had a far more significant effect on public assessments of the seriousness of these problems than did official statistics regarding their prevalence.

But even if concern about crime were strongly associated with its reported incidence, the assumption that anxiety about crime drives support for punitive anticrime policies is questionable. Survey research suggests that neither concern about crime as a social problem nor fear of personal victimization necessarily gives rise to punitiveness. In fact, those who are less afraid of being victimized typically express the highest levels of support for the "get-tough" approach, while those who are more fearful are often less punitive. Rural white men, for example, feel relatively safe but are often staunch supporters of law-and-order policies. Although recent research suggests that increased risk of victimization may be the primary cause of growing punitiveness among African Americans, fear of victimization remains unrelated to punitiveness among whites (Cohn and Halteman 1991). We need, then, an alternative account that can help to explain why public attitudes and beliefs regarding crime and punishment have shifted in a more punitive direction. My research suggests that this trend must be understood as a consequence of the politicization of crime-related problems, a process that began in earnest more than three decades ago.

The rhetoric of "law and order" was first mobilized in the late 1950s as southern governors and law enforcement officials attempted to heighten popular opposition to the civil rights movement. In this rhetoric, civil rights activists were characterized as "hoodlums," "thugs," and "lawbreakers." As civil rights became a national rather than a regional issue, and as welfare rights activists pressured the state to assume greater responsibility for ensuring social welfare and reducing inequality, the battle over state policy intensified. At stake was the question whether the federal government is obligated to assume responsibility for creating a more egal-itarian society.

Without being explicitly identified as such, competing images of the poor as "deserving" or "undeserving" became central components of this debate. By draw-ing attention to the problems of street crime, drug addiction, and delinquency and by depicting these problems as examples of the immorality of the impover-ished, conservatives promoted the latter image.

Over time, race, crime, violence, delinquency, and drug addiction became defining features of those now referred to as "the underclass." The politiciza-tion of the crime problem and the attempt to reconstruct popular conceptions of it were components of a much larger political struggle, particularly the ef-fort to replace social welfare with social control as a principal premise of state policy.

For example, conservative politicians used discussions of the crime issue to ridicule the notion that criminal (or any other "deviant") behavior has socioeco-nomic causes and promoted the alternative view that such behavior is the conse-quence, as former president Richard Nixon put it, of "insufficient curbs on the appetites or impulses that naturally impel individuals towards criminal activities." This neoclassical view that the causes of crime lie in the human "propensity to evil" clearly calls for the expansion of the social control apparatus rather than policies aimed at promoting social welfare. As Nixon concluded, the "solution to the crime problem is not the quadrupling of funds for any governmental war on poverty but more convictions."

Somewhat contradictorily, conservatives also identified the "culture of welfare" as an important cause of "social pathologies" — especially crime, delinquency, and drug addiction. For example, presidential candidate Barry Goldwater argued in the 1964 election campaign that welfare programs are an important cause of in-creased lawlessness and crime: "If it is entirely proper for the government to take away from some to give to others, then won't some be led to believe that they can rightfully take from anyone who has more than they? No wonder law and order has broken down, mob violence has engulfed great American cities, and our wives feel unsafe in the streets."

Over the years, conservatives continued to argue that welfare programs such as Aid to Families with Dependent Children not only "keep the poor poor" but also accounted, along with lenient crime policies, for the rising crime rate. This ar-gument was used in an effort to legitimate reductions in welfare spending and the implementation of increasingly punitive crime and drug policies. As Vice Presi-dent George Bush later put it: "Our current welfare program, originally designed to raise people out of poverty, has become a crippling poverty trap, destroying families and condemning generations to a dependency. . . . Of course, one of the best things we can do for families is obliterate drug use in America . . . [we must therefore make] society intolerant to drug use with stiff penalties and sure and swift punishment for offenders."

In sum, despite their differences, conservative neoclassical and cultural theories of crime and deviance similarly implied the need to adopt policies that would enhance social control, rather than social welfare.

Initially, the Johnson administration countered the conservative anticrime campaign by stressing the social causes of crime and by downplaying the significance of the reported increase in the official crime rate. But, by 1965, liberals began to change course, and, over time, such politicians have become even less likely to challenge the conservative understanding of and approach to the crime problem. Particularly in response to the Reagan/Bush wars on drugs, Democratic party officials made the conservative rhetoric on crime and drugs their own.

The liberal about-face on crime-related problems reflected conservatives' ability to disseminate law and order rhetoric through the mass media, as well as its apparent resonance with electorally important segments of the American public. In my research, I found that the presence of political elites — especially politicians and law enforcement personnel — in news stories that focused on crime (in the 1960s and early 1970s) and drugs (in the 1980s) had a significant effect on the way in which the crime and drug problems were framed. For example, stories in which officials served as primary sources were far more likely to identify "liberal permissiveness" and the loss of "respect for authority" as the main causes of crime than were stories that relied on nonofficial sources. Similarly, drug-related news stories in the 1980s that relied primarily on politicians or law enforcement personnel were much more likely to emphasize the need for greater law enforcement efforts and punishment and were less likely to challenge the assumptions that underlay the war on drugs.

While officials' capacity to shape media representations is not infinite and must be recognized as an achievement (of sorts), officials were quite effective in using the mass media to disseminate images of the crime and drug problems that implied the need for greater punishment and control.

But access to the media does not guarantee the success of efforts to shape popular perceptions, attitudes, and beliefs. The capacity of elites to mobilize public opinion also depends on their ability to select symbols and rhetoric that resonate with deep-seated "myths" and make sense of lived experience. In this case, the neoclassical depiction of crime as a personal and free choice is consonant with the individualistic orientation that is so prominent in American political culture. Similarly, the argument that welfare programs encourage family disintegration taps into (and reinforces) widespread concern regarding the "breakdown" of the family.

It is important to note, however, that support for punitive policies is not evenly distributed across the population. Survey research indicates that the "law-and-order" approach to the crime problem is particularly popular among those who hold racially and socially conservative views. While many such voters are long-time supporters of the Republican party, others are economic liberals who have historically voted Democrat. In-depth interviews with these "swing" voters reveal that racially charged hostility toward those who "seek something for nothing" is widespread and that this hostility informs support for punitive anticrime policies. The strength of these sentiments has had quite significant policy implications, as the Republican and Democratic parties have competed intensely for the loyalty of these "Reagan Democrats" in recent years.

In sum, it is clear that the discourse of law and order has become more entrenched in American political culture. However, it is also clear that political elites have played a leading role in calling attention to crime-related problems, in defining these problems as the consequence of insufficient punishment and control, and in generating popular support for punitive anticrime policies. Those who attribute recent political developments to a preexisting, unequivocal, and universal public desire overlook the contingent and complex nature of political beliefs and attitudes regarding crime and punishment.

This complexity is an important resource for progressives who seek to shift the terms of the debate over crime and social policy in a more humanitarian direction. For example, public support for the notion that crime has social causes and the belief that rehabilitative programs are an effective means of responding to crime suggests that the discourses about "root causes" and rehabilitation may still be deployed with some success.

Research also suggests that concern about the "breakdown" of the family informs assessments of the crime problem and support for punitive anticrime policies (Sasson 1995; Tyler and Boeckmann 1997). So far, this concern has served primarily as a resource for conservatives who decry the decline of "family values" and link this alleged shift to the expansion of welfare and other expressions of permissiveness. But this is not the only way of tapping into popular concern about the family. For example, progressives might stress the ways in which structural forces such as unemployment, low wages, inadequate medical care, and limited access to child care can diminish the capacity of parents to care for their young. The creation of a richer and more meaningful public discourse which includes these and other underrepresented views on crime and punishment is a first step toward the true democratization of crime policy.

NOTE

1. I am indebted to Cullen, Clark, and Wozniak (1985) for this term and for their critique of the view that current criminal justice policies are a direct reflection of popular sentiment.

The Penal System as Labor Market Institution: Jobs and Jails,
1980–1995 (December 1997)
Katherine Beckett and Bruce Western

Because unemployment figures do not take into account working-age people in jail or prison, the dramatic increase in the U.S. prison and jail population has made U.S. unemployment rates look lower than they otherwise would. Most policy analysts, however, attribute apparently low rates of unemployment in the United States to its ostensibly unregulated labor market, rather than to its uniquely high incarceration rate.

When the confined population is taken into account, however, the unemployment rate for males climbs by nearly 2 percent, and considerably more for black males. High incarceration rates thus reduce unemployment estimates in the short run. In the long term, however, they increase unemployment because incarceration significantly reduces later employment prospects.

Across Europe and the United States, the proper role of the government in economic affairs is the subject of intense controversy. Critics of the so-called Continental model contrast high rates of European unemployment with the apparently strong performance of the U.S. labor market. European welfare states, with their generous unemployment benefits and high levels of unionization, are said to be characterized by reduced market flexibility and work incentives and, as a result, heightened unemployment. Even those who support unions and strong welfare states agree that the United States has achieved low levels of unemployment through labor market deregulation, albeit in exchange for rising poverty and inequality.

The estimates of unemployment on which these arguments rest do not include the prison and jail population, which in the United States exceeds 1.6 million people. Our research suggests that when this population, consisting mostly of young, able-bodied men, is included in estimates of unemployment and joblessness, European rates of unemployment were actually lower than those in the United States for 18 of the 20 years between 1975 and 1995. These adjusted figures also show that unemployment rates among African American men have not improved much since the recession of the early 1980s. Thus, it appears that apparently low rates of unemployment in the United States are in part due to the dramatic expansion of the U.S. penal system.

Industrial Relations and the Welfare State

It is often observed, as table 1.5 suggests, that the United States lags far behind Western Europe in industrial relations policy and welfare state development. The comparative weakness of U.S. industrial relations is illustrated by unionization and collective bargaining coverage statistics (columns 1 and 2). The United States has the lowest level of labor force coverage by collective bargaining and the second lowest level of private sector unionization. Social policy is also less developed. While approximately one-quarter of the gross domestic product ("GDP") is devoted to social welfare in the large European countries, U.S. social spending accounts for only 15 percent of GDP (column 3). Coverage of unemployment insurance and spending on employment-related services in the United States are also quite low by comparison (columns 4 and 5).

Penal Institutions and the Labor Market

Social protection mechanisms may be weaker in the United States, but this does not justify the claim that market principles alone drive the superior U.S. employment record. Labor markets are embedded in and affected by a wide array of social arrangements and institutions.

In the United States, for example, market deregulation and welfare state retrenchment have been accompanied by rapid expansion of the criminal justice system. At the peak of the recession of the early 1990s, annual criminal justice spending exceeded $91 billion, dwarfing the $41 billion spent on all unemployment benefits and employment-related services.

Table 1.5. Selected Industrial Relations and Social Policy Characteristics of 12 OECD Countries

	Private Sector Union Density	Collective Bargaining Coverage	Total Social Spending	Unemployment Benefit Coverage	Active Labor Market Spending
Australia	32	80	13	82	.34
Canada	28	38	19	129	.68
Denmark	72	—	28	113	1.56
France	8	92	27	98	.88
Germany	30	90	23	89	1.64
Italy	32	—	25	—	—
Japan	23	23	12	36	.13
Netherlands	20	71	29	105	1.12
Norway	41	75	29	61	1.14
Sweden	81	83	33	93	3.21
United Kingdom	38	47	24	71	.59
United States	13	18	15	34	.25
Average excluding the United States	38	72	24	94	1.03

Notes: OECD = Organisation for Economic Cooperation and Development. Union density and collective bargaining coverage are expressed as a percentage of all employees. Data are for 1988, except for Canada and the Netherlands (measured in 1985) and the United Kingdom (1989). Coverage is expressed as a percentage of all employees. Data are for 1990 except for France (1985), Germany (1992), and Japan (1989). Total social spending is measured as a percentage of GDP. All data are for 1990. Unemployment benefit coverage measures unemployment beneficiaries as a percentage of unemployed recorded in labor force surveys. Data are for 1990–91 except for Denmark (1992) and Sweden (1992). Active labor market spending includes public spending on training, employment services, youth measures, and subsidized employment expressed as a percentage of GDP. Data are for 1990–92.

Sources: Organisation for Economic Cooperation and Development (1991, 1993, 1994*a*, 1994*b*, 1994*c*).

By 1992, the public cost of correctional facilities exceeded $31 billion and 1.63 million people were held in American prisons and jails by 1996 (Gilliard and Beck 1997, p. 1). This was a significant and costly state intervention comparable in size to the large social programs of European welfare states. Indeed, due to low levels of unemployment insurance coverage, more American men were incarcerated in 1995 than received unemployment benefits.

U.S. incarceration rates are even more striking when compared with those of other industrialized democracies (see table 1.6). In 1992–93, the U.S. incarceration rate was five to ten times greater than those of other OECD countries (column 1). These high rates correspond to large absolute numbers (column 2). Prison and jail inmates are counted in the millions in the United States, elsewhere in the tens of thousands.

The Short-Term Effect of Incarceration on Unemployment

By moving more than 1 million able-bodied men of working age into prisons and jails, U.S. criminal justice policy has had profound effects on estimates of em-

Table 1.6. Numbers of Inmates and Incarceration Rates
per 100,000 Adult Population, Selected OECD
Countries, 1992–1993

Country	Incarceration Rate	Number of Inmates
Australia	91	15,895
Canada	116	30,659
Denmark	66	3,406
France	84	51,457
Germany	80	64,029
Italy	80	46,152
Japan	36	45,183
Netherlands	49	7,935
Sweden	69	5,668
United Kingdom	93	60,676
U.S. blacks	1,947	626,207
U.S. whites	306	658,233
United States, total	519	1,339,695
Average excluding the United States	78	26,988

Sources: Bureau of Justice Statistics (1994); Mauer (1994).

ployment trends. Because prison inmates are institutionalized, they are not counted by population surveys as members of the civilian labor force, or even among those "not in the labor force." In the short term, then, incarceration lowers conventional unemployment measures by removing significant numbers of able-bodied men from estimates of unemployment and joblessness.

To remedy this limitation, we analyzed unemployment trends that take account of the size of the incarcerated population.[1] The importance of incarceration as a source of hidden unemployment varies by sex and across countries. More than 90 percent of prison and jail inmates in the United States are male, so we focus on trends in the labor market conditions of men. From a comparative perspective, the short-term effect of incarceration on unemployment is tiny in Europe because incarceration rates are so low (see table 1.7). In most European countries, un-employed males outnumber male prison inmates by between 10 and 20 to one. In the United States in 1995, this ratio had fallen to just under 2.2 (column 3). Differences between the United States and Europe are also reflected in the relative size of the conventional unemployment rate and the adjusted unemployment rate that includes the incarcerated. In most European countries, counting prison in-mates in estimates of unemployment changes the unemployment rate by only a few tenths of a percentage point. By contrast, U.S. prison and jail inmates added 1.5 points to the usual unemployment rate in 1990 (column 5) and more than 2 points by 1994.

Conventional estimates suggest that U.S. unemployment peaked in 1983 at about 10 percent and rose again in the early 1990s, but recovered fairly quickly after each of these recessions. Although European unemployment rates were low

Table 1.7. Male Incarceration and Unemployment Rates in the United States and Western Europe, 1990

	Number Unemployed	Number Incarcerated	Ratio Unemployed to Imprisoned	Unemployment Rate	Adjusted Unemployment Rate	Difference between Conventional and Adjusted Unemployment Rate (in %)
Austria	63	6.0	10.5	3.0	3.3	.3
Belgium	143	6.7	21.5	6.1	6.3	.2
Denmark	121	3.4	35.8	7.8	8.0	.2
Finland	54	3.4	15.8	4.1	4.3	.2
France	935	44.7	20.9	7.0	7.3	.3
Germany	968	49.7	19.5	5.5	5.8	.3
Italy	1,102	11.4	96.7	7.6	7.6	.1
Netherlands	228	6.2	36.9	5.6	5.7	.1
Sweden	36	4.8	7.5	1.5	1.7	.2
United Kingdom	1,155	51.4	22.5	7.2	7.5	.3
United States	3,799	1,087.9	3.5	5.6	7.0	1.5

Notes: Data from all countries are for 1990, except Italy (1986). The unemployed and incarcerated populations are measured in thousands.

Sources: Council of Europe (1992); OECD (1992).

compared with U.S. rates until 1984, conventional estimates of unemployment suggest that European recovery from the recessions of the mid-1980s and early 1990s was relatively weak.

However, employment performance in the United States looks less impressive once the prison and jail population is taken into account. Adjusted estimates that add inmates to the male unemployment count show that labor market inactivity in the United States never fell below about 7 percent in the 1980s. By 1994, the prison and jail population had become so large that (if included in the calculations) it would have added about 2 percentage points to the male unemployment rate. These modified estimates suggest that unemployment in the economically buoyant period of the mid-1990s was about 8 percent—higher than any conventional U.S. unemployment rate since the recession of the early 1980s.

A more detailed examination of the U.S. data shows the impact of incarceration on the labor market experiences of black and white men. Conventional unemployment estimates, and the adjusted measure that takes account of incarceration, are shown in table 1.8. In 1983, when the prison population is added to the unemployment count, the resulting unemployment rate for all men was just one percentage point higher. However, estimates of unemployment among black men in 1983 increased by 4 points to 23 percent. The effect of incarceration on white male unemployment was smaller, raising the rate by about half a percentage point. As the prison population grew through the 1980s, the labor market effects of incarceration become much larger. For all men, average unemployment in the 1990s was lifted to nearly 8 percent. When the incarcerated population is included

Table 1.8. Conventional and Adjusted (Incarcerated Population Included)
Unemployment and Jobless Rates for Men, 1983–1995

	All Men		Black Men		White Men	
Year	Conventional	Adjusted	Conventional	Adjusted	Conventional	Adjusted
Unemployment Rates						
1983	9.7	10.6	19.1	23.0	8.6	9.2
1985–89	5.5	6.7	11.6	16.9	4.7	5.5
1990–94	5.9	7.7	11.3	18.8	5.2	6.3
Jobless Rates						
1983	29.4	29.9	39.5	41.7	28.3	28.6
1985–89	26.2	27.0	34.0	37.0	25.3	25.7
1990–95	27.0	28.1	34.3	38.5	26.2	26.8

Sources: Bureau of Labor Statistics (1990, 1995); Bureau of Justice Statistics, unpublished data.

in estimates of black unemployment, nearly one in five African American men were without a job throughout the 1990s. Incarceration had a similar effect on estimates of black joblessness, a category that includes those no longer looking for work.

In sum, the growth of U.S. incarceration through the 1980s and 1990s conceals a high rate of persistent unemployment and joblessness. Adjusted unemployment figures that include the incarcerated population suggest the United States labor market has performed worse, not better, than European labor markets for much of the past two decades. Incarceration has particularly strong effects on estimates of black unemployment: when inmates are added to jobless statistics, rates of joblessness among black men have remained around 40 percent. It should be noted that because only approximately 5 percent of inmates in the U.S. worked in 1996 producing goods or services for external consumption,[2] omitting inmates engaged in this type of work would not significantly alter these revised estimates of unemployment. However, because our estimates do not reflect reductions in joblessness due to expanded criminal justice system employment, they may significantly underestimate the short-term impact of penal expansion on estimates of unemployment.

The Long-Term Effect of Incarceration on Unemployment

Removal of large numbers of men from the labor force count by incarceration lowers the usual figures for labor inactivity. At the same time, expansion of prisons and jails is likely to increase unemployment in the long run. Research suggests that the job prospects of applicants with no criminal record are far better than those of demographically similar persons who have been convicted and incarcerated. While convicts who acquire educational and vocational skills in prison are able to improve their chances of employment (Irwin and Austin 1994), resources for education and vocational training in prisons and jails have declined, and recent congressional decisions to deny inmates access to Pell grants to pursue higher education suggest that this trend is likely to continue.

Our analysis of data from the National Longitudinal Study of Youth (not presented here) supports the argument that incarceration increases the likelihood of future joblessness. The results of this analysis indicate that being incarcerated as a youth reduces annual employment by about 5 percentage points, or about three weeks per year, controlling for education, work experience, and local labor market conditions. The effect is larger for blacks, whose employment is reduced by about 8 percentage points (more than four weeks in the year) by juvenile incarceration. The effects of youth incarceration on adult employment are even larger than the effects of failure to graduate from high school or from living in a high unemployment area. Even after 15 years, respondents who were incarcerated as juveniles worked between 5 and 10 percentage points less than their counterparts who did not experience incarceration. The effects of adult incarceration on later employment status are even greater, reducing employment by about one-fifth, or about 10 weeks per year. A wide variety of models thus strongly supports the conclusion that incarceration has large and extremely long-lasting adverse effects on the job prospects of ex-convicts.

Conclusion

Comparative labor market research and recent policy debates attribute low levels of unemployment in the United States to an ostensibly deregulated labor market. In contrast, our research suggests that U.S. federal and state governments have made a significant intervention in the labor market by expanding the penal system in the 1980s and 1990s. As a result of the policies associated with the wars on crime and drugs, prisons and jails held around 1.6 million people by 1995. Consisting mostly of young, unskilled, able-bodied men of working age, these confined populations conceal a high level of joblessness that, if included in labor market statistics, would have contributed about 2 percentage points to the male unemployment rate by the mid-1990s. These effects are especially strong for African Americans: labor inactivity is understated by about two-thirds, or 7 percentage points, by the conventional measure of black male unemployment. Despite claims of "Eurosclerosis" and the successful deregulation of the U.S. labor market, our revised estimates show that unemployment in the United States exceeded average European rates between 1975 and 1993.

While incarceration has the immediate effect of lowering conventional estimates of joblessness and unemployment, it significantly increases the chances of unemployment among ex-convicts. With more than 1.4 million men now in prison or jail, current levels of incarceration annually generate the equivalent of a full year of unemployment for more than 200,000 American men. In the aggregate, then, it appears that the high U.S. incarceration rate will greatly reduce the productivity and employment of the male workforce.

How can these findings be reconciled? If incarceration lowers conventional measures of joblessness in the short term but increases unemployment in the long term, why does the U.S. labor market still perform, well according to conventional indicators? The steady expansion of the prison and jail population, combined with high rates of recidivism and reincarceration, helps to explain this paradox. About two-thirds of young state prisoners are rearrested within three years, removing many of those at risk of unemployment from the labor force. With high rates of recidivism and intensified surveillance of ex-convicts, the short-term negative effect of incarceration on unemployment dominates the long-term positive effect. Under these conditions, the appearance of strong employment performance has been assisted by an ever-increasing correctional population.

It has been argued that some European welfare states may also conceal unemployment. However, the dangers of U.S. prison expansion are significantly greater than those posed by European welfare policies. In contrast to welfare institutions, the penal system has unambiguously negative effects on the job prospects of its clients. While many job training programs and employment-related services expand human capital and strengthen social networks, incarceration devastates the market power and productive capacity of potential workers. Moreover, penal expansion exacerbates, rather than alleviates, racial and class inequalities. In sum, the massive expansion of the penal system is a uniquely American mode of state intervention that improves conventional indicators of labor market performance in the short term—but will exact a high social cost in the long run. While some policy analysts celebrate the free market principles of the U.S. model, these same principles should be assessed in light of the significant and coercive reallocation of labor through the expansion of American prisons and jails.

NOTES

1. If the number of unemployed is written U and the total number of civilian employees is written E, the usual unemployment rate is given by: $u = 100U/(U + E)$. To take account of the incarcerated population, P, we also examine the adjusted unemployment rate: $u^* = 100(U + P)/(U + P + E)$.

2. This estimate is based on data provided by the Bureau of Justice Statistics and by Rod Miller of the Bureau of Justice Assistance Jail Work and Industry Center.

Why Are U.S. Incarceration Rates So High? (June 1999)
Michael Tonry

Most explanations of the unprecedented increase in American incarceration rates are inadequate. Crime rate increases, more punitive public attitudes, and postmodernist angst are all only part of the explanation. Those things characterize all Western countries, and, in some, imprisonment rates have long been stable or declining. Where they are rising, absolute levels and rates of increase are dwarfed by those in the United States.

The scale of the phenomenon is distinctly American. It arises partly from American moralism and partly from structural characteristics of American government that provide little insulation from emotions generated by moral panics and long-term cycles of tolerance and intolerance.

American imprisonment rates, 668 per 100,000 residents behind bars at mid-year 1998, are at unprecedented levels compared with those at other times in U.S. history or with current rates in other Western democracies. In other Western countries, between 50 and 135 residents per 100,000 are in prison or jail on an average day. In the United States, one of every 150 people today is in prison or jail; that's six to 12 times the rates in other Western countries (Kuhn 1998).

American punishment policies are especially severe in respects other than imprisonment rates. Only in the United States are constitutional and other safeguards of criminal defendants systematically being reduced; throughout Europe, under the influence of the European Human Rights Convention and Court, defendants' procedural protections have been expanding for the past 20 years. Among advanced Western countries, only the United States retains and uses the death penalty, and with increasing frequency. Only the United States has adopted "three-strikes" and extensive mandatory minimum sentencing laws. Only in the United States are life-without-possibility-of-parole sentences commonplace; elsewhere even most murderers sentenced to life terms are eligible for parole or executive-branch commutation and are typically released after eight to 12 years. Only in the United States are prison sentences longer than one or two years common; in most countries, fewer than 5 percent of sentences are for a year or longer; in the United States in 1994 the average sentence for felons sent to state prisons was 71 months.

All of this is a drastic change from earlier times. In the 1960s, the United States was in the mainstream. The death penalty was withering away, the incarceration rate was dropping and comparable to those in other Western countries, the courts were establishing and elaborating defendants' procedural protections, and crime control was not generally viewed as a partisan or ideological issue.

Now, of course, the United States is unique. This article assesses alternate explanations for why American policies have become so punitive. To avoid having repeatedly to use longer-winded phrases, I refer to this in shorthand as the problem of "American exceptionalism." I discuss five explanations of increasing complexity and conclude that we know why our policies are as they are but that acting on that knowledge requires qualities of political maturity and public civility that do not now characterize U.S. politics.

The first explanation is crudely empirical: that American crime rates are higher or have increased more than other countries' and that punishment patterns and policies are no more than a reflection of that reality. The second is psephological: that opinion surveys show that the public has demanded tougher penalties, and elected officials have bowed to that demand. The third is journalistic: that conservative politicians have cynically used crime, as they have used welfare, immigration, and affirmative action, as "wedge" issues designed to separate white working-class voters from the Democratic party. The fourth is political: that developments of the past quarter century have fragmented the electorate into a melange of single-issue political groups and that politicians have sought broad-based support around emotional issues, such as crime, welfare, and immigration, that offend no politically powerful groups. The fifth is historical: that complex, regularly recurring but poorly understood interactions among crime trends, public attitudes, and policy-making shape contemporary thought and policy debates and that current policies are a predictable result.

No single factor could cause so massive a change in policy. The five explanations do not exhaust the possibilities. Others include widespread public anxieties associated with economic restructuring, the civil rights and feminist movements, increased population diversity, ubiquitous focus on violence by the mass media, the angst associated with postmodernism, and other major social changes. All of these, in various forms, however, affect every Western country and accordingly cannot explain why U.S. policies have become so much more severe than those elsewhere.

Crude Empiricism

The first explanation for why so many Americans are in prison, that our crime rates are higher or faster-rising than other countries', has virtually no validity. Crime rates in the United States in the 1990s are, for the most part, not higher than in other Western countries. We know this from the International Crime Victimization Survey, which has been conducted by national governments in most major Western countries since 1989 (e.g., Mayhew and van Dijk 1997a). For property crimes, the United States is in the middle of the pack. Your chances of having your home burglarized or of having your pocket picked or your car stolen are considerably higher in England and several European countries. For most violent crimes, American rates are among the highest, along with Australia, Canada, Spain, and France, but not the highest. Chances of being robbed or assaulted or the victim of a stranger rape are higher in several other Western countries. Where the United States stands out is in gun violence; our rates of robberies and assaults involving guns, and of gun homicides, are substantially higher than those elsewhere (Zimring and Hawkins 1997). That's important. However, only around a fourth of those sentenced to prison are convicted of violent crimes of any type, so that's not why U.S. prison patterns and penal policies are so different.

If absolutely higher crime rates do not explain American exceptionalism, perhaps crime trends do. Perhaps there is a necessary connection between crime rates and imprisonment rates. When crime rates rise, imprisonment rates follow, and that is why the number of people locked up has increased by five times in the past quarter century, from around 300,000 in 1972 to 1,802,496 at mid-year 1998.

Figure 1.1 shows trends in American imprisonment, homicide, and violent crime rates from 1960 to 1993, and the patterns certainly suggest that violent crime and imprisonment at least initially rose together (more recently, however, imprisonment rates have continued their steep climb, while violence rates have dropped sharply). That there is no such necessary connection, however, is shown in figures 1.2 and 1.3, which show comparable data for Finland and Germany, respectively.

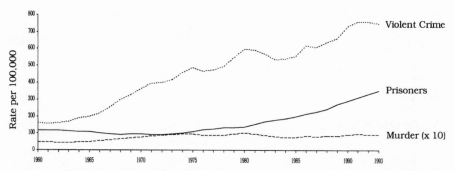

Figure 1.1. Imprisonment, Violent Crime, and Murder Rates per 100,000 Population, United States, 1960–1993. *Notes*: Crime rates are somewhat differently calculated than in Finland and Germany; incarceration rates do not include jail inmates. *Sources*: Bureau of Justice Statistics (various years), *Prisoners in the U.S.* Washington, D.C.: U.S. Department of Justice, Bureau of Justice Statistics; Federal Bureau of Investigation (various years), *Crime in the United States*. Washington, D.C.: U.S. Government Printing Office.

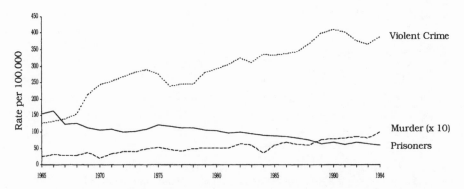

Figure 1.2. Imprisonment, Violent Crime, and Murder Rates per 100,000 Population, Finland, 1965–1994. *Notes*: Violent crime and murder rates are somewhat differently calculated than in the United States; imprisonment rate includes all sentenced prisoners and excludes pretrial detainees. *Source*: Finnish Ministry of Justice.

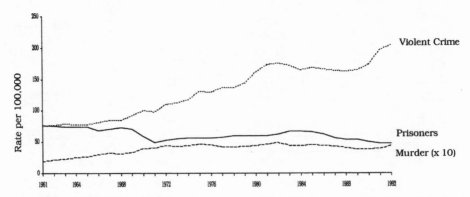

Figure 1.3. Imprisonment, Violent Crime, and Murder Rates per 100,000 Population, Germany, 1961–1992. *Notes*: Violent crime and murder rates are somewhat differently calculated than in the United States; imprisonment rate includes all sentenced prisoners and excludes pretrial detainees. *Source*: German Ministry of Justice.

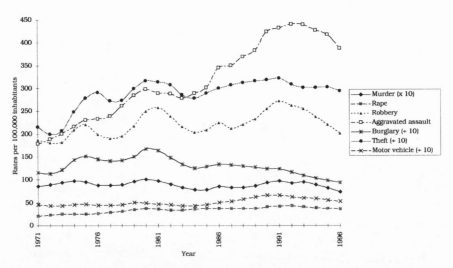

Figure 1.4. Offenses Known to Police, Rates per 100,000 U.S. Inhabitants, 1971–1997. *Note*: Murder rates are multiplied by 10, and burglary, theft, and motor vehicle rates are divided by 10 for purposes of presentation. *Source*: Federal Bureau of Investigation (various years), *Crime in the United States*. Washington, D.C.: U.S. Government Printing Office.

Other countries could have been chosen; the United States is the exceptional case (Kuhn 1997). Although homicide and violent crime rates in Finland and Germany rose as steeply as those in the United States, in Germany the imprisonment rate fell until the early 1970s and remained roughly level thereafter, and in Finland the incarceration rate fell sharply and steadily throughout the entire period. The reasons for those two countries' patterns are different (Lappi-Seppälä 2001; Weigend 2001), but the important point is that they reflect policy decisions that increased incarceration was neither an appropriate nor an effective response to rising crime rates. American politicians decided otherwise. American imprisonment rates rose because American politicians wanted them to rise.

Something wasn't working, and deterrence and incapacitation were the strategies chosen to reduce crime rates. The only problem with this is that the most drastic such strategies were adopted long after crime rates began to fall. As figure 1.4 shows, crime rates for most crimes peaked around 1980, fell through the mid-1980s, rose for a while for reasons largely associated with the crack cocaine epidemic, and have since fallen sharply. The first three-strikes law, however, was enacted in 1993 and the federal "truth-in-sentencing" law, which authorized $8 billion for state prison construction, was passed in 1995. Whatever else these data show, they do not show any simple interaction between crime trends and imprisonment patterns.

Public Opinion

The second explanation is that public opinion survey results sometimes show that "crime" and "drugs" rank first as "America's most pressing problem," that large majorities often express the view that sentencing is too lenient, and that the people demand that criminal punishment be made tougher. On this account, elected officials have merely respected the public will and imprisonment rates have risen as a result.

There are two serious deficiencies in this story. The first is that a mountain of public opinion scholarship and research shows that the "findings" I have reported are fundamentally misleading (e.g., Roberts and Stalans 1997). We know that ordinary citizens base their opinions on what they know about crime from the mass media and as a result that they regard heinous crimes and bizarre sentences as the norms, believe sentences are much softer than they are, and believe crime rates are rising when they are falling. As a result, majorities nearly always report that judges' sentences are too lenient and yet, when asked themselves to propose sentences they would deem appropriate for individual cases, generally propose sentences shorter than those that are actually imposed (Hough and Roberts 1998).

A different body of public opinion research shows that ordinary people have the same complex and ambivalent attitudes toward criminals that judges and lawyers do—simultaneously wanting offenders punished and rehabilitated, willing to see taxes increased to pay for treatment programs but not for prison building, and insistent on prison sentences for the most violent crimes but supportive of other penalties for less threatening offenders (Roberts and Stalans 1997). Thus, the opinion research findings don't actually support undiscriminating policies of unyielding and ever-harsher severity.

The second point about public opinion is more important. Public nomination of crime as the nation's most pressing problem and public support for harsh laws typically follow, not precede, media and political preoccupation with crime. Though politicians who seek favor by demonstrating their toughness nearly always say that they are honoring citizens' wishes, the evidence is that preoccupation by politicians and the media with crime issues is what causes citizens to become concerned. Katherine Beckett (1997a) recently analyzed interactions among media attention to crime and drug issues, politicians' relative emphasis on those issues, and the results of opinion surveys. Content analyses of newspaper and television coverage when compared with public opinion survey results showed a recurring pattern: politicians focused on crime policy, or the media increased their crime coverage, or both, and then, after those things happened, opinion surveys began to show heightened public concern about crime or drugs and heightened support for tough policies. So public support for harsh policies has coincided with their adoption. However, it's not public opinion per se that leads to harsher policies, but politicians' proposals and posturing that lead to changes in public opinion.

Partisan Politics

Crime and punishment have been high on American political agendas since the late 1960s. Before Republican presidential candidate Barry Goldwater raised "crime in the streets" as a partisan issue in his unsuccessful 1964 campaign, public safety was generally seen as one among several important but unglamorous core functions of government, like public health, public transit, and public education. Public officials were expected to do their work conscientiously and well, and systematic knowledge was widely seen as relevant to the formulation of policies and the improvement of institutions and practices. Reasonable people differed over the best approaches for addressing particular problems, but the debates were seldom partisan or ideological. Criminal justice policy was a subject for practitioners and technocrats, and sentencing was the specialized, case-by-case business of judges and corrections officials. In recent decades, however, crime control has been at the center of partisan politics, and policies have been shaped more by symbols and rhetoric than by substance and knowledge. Political scientists and journalists tell the story of how that happened.

Until the 1960s, in most of the South the Democratic party had dominated electoral politics since the end of Reconstruction. Although many southern voters held conservative views on social and racial issues, policy differences were fought out within a state's Democratic party, rather than between parties. The civil rights movement, however, created a fissure within the Democratic party between racial and social policy liberals and racial and social policy conservatives, initially in the South but eventually nationally.

Republican strategists seized the opportunity to appeal to "Nixon [later Reagan] Democrats" by defining sharp differences between the parties on three "wedge issues": crime control, welfare, and affirmative action. On crime control, conservatives blamed rising crime rates on lenient judges and soft punishments and demanded "toughness." On welfare, conservatives blamed rising welfare rolls on "welfare cheats" and laziness and demanded budget cuts. On affirmative action, conservatives blamed white un- and underemployment on "quotas" and urged elimination of affirmative action (e.g., Edsall and Edsall 1991).

Crime's role as a wedge issue has had important consequences. Issues that are debated on television and examined in 15- and 30-second commercials necessarily are presented in simplistic and emotional terms. Matters about which judges and prosecutors agonize in individual cases are addressed in slogans and symbols, which often leads later to adoption of ham-fisted and poorly considered policies.

Notable recent examples include widespread adoption of broadly defined "three-strikes laws," mandatory minimum sentence laws, "sexual psychopath" laws, and the federal sentencing guidelines. Few corrections executives, judges, or informed scholars support such laws in the forms in which they are typically adopted, principally for practical reasons. They are too rigid and often result in unjustly harsh penalties. They are often circumvented by judges and lawyers who believe their application inappropriate in individual cases. They are often redundant, because serious cases nearly always result in severe penalties, anyway.

Many more practitioners and scholars would support such laws if they were narrowly drawn and carefully crafted to encompass only genuinely serious crimes and genuinely threatening offenders. However, in a "sound-bite politics" era, few politicians are prepared to act as voices of moderation and parsimony, and as a result new sentencing laws often lack those qualities.

As important, when crime control became one of the central issues in American politics, it ceased being a specialized policy subject and became instead a symbol or metaphor for, broadly, concepts like "personal responsibility" and vindication of victims' interests and, more narrowly, ideas about criminals' immorality and irresponsibility. A broadly defined sexual psychopath law, three-strikes law, or mandatory minimum sentence law may be ineffective, cruel, or unduly costly, but none of that may matter. If the law's proponents, and voters, view it as a symbol of revulsion toward crime and outrage toward criminals, whether it will work or achieve just results in individual cases is often politically irrelevant. When issues are defined in polar terms of morality and immorality or responsibility and irresponsibility, few elected officials are prepared to be found at the wrong pole.

Few informed people will disagree with the broad outlines of this account. Many liberals might say that the conservative emphasis on toughness was cynical and intellectually dishonest. Many conservatives might respond that they believe that tougher penalties reduce crime rates and that, through public opinion polls and electoral support for "tough-on-crime" candidates, citizens have shown they support such policies. What better basis for policy-making can there be?

In any case, the Right won, and many Democratic politicians have concluded that the only way to defend against sound-bite law-and-order politics, as Bill Clinton is often complimented for having done, is to get to the right of the Republicans (Walker 1998). Of the explanations offered so far, this is the most plausible. It is possible that current American imprisonment policies are merely by-products of an effective electoral strategy. However, that the Right won, whether cynically or honestly motivated, doesn't fully explain American exceptionalism. It doesn't explain why such policies were adopted here, and not in other countries, and now, and not at other times.

Political Fragmentation

What is needed is an explanation for why crime and punishment served so nicely as a wedge issue and why so many elected officials were prepared in recent decades to behave in ways that their opponents and many observers often perceived as demagogic. Social scientists have offered analyses of political and governmental trends of recent decades that attempt to explain why crime has received so much more and more sustained attention from governments and politicians than have other equally important public policy issues.

Sociologists Theodore Caplow and Jonathan Simon (1999) offer two interconnected reasons (among others) why U.S. crime policy has developed as it has. One relates to the paradox that the role of government, particularly the federal government, broadened at a time when public confidence in the capacity of government to achieve public purposes declined. The second relates to the decline of broad-based political coalitions and the development of single-issue politics.

The scope of federal government activity has expanded greatly. For example, the following subjects were largely outside the reach of federal law before the 1960s but today are within it, uncontroversially in principle but with lots of controversy about detail: health care, education, street crime, consumer protection, occupational safety, employment practices, infant and child care, environmental protection, sponsorship of the arts and humanities, and discrimination on grounds of age, race, sex, and disability.

The result, Caplow and Simon (1999) argue, has been a spiral of governmental failure. Related social problems from disorderly schools to illegitimacy are seen as products of failed governmental programs and as sources of crime. The most visible evidence they cite is the massive escalation of costs for virtually all major federal government programs, including health care, education, welfare, and criminal justice, without corresponding increases in benefits. Although none of these systems is widely regarded as conspicuously successful, they are interconnected, and their defects are mutually reinforcing. The extraordinary costs of the health care system prevent any serious effort to alleviate poverty. The deficiencies of the antipoverty programs undermine the public schools. The failures of the schools pour into the criminal justice system.

All of this led to a remarkable collapse of confidence in government. In response to the survey question "How much of the time do you trust the government in Washington to do the right thing," Caplow and Simon (1999) report, 75 percent of a representative national sample in 1964 answered "just about always" or "most of the time." When the same question was put to a similar sample in 1995, only 25 percent gave those answers.

Caplow and Simon's second observation is that American politics have moved away from traditional class and regional divisions and toward a range of "single-issue" movements preoccupied with issues such as abortion, affirmative action, gun control, school prayer, gay rights, and capital punishment. These controversies, Caplow and Simon (1999) note, do not lend themselves to bargaining and compromise. Activists invite people to join the side of good against evil. To anti-abortion activists, abortion is cold-blooded murder. To their adversaries, the right to abortion secures women's ownership of their own bodies. To many gun control advocates, the private possession of firearms is foolish and dangerous; to their adversaries it is the keystone of liberty. All of this makes coalition building difficult and effective implementation of policies even harder.

As a result of political balkanization around moral and absolutist issues, the balance of power in close elections often is, or could be, held by single-issue constituencies, and politicians as a result are reluctant to alienate any of them. Faced with voters who split on so many issues and are profoundly skeptical about the capacities of government, most elected officials promote initiatives that command the broadest support—such as harsh crime, welfare, and immigration policies. The key point is that harsh policies on crime and welfare can be debated in moral terms, respond to broad-based anxieties and empathies, and affront no powerful constituency.

By this point, the explanation for American exceptionalism has gotten pretty complicated. Crime rate levels and changes by themselves don't have much explanatory power. Rising crime rates do provide a plausible basis for heightened public concern about crime, but the best evidence is that ordinary people's views are much more complex, ambivalent, and temperate than is widely recognized. Frightening stereotypes and valid fears provide an intelligible reason why voters respond to "tough-on-crime" rhetoric and appeals but don't explain why politicians in our time chose to campaign on those issues, rather than others. The account of structural changes in American politics is part of the explanation—there is little support in the late 1990s for ambitious broad-based policy initiatives by government, and it is often easier to mobilize support against something than for something. All of these things provide points of understanding, like the dots in a pointillist painting, but they lack a pattern that provides an intelligible picture. That pattern comes from the work of the historian David Musto, which suggests that crime policies, political sensibilities, and the nature of public attitudes about crime are determined by cyclical trends in criminality and responses to it.

Historical Cycles

Historians have long known that crime rates rise and fall over extended periods for reasons that have little to do with crime control policies. The three most influential scholars of the subject—historian Roger Lane (1999) and political scientists Ted Robert Gurr (1989) and James Q. Wilson (Wilson and Herrnstein 1985)—concur in the view that crime rates in the United States, England, Germany, France, and other Western countries have followed a "U" or "backwards J" curve, falling from the second quarter of the nineteenth century through the middle of the twentieth century and then rising until recently. They disagree as to why that happened. Gurr and Lane argue that the century-long decline is associated primarily with the emergence of the industrial economy and the development of bureaucratic institutions, such as schools, factories, and the military, that socialized people into patterns of behavioral conformity, rule observance, and deference to authority. Wilson assigns a major role to religious revivalism in the nineteenth century and a related moral awakening that enhanced character-building processes and law-abidingness. However, none of them attributes the decline primarily to changes in criminal justice system agencies or policies. Many of the major institutions of modern criminal justice systems—professional police, the penitentiary, probation, parole, the reformatory, and the juvenile court—were first established during the long period when rates were falling, but neither then nor now has the fall often been attributed to them.

Drug use and policies also exhibit long-term trends, with periods of prohibitionism in the 1850s, from 1890 through 1930, and from 1980 to the present alternating with periods of greater tolerance. Yale historian David Musto (1987) has shown that antidrug policies interact in predictable ways with patterns of drug use. Seemingly perversely but on reflection understandably, the harshest policies are adopted and the most vigorous prosecutions are carried out after drug use has begun to decline. In our era, for example, self-reported use of marijuana, heroin, and amphetamines peaked for every age group in 1979–80 (for cocaine in 1984–85), and fell steadily thereafter (Tonry 1995, chap. 3), but the harshest federal antidrug laws were not enacted until 1986 and 1988, and the first federal "drug czar" was not named until 1989. If reduced drug use was its aim, the war was being won a decade before it was declared.

The reason all this is understandable is that recreational drug use during prohibitionistic periods is widely seen as immoral and socially destructive. Such attitudes explain why increasing numbers of people stop using and experimenting with drugs and why, after drug use begins falling, comparatively few voices are raised in opposition to harsh policies. Few people, especially elected public officials, are comfortable speaking out on behalf of "immorality." After a while, psychological processes well understood as cognitive dissonance cause many people, perhaps most, to decide that they believe that drug use is immoral and threatening and that there is little to be said in favor of classical liberal values of tolerance.

In more tolerant periods, by contrast, many more people celebrate Enlightenment ideals of moral autonomy and individuals' rights to make choices about their own lives and comfortably oppose harsh laws and policies on those grounds. Something like the recurrent interaction between drug use patterns and drug abuse policy may also characterize interactions between contemporary crime patterns and crime control policies. Two similarities stand out. First, the harshest crime control policies—three-strikes laws, lengthy mandatory minimum sentences, "truth-in-sentencing" laws, increased use of the death penalty—date from the early and mid-1990s, long after crime rates began their steep decline.

Second, few elected officials have been prepared to oppose proposals for harsher laws. Few politicians happily risk being labeled "soft on crime" or "for criminals," rather than for victims. But that's a disparaging account—cowardly, pusillanimous, unprincipled politicians unwilling to stand up for what they believe in the face of cynical and demagogic appeals by their political opponents. Some of that disparagement may be warranted, but it is equally likely that in periods just after crime rates have peaked and begun falling, many more people come to believe that harsh measures are called for and that they will be effective, even if a few years earlier their beliefs were very different.

Harsh laws are often enacted when crime rates are already falling, which enhances people's predisposition to believe that harsh measures work. People who want to make year-to-year comparisons can easily show that the new tougher policies have worked, because crime rates are lower in the years immediately after the change compared with those for the year immediately before. This has happened in relation to New York City's adoption in the early 1990s of "zero-tolerance policing," California's adoption in 1994 of a broadly defined three-strikes law, and the passage in many states in the mid-1990s of "truth-in-sentencing" laws. These may be plausible claims on the part of people who are unaware of long-term crime trends, but, for people who are, they are disingenuous. The year-to-year crime rate declines are at least as likely to be merely the continuation of long-term trends as they are to be effects of policy changes. Nonetheless, such patterns bedevil efforts to devise rational and humane public policies for crime (and for drugs), because they provide plausible support for claims that harsh policies "work."

Scholars have in recent years been trying to make sense of the anomaly that public receptivity to proposals for harsh crime and drug policies remained high in the late 1990s even in the face of substantial and long-term drops in crime rates and in drug use (e.g., Caplow and Simon 1999; Garland 2000). A cynical explanation, mentioned earlier, for which there is some evidence, is that conservative politicians found it in their interest to keep voters' attention focused on an issue about which liberals are reluctant to disagree and that public attitudes and support for harsh policies are simply a predictable response in an era of declining crime rates and moralized policies.

A related explanation is that the mass media have learned that crime pays in terms of a mass public fascination with the darker sides of life and that fears vicariously enjoyed in front of the television or the movie screen are generalized to life outside the home.

A third explanation, consistent with Musto's account of drug policy history and its extension to crime, is that in the 1990s people don't really care about the effectiveness of crime and drug abuse policies but instead support harsh policies for "expressive" reasons. The argument, for which there is some confirmatory public opinion survey evidence (Doob and Marinos 1995), is that people in our time value the denunciatory qualities of harsh laws.

Understanding the Future

Musto's paradigm provides a richer account of American exceptionalism of the past quarter century than do any of the other accounts that I have attempted. It explains why public attitudes are harsher when crime rates are falling than when they are rising, and therefore why law-and-order appeals fall on fertile electoral ground; it explains why politicians feel comfortable appealing to base instincts and proposing policies that in other times would have seemed demagogic and cruel; it explains not only why so few voices are raised in opposition to those policies but also why few people feel a need to speak out in opposition; and it explains why people are inclined to believe that declining crime and drug use rates show that harsh policies work.

There's really nothing unusual about Musto's account of drug policy history and my extension of it to crime policy generally. Historian John Boswell's celebrated history of homosexuality (1980) shows similar cycles of live-and-let-live tolerance and lethal intolerance of homosexuality, and historians of religion and of the arts have documented similarly cyclical patterns. Grant Gilmore has written of the alternation of classical and romantic periods in the arts: "During classical periods, which are, typically, of short duration, everything is neat, tidy, and logical; theorists and critics reign supreme; formal rules of structure and composition are stated to the general acclaim. . . . But the classical period, once it has been formulated, regularly breaks down in a protracted agony. The romantics spurn the exquisitely stated rules of the preceding period; they experiment; they improvise; they deny the existence of any rules; they churn around in an ecstasy of self-expression . . . then, the romantic energy having spent itself—there is a new classical formulation—and so the rhythms continue" (Gilmore 1974, p. 112).

Nor is there anything unusual in the claim that where we stand, and when, influences what we think we think and what we think we believe. The where-we-stand part is something we all recognize in day-to-day life. Wealthy people are more likely to favor low taxes and Republicans than are poor people, who are in turn more likely to favor generous welfare and social programs and Democrats than are the wealthy. Usually, however, we convince ourselves that we have good reasons other than self-interest for believing what we believe.

The when-we-stand part is the same. People in intolerant times are more likely to believe that drug use is immoral and threatening, or that homosexuality is decadent and dangerous, than in tolerant times. Likewise in the arts: during classical periods, people believe they like tradition, regularity, and formalism; in romantic times, they don't. What has any of this to do with understanding American exceptionalism? Everything, for it shows that America's unprecedented and unmatched taste for imprisonment and harsh criminal justice policies has comparatively little to do with them—the offenders who get dealt with one way or another—and everything to do with us. If we took the historical lessons to heart, we might be less quick to adopt harsh crime policies. In our private lives, we know these things, and our folk wisdom celebrates it—don't strike in anger, sit down and count to 10, don't take your frustrations out on your child or your spouse or your employee, write the angry letter but put it aside until tomorrow and see then whether you still want to send it. Whether those private insights will soon shape our public policies remains to be seen.

Early State Guidelines Systems

Washington State Sentencing Changes, 1994–1997
(December 1997)
  Richard D. Van Wagenen

As Washington State moves through its second decade of determinate sentencing, it becomes more apparent each year how responsive such a system can be to public opinion and the political process. Washington's sentencing grid continues to change annually, sometimes by legislation and sometimes by ballot initiative. Previous articles in *Overcrowded Times*, by Roxanne Lieb and David Boerner,[1] have described the changes in Washington sentencing laws since the Sentencing Reform Act took effect in 1984. Those articles chronicle developments through 1994. This essay continues the story through late 1997.

Because Washington had expanded prison capacity to relieve overcrowding after judicial intervention in the early 1980s, it found itself with a temporary surplus of beds in the mid-1980s. The surplus made it easier for the legislature to increase punishment for drug sales, sex offenses, home burglary, and escape between 1987 and 1990. But the surplus quickly disappeared, and Washington began a prison-building program to accommodate population increases from 6,000 in 1988 to more than 12,000 in 1997, with nearly 19,000 inmates projected for 2011.

Three Strikes

When legislators failed to agree on a "three-strikes-and-you're-out" law in 1992, the voters passed one—the nation's first—by a 3-to-1 margin as a ballot initiative in 1993. Unlike some other states' laws, Washington's targets selected only serious felonies. It requires a life sentence, without the possibility of early release, after the third separate conviction of a designated felony. Just over 100 people, mostly robbers in their late 30s, have received life sentences since it took effect four years ago. The state supreme court upheld the "three-strikes" law against a series of constitutional challenges in 1996.

In 1995, the citizens' group that had promoted "three strikes" brought to the legislature a proposal known as "hard time for armed crime," adding sentence enhancements for felonies where the offender was armed with a weapon. Enhancements, which were not subject to "good-time" reduction, ran from six months to 10 years, depending on felony class, number of offenses, and whether the weapon was a firearm. Rather than prepare an alternative to compete with the citizen proposal on the 1995 ballot, the legislature enacted the initiative as proposed. The enhancements are added to about 1.6 percent of felony sentences. Their impact is greatest in cases with multiple counts, because the enhancements run consecutively.

Sex Offenses

Sex offenses have been treated differently from other categories of crimes since the first years of Washington's sentencing reform. In 1984, the legislature authorized a treatment-oriented alternative to prison, available at the court's discretion for first-time offenders not convicted of forcible rape. In 1990, after some highly publicized cases, it added a postprison civil commitment system for "sexually violent predators," who can be confined in a treatment facility indefinitely until they are no longer considered dangerous. A number of other states have enacted similar commitment laws.

Late in 1995, a federal district court struck down Washington's commitment law as unconstitutional. While the state appealed the decision, the legislature enacted a "two-strikes-and-you're-out" law for sex offenders in 1996 and expanded its coverage in 1997. Only two people have been sentenced to life so far under the "two-strikes" law, which targets the most serious offenses.

Another response to the federal court decision was a bill requiring "determinate-plus" sentences for sex offenses. These sentences would consist of a minimum and a maximum — the minimum equal to the determinate sentence under current law, the maximum equal to five years, 10 years, or life, depending on felony class. The parole board, which still exists to deal with pre-1984 offenders serving indeterminate sentences, would set the release date on the basis of public safety considerations.

After this bill passed one house of the legislature in 1997, the sentencing guidelines commission convened a task force to review sex offender sentencing policies. The task force developed an alternative to civil commitment in case the U.S. Supreme Court affirmed the lower court's order. The alternative resembled the "determinate-plus" proposal but was targeted at fewer offenses, required a pattern of predatory behavior, and put the burden on the parole board to release offenders after the determinate sentence unless it found them dangerous.

The governor was prepared to call a special legislative session to pass the task force alternative if the state lost its appeal. But in June 1997, the U.S. Supreme Court upheld Kansas's nearly identical civil commitment law, preventing the release of more than 50 "sexually violent predators" in Washington. The decision may have reduced momentum toward "determinate-plus" sentencing. One of the concerns about the "determinate-plus" proposal is its potential to evolve into an indeterminate system for all felonies, with the current determinate sentences becoming in effect mandatory minimums. Another concern is the difficulty of projecting sentence lengths and prison bed needs with such a system.

In 1997, the legislature increased the standard ranges for the most serious sex crimes, second-degree murder, and manslaughter. The governor vetoed a bill to make sale of methamphetamine a "strike" and another bill requiring consecutive sentences for violent offenses.

Prison Alternatives

Washington has taken long strides toward longer prison sentences in the 1990s, but also a few small steps toward increased use of alternatives to incarceration. The Sentencing Reform Act calls for confinement for violent offenders and alternatives for nonviolent offenders, and the original sentencing grid was largely consistent with these goals. The law permits conversion of jail time to community service, work crew, work release, or home detention on the basis of established conversion ratios. While the grid expresses all sentences as confinement time, the expectation had been that courts would often convert confinement to these alternatives. But there is no enforceable presumption against confinement in any case, and the use of alternatives has not increased over time. Jail and prison time remain the dominant "currency" of sentencing, even for nonviolent crimes.

Drug Offender Sentencing

Nonviolent offenders often go to jail, but they seldom go to prison unless they have long records or have been convicted of selling drugs. In 1987, the legislature disqualified first-time heroin and cocaine sellers from eligibility for a rehabilitative alternative to jail. In 1989, it doubled the standard range to about two years in prison for selling any amount of almost any controlled substance. As the war on drugs stepped up, prisons filled with drug dealers serving short sentences, many of them addicts who had sold small amounts. By 1995, one in four prison inmates was serving a drug sentence.

That year, the legislature enacted a treatment-oriented Drug Offender Sentencing Alternative ("DOSA"), proposed by the sentencing guidelines commission. DOSA gives the court discretion to cut prison time in half, requiring instead treatment in prison and after release, for small-scale heroin and cocaine sellers with no prior felony convictions. This alternative was used in only 15 percent of eligible cases in the first year after enactment and 9 percent in the second year. Reasons include the lack of clarity of some provisions, but more important is the increased availability of other alternatives that offer shorter terms but no treatment. These alternatives include a guilty plea to conspiracy, which carries a shorter sentence, and expanded eligibility for a prison-based "work ethic camp" program, which offers the chance to earn earlier release.

The future of drug sentencing in Washington is uncertain, as DOSA sees little use and legislators face the prospect of competition between small-time drug sellers and an ever-growing "three-strike" population for expensive prison beds. Advocates of drug policy reform, following the lead of California and Arizona, filed a citizen initiative that would have prohibited confinement for possession of controlled substances and prohibited "good-time" release for violent offenses committed under the influence of drugs. Voters decisively rejected this proposal in the 1997 election.

Community Justice Act

Another small step toward expanding alternatives is a proposed "community justice act" that was introduced in the 1997 legislative session. This bill, developed by the state Law and Justice Advisory Council, would allow courts to suspend sentences of a year or less for nonviolent offenders and impose conditions that include community-based "restorative justice" elements. It includes a funding mechanism for state support of local alternatives to jail. Prosecutors and the state employees union have opposed the bill—prosecutors because it allows suspended sentences, state workers because they fear a shift of offender supervision jobs to local government. The Community Justice Act is unlikely to pass soon but may become more attractive as jails get more crowded.

The 1995 "hard time" initiative included a provision that requires the sentencing guidelines commission to publish an annual report on the sentencing practices of individual judges for selected serious felonies. The first published report in 1996 summarized information on standard-range sentences and provided details only on sentences that departed from the range. After criticism from legislators and others, the commission decided to provide much more detail in the 1997 report. The new report describes more than 3,000 sentences in detail but does not include totals or averages. However, journalists and advocacy groups may use these data to "rate" judges, a real concern in a state where they are elected every four years.

Juvenile Sentencing

Washington has been alone in using determinate sentencing in the juvenile courts since 1978. A complex point system produced standard ranges, running from a few days in county detention at the low end to confinement in a state institution until age 21 at the high end. In 1997, the legislature replaced the point system with a simplified grid based on seriousness of offense and criminal history. Lawmakers repealed a presumption against confinement for misdemeanors and an option to avoid state commitment for more serious offenders. They increased enhancements for use of a firearm. They also expanded the list of crimes for which prosecution in adult court is automatic at age 16. The changes in juvenile sentencing took effect for crimes committed after June 30, 1998.

Long-Term Dilemmas

The original goals of Washington's adult sentencing reform in 1981, which took effect in 1984, were proportionality, just punishment, equity, public safety, the chance for rehabilitation, and "frugal use of the state's resources." In a 1996 report to the governor, the sentencing guidelines commission found that the system had by and large met those goals, except for frugal use of resources. Each legislative session has brought longer sentences for crimes featured in news coverage, usually felonies that already drew long prison terms. Lengthening these terms costs nothing in the short run but can cost a lot in the long run. This problem will increase as a 1993 ballot initiative limits state budget growth. The next generation of lawmakers may have to choose between paying for expanding prison populations, driven by sentencing policy choices made in this generation, and paying for education and other services to the generation that follows.

If and when that choice comes, it will be hard to reverse the effect of the decisions made in recent years. There is no evident political appeal in reducing sentences by legislation, liberalizing "good-time" rules, or authorizing wholesale early releases. Policymakers may find a use for the sentencing guidelines commission's "standby" authority to reduce sentence ranges, subject to legislative veto, if the governor declares a prison overcrowding emergency. They may also find a new use for the parole board, which survives to deal with a dwindling number of pre-1984 offenders.

Sentencing reform is supposed to increase accountability, and it has done so for offenders with considerable success. But it has not yet achieved accountability in the use of public resources. In the years to come, the people of Washington and their elected policymakers will have to find a way to decide not just what sentences we want but what we can afford.

NOTES

Detailed information on Washington's sentencing system, including reports on sentences by individual judges, is available from the Sentencing Guidelines Commission, P.O. Box 40927, Olympia WA 98504–0927, or on the Internet at http://www.sgc.wa.gov.

1. These accounts of Washington developments in previous years have been reprinted in *Sentencing Reform in Overcrowded Times: A Comparative Perspective*, edited by Michael Tonry and Kathleen Hatlestad (Oxford University Press 1997).

Ohio Guidelines Take Effect (August 1997)
Fritz Rauschenberg

Amid some fanfare and much fear, Ohio's sentencing reform law went into effect on July 1, 1996. It was the most significant change in Ohio's sentencing law in more than 20 years. The new law resulted from recommendations of the Ohio Criminal Sentencing Commission, which began meeting in 1991 and submitted recommendations to the General Assembly in 1993. It passed in June 1995 and was signed by Governor George Voinovich in August. The effective date was delayed so that officials could be trained and so that legislation could be passed to correct errors in the original version. This article describes the guidelines' implementation and offers preliminary observations on their early days of operation.

The law abolishes indeterminate prison sentencing in favor of a determinate sentence chosen by the judge from a fairly broad range. The sentence announced in court is the sentence to be served. Offenders are eligible for an additional one to 10 years if they are repeat violent offenders. The Parole Authority continues to supervise offenders as they leave prison but is generally not responsible for release decisions. "Good time," which had existed since 1856, was abolished. As a disincentive for misbehavior in prison, the law provided for "bad time."

The law guides judicial discretion, without using a matrix-style grid, and provides one of the most honest truth-in-sentencing laws in the country. Judges are guided toward more or less severe sanctions by a series of purposes, principles, and factors spelled out in the law and by specific guidance based on the level of offense.

The law includes limited appellate sentence review for defendants in cases where a presumption has been successfully rebutted or the judge has imprisoned an offender at the maximum of the range for a given offense level. Similarly, the prosecutor can appeal if a judge imposes a nonprison sentence for a high-level offense. There are also appeals if a sentence is contrary to law or if a pattern of racial disparity is proved.

County governments feared that Ohio's prison doors would be opened and that thousands of felons would end up in county jails. Law enforcement officials feared that changes in drug and theft laws would lead to an unprecedented crime wave, with drug dealers getting away unpunished. Judges were afraid that their discretion had been taken away and that new sentencing rules would overwhelm their already crowded dockets. The appellate courts were threatened by new sentence review procedures that defense attorneys had threatened to use whenever possible.

So What Happened?

While the sentencing legislation was going through the Ohio legislature, the state dramatically expanded its community corrections funding. The number of halfway house slots increased 20 percent, and dollars for nonresidential sanctions increased 10 percent; Ohio's local community-based correctional facilities expanded 44 percent.

For the first time, additional Community Corrections Act money ($5.9 million) was specifically targeted toward offenders diverted from local jails. Ohio's parole supervision operation expanded 27 percent for offenders coming out of prison and facing postrelease control for the first time.

FUNDING The total amount of state money for community corrections (including parole supervision, nonresidential felony sanctions, community-based correctional facilities, jail diversion programs, and halfway houses) grew from just over $102 million in fiscal year 1996 to nearly $132 in fiscal year 1997, when the new sentencing law went into effect. The budget accelerated an already strong state government commitment to community corrections.

Is it enough? The staff of the Ohio sentencing commission and the department of rehabilitation and correction worked hard to make good projections of how many offenders would go into which sanctions. The budget was based on those projections. And a contingency was set up so that if more offenders than expected were diverted, money could easily be transferred from prison operations into community corrections subsidies. In addition, $2 million was set aside to pay for the cost of additional appeals under the new law.

PLANNING The state made $2.2 million available for planning grants to Ohio's 88 counties. The counties had to establish a community corrections planning board and submit a report. While some counties were more effective planners than others, in many counties the judge, sheriff, prosecutor, and county commissioners sat together in a room for the first time. Each county set up the boards, and nearly all used the report to apply for additional community corrections money.

The state department of rehabilitation and correction set up dozens of implementation teams to work on various pieces of the sentencing reform puzzle. It was a daunting task, requiring that parts of the enormous state prison bureaucracy be reconfigured. The department generally proved up to the task, with many new provisions of Ohio's sentencing reform being smoothly implemented.

TRAINING Between the bill's signing and its implementation, sentencing commission members and staff fanned out across the state to train police, prosecutors, defense attorneys, judges, and probation officers.

The commission (with the help of a federal Byrne Memorial grant) prepared training materials, charts, outlines, and manuals that were distributed to anyone who asked. Many statewide professional associations had their own sessions on the new law, inviting commission members and staff to provide expertise. Just about every criminal justice practitioner had access to training.

So, How Has It Gone?

It is still a little early to tell what the impact of the law on the justice system has been. There have been some interesting anecdotes, but little hard data.

Prison intake has indeed declined, by about 4.5 percent. In the first few months officials expected the decline to grow as fewer and fewer offenders were sent to prison who would have been sentenced under the previous law. The decline in intake has not been as large as the 21 percent that we had predicted. The reasons are unclear right now. It is likely that many offenders who were in community corrections under prior law are now being guided toward prison, just as many who were imprisoned under prior law are being guided toward community corrections. Judges seem generally to be following the guidance in the law for prison-bound offenders, and sentences are in line with projections made earlier.

During the debate over the legislation, few issues were more contentious than the appellate review provisions. Defense attorneys said that they would be ethically obligated to appeal everything. The appellate court judges told·us they would be buried in appeals.

It has therefore been a surprise to many observers that there have been very few appeals under the new law, far fewer than originally "guestimated." What makes it even more surprising is that many offenders are coming into prison who are eligible to appeal of right but are not exercising that right. Anecdotal evidence suggests that low-level offenders who get maximum prison terms are not appealing because they are not dissatisfied with what they got, perhaps because the terms are the result of a plea bargain, or perhaps because lengthy local community sanctions are seen as more onerous.

What Does This Mean for Prison Crowding?

Those who worked on the population projections for the new law anticipated a drop in prison population. That drop has not occurred. The main reason for this is that the parole board has become stingier in granting releases to those imprisoned under the old law. Some of this is to be expected—the old-law prisoners who remain are often the worst offenders and therefore less likely to get parole.

However, even if the current prison population matched our projections exactly, the long-term trend in prison population is up. In 1997 Ohio had 46,296 prisoners in 29 prisons, with a total rated capacity of 34,337. Another seven prisons are on the drawing board, which should increase capacity by 5,450 beds.

Several things loom on the horizon for Ohio's prison population. The legislature passed Ohio's first felony drunk-driving law, with mandatory prison terms for fifth-time offenders. It also passed a "Megan's law" targeting sex offenders, coupled with potential life sentences. Both will replace some of the offenders diverted from Ohio's prison population by the sentencing reform law.

There is a great deal of interest in evaluating the impact of Ohio's sentencing reform. Once some time has passed and technical hurdles of data collection and attribution have been cleared, there should be a more precise sense of its effects. The sentencing commission has a duty to monitor the effects of Ohio's reforms and report to the legislature.

In the meantime, the commission is finishing its work on misdemeanor sentencing, with recommendations to go to the legislature in 1997. That package will probably include an overhaul of Ohio's traffic laws, and a reworking of the way fine money is distributed. The commission is also just beginning work on its recommendations on rewriting Ohio's juvenile laws.

Pennsylvania Revises Sentencing Guidelines (August 1997)
Cynthia Kempinen

Revised Pennsylvania guidelines took effect on June 13, 1997. Building on a major overhaul in 1994, the changes expand the range of offenders for whom intermediate punishments are authorized and accompany a substantial increase in state funding for community-based penalties. The 1994 revisions, which similarly authorized expanded use of intermediate punishments, have succeeded in their goal of diverting low-risk offenders from jail and prison to less restrictive punishments. This article describes the 1994 changes and their effects and discusses subsequent developments that led to the 1997 amendments.

Pennsylvania's first set of guidelines took effect in July 1982. After a decade's experience, the Pennsylvania Commission on Sentencing initiated a reassessment of the guidelines that resulted in a complete overhaul that took effect in August 1994. The reassessment was brought about by several factors, including high departure rates for some offenses, prison overcrowding, and relations between guidelines for drug and nondrug offenses.

The 1994 Changes

The commission formed a reassessment subcommittee to examine the guidelines in depth and to present recommendations for changes to the entire commission. The subcommittee included four commission members—an urban judge, a district attorney, a defense lawyer, and a legislator; to provide broader-based input, it also included representatives from corrections, probation and parole, and rural judges.

The reassessment resulted in numerous changes that included increasing the number of offense gravity categories from 10 to 13 to allow for greater distinctions among offenses, giving more weight to prior violent offenses in the calculation of prior-record scores, and creating new prior-record categories that target serious repeat and violent offenders.

The commission also divided the guidelines matrix into four sentencing levels to identify the purposes the commission wished to achieve in each level and the appropriate sentencing options to be used to accomplish those purposes. As the presumptive sentence ranges are proportionate to the gravity of the current offense and the extent of prior record, retribution is the primary purpose. The commission, however, also adopted secondary purposes for each level to take account of other goals, including rehabilitation, deterrence, and incapacitation.

Two major changes were made. One was to provide harsher penalties for violent offenders and, in doing so, to make greater distinctions between violent and non-violent offenders. The second was to refine the concept of "intermediate punishments" and to extend their use. Both changes provoked controversy. The violent offender changes became the focus of 1997 revisions that are discussed later. The intermediate punishment changes raised questions about the meaning of "intermediate punishment," and how the changes were to be funded.

What Is Intermediate Punishment?

When the legislature authorized intermediate punishments ("IP") as an independent sentencing option in 1990, one immediate concern was the similarity between programs included under IP and those traditionally associated with probation. This issue became more pronounced in 1994 when the commission sought to expand use of intermediate punishments.

One major distinction was the type of offender targeted. By statute, probation is for offenders who would not otherwise be incarcerated—when the crime included no serious harm, the defendant is generally law-abiding, the behavior is unlikely to recur, and confinement is deemed unnecessary or would cause excessive hardship. Intermediate punishments are for offenders who would otherwise be sentenced to confinement but who have not committed violent crimes. Thus, the intent was that IP programs would entail more structure and more intensive supervision for otherwise jail-bound offenders who were a "higher-risk" population than probation traditionally handled.

Since the IP legislation provided that a number of programs could be grouped together in a package to be used in lieu of incarceration, the legislature approved the use of a wide range of programs of varying degrees of restrictiveness. The goal was to permit the use of the less restrictive programs under an IP sentence only in conjunction with more restrictive programs. It would have been inappropriate and politically risky to substitute entirely nonrestrictive programs for incarceration. Unfortunately, this was not clearly stated in the text of the legislation, which resulted in a great deal of confusion regarding differences between probation and IP.

The legislation also required each county to develop an intermediate punishment plan that identified programs that would qualify for IP in accordance with regulations developed by the Pennsylvania Commission on Crime and Delinquency ("PCCD"). In order for a judge to be able to impose an IP sentence, the county's plan had to be approved by PCCD. Further, counties had to apply to PCCD for IP program funding and demonstrate that they planned to use the funds in accordance with standards developed for the various programs. Thus, mechanisms were in place to ensure that a given program qualified as IP and that a distinction was made between IP and probation.

Guideline Recommendations for IP

The legislation directed the commission to identify offenders appropriate for IP. On the basis of the commission's understanding of the statute, the 1994 revisions refined the concept of intermediate punishments by dividing IP programs into two categories according to their restrictiveness. The more restrictive programs, such as inpatient treatment and electronic monitoring, were classified as restrictive intermediate punishments ("RIP"). The less restrictive, such as community service or restitution, were referred to as restorative sanctions ("RS"). RS also included standard probation.

Subdividing IP enabled the commission to provide more appropriate sentence recommendations for various types of offenders. Further, the programs under RIP were the ones governed by the PCCD regulations and identified as most appropriate for IP funding.

One notable change in the 1994 guidelines was the allowance of RIP for certain offenders who fell in the area of the matrix in which the presumptive sentence was incarceration. However, before a judge could impose RIP in lieu of incarceration, the guidelines required that the offender undergo a drug and alcohol assessment/evaluation. If the offender was found to be in need of treatment, substance abuse treatment became the only RIP option available. The emphasis on drug and alcohol treatment resulted from insistence by district attorneys that offenders receive drug treatment in licensed programs. Otherwise, jail was the only option.

Funding

A major concern throughout the adoption and implementation of the guidelines was the inadequacy of funding for intermediate punishments. The commission worked hard to secure funding, and $5.3 million was allocated for IP in the 1994–1995 state budget. That, however, was well below the $10.6 million estimated to be necessary. The counties were concerned that the guidelines would result in many more offenders being eligible for IP than the number of available program slots. This, coupled with the anticipated shift of offenders from state prisons to county jails, would increase county jail populations. The district attorneys contended that the commission's estimates concerning the number of people eligible for community programs were much too low. They also argued that there should have been a stronger link between the adoption of the guidelines and the provision of adequate state funding to support IP programs. To complicate the situation, there was a difference of opinion regarding the appropriate use of the $5.3 million. While the district attorneys had expected the funding to be used only for substance abuse programs, the appropriation was not restricted in that way and could be used to support any approved IP program.

Discussions ensued, and the commission worked to develop better estimates of how many people would receive IP and the cost implications. Extensive work was also done to determine a realistic price tag for a comprehensive program of drug treatment and supervision, since this was the IP sentence that had the greatest support. The result was a new estimate of the number of individuals likely to receive drug treatment and a revised price tag of an additional $26.5 million a year, with the existing state funding of $5.3 annually to be used to support other types of approved IP programs. The estimates received broad-based support, and the district attorneys (along with others) worked with the legislative and executive branches to obtain adequate ongoing funding.

Impact of the 1994 Guidelines

The revised 1994 guidelines were projected to reduce the growth of the prison population as a result of the recommendations that certain drug delivery and felony theft offenders be given jail rather than prison sentences. To accommodate the shift of these offenders to the county jails, the revised guidelines recommended community-based programs, rather than jail, for certain offenders convicted of drug possession and misdemeanor theft.

The commission found itself in the awkward position of having guidelines in place while counties lacked funding to carry them out. This raised doubts whether the guidelines could achieve their goals of reserving scarce prison space for violent offenders by redirecting nonviolent offenders from the state prison system to the county jails and expanding the use of community-based sentencing options for offenders who could benefit from alternatives such as substance abuse treatment.

Early monitoring data indicate that the projected shifts are occurring. Table 1.9 compares the sentences imposed for these targeted offenses in 1994 and 1996. For drug and theft offenders targeted to be diverted from prison to jail, there was a decrease in prison admissions. For example, for mid-level traffickers in heroin and cocaine (involving between two and 100 grams), the percentage sentenced to prison fell from 72 percent in 1994 to 57 percent in 1996. For felony retail-theft offenders, the percentage of offenders sentenced to prison dropped from 23 to 6 percent.

Table 1.9 shows that diversion from jail also occurred for offenses targeted for removal from jail. The shift occurred for drug deliveries involving a small amount of marijuana (from 66 percent to 37 percent) and for misdemeanor theft (from 38 percent to 33 percent). For these offenses, the guideline recommendation became RIP or RS, depending on the offender's prior record. While judges appear

Table 1.9. Comparison of 1994 and 1996 Sentences Imposed in Pennsylvania

Offense	Prison	Jail	IP	Probation	RIP	RS
	Major Offenses for Which Shift from Prison to Jail/RIP Expected					
Drug delivery (heroin, cocaine, PCP, METH)						
Less than 2 grams						
1994	1,380 (34%)	2,002 (50%)	77 (2%)	583 (14%)	—	—
1996	752 (24%)	1,600 (52%)	—	—	127 (4%)	613 (20%)
2–100 grams						
1994	2,078 (72%)	610 (21%)	9 (0%)	197 (7%)	—	—
1996	804 (57%)	500 (35%)	—	—	20 (1%)	96 (7%)
Felony theft						
Retail theft						
1994	362 (23%)	766 (48%)	39 (2%)	426 (27%)	—	—
1996	78 (6%)	686 (55%)	—	—	53 (4%)	426 (34%)
Theft (more than $2,000)						
1994	709 (21%)	1,417 (42%)	55 (2%)	1,231 (36%)	—	—
1996	321 (12%)	1,251 (48%)	—	—	55 (2%)	994 (38%)
	Major Offenses for Which Shift from Jail to RIP/RS Expected					
Drug delivery (marijuana)						
Less than 1 lb.						
1994	118 (10%)	799 (66%)	43 (4%)	246 (20%)	—	—
1996	69 (6%)	400 (37%)	—	—	93 (9%)	528 (48%)
Drug possession						
1994	61 (2%)	1,189 (30%)	76 (2%)	2,621 (66%)	—	—
1996	73 (2%)	1,011 (31%)	—	—	82 (2%)	2,124 (65%)
Misdemeanor theft						
1994	455 (6%)	2,883 (38%)	104 (1%)	4,062 (54%)	—	—
1996	310 (5%)	1,933 (33%)	—	—	225 (4%)	3,317 (57%)

Notes: IP = Intermediate Punishments; RIP = Restrictive Intermediate Punishments; RS = Restorative Sanctions

to be following the recommendations for RS (which reflects mostly traditional probation sentences), the shift in sentencing to RIP was less pronounced. Of course, a major concern continued to be that funding was not adequate to assure full implementation of the RIP recommendations. The commission continued to work to secure more funding, while considering guideline revisions that would expand RIP use further.

1997 Guidelines Revisions

After the adoption of the 1994 guidelines, the commission began to work on further revisions. (Figure 1.5 shows the revised matrix that took effect June 13, 1997.) The need to make adjustments was initially the result of arguments by district attorneys that the presumptive sentences for some violent offenders were still not harsh enough. There were also a number of new laws passed as a result of a Special Session on Crime. One of the most notable pieces of new legislation was a "three-strikes" bill that revised mandatory sentences for violent offenders. The commission worked to make the guideline recommendations and the "three-strikes" legislation consistent and, in doing so, to address the prosecutors' call for harsher penalties for violent offenders. Commission staff had worked with the legislature in drafting the "three-strikes" legislation, and the offenses included in that statute parallel closely the offenses included in the upper tier of the guidelines (i.e., offense gravity scores 9 to 14) that require a state prison sentence. To the credit of both the legislature and the governor, who encouraged a well-thought-out, rational "three-strikes" policy, Pennsylvania enacted one of the most reasonable "three-strikes" bills in the country.

Another major change incorporated in the 1997 guidelines was further expansion of RIP. The 1994 guidelines allowed RIP for certain offenders who would otherwise have received a county jail sentence (LEVEL 3). The 1997 guidelines expanded this concept to allow for a RIP exchange for certain "state" offenders (LEVEL 4). These are offenders for whom the guideline recommendation would result in a maximum sentence of between two and five years. While normally such offenders are sent to state prisons, the judge can designate that they serve the sentence in the county jail. The rationale was that the statute includes offenders who "would otherwise be sentenced to a county facility." In the definition of IP eligibility, the procedures for sentencing an offender to RIP in lieu of incarceration at LEVEL 4 are the same as those discussed earlier for LEVEL 3.

The latest guideline revisions were submitted for legislative approval in March 1997 while the 1997–1998 budget was being negotiated. In April, the legislature allocated an additional $10 million for drug and alcohol IP programs in the 1997–1998 budget, along with the original $5.3 million for other types of IP programs. While less than half of the original request, this was a victory in a time when the corrections system already consumes a significant portion of the state budget. The guidelines met with legislative approval and became effective June 13, 1997.

The commission, along with PCCD and the Pennsylvania Department of Health/Office of Drug and Alcohol Programs, will review applications from counties for distribution of the $10 million. This competitive application process should

Prior Record Score										
	OGS	0	1	2	3	4	5	RFEL	REVOC	AGG/MIT
LEVEL 5 State Incar	14	72–240	84–240	96–240	120–240	168–240	192–240	204–240	240	+/- 12
	13	60–78	66–84	72–90	78–96	84–102	96–114	108–126	240	+/- 12
	12	48–66	54–72	60–78	66–84	72–90	84–102	96–114	120	+/- 12
	11	36–54 BC	42–60	48–66	54–72	60–78	72–90	84–102	120	+/- 12
	10	22–36 BC	30–42 BC	36–48	42–54	48–60	60–72	72–84	120	+/- 12
	9	12–24 BC	18–30 BC	24–36 BC	30–42 BC	36–48 BC	48–60	60–72	120	+/- 12
LEVEL 4 State Incar/ RIP trade	8 [F1]	9–16 BC	12–18 BC	15–21 BC	18–24 BC	21–27 BC	27–33 BC	40–52	NA	+/- 9
LEVEL 3 State/Cnty Incar RIP trade	7 [F2]	6–14 BC	9–16 BC	12–18 BC	15–21 BC	18–24 BC	24–30 BC	35–45 BC	NA	+/- 6
	6	3–12 BC	6–14 BC	9–16 BC	12–18 BC	15–21 BC	21–27 BC	27–40 BC	NA	+/- 6
LEVEL 2 Cnty Incar RIP RS	5 [F3]	RS–9	1–12 BC	3–14 BC	6–16 BC	9–16 BC	12–18 BC	24–36 BC	NA	+/- 3
	4	RS–3	RS–9	RS–<12	3–14 BC	6–16 BC	9–16 BC	21–30 BC	NA	+/- 3
	3 [M1]	RS–1	RS–6	RS–9	RS–<12	3–14 BC	6–16 BC	12–18 BC	NA	+/- 3
LEVEL 1 RS	2 [M2]	RS	RS–2	RS–3	RS–4	RS–6	1–9	6–<12	NA	+/- 3
	1 [M3]	RS	RS–1	RS–2	RS–3	RS–4	RS–6	3–6	NA	+/- 3

Key:
AGG	= aggravated sentence addition	MIT	= mitigated sentence subtraction
BC	= boot camp	OGS	= offense gravity scale
CNTY	= county	RFEL	= repeat felony 1 and felony 2 offender category
F	= felony	REVOC	= repeat violent offender category
INCAR	= incarceration	RIP	= restrictive intermediate punishments
M	= misdemeanor	RS	= restorative sanctions
		< ; >	= less than; greater than

Figure 1.5. Pennsylvania's Guideline Recommendations (June 13, 1997). *Notes*: Shaded and cross-hatched areas of the matrix indicate restrictive intermediate punishments may be imposed as a substitute for incarceration; when restrictive intermediate punishments are appropriate, the duration of the restrictive intermediate punishment program shall not exceed the guideline ranges; when the range is RS through a number of months (e.g., RS-6), RIP may be appropriate. *Source*: Pennsylvania Commission on Sentencing.

result in full funding of drug and alcohol IP treatment for targeted offenders in selected counties. An evaluation is being developed to study the effects of the use of comprehensive treatment and supervision as an alternative to incarceration. Time will tell how successful the new programs are in meeting their goals.

North Carolina

North Carolina Prepares for Guidelines Sentencing
(February 1994)
Ronald F. Wright

In July 1993, the North Carolina legislature enacted new sentencing reform legislation. This was the state's second recent effort to overhaul sentencing. The first, in 1979, worked roughly as intended for its first few years but soon fell apart. Beginning in January 1995, North Carolina will begin using presumptive sentencing guidelines similar to those in Oregon, Washington, Minnesota, Kansas, and Pennsylvania. The legislation abolished parole release.

The politics of sentencing reform in North Carolina have been unusual. Because of concern for prison population and costs, key legislators, unlike legislators in many states, have not called for ever harsher penalties. Unlike Kansas and Pennsylvania, for example, where legislatures rejected initial guidelines proposals because they were not severe enough, North Carolina legislators rejected sentencing commission proposals because they would have placed too great a burden on stretched corrections resources.

Criminal justice officials can expect the new system to bring relief to a severely damaged and barely credible system. Like those in Texas and Florida, North Carolina prisons have had revolving doors through which prisoners were released to accommodate new admissions and to comply with a population cap. Nonetheless, the sentencing commission and the Department of Correction ("DOC") must also brace themselves for difficult problems during the transition period before guideline sentencing begins, and in the early years of guideline operation.

During the transition period, DOC must respond to a potential loss of 3,000 prison beds (out of about 21,000 now in use). A 1986 consent decree is responsible for this loss of beds: in 1994, minimum square footage per prisoner goes up from 35 feet to 50 feet. The sentencing commission must also design and execute a training program for judges, lawyers, and court officials and keep the General Assembly informed about guidelines changes that may be proposed during a special session on crime.

The 1979 Reforms

The 1979 Fair Sentencing Act specified presumptive sentences for each felony. Judges could sentence offenders to longer or shorter prison terms if they explained their reasons. The Act abolished parole release, but the legislature restored "emergency" parole power a few years later.

The Act promised to bring more uniformity and predictability to sentencing, but it delivered on these promises only for the first few years. As state population and convictions rose, the presumptive sentences produced overcrowded prisons. A federal lawsuit over prison conditions ended in 1986 in a consent decree: the state agreed to a prison population cap (now embodied in statute).

The increase in convictions, the presumptive sentences, the population cap, and the failure to build new prisons combined to force the state to release prisoners early by use of a variety of "back end" measures. Sentencing judges became frustrated as they watched the gap grow between the sentences they imposed and the times served. They responded by imposing sentences longer than the presumptive levels, and the gap grew larger still.

As time served for active sentences declined, offenders sentenced to suspended terms with onerous conditions began to opt for active terms or to violate the terms of their probation. This, of course, further worsened crowding.

The Commission and Its Proposals

In 1990, the General Assembly created a Sentencing and Policy Advisory Commission and charged it to propose changes in this deteriorating system. After two years of study, the commission proposed a sentencing structure now familiar in other guideline states.

The proposed guidelines ranked felony offenses into nine levels of severity, giving a clear priority in prison space to violent offenders who had caused bodily harm and directing most property offenders into nonprison sanctions. Misdemeanors were ranked into three levels of severity in order to prevent uncontrolled use of jails to bypass limits on the use of prisons.

The offense seriousness rankings created the vertical axis of a sentencing grid, a format now used in almost every guideline state. The criminal record of the offender—the second major variable in the sentence—created the horizontal axis. The commission's proposal assigned points for every prior felony or misdemeanor, with more points assigned for more serious offenses (as in Washington State).

The sentencing grid sorted offenders into six different prior record levels. The proposed point system accelerated sentence lengths quickly as prior records lengthened. A simplified point system measured the prior criminal records of misdemeanants.

Most cells in the proposed grid specified a "community" punishment (such as outpatient drug treatment or unsupervised probation, providing minimal control of the offender), an "intermediate" punishment (nonprison sanctions requiring more intensive supervision), or an "active" punishment (a prison term). Community sanctions were available for the least serious crimes and the least extensive prior records. Some cells on the border between types of sanctions authorized judges to choose between them.

The commission's proposal gave judges no power to depart in unusual cases if the grid specified only one disposition. An active term could not be reduced to an intermediate sanction. The only departure power granted to the judge was to set the *duration* of the sentence outside the range specified in the grid box. The judge could choose from an aggravated or mitigated range (spanning 25 percent above and below the presumptive range) after explaining on the record why the case was unusual. Such decisions would be subject to appellate review.

After the commission provided an interim report to the General Assembly, key legislators sent a clear signal that new prison costs should be kept to a minimum. A new statute instructed thecommission to submit at least one proposal that required no immediate prison construction beyond new facilities already financed by a recently (and narrowly) approved bond issue.

The commission complied grudgingly. It submitted and endorsed the plan already described, which called for more than 10,000 new prison beds over five years: an increase in the felony population from 23,000 to 31,000, along with the space needed for the longest misdemeanor sentences. A minority report called for significantly greater reliance on prison.

The commission also submitted, without endorsement, a standard operating capacity ("SOC") plan that did not require any new growth in prison capacity during the first few years. The SOC plan did, however, forecast a slower expansion of about 9,000 beds over 10 years. The SOC plan reduced prison requirements by reducing the influence of prior record and by reducing durations in all cells.

The New Legislation

A relatively small Democratic leadership group in both the House and the Senate had drafted the statute creating the commission and had pointed it toward guideline sentencing. The same group dominated the debate over the commission's final proposals. It soon became clear that the SOC plan would receive the closest attention in both houses. In a legislative session dominated by a search for health care and education dollars, there was no sentiment, within the leadership group or elsewhere, for funding much new prison construction.

There was serious question, however, whether the legislature would approve the concept of using sentencing guidelines to control prison population. Because the package eliminated parole release, the parole commission became its most influential critic.

The parole commission relied on anecdotal evidence to argue that sentencing guidelines in other systems have exacerbated prison crowding. More plausibly, the commissioners warned that predictions of future prison populations cannot be exact and that some "safety valve" might be necessary. Finally, they pointed out that none of the proposals made any attempt to tie sentence lengths to the predicted dangerousness of individual offenders or to hold the most dangerous offenders for the longest times.

The legislature chose the public visibility and certainty of sentencing guidelines over the ability to hold potentially dangerous offenders for more indefinite terms. The parole commission's arguments, however, produced an important change. The final legislation provides for six months mandatory postrelease supervision for all felons convicted of the most serious classes of offenses. Violators can be returned to prison for up to nine months.

Other deviations from the sentencing commission proposal tended to reduce the system's reliance on prison. Where the commission had treated attempted crimes and completed crimes as equivalent in seriousness, the legislation placed attempts one level below the completed crime.

Where the commission had given judges no power to change a disposition specified in the guidelines, the legislation allowed judges to depart from a prison sentence and impose an intermediate punishment where there is "extraordinary mitigation." Finally, where the commission had remained silent on the duration of nonprison sanctions, the legislation established ranges of possible lengths for probation terms. One effect will be to prevent judges from imposing such onerous probation terms that low-level offenders choose prison far more often than probation. Imposing guidelines on probation use acknowledges that probation, like prison, is a scarce resource and that funding for the system must match its anticipated use.

Hence, the legislature and the commission continued the roles they established earlier in the process. The commission called for faster growth in the prison system, and the General Assembly held out for cheaper alternatives to prison. In light of the greater insulation of the commission from political pressure, it is somewhat surprising that the General Assembly took the less politically popular position.

Although the legislature emphasized intermediate sanctions, it did not increase funding to match the anticipated needs. If caseloads increase for probation officers or other program officials, intermediate sanctions may become no more intrusive than community sanctions and lose their already shaky credibility with the public.

Department of Correction Challenges

From DOC's point of view, the greatest disappointment is that the guidelines' effective date was pushed back from January 1994 to October 1994. This means one more year of operating a system that makes prison officials appear foolish or negligent. The accelerated early release practices of recent years will continue. There will be virtually no imprisonment for misdemeanors, and the gap between prison terms announced and actual times served will grow.

DOC must also deal with a public relations dilemma. The 1986 consent decree called for a further reduction in prison crowding by early 1994, with minimum allowable square footage per inmate up from 35 to 50. This will mean a temporary loss of roughly 3,000 prison beds. The attorney general is seeking federal court approval to keep the square footage at 35. The governor has explored the possibility of sending prisoners out of state.

Both the commission proposal and the legislation anticipated the loss of beds. It coincides, however, with a cluster of highly visible crimes, including the murder of Michael Jordan's father, committed by offenders with prior felonies, some released early from prison. These events may create pressure to rethink the new sentencing legislation before it takes effect, perhaps to reinstitute authority to hold dangerous inmates longer.

To complicate matters further, merchants in Durham have filed a lawsuit in state court, seeking to invalidate the statutory prison cap under the North Carolina constitution. They claim that the "prisons" clause in the constitution ("Such . . . correctional institutions . . . as the needs of humanity and the public good may require shall be established and operated by the State") requires the state to respond to any prison bed shortage by building new prisons, not by shortening terms. If the court were to rule for the plaintiffs, it could call into question the constitutionality of the sentencing guidelines themselves. The guidelines, like the statutory prison cap, ration prison space, rather than expand prison capacity.

Short-Term Challenges for the Commission

The governor recently called an emergency session of the legislature to address crime, and the odds of further changes in the sentencing guidelines have increased. The legislature could advance the effective date or change the classifications of particular crimes. It will almost certainly authorize new prisons.

The commission must anticipate various proposals for change and inform legislators about the systemic consequences of each. This is bound to distract them from another critical task—training judges, court personnel, and attorneys who will be using the guidelines. Two forces have made training unduly difficult.

First, the training will take place in an atmosphere of cynicism. The state has operated under a partially structured but failed sentencing regime for the past 10 years. Judges will need to be convinced that this reform has greater prospects of success than its predecessor.

Second, the training will take place amid apprehension about sentencing guidelines, deriving mostly from controversies associated with the federal guidelines. Few court personnel and attorneys in North Carolina have firsthand experience with the federal guidelines, but they have heard plenty of complaints about them.

Long-Term Challenges

After the guidelines take effect, the commission's most important duties will be to monitor the system and anticipate any adjustments needed. Three areas will bear watching.

First, the commission must monitor the habitual felon provisions closely. Under the commission's proposal, any offender convicted of three prior felonies could be charged separately as a habitual felon, a Class D felony. The General Assembly limited this provision, by insisting that at least two of the three prior felonies be more serious than a Class H or I felony (the two least serious classes). Still, offenders in more than one-quarter of the guideline cells could have their sentences enhanced as habitual felons.

In the past, difficulties in proving prior felonies with authenticated records limited the use of the habitual felon statute. The new system, however, creates more incentive, and, combined with the state's commitment to a cutting-edge information system, it may lead to an explosion in habitual felon charges. Moreover, prosecutors are hoping to convince the legislature to amend the statute to broaden the number of eligible felons.

The commission must also remain mindful of drug charges that carry mandatory minimums. The guidelines do not cover drug trafficking or drunk driving charges. A big change in the number of drug convictions could strain the prisons, as has happened in the federal system. In the long run, it may be necessary to include drug trafficking and drunk driving within the guidelines system. Both were considered too controversial to include in the initial legislative package.

Finally, certain forms of judicial discretion must be monitored closely. The most important involves multiple offenses. Under the new statute, the court retains complete discretion to impose consecutive or concurrent sentences for multiple convictions. If judges start to impose consecutive sentences more often, prosecutors will respond by multiplying charges. The population estimates that underlie the sentencing durations in the grid will become meaningless, and the system will spin out of control.

Judges also control the future of structured sentencing through their use of "border blocks," the areas in the grid giving them discretion to choose between active prison terms and intermediate punishments. If the judges choose active terms at a much higher rate than in the past, the commission's population projections will lose touch with reality.

When adjustments become necessary to keep the system afloat, the commission will not be able to make those adjustments alone. The enabling legislation gives the commission no independent power to amend its guidelines. It can only make recommendations to the legislature. Since the General Assembly meets in full session only every two years, it may be impossible to respond quickly to problems. Even if the commission can get a timely response from the legislators, they may not be able to obtain a satisfactory answer.

Because of lessons drawn from the failure of the 1979 Act, it may be possible for North Carolina to keep a consistent approach to sentencing, to fund the strategy adequately, and to finetune the system as conditions change. The presence of the sentencing commission to frame and inform debate might make a difference this time.

Sentencing Changes in North Carolina (June 1996)
Robin L. Lubitz

Over the past several years, North Carolina has dramatically reshaped how offenders are sentenced, how prison resources are prioritized, and how correctional dollars are spent. The effects of these changes are now becoming evident and point to a more rational, accountable, and cost-effective criminal justice system.

The catalyst was the passage of the State's Structured Sentencing Act ("SSA"). This legislation was based on recommendations developed by the North Carolina Sentencing and Policy Advisory Commission and took effect late in 1994. Through a system of sentencing guidelines, the SSA established truth in sentencing, increased consistency in sentencing, and redirected the flow of offenders into prison and community-based corrections. At the same time, the state enacted a State-County Criminal Justice Partnership Act. This legislation, modeled after community corrections acts in other states, was designed to encourage the creation of county-based correctional programs responsive to local needs. Surrounding the adoption of both acts was a flurry of activity to restructure program eligibility requirements, redesign forms and procedures, train court and criminal justice personnel, and revamp information systems.

Initial Impact

STRUCTURED SENTENCING MONITORING SYSTEM · The sentencing commission has ongoing responsibility to monitor sentencing practices under the new law, to report sentencing information, and to make recommendations for modifications to the law when necessary. To this end, the commission worked closely with the Administrative Office of the Courts to develop and implement its *Structured Sentencing Monitoring System*. This system piggybacks on the state's existing automated court information system. This monitoring system has been in operation since January 1, 1995, and provides detailed data on all sentenced felons and misdemeanants. Sentencing data have now been collected and analyzed for 1995 and demonstrate that the SSA is beginning to achieve its goals.

ESTABLISHING TRUTH-IN-SENTENCING   Under the SSA, felons are required to serve 100 percent of the minimum sentence imposed by the court and may serve up to 20 percent longer. In the years leading up to passage of the SSA, there was a steady decline in the average percentage of sentence served. In 1987, the average felon served 40 percent of the sentence imposed. By 1991 this figure had dropped to 24 percent, and by 1993 it was less than 19 percent. Figure 1.6 shows the average percentage of sentence served from 1986 through 1993 and shows the corresponding percentage for structured sentencing cases in 1995. For purposes of statistical

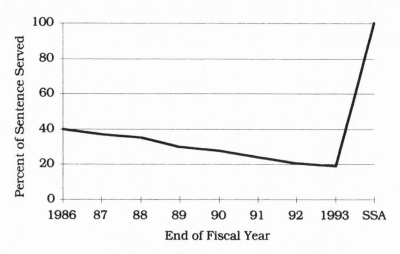

Figure 1.6. Average Percentage of Sentence Served. *Note*: SSA = Structured Sentencing Act (1995).

comparison, 1993 was used as the base year because this was the last full calendar year before implementation of the SSA.

PRIORITIZING THE USE OF PRISON RESOURCES   Under the SSA, prison is mandatory for the most serious violent felonies, such as murder, rape, kidnapping, and armed robbery, and for career offenders, but nonviolent offenders with little or no prior record are channeled into community-based intermediate punishments. This has resulted in a significant shift in the number and type of offenders sentenced to prison. The percentage of violent offenders receiving prison sentences has increased from 67 percent to 81 percent, while the imprisonment rate for nonviolent offenders has decreased from 42 percent to 23 percent. Because many more offenders fall into the latter category, the overall rate of imprisonment has substantially declined. Table 1.10 shows changes in imprisonment rates by class of crime, comparing sentences imposed in 1993 with those imposed in 1995 under the SSA. It demonstrates substantial increases for violent crime classes (B1 through E) and substantial decreases for the nonviolent crime classes (Classes F through I).

INCREASING TIME SERVED FOR VIOLENT AND CAREER OFFENDERS   Although fewer offenders go to prison under the SSA, those who do will stay longer. Overall, average time served for felons is expected to increase from about 16 months for those sentenced in 1993 to 37 months for those sentenced under the SSA in 1995. For violent offenses, average time served is expected to increase from 56 months in 1993 to 87 months for offenders sentenced in 1995 under the SSA. Table 1.11 shows changes in average time served by class of crime, comparing sentences imposed in 1993 with those imposed in 1995 under the SSA. The table shows substantial increases for most classes of crimes, especially violent crime classes (B1 through E).

BALANCING SENTENCING POLICIES WITH PRISON RESOURCES   A cornerstone of the SSA is that sentencing policies must be balanced with correctional resources (both prison and community corrections). To support the SSA, the General Assembly

Table 1.10. Percentage Receiving Prison Sentence

Offense Class	1993	Structured Sentencing 1995
A	100%	100%
B1	100	100
B2	97	100
C	84	100
D	93	100
E	52	53
F	47	37
G	65	58
H	45	25
I	31	8

Table 1.11. Average Months Served in Prison

Offense Class	1993	Structured Sentencing 1995
A	Life with parole	Life without parole
B1	240 months	301 months
B2	92 months	171 months
C	55 months	94 months
D	73 months	75 months
E	25 months	35 months
F	23 months	23 months
G	22 months	18 months
H	12 months	13 months
I	7 months	9 months

funded a significant expansion of prison capacity. When all currently funded prison construction is completed late in 1997, the state will have prison capacity for about 35,000 inmates. This will be sufficient to carry out the new sentencing policy until about the year 2004 (assuming no further changes to sentencing law). In the meantime, however, the state is experiencing a temporary shortage of prison capacity (some prisoners are being housed in out-of-state facilities), which was predicted by the sentencing commission and results from a decline in parole releases for offenders still in the system under the old law.

BALANCING SENTENCING POLICIES WITH COMMUNITY CORRECTIONS RESOURCES The SSA has expanded sentencing options so that the choice of punishment is no longer limited to prison or probation. Large numbers of nonviolent offenders are now channeled into intermediate punishments. To achieve truth in sentencing, prison sentences must be supported by adequate prison capacity, and, equally important, nonprison sentences must be supported by meaningful community-based punishments that control and treat offenders, while helping to restore the victim and the community.

With the passage of the SSA, the General Assembly provided funding to hire more than 500 new probation officers. This additional staff was intended to reduce caseloads and to permit closer supervision and control over offenders sentenced to community-based punishments. At the same time, the Division of Adult Probation and Parole has undertaken an ambitious reorganization of its structure and procedures. The division has developed new methods for classifying offenders, for tightening or loosening controls, for adding or removing sanctions, and for handling technical violations. As a result, there has been a 25 percent reduction in admissions to prison resulting from probation violations (12,496 such admissions in 1993 compared to 9,320 in 1995).

As part of the overall sentencing reform package, the General Assembly funded the State-County Criminal Justice Partnership Act at $12 million per year. Under this Act, counties can create advisory boards to assess their local correctional program needs and to submit applications for funding to the state. These programs must be targeted for pretrial offenders, offenders sentenced to intermediate punishments under the SSA, or offenders under postrelease supervision. These programs are generally treatment oriented and are intended to supplement, but not replace, the strict supervision and control provided by state probation officers.

To date, 82 of North Carolina's 100 counties have applied for funding through the State-County Criminal Justice Partnership Act, and 70 counties have had programs funded, with 12 still pending. Currently funded programs include 41 day-reporting centers, 18 pretrial release programs, 16 stand-alone substance abuse treatment programs, and three stand-alone work/employment programs. In addition, 75 residential substance abuse treatment beds have been funded.

The most frequently funded program is day reporting. Although the particulars of each day-reporting center vary, all establish a highly structured day or evening environment that requires offenders to work, perform community service, receive substance abuse treatment, or participate in educational and vocational development programs.

Implementation and Related Issues

To prepare for the new law, the sentencing commission (in conjunction with the Administrative Office of the Courts and the University of North Carolina's Institute of Government) undertook an ambitious education program. Training and reference manuals were prepared and distributed, forms and procedures were redesigned, and educational seminars were conducted across the state. More than 2,000 judges, prosecutors, defense attorneys, court clerks, probation officers, and other criminal justice personnel attended the seminars.

ADJUSTMENTS TO THE LAW   The training seminars provided an opportunity for the sentencing commission to receive feedback from criminal justice practitioners. The information helped the commission identify potential problem areas and propose solutions. Consequently, the commission made several recommendations to the General Assembly in 1995 for adjustments to the SSA. Several were enacted and took effect at the end of 1995. The adjustments increased sentence lengths for certain violent offenses and gave judges more discretion to impose prison sentences for certain first-time property offenders. At the same time, the General Assembly appropriated the necessary funds to support these changes on the basis of impact estimates provided by the commission.

OBSTACLES AND PROBLEMS   The shift to the new law did not occur without some problems and resistance. The SSA not only required practitioners to learn new laws and procedures but also required a shift in thinking about what a sentence meant and when a particular sentence was appropriate. It also placed an additional responsibility on prosecutors to obtain and present criminal history information for all felons. Complicating matters further, the old law continued to apply to offenses committed prior to the effective date of the SSA. This meant that two very different sets of sentencing laws, procedures, and philosophies were temporarily operating concurrently. Over time, however, these initial difficulties were overcome, and the vast majority of offenders are now subject to the SSA. Dire predictions of slowdowns in court processing and increases injury trials failed to materialize.

Perhaps most challenging has been the transition to truth in sentencing. Because of the elimination of parole and other early-release mechanisms, sentences now appear shorter than in the past. This has been a difficult adjustment for some in the criminal justice system. Some judges were uneasy imposing shorter-sounding sentences, even though they knew that in most cases offenders would serve more time. Not surprisingly, a few outside the criminal justice system tried to take political advantage and to paint the SSA as lenient. Fortunately, the media have been generally responsible in reporting the facts and in setting the record straight. Such charges are clearly contradicted by increases in incarceration of violent and career offenders, longer average times served by nearly all felons and misdemeanants, and substantial increases in prison populations and capacities.

UNEXPECTED FINDINGS   Overall, there were few surprises during the first year of the SSA, and sentencing patterns closely conformed to predictions. One unexpected finding, however, was a decline in incarceration rates for Class F and Class G felons. Offenses in these two classes commonly involve serious property loss, serious societal injury, or significant personal injury. Because the SSA does not limit judges' discretion to impose incarceration for these crimes, these reductions cannot be directly linked to the SSA. These declines may, however, be explained by the expanded availability of intermediate punishments and may signal an unexpected willingness of judges to impose intermediate punishments in lieu of prison.

PUBLIC OPINION   As part of a grant from the Edna McConnell Clark Foundation, North Carolina contracted with John Doble Research Associates, Inc., to conduct a public opinion survey of the views of the people of North Carolina about crime and corrections.[1] The results supported the goals of the SSA. A vast majority of those surveyed supported the concept of truth in sentencing—even if sentences sounded shorter. A vast majority also supported the idea of structuring sentences so that offenders with similar prior records who commit similar crimes receive similar sentences. Large majorities supported longer prison terms for violent criminals and use of community-based alternatives to prison for nonviolent offenders. All these concepts are encompassed within the SSA.

Conclusions

The SSA is working as planned and is beginning to accomplish its goals. Truth in sentencing has been established, and the revolving prison door has been shut. Violent offenders are more likely to go to prison and will serve more time once there. Nonviolent offenders are less likely to go to prison and instead are being channeled into an array of less expensive intermediate punishments. When current construction is completed, the state's prison capacity will match projected prison populations, thus bringing sentencing policies and correctional resources into balance. The state has also significantly increased its probation force to provide more meaningful control and supervision of offenders in the community. Last, through the State-County Criminal Justice Partnership Act, the state has funded additional community-based correctional programs designed to help reduce future crime by providing treatment, education, and work opportunities for offenders and requiring offenders to compensate the victim and the community.

NOTE

1. The survey was conducted during August 1995 and involved telephone interviews with a random sample of 810 North Carolina adults. *Crime and Corrections: The Views of the People of North Carolina* (October 1995), Doble Research Associates, Inc.

Flexibility in North Carolina Structured Sentencing, 1995–1997
(December 1998)
  Ronald F. Wright

North Carolina revamped its sentencing practices in the early 1990s and began to operate its new system in October 1994. With data now available from three full years of sentencing under the new system—calendar years 1995 through 1997—it is possible to make a few preliminary observations about the effects of the legal changes.

It appears that the sentencing structure, at least at this early stage, is accomplishing its major objectives. The system is effectively rationing prison sentences: fewer offenders are serving prison terms, while those who do go to prison (mostly violent and repeat offenders) are serving longer terms. The sentencing rules also allow for resource planning: prison populations and the use of community and intermediate sanctions are remaining within predicted ranges.

The early experience also shows the persistent need for flexibility in a sentencing system. The North Carolina system lacks some forms of flexibility that are available in most other systems. In particular, North Carolina sentencing judges do not have the power to "depart" from the prescribed sentence range in unusual cases.

The need for sentencing flexibility in unusual cases has become a recurring source of pressure to amend the guidelines in the legislature, particularly in connection with assault crimes. Concerns about a subset of unusual assault crimes convinced legislators to amend the sentencing laws in 1995 and 1996. The legislature created new categories of assault crimes and gave sentencing judges more discretion to impose an active prison sentence.

While the lack of sentencing flexibility has shaped the legislature's work in important ways, the same is not true for sentencing judges in North Carolina. Early charging and sentencing patterns suggest that judges have gotten along without departures for most categories of cases. The departure power is useful but not essential for sentencing flexibility: the sentencing judge in North Carolina does have a choice among different dispositions for several key groups of offenses and offenders. While judges for the most part have continued to sentence as they did in the past, in a few classes of cases sentencing judges are changing their traditional sentencing patterns.

Degrees of Binding Rules

Sentencing laws can have different degrees of binding effect on sentencing judges. In some jurisdictions with so-called voluntary sentencing guidelines, judges who sentence within the statutory bounds for the offense but outside the range recommended in the guidelines do not suffer any consequences. There is no obligation to explain the nonguideline sentence, no heightened risk of reversal on appeal, and no increased risk that the parole authority will release the offender before the end of an announced prison term.

Other jurisdictions give some degree of binding power to the sentencing rules. A judge who departs from the guidelines might have to explain the departure and face informal disapproval (perhaps from other sentencing judges) if the departure is not justified. This is the mechanism at work in Virginia and Delaware. Other states (such as Pennsylvania and Minnesota) give even more binding power to their sentencing guidelines by making it easier for an appellate court to overturn a sentence that falls outside the ordinary guideline range. Different formulations of the statutory instructions to appellate courts can give different degrees of binding authority to sentencing rules.

North Carolina gives its sentencing rules more binding authority than most other states. The crime of conviction falls into an applicable "offense class," Class A through Class I felonies (Class I includes the least serious felonies), and Class A1 through Class 3 misdemeanors. The offender's prior convictions determine the "prior record level." A sentencing grid uses these two factors to direct the sentencing judge to a box on the grid containing the relevant sentencing options.

First, the box indicates the proper disposition: "A" for active prison terms, "C" for community sanctions (such as fines or community service), and "I" for intermediate sanctions (such as residential drug treatment centers) that restrain the offender's liberty more severely than community sanctions do. Most of the boxes in the sentencing grid contain only one letter, designating one disposition. A few boxes allow the judge to choose between A and I or between I and C. These are called "border boxes" because they lie on the border between boxes providing exclusively for A, I or C punishments.

North Carolina does not allow sentencing judges to depart from the disposition that appears in the relevant box on the grid. If the relevant box is a border box, the judge has a choice. But, unlike the judges in other states, the North Carolina judge does not have the power to choose a disposition outside the box, even for cases the judge considers to be unusual. While there is a provision for using an intermediate sanction for a case of "extraordinary mitigation," the statutory definition is so narrow that it is virtually never used (N.C.G.S. §15A-1340.13[g]).

The system also limits the judge's power to select the duration of the sentence. Each box contains three ranges of months: a presumptive range (say, 17–21 months), an aggravated range (say, 21–26 months), and a mitigated range (say,

13–17 months). If the judge chooses a duration within the presumptive range, no justification is necessary. However, if the judge wants to select a sentence from the aggravated or mitigated ranges, he or she must find that an acceptable aggravating or mitigating factor is present in the case.

A sentencing judge can move between the presumptive range and the aggravated or mitigated ranges with virtually no risk of reversal on appeal. Taken together, these ranges offer the sentencing judge a fairly wide set of options. But, once again, the judge has no authority to go above the aggravated range or below the mitigated range, even for a highly unusual case.

Benefits of Binding Rules

The lack of departure power for judges in the North Carolina system makes it easier for the sentencing commission to change judicial behavior. If the rules call for a change in historical sentencing practices, the judges cannot openly depart from those rules.

The North Carolina system did aim to change certain sentencing practices. The rules were designed to direct more prison resources toward cases involving physical violence and to use less prison space for property offenders. The data from 1995–1998 indicate that the rules are accomplishing this goal. During fiscal year 1993–1994, just prior to the beginning of structured sentencing, 48 percent of the felony convictions (about 22,000) resulted in an active prison sentence. During calendar year 1995, 29.2 percent of the felony convictions resulted in active prison terms. By calendar year 1997, 33.6 percent of the roughly 22,000 convictions ended in active terms. Thus, both the number of entrants to the prison system and the proportion of convictions resulting in active terms dropped immediately after the start of structured sentencing and have stayed much lower than they were in 1993–1994.

The other half of the rationing formula has also worked as predicted: the smaller number of entrants to the system has made it possible to lengthen the time served for those who do go to prison. The average length of time served is up. In 1993, the average sentence length actually served for active prison terms in felony cases was 17.3 months. In calendar year 1997, the mean length of the minimum active sentence to be served for a felony was 31.5 months. The rationing system not only limits the number of entrants; it also designates which classes of offenders will receive high priority for prison space. A higher proportion of violent offenders now serve prison terms, because a lower proportion of nonviolent offenders now go to prison.

The structured sentencing rules have also changed judicial use of community and intermediate sanctions. During fiscal year 1993–1994, judges sentenced about 11,000 felony offenders to nonprison sanctions. By calendar year 1997, those nonprison sentences had increased to more than 14,000 (8,999 for intermediate sanctions and 5,663 for community sanctions), despite no substantial increase in the overall number of convictions. Most of the increase came in the use of intermediate sanctions, because the 1994 legislation funded new program slots for these punishments.

Legislative Changes in Assault Crimes

Any sentencing system must be able to adapt to changing patterns of offenses and to changing public concerns. In North Carolina, most of the changes during the first three years of operation have come from the sentencing commission and the legislature. Some of the most important changes took place with assault crimes, which encompass a large number of convictions.

When the sentencing commission began to teach judges, prosecutors, and probation officers how to use the new structured sentencing rules before their effective date in October 1994, it became clear that there was a problem with the assault sentences. The prosecutor could charge a Class E felony for the most serious assaults: those committed with a deadly weapon, combined with an intent to kill, or an infliction of serious injury (N.C.G.S. §14-32). The presumptive sentence range for Class E felonies was 20–25 months for those with no criminal history. If the assault involved all three elements (deadly weapon, intent to kill, and serious injury), it could be a Class C felony, with a presumptive range starting at 58–73 months. Most other assaults, however, qualified only as Class 1 misdemeanors (N.C.G.S. §14-33). No active prison term was possible for these offenses unless the offender had at least one prior conviction; the maximum term was 120 days for those with the most serious prior records. This left a discontinuity between the available punishments for a few serious assaults and all other assaults. The gap was especially troubling to many judges when they considered the domestic assault cases that they saw on a regular basis. These domestic assault cases were misdemeanors.

As a result of this input from prosecutors and judges, the commission recommended some changes in assault crimes and in the punishment grid more generally. The legislature adopted that package in 1995 and added a few wrinkles of its own. It created a new intermediate class of assault crimes involving "habitual misdemeanor assaults" (N.C.G.S. §33.2). A person convicted of misdemeanor assault and who had also been convicted of five previous misdemeanors (at least two of them assaults) would be punished as a Class H felon. Because the grid boxes for Class H felonies did not allow active prison terms for offenders with no criminal history, the legislature also amended the grid. Class H felons with no prior criminal record (and these included larceny and breaking-and-entering defendants) could now receive a presumptive term of five to six months. The legislature also created an entirely new level of misdemeanor offense — Class A1 misdemeanors — and made active jail terms (up to 60 days) available even for those with no prior criminal record. Assaults that inflicted serious injury or that involved use of a deadly weapon would qualify as Class A1 misdemeanors, while other assaults dropped down to Class 2 misdemeanors.

The legislature followed up on these changes to the assault laws in 1996. The new law increased again the number of assault crimes that prosecutors could charge as low-level felonies rather than misdemeanors. It converted certain assaults (those inflicting serious bodily injury, such as permanent impairment of a bodily member or a substantial risk of death, N.C.G.S. §14-32.4) from Class A1 misdemeanors to Class F felonies. Class F felonies carry a presumptive active term of 13–16 months for those with no prior criminal record.

The number of assaults charged as felonies under these new statutes has remained low so far. In 1997, 49 charges resulted in conviction under the Class H "habitual misdemeanor felon" statute, while 13 convictions resulted under the Class F "serious bodily injury" statute. By comparison, the number of misdemeanor assault charges resulting in conviction under the Class A1 statute remained high, just as it had been under the 1994–1995 law. There were 18,764 Class A1 misdemeanor assault convictions in 1997. The less serious Class 2 misdemeanor assaults amounted to 10,702 convictions.

Amendments to the assault crimes were driven by the need for flexibility. If judges had the power to sentence outside the grid box in unusual cases, the judges themselves could have responded to the most troubling of the misdemeanor assaults under the 1994–1995 structure. The tiny number of cases charged under the new felony assault laws indicates that a small subset of the most serious assaults were responsible for the statutory changes.

The need to create flexibility in sentencing options has been only one among several different sources of legislative change over the past three years. The 1998 legislature completely overhauled the juvenile justice system. The 1996 and 1997 sessions included the usual fare of new crimes created, such as bombing or burning a church, selling handguns to minors, or exploiting a child sexually by computer. The legislature has also enhanced penalties (more than once) for some of the most serious offenses, including a gun enhancement statute for felonies in Classes A–E. These enhanced penalties, unlike the assault crimes amendments, do not give sentencing judges a greater range of options; they simply increase all the available sentences.

Judicial Discretion in Border Boxes

Judges played a crucial role in signaling the need for changes in assault punishments. Their sentencing patterns over the past three years, however, have not signaled the need for other major changes in the structure.

Despite the tight controls on judicial sentencing decisions under North Carolina law, there are still times when the judge can exercise discretion. For one thing, the judge can choose between two dispositions (and, in one instance, three dispositions) whenever the relevant box on the sentencing grid is a "border box." Data from the first three years of sentences under the new system show some small shifts in the judges' willingness to impose active prison terms. Where judges have some choice under the system, they have used prison a bit less often for a few less serious offenses.

Table 1.12 indicates the changes between 1992 and 1997 in the percentage of cases where judges impose active prison terms for selected crimes. I have selected crimes with the largest number of cases, where the judge today retains discretion

Table 1.12. Percentage of Convictions Resulting in Active Prison Term, by Crime Type for 1992–1997

Crime	FY 1992–1993	FY 1993–1994	1995	1996	1997	% Change 1992–1997
Forgery, Class I	36	38	11	10.4	9.4	−73.9
	($n = 1,013$)	($n = 959$)	($n = 572$)	($n = 862$)	($n = 875$)	
Fraud, Class I	13	14	10.6	6.4	9.8	−24.6
	($n = 145$)	($n = 163$)	($n = 104$)	($n = 202$)	($n = 246$)	
Larceny, Class H	47	47	25.8	25.4	33.4	−28.9
	($n = 1,240$)	($n = 1,150$)	($n = 890$)	($n = 1,246$)	($n = 1,513$)	
Breaking and Enter-	51	50	29.3	28.9	35.6	−30.2
ing, Class G	($n = 3,929$)	($n = 3,430$)	($n = 2,275$)	($n = 2,971$)	($n = 2,769$)	
Burglary 2d degree,	96	94	54.9	44.8	55.4	−42.3
Class G	($n = 78$)	($n = 69$)	($n = 122$)	($n = 143$)	($n = 157$)	
Common Law Rob-	67	70	53.1	49.6	51.9	−22.5
bery, Class G	($n = 996$)	($n = 926$)	($n = 620$)	($n = 832$)	($n = 872$)	
Kidnap, Abduction,	88	87	75	75.9	78.8	−10.5
Class F	($n = 81$)	($n = 87$)	($n = 76$)	($n = 87$)	($n = 151$)	
Involuntary Man-	68	64	72.7	57.4	60.3	−11.3
slaughter, Class F	($n = 89$)	($n = 80$)	($n = 33$)	($n = 61$)	($n = 73$)	
Voluntary Manslaugh-	71.3	84.3	81.6	70.3	76.5	+7.3
ter, Class E	($n = 108$)	($n = 115$)	($n = 49$)	($n = 101$)	($n = 115$)	

Note: n = total convictions for crime.

over the disposition and the data allow comparison between the old system (fiscal years 1992–1993 and 1993–1994) and the new system (calendar years 1995–1997). For each of these crimes, judges retain the discretion to choose an active prison term for at least some cases (for the Class I crimes, only for those offenders with more extensive prior criminal records). For all but one of these crimes, the percentage of active prison terms has gone down. The changes for common law robbery, burglary in the second degree, breaking and entering, larceny, and forgery are statistically significant at the 1 percent level.

Although judges had the option of imposing an active prison term under the new sentencing laws, they shifted to less use of prison for a few felonies within Classes G, H, and I. Judges probably chose the nonprison sanctions because the new structured sentencing laws made intermediate sanctions available for a greater number of offenders (rather than the less intrusive "community" sanctions). When intermediate sanctions were not realistically available because they were not funded, the judges chose prison over community punishments. The extra funding for intermediate sanctions appears to have paid off in less use of active prison terms for these crimes.

The statistics also show some changed sentencing patterns in particular "border boxes" on the grid between 1995 and 1997. Table 1.13 displays the percentages of active prison terms, intermediate sanctions, and community punishments for cases that fell within several border boxes during the first three years of structured sentencing. The table displays only those border boxes that saw changed propor-

Table 1.13. Change in Percentage of Convictions Resulting in Active and Intermediate Sentences, Selected Border Boxes, 1995–1997

Offense Class	Criminal History	Disposition	1995	1996	1997	% Change 1995–1997
H	1	Active	NA	2.9	7.7	
		Intermediate	43.6	39.4	36.4	−16.5
		Community	56.4	57.7	55.8	
			(n = 1,982)	(n = 3,054)	(n = 2,917)	
H	4	Active	76.8	70	71	
		Intermediate	23.2	80	29	−7.5
			(n = 708)	(n = 967)	(n = 1,031)	
I	2	Intermediate	49.3	44.8	43.6	
		Community	50.7	55.2	56.4	−11.6
			(n = 1,683)	(n = 2,613)	(n = 3,083)	
I	6	Active	45.7	80.2	83.8	
		Intermediate	54.3	19.8	16.2	83.4
			(n = 70)	(n = 81)	(n = 68)	

Note: n = total convictions for grid box.

tions of active or intermediate sentences that were statistically significant at the 1 percent level.

The change in the box for Class H offenses committed by offenders with criminal history category 1 (the "H/1" box) between 1995 and 1997 appears to involve a shift away from intermediate sanctions toward active terms. This took place because of the changes in assault laws in 1995. Starting in 1996, an active prison term became available to judges sentencing offenders in the H/1 box. This change led judges to sentence some offenders to active terms when they would have received intermediate sanctions under the old law. However, most of the new active terms were not imposed in assault cases, the original focus of the statutory changes. Recall that 1997 saw only 49 convictions for Class H assault, while about 225 defendants in the H/1 grid box received active terms.

The H/4 and the I/2 boxes each reveal a shift from a more intrusive to a less intrusive sanction over the first three years of guideline sentences. Sentences in the H/4 block shifted from active to intermediate sanctions, while some of the I/2 sentences changed from intermediate to community sanctions.

The I/6 box involves the least serious crimes committed by those with the most extensive criminal histories. This is the only border box where judges have shifted to a more intrusive disposition over the first three years of the system with no prompting from the legislature. This change in practice may reflect a choice by sentencing judges to place great weight on an extensive criminal history, even for less serious offenses. However, given the similarity of the numbers for 1996 and 1997, it may be that the change between 1995 and 1997 was simply an anomaly.

In sum, in those border boxes where North Carolina sentencing judges have choices over the disposition of cases, they are by and large choosing the same dispositions that they chose before the new system took hold in October 1994. They have not changed their patterns much over the first three years of structured sentencing, either. Where the few noteworthy changes have appeared, they tend to shift from more intrusive to less intrusive punishments.

Judicial Discretion in Selecting Duration

There is very little evidence of changing judicial practice between 1995 and 1997 in selecting the proper duration of the sentence. Under the North Carolina sentencing structure, the judge may choose among a presumptive range, a mitigated range, and an aggravated range. A sentence outside the presumptive range requires a special justification, but the list of possible justifications is long. Moreover, an extensive body of case law developed under the prestructured-sentencing law (known as the Fair Sentencing Act) and established many reliable grounds for going outside the presumptive range. North Carolina appellate courts have made it clear that they will not actively review the reasons a sentencing court gives for choosing a sentence in the mitigated or aggravated ranges.

Despite the sentencing judges' wide discretion in using these ranges, data from 1995–1997 show a restrained and steady use of mitigated and aggravated ranges. The percentage of cases falling within the presumptive range was 81 percent for 1995, 83 for 1996, and 81.2 for 1997. The percentage of cases falling within the aggravated range was 10.3 percent for 1995, 7.4 for 1996, and 8.2 for 1997. For the mitigated range, it was 8.7 percent in 1995, 9.5 in 1996, and 10.6 in 1997. Judges were more likely to stay within the presumptive range for less serious felonies (Classes G through I) for which they sentenced more offenders.

The number of aggravated and mitigated durations in North Carolina is comparable to the proportion of "departure" cases (those sentenced outside the sentencing guidelines) in other presumptive guideline jurisdictions, such as Minnesota. These patterns do not indicate any restiveness among sentencing judges. If the judges believed that sentences were set systematically too low or too high for some classes of offenses, we would see cases clustering in the aggravated or mitigated ranges.

That we cannot yet see widespread changes in sentencing practices does not mean that they will not happen or that they are not happening now. This survey is based on only three years of data from sentencing courts. It does not account for possible changes in prosecutorial charging practices. Nevertheless, the early experience in North Carolina does confirm that the legislature remains concerned about the sentencing flexibility of judges. The judges, for their part, have not yet used their real but limited flexibility to signal the need for changes in sentencing practices.

Penal Developments in Europe and Japan

Populist punitivism has had less influence in Europe and Japan than in the English-speaking countries. The reason for this may be that most or all criminal justice officials in these countries are career civil servants, and thus by circumstance and professional values somewhat insulated from short-term political pressures. Or it may be that political and social values still retain strong social democratic strains that acknowledge economic and social disadvantage as powerful predictors of criminality and thus make a penal policy of singleminded punitiveness seem too simple. Whatever the explanations, few European countries (or Japan) have emulated U.S. crime control policies.

There is no question that, as many of the articles in this chapter describe, public attitudes toward crime have in many countries become more punitive or that officials and policymakers have in various ways taken account of those sentiments. In the Netherlands, for example, judges' sentences have become more severe, the government has adopted community penalties policies intended to communicate greater firmness, and the prison population has since 1975 increased as rapidly as that in the United States. Overall, though there are numerous exceptions, there is a trend toward rising prison populations.

However, the most conspicuous imprisonment policy pattern in recent decades among the countries discussed in this chapter is the lack of a pattern. In Japan, crime rates fell steadily and imprisonment rates with them. In Finland, imprisonment rates fell continuously, but crime rates increased about as quickly as elsewhere in Europe. In the rest of Europe, crime rates rose substantially from the 1970s until the early or mid-1990s and then stabilized or fell. Despite that common crime pattern, there is no common imprisonment pattern. In incarceration rates, Holland's and Portugal's rose sharply, Germany's and the Scandinavian countries' fluctuated, and France's and Italy's oscillated.

There are wide differences in sentencing patterns. In Finland and Sweden, the likelihood of imprisonment following conviction is high, but most sentences are measured in day or weeks and only a few in years. In Germany and Austria, the likelihood of imprisonment is much lower; sentences under six months are disfavored, because they cause great disruption to offenders' lives but accomplish little, so there are few short sentences.

The most active penal reform activities in many European countries involve community penalties or, as they are still often in Europe called, "alternatives to incarceration." The latter term is out of fashion in English-speaking countries because it has the connotation of softness and because it implies that incarceration is something to be regretted and avoided. The terms "community penalties" and "intermediate sanctions" are widely used in English-speaking countries to communicate that these are tough penalties in their own right and not mechanisms to allow people to avoid the rigors of prison.

Conversely, U.S. exports like boot camps, three-strikes laws, and truth in sentencing, whose appeal is at least partly punitively symbolic, have not anywhere in Europe been adopted.

The major penal reform realms in Europe have centered on front-end diversions and on community penalties (to use the U.S. term). Germany developed conditional dismissal, sometimes called prosecutorial fines, to implement its policy of reducing use of short prison sentences. Initially for a defined subset of relatively minor offenders, but now for a much broader group including some who have committed very serious crimes, German prosecutors can dismiss criminal charges on condition that the suspect accept the penalty, usually a fine, that would have been imposed if he had pled guilty. A large fraction of German criminal cases are disposed of in this way, and the practice has since been adopted and widely used in Austria, Belgium, Holland, and Portugal.

Many countries have adopted new forms of community penalty. Day fines, fines scaled simultaneously to the offender's daily income and to the severity of his crime, began in Scandinavia but were adopted in Germany in the 1970s and soon spread to several other countries. Community service as a diversion from prison began in California in the 1960s (though in California and the United States generally it soon withered away except as a probation condition) and was adopted in England in the mid-1970s. From there it quickly spread to Scotland and Holland and then to other European countries. Electronic monitoring, first tried in the United States in the 1980s and ubiquitous there by the early 1990s, did not catch on in Europe until later, despite English pilot projects in the late 1980s. Sweden was the innovator, using electronic tagging (as it is called in Europe) as part of a new prison early-release program. This was evaluated, deemed successful, and soon replicated in Holland and England.

And no doubt elsewhere. The difficulty in writing about penal policy in Europe is that there are many countries with many languages, and relatively little is written in English. This is a problem for an English speaker, but the problem would be even greater for a speaker of French or Italian or Norwegian, for whom even less published work on other countries would be available in the researcher's native language.

The generalizations offered in this introduction are based on the articles in this volume and things I've learned from my readings and travels elsewhere. There is much to be learned from looking across other countries' borders to see how they deal with the timeless human problems of crime and punishment. I hope others will continue the efforts made by the late *Overcrowded Times* to encourage and publish writings on yet more countries so that we may continue to learn from one another.

Incarceration Rates across the World (April 1999)
André Kuhn

Increases in prison populations are an important concern in many democratic countries. Rising crime rates are often invoked to explain those increases, but this cannot be the primary explanation, because there is no general relationship between crime rate trends and prison populations. Independent of crime rates, increased numbers of prisoners can result from increasing numbers of persons receiving confinement sentences or from longer sentences being imposed. The main indicator of comparative numbers of inmates is the incarceration rate. It is obtained by calculating the number of prisoners on a specific date or as an annual average relative to the number of inhabitants. Generally, this is expressed as the number of inmates per 100,000 inhabitants. It varies today from about 20 in Indonesia to about 685 in the Russian Federation. In Western Europe it varies between 35 (Cyprus) and 145 (Portugal), and in the United States there were at midyear 1998 about 668 inmates per 100,000 population (Bureau of Justice Statistics 1999a).

Comparison of different countries' incarceration rates and explanation of differences among them are not easy tasks. Prison population changes result from complex behavioral, cultural, and political processes that are affected by the frequency and seriousness of offenses, police efficiency, the strictness of the law, and the way judges carry it out. Furthermore, the incarceration rate is often established by the national authorities, without any international control. As a result, this article tries to show national trends in prison population, rather than to analyze differences between countries.

A number of generalizations emerge from examination of penal patterns in the countries discussed. First, though crime rates increased substantially in most industrialized countries in the 1970s and 1980s, there is no standard of incarceration rate patterns. Finland and Japan have experienced declining rates for several decades, the United States has experienced unbroken increases since 1973, and other countries' patterns vary between those extremes. Second, while a variety of measures to reduce imprisonment rates have been tried and have succeeded in the short term, there does not appear to be any generally successful long-term "technical" solution. Third, prison population trends are powerfully shaped by countries' cultures and histories and by contemporary politics and ideologies; whether imprisonment use changes inevitably must follow or can themselves lead penal attitudes remains to be seen.

The Netherlands

The Netherlands illustrates the recent increase in incarceration rates in many European countries. Although the Netherlands is well known for its low incarceration rate, its prison population increased from 28 prisoners per 100,000 population in 1983 to about 74 in 1997, an increase of 164 percent (figure 2.1). The increase is attributable largely to longer sentences for sentenced offenders, rather than to growth in the numbers of sentenced or pretrial inmates (Tubex and Snacken 1995).

Switzerland

Prison population data are available in Switzerland for the years 1890–1941 and since 1982, when the federal statistics agency initiated a central data bank on the correctional system. Prisoners are divided into two major groups: sentenced and nonsentenced.

As figure 2.2 shows, the Swiss incarceration rate fell by half between the 1930s and the 1980s, suggesting that the contemporary criminal justice system is less severe than formerly. Between 1982 and 1997, however, the average length of sentences increased by 132 percent, from 74 to 172 days, while the median term increased by only 50 percent, from 28 to 42 days. This suggests that sentences stayed short but that longer ones become substantially longer.

Italy

The overall Italian incarceration rate between 1983 and 1997 appears to have experienced three periods of relative stability (see figure 2.3). This is true but

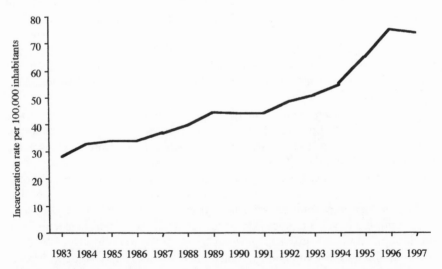

Figure 2.1. Incarceration Rate per 100,000 Inhabitants in the Netherlands, September 1, 1983–1997. *Sources:* Council of Europe (1983–1996), *Prison Information Bulletins;* Database S.PACE for 1997.

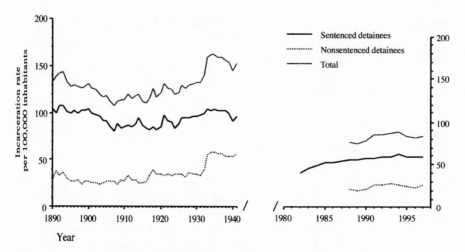

Figure 2.2. Incarceration Rate per 100,000 Inhabitants in Switzerland, 1890–1941 and 1982–1997. *Sources*: Killias and Grandjean (1986); Office fédéral de la statistique.

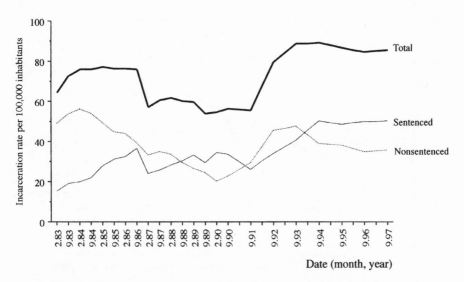

Figure 2.3. Incarceration Rate per 100,000 Inhabitants in Italy, 1983–1997. *Note*: Non-sentenced detainees include all inmates awaiting a first or an appeal trial. *Sources*: Council of Europe (1983–1996), *Prison Information Bulletins*; Database S.PACE for 1997.

misleading, as it hides a tripling of the sentenced incarceration rate. The pretrial detention rate, by contrast, is lower in 1997 than in 1983. The three plateaus are largely the result of a 1986 amnesty. Between September 1, 1986, and February 1, 1987, the overall incarceration rate dropped from 76.3 to 57.4 prisoners per 100,000 inhabitants, mainly because of the December amnesty.

Italy's example shows that an amnesty can significantly reduce the incarceration rate in the short term. The question is whether this can work in the middle and long terms. The data suggest that an amnesty is incapable of reducing prison population for any length of time, as the sentenced prisoner rate quickly returned to the pre-amnesty level. The overall incarceration rate did not rise for a time after the amnesty because of a decreasing pretrial detention rate. This was partly the result of a change in pretrial detention law, which abolished compulsory arrest and introduced stricter conditions for pretrial detention.

Between 1991 and 1997, the total incarceration rate increased significantly, from 56 to 86 per 100,000. This seems to be an effect of illegal Albanian immigration, enlargement of the anti-Mafia fight after the assassination of judges, and anticorruption operations led by the magistrates.

France

France is a special case. Were total, sentenced, and pretrial detention populations shown as a three-year running average, the rates would be shown as gently undulating but essentially flat lines. Instead, as figure 2.4 shows, the rates have been highly erratic. This is the result of a series of amnesties and pardons.

Between January 1, 1968, and January 1, 1975, there was a reduction of approximately 25 percent because of a combination of several statutes. These include June 30, 1969, and July 16, 1974, amnesty laws, introduction of partially suspended

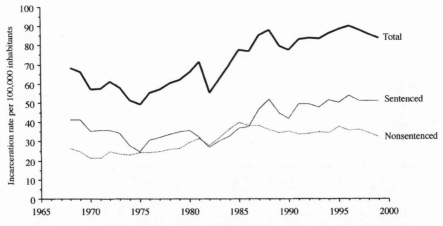

Figure 2.4. Incarceration Rate per 100,000 Inhabitants in France, 1968–1999. *Notes*: Nonsentenced detainees include all inmates awaiting a first or an appeal trial; prisoner rates are recorded on January 1. *Source*: Database SEPT, Ministry of Justice, Paris.

sentences on July 17, 1970, a December 29, 1972, law instituting stays of sentences and giving judges power to grant release on parole to those sentenced for less than three years, and an October 3, 1974, decree that granted sentence reductions to prisoners who were not part of summer 1974 insubordination movements.

The number of prisoners then increased continuously from 1975 to 1981. A July 1981 presidential pardon and an August 1981 amnesty law temporarily curtailed the increase, but the numbers increased even more from 1982 to 1988. Following the presidential election of 1988, general pardons and one more amnesty were pronounced. A general pardon was also granted on the occasion of the French revolution bicentennial in 1989. Despite all those measures, the incarceration rate increased from 78.0 to 90.4 per 100,000 between 1990 and 1996, a growth rate of 15.9 percent. The French experience suggests that amnesties and other pardons can temporarily mask upward structural trends in prison populations but do not provide long-term solutions.

Nonetheless, since 1996 the French figures have decreased, mainly as a result of decreasing entries into pretrial detention because of recent tolerant attitudes toward immigration. This suggests that even as sentences become longer, the incarceration rate can decrease because of the diminution of entries into prison (see Kensey and Tournier 1998).

Greece

Since 1911, the Greek penal code has allowed judges to replace some prison sentences with fines. If an offender is found guilty, the judge must first determine an appropriate prison term. If the term is not higher than a certain limit, the sentence is automatically converted into a fine, and if it is not higher than another limit, the judge may convert it into a fine. In 1911, the automatic conversion limit was set at six months (every prison sentence of less than six months had to be converted into a fine unless special deterrent considerations did not permit the conversion), and the discretionary conversion limit was set at 12 months (every six- to 12-month sentence could be converted under some conditions).

In 1984, the discretionary conversion limit became 18 months. In 1991, the automatic conversion limit was extended to 12 months and the discretionary one to 24 months (Lambropoulou 1993).

Figure 2.5 shows that there was an increase in incarceration rates from 37 to 71 per 100,000 between 1984 and 1994, despite the 1984 and 1991 changes. The replacement of short terms of imprisonment with fines did not decrease the prison populations but coincided with an upward shift.

Germany

Figure 2.6 shows the German incarceration rates from 1960 to 1992. Following criminal law changes in 1969, use of short terms of imprisonment was limited by statutory changes that discouraged imposition of prison terms of six months or less. This temporarily reduced the incarceration rate. The prison population grew quickly again, however, because of an increase in the lengths of some sentences.

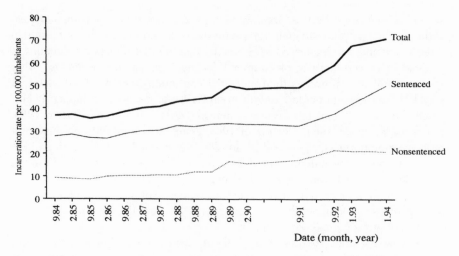

Figure 2.5. Incarceration Rate per 100,000 Inhabitants in Greece, 1984–1994. *Note*: Nonsentenced detainees include all inmates awaiting a first or an appeal trial. *Sources*: Council of Europe (1983–1994), *Prison Information Bulletins*.

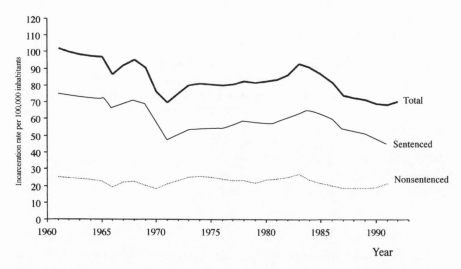

Figure 2.6. Incarceration Rate per 100,000 Inhabitants in Germany, 1961–1992. *Note*: Prisoner rates per 100,000 inhabitants on January 1 in former West Germany. *Sources*: Statistisches Bundesamt Wiesbaden.

By 1973, there were twice as many sentences between six and 12 months as in 1968, and by 1983 there were three times as many. Judges seem to have substituted longer sentences for some of the short sentences they could no longer impose.

Between 1983 and 1991, the German incarceration rate fell significantly, from 93.3 to 69.2 per 100,000. This phenomenon has not been fully explained by criminal policy specialists, although it may be attributable, in part, to a change in judges' and prosecutors' attitudes. Nonetheless, according to the Council of Europe's S.PACE data, the German incarceration rate increased between 1990 and 1997 by 15.7 percent to 90 prisoners per 100,000 inhabitants. This remains, however, below the 1983 level.

Austria

Figure 2.7 shows Austrian data on incarceration from 1970 to 1994. The use of sentences of less than six months was limited in 1975. As in Germany, this measure does not seem to have been a long-term solution allowing the lowering of the incarceration rate. The decrease in 1975 stabilized rates through 1980, after which there was an increase.

But the most interesting aspect of figure 2.7 is the second decrease, from 1985 to 1990, which is mainly the result of the establishment of partly suspended sentences and the reduction of the eligibility date for parole release from two-thirds of the sentence to half.

The total incarceration rate was relatively stable until it fell from 96 per 100,000 inhabitants, in February 1988, to 77, in September of the same year. This occurred mainly because the law reducing the parole eligibility date came into force on

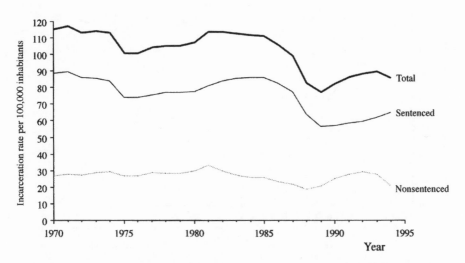

Figure 2.7. Incarceration Rate per 100,000 Inhabitants in Austria, 1970–1994. *Note*: Annual average prisoner rates per 100,000 inhabitants. *Source*: Austrian Ministry of Justice.

March 1, 1988. Nearly 1,500 prisoners were released (those who had served more than half but less than two-thirds of their sentences). But the extension of parole release seems also to have had a perverse effect: according to Austrian authorities, release on parole has become less common. Thus, the reduction of the parole eligibility date was offset by decreased use of parole. Therefore, the relative stability (in spite of some fluctuations) in the incarceration rate following the drop in 1988 seems mainly to be attributable to the introduction of the partly suspended sentence.

Portugal

Figure 2.8 shows Portuguese incarceration data from 1983 to 1998. A new penal code came into force on January 1, 1983, largely inspired by German law, which limited the use of short-term imprisonment and aimed to replace most short-term sentences with other sanctions. Instead, there was an 81 percent increase in incarceration rates from 53 to 96 per 100,000 between 1983 and 1986.

Here again, limiting use of short terms of imprisonment did not reduce the prison population, because the length of sentences increased (Lopes Rocha 1987). The sharp reduction in 1986 occurred mainly because of an amnesty. The stability of the overall incarceration rate between 1986 and 1990 resulted from an offset between increasing rates for sentenced offenders and decreasing rates for pretrial detainees. The latter resulted from a new procedure act, which limited use of pretrial detention. In 1991, another amnesty reduced the incarceration rate, but the rate resumed its growth after 1992 to become one of the highest in Western Europe. In 1994, yet again, an amnesty was enacted, and the incarceration rate

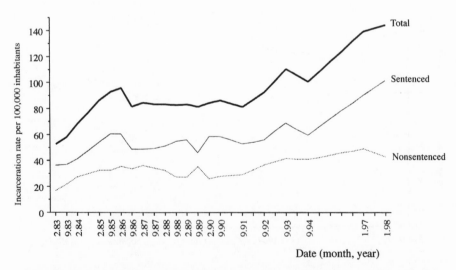

Figure 2.8. Incarceration Rate per 100,000 Inhabitants in Portugal, 1983–1998. *Sources*: Council of Europe (1983–1996), *Prison Information Bulletins*; Database S.PACE for 1998.

decreased. However, Portugal definitely achieved Europe's highest incarceration rate after a new penal code entered into force on October 1, 1995.

Finland

Finland, unlike any other European country discussed here, has long had a decreasing incarceration rate, as figure 2.9 shows. Twenty years ago, the Finnish incarceration rate was one of the highest in Europe. Today, with about 60 inmates per 100,000 population, Finland has one of the lowest. Thus, incarceration rates are not inevitably fated to increase.

Finland has moved gradually toward a criminal justice system based on general prevention, which holds that it is important that criminals are caught and punished and that the severity of the sanction is, in comparison, a minor issue (Törnudd 1993, 1997). The Finnish criminal justice system, therefore, emphasizes the certainty of the sanction, rather than its severity. That philosophy, according to which it is not useful to sentence an offender to several months of deprivation of liberty if several weeks will equally effectively demonstrate society's condemnation, has affected incarceration rates.

Another important explanation is that Finns shared an almost unanimous conviction that Finland's internationally high incarceration rate was a disgrace and therefore decided to "normalize" it. As a result, the average length of prison terms for some offenses was reduced, release on parole was facilitated, an increase was achieved in the proportions of fines and suspended sentences imposed, and the average length of prison sentences served steadily declined. Between 1976 and

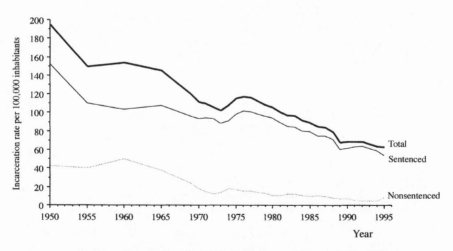

Figure 2.9. Incarceration Rate per 100,000 Inhabitants in Finland, 1950–1995. *Notes*: Annual average prisoner rate per 100,000 inhabitants; sentenced inmates are those who have been condemned to a prison term; nonsentenced inmates include pretrial detainees and fine defaulters. *Source*: Finnish Department of Prison Administration.

1992, the incarceration rate decreased from 118 to 70 per 100,000 population, annual admissions fell from 13,457 to 9,851, and the median length of sentence decreased from 5.1 to 3.6 months. The average length of prison sentence served by murderers declined from 16 to 12 years. Today, Finland has an incarceration rate of about 60 inmates per 100,000 inhabitants, sentences of up to two years can be suspended, a prisoner can be released on parole after having served one-half of the sentence, the maximum fixed-term prison sentence is 12 years (or 15 years for combined sentences). Murder, however, is punishable by life imprisonment. All these changes were introduced without major or abnormal changes in the crime rate or recidivism.

Thus, the Finnish case shows that a government that wants to decrease its prison population can do so. The problem is knowing which measures to take to achieve that end. Most European countries that have tried to do this have abolished short prison terms or replaced them with alternative sanctions, but Finland's experience demonstrates a different strategy. The minimum sentence is 14 days, and the system is built on only three basic sentencing alternatives: unconditional imprisonment, conditional (suspended) imprisonment, and fines (set on the basis of the day-fine system). Community service was introduced nationwide only in 1996.

Japan

As figure 2.10 shows, Japan, like Finland, has experienced decreasing incarceration rates since 1950 and now has one of the lowest incarceration rates (37 per 100,000

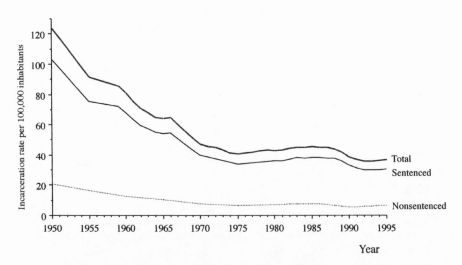

Figure 2.10. Incarceration Rate per 100,000 Inhabitants in Japan, 1950–1995. *Note:* Annual average of daily prison population. *Source:* Japanese Ministry of Justice and Government of Japan (1965–1995), *Summary of the White Paper on Crime.*

in 1995) among the industrialized countries. A simplistic explanation for the low incarceration rates in Finland and Japan is that they are homogeneous countries with very few foreigners. The real reasons are much more complicated and do not depend on a single factor.

Japan's World War II defeat affected its prison populations. Between 1945 and 1950, Japan experienced severe distress. Postwar starvation and socioeconomic chaos led to an increase in the crime rate. The result was that Japan's incarceration rate peaked in 1950 but dropped precipitously thereafter as a consequence of a tremendous decrease in the crime rate, especially in the numbers of reported homicides and robberies. In addition, the sentencing policy in the courts changed to emphasize more noncustodial sentences. (See also Hamai [1999] for fuller discussion.)

Notions of a hierarchical social order remain important in Japan today: knowing one's place in the societal scheme, fulfilling the Confucian obligations that the ruler be benevolent and the ruled be obedient, and holding the respect of others by maintaining social harmony, even at the expense of self-interest, remain widely held norms. The lawbreaker is expected to be repentant and to undertake self-correction (Johnson 1996, p. 5). It is, therefore, understandable that the criminal justice system is "lenient" toward offenders who express repentance and show willingness and capacity for self-correction. Legal standards and procedures permit extensive diversion of defendants from trials and suspended prison sentences. That partly explains the incarceration rate, which is much lower than would be expected from the incidence of crime in Japan. Another explanation is that prison terms are relatively short. Among adults given prison terms in 1994, 28.8 percent received terms of less than one year, 40.6 percent received terms between one and two years, 17.8 percent received terms of two to three years, 9.2 percent received terms of between three and five years, and 3.5 percent received terms of more than five years in prison. The very low pretrial detention rate seems to be related to the speed and efficiency of the Japanese criminal justice system.

Japan decreased its prison population principally by reducing the number of entries into prison from 64,112, in 1951, to 31,122, in 1989. The incarceration rate dropped despite growth in the mean length of sentence from 17.5 months in 1970 to 20.9 months in 1990 and despite a rising crime rate.

Australia

The Australian incarceration rate has been increasing, especially since 1984. Nevertheless, as figure 2.11 shows, the Australian nonsentenced prisoner rate is low compared with those in most Western countries (though it may still be considered high if compared with those in other Asian and Pacific countries; see Biles 1995).

The Australian trend is mainly a result of the evolution of the New South Wales prison population. The latter accounts for almost 40 percent of the total prison population in Australia and showed a 36.7 percent increase between 1988 and 1996, pulling the national trend upward. That same year (1988), a new conservative state government was elected and introduced "truth-in-sentencing" legisla-

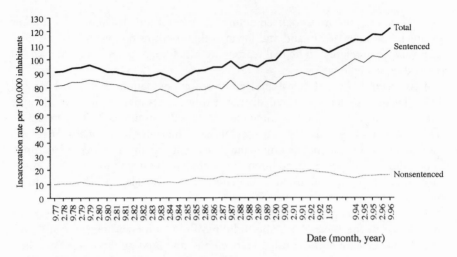

Figure 2.11. Incarceration Rate per 100,000 Adult Inhabitants in Australia, 1977–1996. *Note*: Monthly average prisoner rate per 100,000 adult population. *Source*: Australian Institute of Criminology and National Correctional Services.

tion so that the sentences served by offenders corresponded to the sentences imposed by the judges. The new legislation had a huge impact on sentence lengths, which increased dramatically (Gorta 1997).

Since politicians from across the country have noticed that "get tough on crime" campaigns win elections, and since a "three-strikes-and-you-are-in" law took effect in New South Wales in 1995, the Australian prison population is not expected to decrease in the near future.

United States

It is common knowledge that the U.S. incarceration rate is one of the highest in the world. But that was not true 30 years ago. The incarceration rate was much lower and remained relatively stable until the 1970s.

About 25 years ago, as figure 2.12 shows, the U.S. incarceration rate started to rise sharply. The number of inmates in the nation's jails and prisons more than tripled between 1978 (452,790 inmates) and 1994 (1,507,202 inmates), even though crime rates had decreased substantially since their high points in 1979–1981.

Increases in crime are often invoked to explain increasing prison populations. In recent years, though, many criminologists have concluded that imprisonment rates are to a great degree a function of criminal justice and social policies that encourage or discourage the use of incarceration. "Crime rates rise and fall according to laws and dynamics of their own and sanction policies develop and change according dynamics of their own: these two systems have not very much to do with each other" (Törnudd 1993, p. 27).

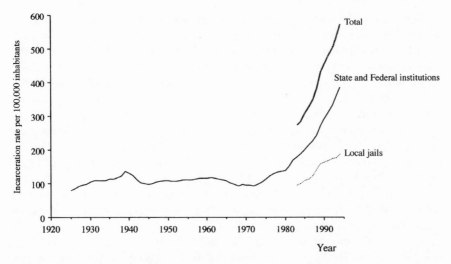

Figure 2.12. Incarceration Rate per 100,000 Inhabitants in the United States, 1925–1994. *Sources*: Bureau of Justice Statistics (1996); *Sourcebook of Criminal Justice Statistics (1995)*, Washington, D.C.: U.S. Department of Justice.

There is no doubt that the American criminal justice system is much more punitive than the European systems. In the United States, the average length of sentence for inmates admitted in 1993 was 75.6 months, and the average length of time served by inmates released in 1993 was 26.0 months. By comparison, in Europe the 1993 average length of imprisonment varied between 11.4 months in Portugal and 1.1 month in Denmark. Even allowing for differences in crime rates, sentencing severity is much higher in the United States than in Europe.

Unfortunately, like those in Australia, American politicians know that "get tough on crime" campaigns win elections. Since their main focus is to be elected, they are often not interested in the long-term health of the American society. Even worse, many American prosecutors and judges hold similar short-term views. Many are elected and some compete for votes by promising to meet punitive populist demands.

Prisoner Rates in Perspective

The data reported in this article show both distinct differences in national trends and some predominant patterns.

Four different incarceration trends stand out. First, the United States is unique in its steep and continuous increase in incarceration rates since 1973. Second, several countries, notably Portugal, Australia, and the Netherlands, have long had fluctuating but generally sharply rising rates. Third, a plurality of countries, exemplified by Germany, Austria, and France, have used a variety of measures to maintain rates that have over the long term of the past 20 years neither changed dramatically nor shown any clear pattern. Finally, at the opposite pole from the United States, Finland and Japan have both enjoyed falling rates for many years.

How can such national differences be explained? According to Young and Brown (1993), the view that variations in prison populations are explicable in terms of criminal justice policies is "simplistic and largely unhelpful." They argue that policies adopted to reduce the prison population often do not have the intended effect and that pressures within the criminal justice system itself or within the wider socioeconomic and political context are much more important. Attitudes toward punishment, they argue, are driven by a range of deeply rooted cultural factors in a society's history, values, and socioeconomic structure. "Ultimately, effecting very substantial shifts in the use of imprisonment . . . involves changing a range of sociocultural attitudes and values that go well beyond the technical penological agenda" (Young and Brown 1993, pp. 39, 45).

It is no doubt true that attitudes toward punishment are related to cultural background. But saying that deep social changes are the only way to work toward a general evolution of attitudes and thus to diminish prison populations means that public opinion must be changed first and that criminal justice system changes will then follow. But the existing correlation between public opinion and severity of sanctions could also be reversed. In other words, the severity of sanctions may influence public opinion; the latter may adapt itself to the delivered sanctions (Beckett 1997*b*). That's why I believe prison terms can be shortened (and public opinion changed) through changes in criminal justice policies. The Finnish case is the prime example of a voluntary decrease in prison populations and of the amazing adaptability of the criminal justice system (Törnudd 1993, p. 23).

If sentence length is a key variable in understanding relative rates of incarceration, and if the goal is to reduce the incarceration rate, means must be found to reduce long-term imprisonment. That could be done by the extension of the use of parole release and the introduction of partly suspended sentences (as in Austria). It could be achieved by changes in attitudes and punitiveness of judges (as in Germany, Finland, and Japan). Or it could be done by a general reduction in the terms of imprisonment imposed. Sentences would become shorter and would weigh less on prison populations, which would consequently be reduced.

The differences between Europe and the United States are largely ideological. Americans tend to accept the proposition that human beings are possessed of free will and are capable of making rational choices. They are generally receptive to the idea that people succeed or fail as a result of their own initiative. That ideology views crimes as the moral failure of individuals who freely elect to commit crimes and who can therefore be held to account for their behavior. In this light, punishment ought to be designed to increase the costs of crime to such an extent that rationally acting individuals will no longer have incentives to commit crimes. Europeans more often view human behavior as more than just a function of free will and see human behavior as influenced by social circumstances such as education, peer relationships, and many other variables. All are important factors in the progression of events that lead to crime. Their view of crime as a product of both social and individual circumstances inclines Europeans more readily to accept responses to crime that include rehabilitative measures. That reflects the moral understanding that if individuals cannot be held solely responsible for what they become and what they do, society has an obligation to try to correct the influences or the conditions which may have led an individual into crime (Durham 1994).

Scandinavia

Penal Sanctions and the Use of Imprisonment in Denmark
(December 1998)
   Britta Kyvsgaard

Denmark is one of the few Western countries in which incarceration rates have not increased substantially in the 1990s. Crime rates have been relatively stable for a decade, as has the prison population. Prison admissions have increased but have been offset by a decline in average sentence lengths. New sanctions have been established, but the basic structure of the sanctioning system has changed little.

The Danish penal system can be characterized as being rather traditional. The penal sanctions predominantly used have been in use for most of the twentieth century. The most widely used sanction is the fine, which in 1997 was ordered in 53 percent of all criminal code cases and in 93 percent of all other penal cases (mostly traffic code violations). Imprisonment and suspended sentences constituted 19 and 18 percent, respectively, of criminal code cases. Withdrawal of charges, an option primarily for offenders less than 18 years of age as a way to keep young ones outside the sanctioning system, is used in nearly all the remaining criminal code cases; 6 percent of criminal code cases result in withdrawal of charges. Formally, withdrawal of charges is not a penal sanction, but in practice it functions very much like a suspended sentence.

Parole is widely used. Today, 85 percent of all inmates with a prison sentence of three months or longer are released on parole, usually after serving two-thirds of the sentence but sometimes earlier. Half of parolees are supervised by the probation service, normally for one year; the rest are subject to no special conditions.

Offenders under suspended sentences and withdrawals of charges may also be subject to supervision. Approximately one-fifth each of offenders on suspended sentences and of offenders who have had their charges withdrawn are subjected to supervision.

Recent Changes

The Danish penal system has, however, innovated a bit in recent decades, and the renaissance of the old ideas of treatment and rehabilitation has, especially in the last few years, influenced criminal policy.

In 1973, the possibility of serving a prison sentence in an institution outside the criminal justice system was introduced. Permission to serve a sentence in this way is granted in case of a special treatment need and—to avoid the harmful effects of imprisonment—very often also to offenders less than 18 years of age.

Community service orders, introduced on an experimental basis in 1982, were made statutory in 1992. Community service is not a separate sanction but is a condition of a suspended sentence.

Since 1990, persons convicted of drunk driving and in need of treatment for alcohol abuse have been able to avoid a short prison sentence, provided they submit themselves to treatment.

Another new type of community sanction, the "youth contract," was tested between 1991 and 1993. Offenders between 15 (the minimum age of criminal responsibility) and 17 are obliged to participate in designated activities. The youth contract was made permanent in 1998 as a condition that can be attached to a withdrawal of charges.

A treatment program as an alternative to incarceration for drug-abusing offenders began on an experimental basis in 1995. Similarly, a treatment program for nonviolent sexual offenders, partly community based, was started in 1997 on an experimental basis.

From a policy perspective, the recent changes are important but from a practical perspective are less so. Except for the treatment program for drunk driving, which is applied in 40 percent of eligible cases, the new community sanctions and treatment programs have as yet only marginally influenced penal practice. The traditional penal sanctions and the traditional ways of serving a sentence still dominate.

Crime and Imprisonment Trends

Since 1950, the number of reported criminal code offenses has increased by nearly 400 percent. The increase was especially pronounced from the mid-1960s to the mid-1980s. Since the late 1980s, the number of reported crimes has been stable.

As imprisonment is in practice primarily for criminal code offenses, one might expect the prison population to have increased. This, however, has not happened. In the years just after World War II, the number of prisoners was rather high due to incarceration of collaborators. Since the early 1950s, the average daily prison population has remained relatively constant, with only minor and temporary fluctuations. In 1997, the number of daily prisoners was equivalent to 64 per 100,000 of the population.

Both practical and political reasons help explain this discrepancy between the increased crime rates and imprisonment patterns.

PRACTICAL REASONS   The number of prison cells is of utmost importance in limiting an increase in the number of prisoners. Danish prison policy, unlike that in the United States, does not allow overcrowding in prisons. If the capacity of the prisons is too small, persons sentenced to imprisonment must wait their turn.

Historical analyses show that increased numbers of prison sentences have led to policy changes, and this is the case in recent years. In the late 1970s, the number of persons waiting to serve a sentence was very high and led to decriminalization of drunk driving and of property offenses in the beginning of the 1980s. An expansion of the proportion of prison sentences eligible for parole was simultaneously introduced and similarly served to reduce pressure on prison capacity. In spite of these changes, the number of persons waiting to serve a sentence did not fall to an acceptable level. This is why a policy encouraging pardons for persons who had been waiting to serve a sentence for at least one and a half years was implemented in 1984.

SENTENCING POLICY Changes in sentencing policy can be tracked back to 1980 but not further due to changes in the crime statistics.

Even though prison population trends do not track changes in the number of reported criminal code offenses, increases in the total number of criminal code sanctions do. Or rather—one could say—more than so, as the number of sentences has increased more than the number of reported offenses. The stable level of the prison population is thus due not to inefficiency or indulgence but to changes in sentencing policy.

From 1980 to 1997, the number of criminal code sanctions increased 66 percent, which is largely the result of an increase in use of fines, as the number of fines has more than doubled since 1980. The number of prison sentences for criminal code offenses has also increased but much less—29 percent. The reason this increase in the number of prison sentences is not reflected in the number of prisoners is that lengths of prison sentences have decreased correspondingly. The lengths of prison sentences have long been comparatively short; most are less than six months. In 1997, the average sentence for criminal code offenses was six months.

The tendency is thus toward less punitive and—in the case of imprisonment— shorter sentences, but not toward lesser use of penal sanctions. This can to some degree be explained by amendments to the criminal code, including the decriminalization of property crimes in the beginning of the 1980s. But shortening of sentences has continued beyond the developments of the late 1980s and early 1990s. No clear analyses of this situation have been carried out, but, at least to some degree, it reflects a less punitive attitude in the Danish penal system toward the many property crimes. This change of attitude, however, is not found in all instances.

CRIMINAL POLICY Why have problems of prison capacity not led to the building of more prisons, as in the United States and elsewhere, including England (Morgan 1998) and Holland (Junger-Tas 1998)? Economic considerations are one explanation, as the cost of prison building is high. This explanation, however, cannot stand alone. The human cost of increased imprisonment and lack of belief in the effectiveness of incarceration are just as important.

Crime control policy has traditionally not been an issue in Danish politics, and this is probably the most significant reason that prison populations have not increased. Policy has long been set by government officials who believe in humane crime policies, and, until recently, crime has not played an important role in election campaigns and in political discussions. In addition, criminal justice officials are not elected but are civil servants. Finally, a more punitive crime policy has not attracted majority support in the Parliament.

New Worries?

Crime policy is now becoming a more important political issue. The Social De-mocratical party, now in power, is trying to regain lost ground on the basis of crime policy issues as political analysts point to voters' dissatisfaction with a too lenient criminal policy. The examples of Tony Blair in England and of Bill Clin-ton in the United States may also have influenced this policy. So far, however, only minor changes have been carried through.

The prime area for change is violence. Even though the number of victims of violence has declined, opinion polls repeatedly show huge concern about violence and have caused politicians to react. During the 1990s, extensive programs con-taining both preventive and punitive measures aimed at reduced violence were put forward.

Sentencing practices seem to be changing in ways that go beyond the new laws. The courts have apparently reacted to the political signals and during the 1990s have increased use of imprisonment for violence. The increase in the number of prison sentences during the 1990s is solely a result of this change in sentencing practice.

The crime policy scene is now being invaded by right-wing political parties trying to gain voters by demonstrating the will to combat violence and youth crime with measures of a punitiveness thus far unknown in Denmark. From a pessimistic point of view, the situation threatens to destroy Denmark's liberal crime policy. From an optimistic point of view, this competition in demonstrating toughness may turn out to be an advantage if it pushes the Social Democratic party back to a more humane approach in order not to be confused with its political opponents.

Sentencing Law, Policy, and Patterns in Sweden (October 1999)
Nils Jareborg

When the current Swedish Criminal Code came into force in 1965, the sentenc-ing law was significantly influenced by special-preventive considerations. Since then, the law has undergone many changes. The most important occurred in 1980–1981 (abolishing indeterminate incarceration of dangerous recidivists and of juveniles), 1988 (introducing an elaborate set of sentencing rules, based on just-deserts principles), and 1998 (introducing community service and electronic mon-itoring as permanent modes of sanctioning and new rules on parole and on in-carceration of juveniles). This article provides a brief overview of the structure of Swedish sentencing law and policy and describes recent sentencing patterns.

Sentencing Law and Policy

Only imprisonment and fines are called "punishments." The other general sanc-tions, including probation, conditional sentences, and commitments to special care, are called "other sanctions for crime." Forfeiture and such things as revo-cation of a driving license are technically not sanctions for crime but so-called special consequences of crime.

Under Swedish law, sentencing has two quite different components: the choice of sanction, that is, selecting the appropriate type of sanction, and the measurement of punishment, that is, meting out a term of imprisonment or fines in the particular case. Since "other sanctions for crimes" are not punishments, by definition the "measurement of punishment" component does not apply to them.

Penalty scales are attached to the provisions on specific crimes in the criminal code or elsewhere, with specified maximum and minimum sentences. In addition, many types of offenses are divided into seriousness levels. For example, the punishment for petty theft is imprisonment for from 14 days to six months or fines; the punishment for theft is imprisonment for from 14 days to two years; and the punishment for grand theft is imprisonment for from six months to six years. The scope of the penalty scale is supposed to reflect the relative seriousness of the specific type of offense.

If someone is to be sentenced for more than one offense, a composite penalty scale must be constructed. Thus, the maximum for aggravated robbery is 10 years' imprisonment, and the maximum term for two or more aggravated robberies is 14 years. In most cases, the offender is sentenced to one sanction without explicit account being taken of the sanction he would have received for each separate offense.

Penal Value

Penal value is the basic concept used in the 1988 sentencing law. Penal value has to do with seriousness of crime, and seriousness of crime is normally analyzed as a function of the criminal conduct's harmfulness and the offender's culpability (manifested in the offense). This idea is captured in the legislation, which indicates that other types of factors can also affect the penal value. Previous criminality is, however, explicitly excluded as a relevant consideration.

What besides harmfulness and culpability can influence the penal value? The committee that prepared the reform accepted one departure from strict proportionalist thinking: for internationally connected criminality, the penal value to some extent also depends on penalty levels in other countries. And a further departure was envisaged in the Bill to Parliament: in certain cases (no example given) the penal value could be enhanced due to increased frequency or perniciousness of the type of crime.

These two amendments to the idea of penal value have considerable practical importance. Most notably, as a result of these two factors, the severity of sentences for drug offenses is clearly out of proportion to the seriousness of the crime.

Sentencing Options

Swedish law offers fewer sentencing options than do most other countries. Fines and imprisonment constitute the large majority of sanctions imposed. Community penalties are relatively underdeveloped.

FINES   There are three types of fines. Traditional fines are used for petty, mainly minor traffic, offenses. Standard fines are determined according to a special basis of computation; this model is rarely used. Most important are the day fines, settled as the product of a number of days and the size of the day-fine unit. These range from 30 to 150 days (200 for multiple offenses). The daily amount, determined in accordance with the financial situation of the accused, ranges from 30 to 1000 Swedish kroner ("SEK"). (U.S. $1 is a little more than 8 SEK; thus, the highest day-fine sum for multiple offenses equals about $25,000 U.S.)

The court may, under some circumstances, convert unpaid fines into imprisonment for from 14 days to three months. The conditions for conversion are strict, and in practice almost no one goes to prison for default in paying fines.

PRISONS   Imprisonment is always regarded as more severe than fines; that is, in measuring punishment, fines cannot (conceptually) be an alternative to imprisonment. A fixed term of imprisonment (for one offense) may not be longer than 10 years nor shorter than 14 days. The maximum possible term for a recidivist who has committed more than one offense is 18 years. Life sentences are mainly used in cases of multiple murders or aggravated espionage. They are without exception converted by grace (pardon decided by the government) into a fixed prison term of from 16 to 20 years.

Under new rules on conditional release, prisoners are to be released when they have served two-thirds of the sentence (but not less than one month). The parole period is one year, or any longer period that may remain of the sentence.

Prison terms of up to three months may be served in the form of partial house arrest (intensive supervision through electronic monitoring). The main advantage of this is that the prisoner can keep his job. It is mainly used in cases of drunk driving and not very serious assaults. The decision to use intensive supervision as a form of imprisonment is made not by the court but by the correctional authorities.

ALTERNATIVES   The main alternatives to imprisonment are conditional sentences and probation. A conditional sentence is not a suspended prison sentence. It is more like a conditional discharge with a probationary period of two years, normally combined with day fines, a community service order, directives to pay damages or assist in mitigating harms caused, or some combination.

Probation is used instead of a conditional sentence if there is reason to suppose it can help the offender avoid committing new crimes. The choice is typically made on pragmatic grounds (depending on whether the offender needs support, help, or treatment); the special-preventive flavor of the legislation is somewhat deceptive. The probationary period is three years. The offender is supervised for one year and is normally subjected to a number of directives and restrictions. Probation may be combined with day fines, a community service order, so-called contract care for addicts, or a prison term of from 14 days to three months.

For certain categories of offenders, all these sanctions may be replaced by commitment for special care: care within the social welfare services (for offenders in the age group 15–20 years), special care for addicts, or psychiatric care (for those who suffer from a severe mental disturbance).

If the court finds that an offender who was 15, 16, or 17 years at the time of the offense should be sentenced to imprisonment, the court should in most cases order that the offender instead be incarcerated in a special institution for closed youth care (for not less than 14 days and not more than four years).

An assessment of the penal value of a concrete crime is of importance not only for the measurement of punishment but also for the choice of sanction. It is, however, impossible to go into details within the scope of this article (for details, see Jareborg 1995). Here, only two questions are addressed.

Previous Criminality

Previous criminality is understood to be criminality that has resulted in a court sentence, a prosecutor's summary punishment by fine, or a prosecutor's decision to forgo prosecution.

Previous criminality plays a major role in the choice of sanction. It may affect the choice between imprisonment and conditional sentence or probation (or commitment for special care), between conditional sentence and probation, between probation with a fine and without a fine, between probation with and without community service, and between probation with a fine or community service and probation with imprisonment. Repeated criminality may also result in revocation of parole. New criminality within the parole period can result in complete or partial revocation.

Finally, previous criminality may influence ("to a reasonable extent") the severity of punishment if it has not been taken "appropriately" into account in the choice of sanction or revocation of parole. There may be nothing to revoke, or the new crime may be so serious that imprisonment is the only option. In practice, the authority to increase the punishment is rarely used, and mainly in cases of very serious repeated criminality.

Imprisonment versus an Alternative

The alternatives to imprisonment are conditional sentences and probation. In choosing sanctions, imprisonment is considered more severe than conditional sentences and probation. (In relation to fines, however, imprisonment is not considered more severe than conditional sentences and probation.) This rule lays a foundation for a presumption against the use of incarceration. The following considerations flesh out this presumption.

The use of imprisonment is prohibited if the crime was committed under the influence of serious mental abnormality (there is no insanity defense; however, a legislative committee has recently proposed that such a defense be reintroduced).

The court is urged to pay special heed to circumstances that suggest a less severe sanction than imprisonment. In so doing, the court should consider particular mitigating circumstances (those that do not affect the penal value), normally referred to as "equity reasons."

The presumption against imprisonment loses its force in the following way: as "a reason for imprisonment the court may consider, besides the penal value and the nature of the criminality, the accused's previous criminality." Explanatory notes state as a guideline that a penal value of one year or more suggests that imprisonment should be used (unless the just-mentioned so-called equity mitigation suggests otherwise). The reference to the nature of the crime makes it possible to choose imprisonment instead of conditional sentence or probation for general-preventive reasons. Unfortunately, the courts tend to add new sorts of crimes to this category, which by tradition includes frequent offenses such as drunk driving, unprovoked assault, and minor drug offenses. Finally, repetition of criminality of intermediate gravity will eventually lead to imprisonment.

For young offenders, the presumption against imprisonment is to a certain extent restored. If at the time of the crime the offender was 18 to 20 years old, there must be special reasons for imposing imprisonment. Penal value is one important factor, but the nature of the crime and previous criminality are also relevant. If the offender was between 15 and 17 years old, the presumption against imprisonment is extremely strong. There must be extraordinary reasons, in practice a very high penal value (3–5 years). Fewer than 50 persons per year in this age group have been sentenced to imprisonment, and they receive huge deductions due to so-called youth mitigation. (In the future, most offenders of this category will be sentenced to closed youth care.) The normal disposition for offenders of this age is commitment for care within the social welfare services.

There are other ways to escape imprisonment. Most important, one provision enumerates special reasons for probation, such as that the offender's personal or social circumstances have significantly improved in a way that may be assumed to bear a relationship to his criminal career, that he has undertaken to undergo special treatment (contract care), or that he has consented to a community service order. As far as the penal value is concerned, judicial practice suggests that the one-year guideline is replaced by a two-year guideline.

Sentencing Patterns

The population of Sweden is 9 million. The prison system provides places for approximately 5,000 persons, including 1,300 for pretrial detention. Some 300 are used for women.

More than 1 million crimes are reported annually to the police. This does not include some minor traffic offenses. Two-thirds of reported crimes are not cleared up.

There were 163,000 convicted persons in 1988 and 124,000 in 1997. These numbers include those who received a waiver of prosecution (which presupposes that a crime was committed) — 19,300 in 1988 and 13,700 in 1997. However, these figures do not include summary police fines for traffic and smuggling offenses, which totaled 195,000 in 1988 and 192,300 in 1997. In 1997, 773 women were sentenced to imprisonment. Table 2.1 shows the distributions of sentences in those years.

Table 2.1. Distribution of Sentences in Sweden, 1988 and 1997

	1988	1997
Prosecutorial fines	75,500	56,000
Court fines	30,000	21,500
Imprisonment	16,500	13,700
Probation with imprisonment	900	300
Probation with contract care	300	1,000
Probation with community service	—	500
Probation (other)	5,300	4,400
Conditional sentence	10,300	8,000
Commitment to special care	1,200	2,600
Old sentence used for new crimes	3,200	2,200
All	143,200	110,200

Source: Kriminalstatistik 1997. Brå-rapport 1998:3. Stockholm.

The average daily prison population (including those in pretrial detention and those subjected to electronically monitored intensive supervision) is approximately 58 per 100,000 population, which is comparatively low. It should, however, be noted that Sweden has experienced a decrease in prison sentences for drunk driving (fewer cases are reported), violent crimes, and property crimes. Recent statutory changes toward greater harshness (such as abolishing half-time conditional release and prescribing greater emphasis on short prison sentences because of the "nature of the crime") have been balanced by a decreasing number of sentences (unrelated to reported crime, except as regards drunk driving).

Table 2.2 shows prison sentences imposed in 1997. The modal sentence is one month, the median between one and two months, and the mean 6.4 months (these are gross numbers and are not adjusted for shortening by conditional release). Of all sentences imposed, only 9.7 percent were for more than one year. In 1997,

Table 2.2. Prison Sentences Imposed in Sweden, 1997

Less than 1 month	382
1 month	4,602
More than 1 month, not more than 2 months	4,602
More than 2 months, not more than 3 months	1,473
More than 3 months, not more than 4 months	999
More than 4 months, less than 6 months	251
6 months	1,016
More than 6 months, less than 1 year	1,147
1 year	563
More than 1 year, not more than 2 years	834
More than 2 years, not more than 4 years	430
More than 4 years	206
Life imprisonment	9

Source: Kriminalstatistik 1997. Brå-rapport 1998:3. Stockholm.

3,800 offenders (250 women) served their prison sentences as electronically monitored intensive supervision.

Norway Prison Use Up Slightly, Community Penalties Lots
(February 1999)
Paul Larsson

Use of prisons in Norway has grown steadily since the early 1980s. This increase is reflected in both open and closed prison units. The number of persons awaiting imprisonment, the "prison queue," a phenomenon from the late 1980s, is now history. There has also been an increase in the use of community sanctions, mainly CSOs, and ticket fines and a reduction in the use of suspended sentences (conditional imprisonment). In relative terms, the increase has been highest in the use of ticket fines and CSOs, and use of conditional and unconditional prison has declined. However, there are no indications that the number of people under state control is going to fall in the near future. Use of both prisons and community sanctions is likely to grow.

Norway is a small and homogeneous country (4.4 million in 1998). Culturally, it is closely connected to other Nordic countries like Sweden and Denmark, but historically it has also been close to the "big brothers," Britain and Germany. These ties are reflected in Norway's penal policy, which from an American perspective is rather tolerant. This tolerance, combined with a society marked by few conflicts,[1] has produced a low incarceration rate and (more or less) general agreement that prison should be used as a last resort. Just-deserts theory never caught on in the 1970s or 1980s; instead, the dominant ideology has been general deterrence.

Norway has nearly all the hallmarks of a low-crime country. Economic differences have traditionally been small. Norway is racially and religiously homogeneous, and its many small towns and few big cities preserve a rural identity. The postwar period has been characterized by nearly full employment. Use of alcohol and drugs is modest. The dominant welfare ideology has to a large degree provided help for the worst off.

However, the stable and tolerant picture is under pressure. Norway has for the past 20 years become increasingly integrated into the global economy and market. There are growing class differences and inequalities. The welfare state is under attack.

Crime Rates

As table 2.3 shows, crime in Norway has risen steadily since the early 1960s. There was a decrease in reported crimes in the first years after World War II, but that bottomed out by the beginning of the 1960s. However, crime rate growth has fallen in the 1990s.

Property offenses have been the principal component of the overall increase. This is generally interpreted as a consequence of there being more goods to be

Table 2.3. Reported Crimes, 1960–1995, Selected Years

	1960	1970	1980	1990	1995
Total crimes	38,700	65,080	121,565	235,256	269,366
Larceny	26,049	46,071	95,011	175,165	186,165
Homicide	14	6	31	42	32

Source: Norwegian Crime Statistics (1995).

stolen — more cars, cameras, and other consumer goods. In addition, insurance companies in the early 1970s established policies requiring that owners report stolen goods to the police in order to recover for their loss. This no doubt increased reporting to the police.

As in other Western societies, crime by youth has dominated recent increases in reported offenses. There was stability, followed for a short period by a decrease since the mid-1980s, in the growth in crime by the youngest. Charged persons are now older on average than they were 15 to 20 years ago.[2]

Drug crime is one category that has grown rapidly. There used to be few such cases. In 1970, 3 percent of reported offenses were drug cases; by 1994, this figure had risen to 19 percent. In 1980, approximately 2,000 drug cases were investigated; by 1996, the number had passed 20,000. This seems mainly to reflect the war on drugs and provision of huge resources and means to the police to tap phones, raid houses, and so on. However, research on drug habits by youngsters shows stability in use and experimentation.

Norway is a peaceful country with few violent offenses. The number of killings, murders, and other serious violent acts has long been low by Western standards. The homicide rate per 100,000 in 1995 was 0.74 but in recent years approximately has risen to 1 per 100,000. The U.S. numbers are 8–9 times higher, and the Canadian numbers are 2–3 times higher (Hagan 1994).

There has been an increase in the number of reported violent crimes since the 1970s. In 1985, 5,700 crimes of violence were investigated; by 1996, the number had reached 17,000. It is unclear whether the increase is "real" or instead reflects growing concern about sensitivity to violence. Olaussen (1995) has reported victimization data that show that the main increase in self-reported violent crimes comes from minor acts. There seems to be increased concern about personal threats and minor deeds. Some of the violence increase results from new routines in the recording of violence by the police and from the introduction of new regulations concerning violence. But there are also signs of an increase in more serious violent crime, some related to use of alcohol in public.

Use of Imprisonment

The Nordic countries are known for their relatively small numbers of prisoners. The average numbers per 100,000 inhabitants were 55 in 1990 and 59 in 1995. As table 2.4 shows, the use of imprisonment has increased steadily since 1980. From 1975 to 1980 there was a small reduction, after which there has been expansion.

Table 2.4. Average Daily
Number of Prisoners, 1975–
1995, Selected Years

1975	1,913
1980	1,797
1985	2,104
1990	2,379
1995	2,605

Source: Norwegian Crime Statistics
(various years).

One interesting side of this development is the comparative growth in the proportions of open and closed units. As table 2.5 shows, nearly all the increase has been in open units. There was a small decline in the use of closed units in the 1980s, but this was reversed in the 1990s. In the same period there was a steady increase in open prison units.

In the 1980s and early 1990s, Norway experienced a phenomenon called "prison queues." In the summer of 1992, 4,295 *sentences* had not been served because prisons were full (Larsson 1993). The official numbers did not say how many *persons* were waiting. This number was lower because some offenders had more than one sentence to serve. Fifty percent were convicted drunken drivers, and the average sentence was less than 60 days. This "queue" is now history.

The most important reason for the growing number of prisoners is not increased prison admissions but increased sentence lengths. Norway has, like other Western countries, devoted great resources to the "war on drugs." Sentences in drug-related cases are long compared with those in most other European countries. In 1984, the maximum penalty in such cases was raised to 21 years—which is the maximum sentence in Norway. The war on drugs resulted in the use of long sentences also in minor cases. In 1990, there were 37 sentences of 7 years or more; 16 of these were for drugs, and 17 for homicide. In 1996, there were 28 sentences longer than 7 years. Of these, 13 were drug sentences, and 13 were for homicide. The average prison sentence in Norway is short, so these long drug sentences are in many ways abnormal. More than half of prison sentences are shorter than 90 days.

Table 2.5. Prison Units, 1980–1995, Selected
Years

	1980	1990	1995
Open	384	736	885
Closed	1,790	1,643	1,869

Source: Larsson (1993).

Community Sanctions

Norwegian courts have long made extensive use of suspended (conditional) sentences. As many as 35–40 percent of all sentences in criminal cases used to be suspended (conditional). Offenders were given a prison sentence in court, but this was then made into a suspended sentence with certain conditions and a time limit (usually two years).

There has been a slow but steady decline in the use of suspended sentences for three or four decades. Today the share of suspended sentences is approximately one-third of the total number of sentences in criminal cases (17,600 in 1995).

Traditionally, the repertoire of so-called community sanctions has been limited. One such sanction is a suspended sentence with supervision by the probation service. The use of supervision in connection with parole and suspended sentences has been debated since at least the 1970s. The criticism was directed at the supervision. This was randomly executed, and control of the offender was superficial. Very few breaches of conditions were reported to the police, especially for probationers. Use of supervision as a part of the punishment was criticized. Critics argued that supervision should be voluntary and consist of help and support. This might be one reason for reduction of supervision over the past 25 years.

Community service is the most used "new" community sanction. It was introduced in 1984 as a pilot project and made a regular sentence in 1991. The number of sentences grew considerably from the end of the 1980s, as table 2.6 shows, peaking in 1994 and dropping slowly since then. Community service has been criticized as a soft sanction and not to be trusted as a real alternative for prison. The probation service workers are often seen as "do-gooders" with little credibility in the courts or the police. A reason for this is a widespread belief that the service does not rigorously control offenders and that control should be intensified and community service made more demanding.

The latest community-sanctions development is publication of the white paper "On the Probation and Prison Service" (Justis-og politidepartement 1998). Among its proposals is the introduction of intensive supervision and electronic monitoring. These new sanctions were seen as a positive addition to existing community sanctions by the majority in Parliament. A pilot electronic-monitoring project based on a Swedish program is being planned.

Table 2.6. Community Service Orders, 1984–1996, Selected Years

Year	
1984	24
1989	268
1991	760
1994	1,026
1996	900

Sources: Larsson (1993); Norwegian Crime Statistics (1996).

Trends in Penal Sanctions in the 1990s

So, what are the most important trends in the developments in the use of penal sanctions in Norway in the 1990s? These are differentiation, closing the "gap" between community sanctions and prison, polarization, a return to treatment ideologies, and a steady expansion in the use of prison and community sanctions.

Toward the end of the 1980s, the idea of a more differentiated sanction system was introduced. The basic idea was that there were too few sentencing alternatives. Offenders were in prison, or they were not; there was no in-between. The proposed system had five levels: high-security prisons, ordinary closed prison units, open prison units, boarding or halfway houses, and community sanctions.

This system would enable the offender to work his way from the closed units to the open alternatives. This is seen as a model that will help offenders adjust better to their release and give incentives for good behavior. Few have mentioned the opposite possibility that offenders, by breaching conditions, may instead work themselves back into the system.

This multilevel system is blurring the differences among the different alternatives. At the same time, it is an answer to the cry for closed-security units for "the dangerous" and for troublesome prisoners. There is a blurring of boundaries between programs inside and outside the prison, a growth in open prison units, and a move toward more intrusive and tightly controlled community sanctions. The community sanctions are getting more prisonlike, while the prison slides into the society.

There has been a shift back toward the treatment ideology. Cognitive skills training, or "New Start" as it is labeled in Norway, is now in use in the prisons. This model is also used on released prisoners to aid their readjustment to society. There are different programs for sex offenders and drunken drivers that can be used as community sanctions on release from prison. Reality therapy and consequence pedagogics, which is the ideology behind the probation officers' work on community service, share similarities with the mentioned treatment programs. The main idea is that the individual is responsible for his actions and that most of what we call crime is committed by irresponsible individuals whose way of thinking is wrong.

There is also much public reference to monsters and dangerous criminals. The image of *the* threat has changed. There have been waves of panic concerning bikers (Hell's Angels and Bandidos), sexual offenders, drug smugglers, Russian and Yugoslavian "Mafia," and robbery and violent offenders. There has been a cry in the media for longer prison terms and more secure prison units for the mad and bad.

There are clear signals from the political elite that one aim in the coming years is to open new prison units. It is said that 300–400 new cells will be needed over the next three to five years (Innst. S. nr. 6 1998–99). At the same time, new intermediate community sanctions are being introduced.

NOTES

1. Many might say the lack of conflicts makes for a boring society. Since World War II, Norway has experienced a social stability that few other non-Nordic countries can match.

2. This may have something to do with increased efforts to divert juvenile delinquents from the courts.

Sentencing and Punishment in Finland (December 1994)
Patrik Törnudd

Finnish sentencing policies have for many years been stable and uncontroversial, and the numbers of those in prison have steadily declined. The stability results from widespread commitment to the values of proportionality and predictability in sentencing. The decline results from a concern that Finnish prisoner numbers were high compared with those in other countries and from a commitment over many years to reduce imprisonment.

For various historical reasons, emphasis on the rule of law and written legal norms is particularly strong in Finland. The discretion of the police, the prosecutors, and the judiciary is circumscribed in many ways. Plea bargaining is unknown in Finland—offenses of which people are convicted are expected to correspond to the offender's actual behavior. Within the criminal justice system, a high value is set on the principles of proportionality and predictability (Joutsen 1989).

Finnish Criminal Justice Ideology

The rationale of the criminal justice system is usually thought to be *general prevention*—not *general deterrence*. Outside Finland, those terms are used as synonyms by many people. In Finland they have distinctly different meanings, and the preference for general prevention over general deterrence has important implications. In the Nordic countries, the concept of general prevention is strongly connected with the idea that a properly working criminal justice system has powerful indirect influences on people's beliefs and behavior. General deterrence is an element of general prevention, but the deterrence mechanisms are not necessarily the most important ones in maintaining respect for the law. It is, however, necessary that citizens perceive the system to be reasonably efficient and legitimate. Such a system promotes internalization and acceptance of the social norms that underlie the prohibitions of the criminal law (Anttila 1986).

This emphasis on the justice system's indirect effects has made it possible for Finns to reject *both* harsh punishments and highly individualized sanctions based on coercive treatment. The expectation that a properly working criminal justice system must meet certain *minimum* requirements—standards of certainty and adequacy of punishment, legitimacy of procedure, and appropriateness in the scope of the criminal law—is, in a sense, *static*. Such requirements are not directly translatable into theses about the efficacy or desirability of *changes* in the system. A strong belief in general prevention as the guiding rationale of the criminal justice system thus does not imply that changes in policy, such as increases in the severity of punishment, would be widely seen as an appropriate or cost-effective means of controlling the level of crime.

The idea of a just proportion between crime and punishment is, according to this view, an indispensable quality of a properly working criminal justice system. One important function of the proportionality principle is to set an upper limit to the penalty for any given offense. The ideas of fairness and justice within the system are also seen as absolute values. But the principal aim of the criminal justice system is not retribution or "doing justice" but the control of crime through the indirect and long-term mechanisms already outlined.

While the idea of system-based general prevention is strong in all Nordic countries, it has the widest support in Finland. The rehabilitative ideal, which until recently was very popular in Sweden, never gained wide support in Finland. Nor can a system that sees the establishment of *upper* limits to punishment as a primary goal leave much room for purely incapacitative measures. Finnish law contains provisions for very dangerous, violent offenders, which authorize their continued detention in prison after the completion of their sentences, but the provisions are not used and are likely, according to recent reform proposals, to be repealed.

The Sanction System

Finnish laws provide relatively narrow ranges to govern judges' sentencing decisions (and parole release serves to reduce the durations of prison stays). The statutes on theft provide an example. The basic statute on simple theft (section 28:1 of the Finnish Penal Code) states that the offender shall be sentenced to "a fine or to prison for at most one year." If, on the basis of the value of the stolen goods or certain other criteria, the offense is found to be an aggravated one (28:2), the available punishments range from four months to four years of imprisonment. Petty theft is dealt with in a separate statute that allows only fine sentences.

Unlike many other European countries, the Finnish penal system is built on only three basic sentencing alternatives: *fines* (set on the basis of the day-fine system that was introduced in 1921), *conditional (suspended) imprisonment*, and *unconditional imprisonment*. Table 2.7 indicates the use of the basic sanction options in 1991 for selected offenses.

A conditional sentence of imprisonment can be combined with an unconditional fine—this option was used in 1991 in 37 percent of all conditional prison sentences for offenses against the penal code. Fines can be set by the court, but for less serious offenses the police set a summary day fine, which later is approved by the public prosecutor in a routine procedure.

Waiver of punishment (the offender is found guilty but because of his youth or other extenuating circumstances is absolutely discharged) is also a possibility; this option was highly restricted until a 1991 amendment increased its scope.

Community service, introduced in some districts on a trial basis in 1991 and extended nationwide in 1994, allows the court to convert an unconditional sentence of imprisonment to community service. Current reform plans may create

Table 2.7. Sanctions Imposed in 1991 for Selected Offenses

	Theft Offenses %	Assault Offenses %	Drunk Driving %	All Penal Code Offenses %
Waiver of punishment	1.0	1.9	0.2	1.1
Fines set at trial	16.6	75.8	43.8	39.8
Summary fines	64.6	—	—	31.4
Conditional imprison-ment	7.4	13.2	38.7	16.3
Unconditional impris-onment	10.4	9.1	17.3	11.3
Total	100.0	100.0	100.0	99.9
	(n = 32,209)	(n = 7,621)	(n = 24,054)	(n = 97,636)

Notes: Figures refer to the persons who were sentenced (n = 65,928) or absolutely discharged through waiving of punishment (n = 1,118) in general courts of first instance or who were fined in a summary procedure (n = 30,647) in 1991. The total number of offenders was almost 98,000, and the total number of separate sentences approximately 135,000. The offenders are grouped according to the most serious offense.

additional sanctions for juvenile offenders who were under 18 at the time of the offense (Lappi-Seppälä 1994, p. 203).

Before 1976, the conditional sentence was reserved for first offenders and young offenders. Current law recognizes prior criminality as a criterion that in some cases may preclude suspension of sentence, but the main emphasis is on the gravity of the offense. An amendment in 1989 provides that persons under 18 at the time of the offense should be given an unconditional sentence only under exceptional circumstances. Prison sentences of more than two years cannot be suspended, but recent proposals have been made to remove this restriction.

Statutory Sentencing Standards

Apart from statutes that authorized reductions of sentences for young offenders, partially insane offenders, and certain acts of self-defense or duress, the only general sentencing rules that formerly affected the length of the prison sentence were statutes on recidivism, which stipulated extended sentences for repeat offenders. The recidivism provisions were abolished in 1976 and replaced with a set of sentencing rules (Chapter 6 of the Finnish Penal Code).

The current statutes direct the courts to take into account the goal of uniformity of sentencing and all grounds for increasing or decreasing the severity of the punishment. The law specifically lists four aggravating considerations: the degree to which the criminal activity was planned; whether the offense was committed by a member of a group organized for serious offenses; whether the offense was committed for remuneration; and the previous criminality of the offender if similarity between the offenses shows that the offender is particularly heedless of the prohibitions and commands of the law.

A separate statute provides three grounds for mitigating punishment: presence of significant coercion, threat, or similar action; exceptional and sudden temptation or a similar factor that lowered the offender's ability to obey the law; and the offender's voluntary efforts to prevent or compensate for the offense or aid in clearing up the offense.

A separate provision, rarely used (only 20 times in 1991), also allows the court to reduce the sentence because of such consequences of the offense and the trial as loss of job, heavy damages, adverse publicity, or serious personal injury.

Sentencing Practices

Table 2.8 illustrates recent sentencing patterns in Finland. It shows by offense the proportions of unconditional sentences among all sentences and their mean lengths. The data in table 2.8 represent sentences per conviction offense, not aggregate sentences received by offenders for all current offenses. Summary fines are not included. The crime-specific data here do not include sentences for attempted offenses.

Long sentences are used sparingly—only 1.4 percent of all unconditionally sentenced offenders in 1991 received a prison sentence of four years or longer. A few persons each year are sentenced to life imprisonment for murder.

The parole rules assume that first-time offenders can be paroled after serving one-half of the sentence. Special rules for young offenders allow earlier release. Adult repeat offenders must serve at least two-thirds of the sentence. The paroling practices are fairly uniform and predictable.

A Trend toward Less Imprisonment

As table 2.8 shows, there has been a trend toward fewer and shorter sentences of unconditional imprisonment. Theft offenses in particular have undergone significant changes. Theft offenses dealt with in court are more seldom than in earlier

Table 2.8. Unconditional Prison Sentences in Finland, 1980, 1986, and 1991

	Unconditional Prison Sentences (in % of all sentences)			Average Length of Unconditional Sentence (in months)		
	1980	1986	1991	1980	1986	1991
Simple theft	44.2	39.5	36.2	3.4	2.7	2.0
Aggravated theft	74.0	69.1	68.7	10.8	10.3	7.7
Simple assault	16.7	11.5	9.2	3.1	2.6	2.2
Aggravated assault	50.4	58.7	54.9	15.0	13.3	13.0
Fraud	51.6	42.7	32.4	3.5	3.4	2.8
Aggravated drunk driving	25.0	31.9	33.5	3.0	3.0	2.9
Forcible rape	46.6	72.0	78.2	20.5	23.3	19.5
Intentional homicide	100.0	98.0	99.0	88.7	92.9	94.7
All penal code offenses	23.1	23.0	21.8	5.0	4.4	3.7

Note: Summary fines and sentences for attempted offenses are not included.

times considered to be aggravated. At the same time, the number and proportion of petty theft offenses handled by a summary day fine has dramatically increased; those data are not reproduced in table 2.8, which shows the percentages of offenders, by offense, who receive prison sentences (table 2.7 provides data on all sentences imposed, by offense). Much of the increase in petty theft results from growing numbers of shoplifting offenses.

Violent offense patterns have not changed significantly. The sentencing practices as regards intentional homicide are stable. The average age of rape offenders has increased, which is reflected in an increasing proportion of unconditional sentences, but the mean length of rape sentences has not increased.

When an offender is charged with multiple offenses, the courts before 1992 determined the proper sentence for each offense and then combined them according to certain rules. The new seventh chapter of the penal code, which took effect in 1992, instructs the courts to pass one single punishment for the main offense, and the secondary offenses are treated as aggravating circumstances.

The prison population is declining. In 1980 Finnish prisons received 10,112 persons (including remand prisoners and fine defaulters). The average daily population was 5,088, or 106 inmates per 100,000 inhabitants. In 1992, only 9,851 persons entered Finnish prisons, the average population was 3,511, and the prisoner rate had dropped to 70 per 100,000 inhabitants.

Explaining the Trend

Why has the average severity of sentences, particularly for property offenses, declined? Crime rates have steadily increased in most offense categories, and the gravity of the offenses has not declined. The average age of the offender population has slightly increased.

Use of prisons has declined because Finnish policy makers decided prison use *should* decline. In the 1960s, Finnish crime specialists became aware that the Finnish prisoner rate was abnormally high compared with that in other Nordic and Western European countries. Sentences for property crimes were considerably harsher than those in other Nordic countries. Scholars, civil servants, judges, and others involved in the system reacted strongly to these findings and called for reforms.

The decision to "normalize" the Finnish sanctioning system produced changes in crime definitions, in authorized sentences in the penal code, in the rules governing the choice and the severity of sanction, and in the parole system. Many of these reforms were enacted in the 1970s, including introduction of new statutes on theft in 1972, on drunk driving in 1976, and on conditional sentences in 1976 (Törnudd 1993). The effects were apparent throughout the 1980s.

Other reforms were parts of the still ongoing reform of the Finnish Criminal Code. One important change in 1991 promoted the use of very short sentences of imprisonment measured in days. The theft statutes were modernized in 1972; all authorized punishments for property offenses were reduced. The effects of this change were visible in the judicial statistics for the year 1991 (Oikeustilastollinen 1993, pp. 102–6).

The Finnish experience shows that—given the political will—the use of imprisonment can be substantially reduced without introducing new alternative sanctions. A necessary requirement has been the fairly stable and coherent criminal justice ideology of Finland and the relative lack of public controversy about it.

Recent Trends in Finnish Sentencing Policy (October 1999)
Tapio Lappi-Seppälä

In the early 1950s, the incarceration rate was four times higher in Finland than in the other Nordic countries—about 200 prisoners (including pretrial and sentenced) per 100,000 inhabitants, compared with around 50 in Sweden, Denmark, and Norway. In the 1970s, Finland's rate continued among the highest in Europe. However, a steady decline started soon after World War II and continued with only minor interruptions. By the early 1990s, Finland had reached the Nordic level of about 70 prisoners per 100,000 residents. The decline resulted from several factors, including changes in court practices and legislative reforms that reduced penalty scales and offered new sentencing alternatives. Behind this change were a consistent long-term penal policy and a political will to bring down the incarceration rate. These factors have been discussed elsewhere (Törnudd 1993; Lappi-Seppälä 1998*a*).

Crime Rates and Prison Rates in the Nordic Countries

Such a profound change in the use of imprisonment naturally raises questions about its effects on crime rates. There are several well-known methodological difficulties in measuring causal relations between crime rates and prison rates (and other changes in sentence severity; see, e.g., von Hirsch et al. 1999, pp. 17–23). However, the possibility of comparing countries that share strong social and structural similarities but have different penal histories provides an unusual perspective. The Nordic experiences provide an opportunity to see how drastic changes in penal practices in one country have been reflected in crime rates, compared with countries that have kept their penal systems more or less stable. Figure 2.13 shows incarceration and reported crime rates in Denmark, Finland, Norway, and Sweden, from 1950 to 1997. There is a striking difference in the use of imprisonment, and a striking similarity in trends in recorded criminality. That Finland has substantially reduced its incarceration rate has not disturbed the symmetry of Nordic crime rates. The figures also confirm the general criminological conclusion that crime and incarceration rates are fairly independent of each other; each rises and falls according to its own laws and dynamics.

Penal Changes in the 1990s

The three basic sentencing options in Finland have traditionally been fines, conditional imprisonment (suspended sentence), and unconditional imprisonment. Fines are imposed according to the day-fine system. The number of day fines is

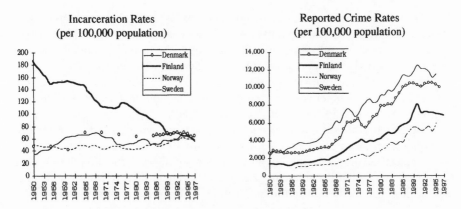

Figure 2.13. Incarceration and Reported Crime Rates in Denmark, Finland, Norway, and Sweden, 1950–1997. *Source*: Lappi-Seppälä 2001.

determined on the basis of the seriousness of the offense, while the amount of a day fine depends on the offender's income (basically one-third of the daily income before taxes). A sentence of imprisonment may be imposed for a determinate period (at least 14 days and at most 12 years) or for life. A life sentence is mandatory for murder. Sentences of imprisonment of at most two years may be imposed conditionally. A conditional sentence may be activated if, during the probation period, the offender commits a new offense for which he or she is sentenced to imprisonment. In addition, there are special arrangements for young offenders between 15 and 17 years of age. Finally, a legal institution called "waiving of measures" gives the police, the prosecutor, or the judge power to waive further measures under certain circumstances (see in more detail Lappi-Seppälä 2001).

This basic structure of the sentencing system has remained relatively stable during recent decades. The only major change has been the introduction of community service. This took place first on an experimental basis in 1991. In 1994, the system was extended to the entire country, and community service became a standard part of the Finnish system of sanctions. Community service is imposed instead of unconditional imprisonment for up to eight months. In order to ensure that community service is used in lieu of unconditional sentences of imprisonment, a two-step procedure was adopted.

First, the court is supposed to make its sentencing decision in accordance with the normal principles and criteria of sentencing, without considering the possibility of community service. *If* the result is unconditional imprisonment, *then* the court may commute the sentence to community service under the following conditions: the convicted person must consent to the sanction; the offender must be capable of carrying out the community service order; and recidivism and prior convictions may disqualify the offender.

The duration of community service varies between 20 and 200 hours. In commuting imprisonment to community service, one day in prison equals one hour of community service. Thus, two months of custodial sentence should be commuted to roughly 60 hours of community service. If the terms of the community service order are violated, the court normally imposes a new unconditional sentence of imprisonment. Community service does not contain any additional supervision aimed at controlling the offender's other behavior in general. The supervision is strictly confined to compliance with working obligations.

The rationale was that community service should be used only in cases where the accused would otherwise have received an unconditional sentence of imprisonment. As figure 2.14 shows, this aim was achieved.

The number of community service orders has increased, and the number of unconditional prison sentences has decreased. In 1998, the average daily number of offenders serving a community service order was about 1,200, and the number in prison was 2,800. It is therefore reasonable to argue that, within a short time, community service has proven to be an important alternative to imprisonment.

Recent Prison Statistics

Between 1975 and 1990, the Finnish incarceration rate fell about 40 percent (see figure 2.13). The downward trend continued during the 1990s. Between 1990 and 1998, the incarceration rate fell by 20 percent (from 69 to 55). The annual number of admitted prisoners decreased by 34 percent, from 8,800 in 1990 to 5,800 in 1998. During the same period, the average length of the effective prison term increased from 4.7 months in 1990 to 5.8 months in 1998, explaining why the number of prisoners admitted annually decreased more rapidly than the number of prisoners (see table 2.9).

In the early 1990s, three of four prisoners released each year had served less than six months, and a little over 10 percent had served a little more than one year. In 1998, a little over 60 percent had served less than six months and about 20 percent more than one year.

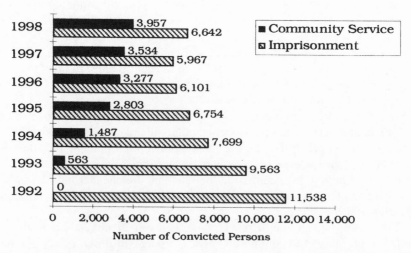

Figure 2.14. The Use of Imprisonment and Community Service in Finland, 1992–1998. *Source*: Lappi-Seppälä 1998*b*.

Table 2.9. Prison Rates in Finland, 1975–1998 (annual averages)

	Prisoners	Rate per 100,000 Inhabitants	Prisoner Admissions	Average Stay in Prison (in months)
1975	5,469	116	13,457	4.9
1980	5,085	106	10,114	6.0
1985	4,411	90	9,307	5.7
1990	3,441	69	8,831	4.7
1991	3,467	69	8,874	4.7
1992	3,511	70	9,851	4.3
1993	3,421	67	9,435	4.4
1994	3,275	64	8,711	4.5
1995	3,248	63	7,755	5.0
1996	3,197	62	6,594	5.8
1997	2,974	58	6,201	5.7
1998	2,809	55	5,803	5.8

Source: Prison Administration, Ministry of Justice.

Both the downward trend in the incarceration rate and the upward trend in time spent in prison largely result from the introduction of community service. This new alternative reduced the number of prison sentences, especially short prison sentences. The average length of stay in prison became longer as shorter prison sentences were converted to community service orders. In 1990, there were no community service sentences. In 1994, 2.4 percent (1,487) of sentences were to community service, a proportion that reached 6.8 percent (3,957) in 1998.

Sentencing Trends

Leaving aside changes caused by the community service order, sentencing practices have been stable in the 1990s. The overall level of sanctions and the relative use of basic sentencing alternatives have not altered much. Of all criminal cases brought before the court, a clear majority result in fines (60 percent) or a conditional sentence (20 percent). About 10 percent of offenders are sentenced to imprisonment (usually between 3 and 6 months) and some 6–7 percent to community service. In fewer than 2 percent of the cases does the court waive further sanctions (nonprosecution is not included in these figures).

Sanction severity is relatively low in Finland, especially from an American perspective. Most intermediate-level offenses such as theft, assault and battery, fraud, and drunken driving are punished by fines or conditional sentences. Prior convictions will, however, lead to short prison sentences in these offense categories. Murder leads either to a life sentence or, in case of diminished responsibility, to a prison term of 10–12 years. Manslaughter leads to a prison term of 10–12 years. The average penalty for aggravated robbery is about three years, for rape around two years, for aggravated assault around one year, and for aggravated theft and a normal type of robbery a little less. In the last category of cases, first offenders usually receive conditional sentences.

Practically all prisoners are released on parole. First-time prisoners are released after half of the sentence, others after having served two-thirds of the sentence. Young offenders are released after having served one-third of the sentence. Offenders serving life sentences are pardoned by the President of the Republic after a prison term of 10–12 years. The period of parole is the remaining sentence, but at least three months and at most three years. In practice, parole may be revoked only if the offender commits a new offense during this period. Twenty to 30 percent of those released on parole are placed under supervision.

Rational Criminal Policy—or Symbolic Politics on Crime and Criminality?

Finnish policy may be characterized as both rational and humane (see Törnudd 1996 and Lappi-Seppälä 2001). Whether this will continue, of course, remains to be seen. Elsewhere in the world, criminal policy has increasingly become entangled in partisan politics, with results that often are less than desirable. The rule of thumb seems to be that the higher the level of political authority at which crime policy is considered, the more simplistic the approaches that are advocated. This can be seen in programs and slogans compressed into two or three words, such as "three strikes," "prison works," "truth in sentencing," "war on drugs," "zero tolerance," and so on. This, in turn, leads to a tendency to offer simple solutions to complex problems and to pander to punitive (or presumably punitive) public opinion with harsh tough-on-crime campaigns. A common feature is that the solution to social problems is sought in the penal system, where it cannot be found. Criminality is seen not so much as a social problem connected to social and structural factors as a problem caused by evil individuals, a problem that can be eliminated by shutting those people away in institutions.

It may be that international currents are so strong that it is only a question of time before Finland is caught up in this development. For example, it is evident that national criminal justice policies in Europe will increasingly be influenced by the European Union. In the hands of euro-politicians, criminal policy is often just another tool of general politics, a way to transmit "symbolic messages," a way to "take a stand," a way to "make strategic choices." Instead of balanced reasoning and the weighing of different strategies and their pros and their cons, criminal justice policies are often determined by a simple political need to "do something." This is one reason why a large segment of Nordic scholars in criminal law are quite skeptical of attempts to harmonize criminal law (see Greve 1995; Träskman 1997).

But even though isolated signs of such an approach can also be seen in the Finnish debate, developments in Finland, at least so far, do not give cause for great concern. The total reform of criminal law launched in 1980 should be completed by the year 2000. Throughout, the reform has been carried out in the spirit of neoclassical criminal law, with respect for principles of due process and for legal safeguards. The reassessment of individual offenses has been carried out primarily by lowering ranges of authorized penalties, the primary exception being increases for some economic crimes. The reform of the penal system has included expansion of community-based measures. Also, the first national crime prevention program, approved by the government in 1999, puts its focal point on situational and local crime prevention. For the time being, it remains hard to imagine that the claim that "prison works" will soon find its way into Finnish political campaigns.

Germany

Sentencing and Punishment in Germany (February 1995)
Hans-Jörg Albrecht

Sentencing policies and practices in Germany have changed substantially since 1970 as a result of a substantial shift from imprisonment to fines, probation, and various diversionary programs. The prison population declined from 56,870 in 1963 to 34,398 in 1994. Unsuspended sentences to imprisonment fell from 92,576 in 1967, fluctuated between 30,000 and 40,000 in the 1970s and 1980s, and totaled 32,359 in 1991 (5 percent of all penalties). Fines, by contrast, have been ordered in 82 to 84 percent of cases since 1970 (83.8 percent in 1991).

This article explains how and why those shifts occurred and describes modern German case disposition from presentencing through parole, with primary emphasis on the adult system.

Sentences for Adults

Each offense in the German Criminal Code ("G.C.C.") carries a minimum and a maximum penalty. The main penalties are day fines and imprisonment. The number of day fines varies with the seriousness of the offense, from five to 360. The size of one day-fine unit (which may vary between 2 DM and 10.000 DM, or $1.30 and $6,700) must be adjusted to the offender's (daily) net income. On default, imprisonment has to be imposed (with one day equaling one day fine). Under particular circumstances (59 G.C.C.), the court may caution the offender and postpone the imposition of a day fine. The minimum prison term is set by statute at one month and the maximum at 15 years. Life-term imprisonment is restricted to murder. Under a 1992 amendment (42a G.C.C), confiscation of property may be imposed in addition to a sentence of imprisonment of more than two years and may amount to the total value of the defendant's assets.

German criminal law also allows for so-called measures of rehabilitation and security that are not dependent on personal guilt but depend solely on the degree of dangerousness exhibited by an offender and the corresponding need for preventive action. These are based on the consideration that proportional punishment may be insufficient for very dangerous offenders who are likely to recommit very serious crimes.

Under very restrictive conditions, the court may order additional detention in a detoxification center (for a maximum of up to two years), indeterminate detention in a psychiatric facility (in case of insane offenders and very serious crimes), or an additional incapacitative sentence (the first time detention is ordered, a

maximum of 10 years applies; if ordered a second time, detention is indeterminate). Finally, revocation of the driving license may be ordered as a measure of
security.

In quantitative terms, these measures do not play a significant role, with the
exception of withdrawal of the driving license. An incapacitative sentence is imposed in some 30 cases per year; approximately 500 offenders are sentenced to
indeterminate detention in a psychiatric facility, and 700 offenders are detained
in detoxification centers. Incapacitative sentences are under heavy criticism because of problems of establishing dangerousness and the assumption of excessive
punishment (Kaiser 1990).

Young Offenders

Sentencing options available in German criminal law differ according to the offender's age. Juveniles (14–17 years) are dealt with by a system of juvenile criminal
justice. Eighteen- to 20-year-olds are presumed to be adults and therefore to be
fully responsible. However, under certain conditions, defined in 105 Youth Court
Law, young adults may be prosecuted and sentenced as if they had been juveniles
when committing the crime. For juvenile offenders, rehabilitation must be sought,
while in adult criminal law the basic statute on sentencing (46 G.C.C.) requires
punishment to be proportional with the guilt of the offender and the seriousness
of the offense.

In practice, treatment of older adolescents as adults is the exception, not the
rule. At the beginning of the 1990s slightly more than 60 percent of all young
adults were sentenced as juveniles, including 80 percent of those sentenced for
sexual crimes and property offenses and virtually all young adults sentenced for
robbery and homicide.

The adult penal code penalty ranges do not apply to juveniles. Nor do day
fines or adult imprisonment. Youth court sanctions consist of educational measures
(e.g., community service, participation in victim-offender-mediation), "disciplinary
measures" (e.g., short-term detention up to four weeks), and youth imprisonment
with a minimum of six months and a maximum of five years (in cases of very
serious crimes imprisonment may be extended to 10 years).

Sentencing Adults

German criminal law provides for a two-step procedure in the sentencing of adults.
The first requires a decision on the amount of punishment that is proportionate
to the offender's guilt and the seriousness of the offense (46 G.C.C.). Rehabilitation and deterrence may be pursued only within a narrow range of penalties
deemed consistent with the principle of proportionality. Although sentencing statutes are not very explicit on the relations among sentencing goals or on mitigating
and aggravating circumstances, doctrine and court practice widely agree that rehabilitation and deterrence cannot justify sentences outside the range determined
by the principle of proportionality. However, the problem of how proportionality
can be established and how control of proportionality by superior courts can be

exerted is not resolved (Albrecht 1994). Finally, sentencing is determinate (German adult criminal law, although heavily influenced by the idea of rehabilitation, never allowed for indeterminate sentencing).

The second step requires a decision on whether punishment should be imposed as a day fine, a suspended prison sentence, or an immediate sentence of imprisonment. In this decision, not individual guilt or seriousness of the offense but individual and general prevention should play the decisive role.

The most important changes occurred in 1969 and 1975, when legislation was introduced (47 G.C.C.) ordering that (day) fines should have priority over short-term imprisonment (of less than six months) with rare exceptions. The rationale was that short-term imprisonment was incompatible with respect to rehabilitation because of the short period available for treatment and the corruptive effects of the prison environment. These policies manifest the view that first-time offenders and those who commit crimes of a nonserious nature should receive fines, while longer prison sentences should concentrate on a small group of heavy recidivists, as well as those who have committed serious crimes.

Prison sentences of one year or less require regular suspension in case of low risk of recidivism (56 G.C.C.). Sentences of up to two years may be suspended if the offender presents a low risk of recidivism and the particular circumstances of the offense or the offender justify a suspended sentence. In case of suspension, a period of probation of up to five years must be determined, and the offender may be placed under the supervision of a probation officer. Conditions include community service, a summary fine, or compensation paid to the victim. If conditions are not met or if the offender commits a new crime, suspension may be revoked, and the original prison sentence has to be served.

The Prosecution System

Judges' sentencing decisions are but a small part of the system that determines the type and size of punishment an offender receives. The public prosecutor's office plays an important role. Since the mid-1970s, the discretionary powers of the public prosecutor to dismiss criminal cases have expanded considerably. German Procedural Code 153a empowers the prosecutor to dismiss minor cases if the offender accepts punitive conditions determined by the prosecutor (a fine, community service, compensation).

A March 1993 law empowered the prosecutor to dismiss a case if the offender's guilt does not necessitate a penalty. This was motivated by economic problems due to German reunification. Because rebuilding the justice system in the East requires enormous resources, the need was felt to streamline criminal procedures further in order to reduce costs. Budget concerns have outweighed legitimate interests in maintaining proper lines between the public prosecutors' task of investigating and indicting criminal cases and the judges' task of imposing criminal punishments.

The public prosecutor can choose between two procedures in bringing a case to court. One is the regular criminal trial. However, a simplified procedure may be initiated that consists solely of written proceedings. If the prosecutor concludes that guilt can easily be proven and that a day fine is sufficient punishment, a penal order providing for a day fine may be proposed to the judge. If the judge agrees, a penal order is mailed to the suspect, who is entitled to appeal. In the case of ordinary crimes (approximately 1.3 million cases per year), 30 percent are dismissed, 40 percent are dealt with by simplified procedures, and the rest receive a full trial (30 percent).

The procedural option of simplified procedures was extended in 1993. Now, if the offender had a defense counsel, the public prosecutor may propose a suspended sentence of imprisonment of up to one year in a simplified procedure. Since only 6 percent of all criminal penalties today involve prison sentences of more than one year, in theory a full trial (and sentencing by the criminal court) could be restricted to a minor part of all offenders. Economic pressures and administrative convenience thus have supported the trend toward noncustodial sentences (especially day fines).

Parole

Time served by imprisoned offenders and the type of penalty ultimately executed may deviate considerably from the disposition made by criminal courts. According to 57 G.C.C., a prisoner may be paroled after having served two-thirds of the prison sentence; under exceptional circumstances parole may be granted after half of the prison term. Several important changes should be mentioned. In 1977 the Prison Law established a system of correctional courts with authority over parole. In case of life-term imprisonment, the constitutional court ruled that regular statutory parole must be available for prisoners sentenced to life imprisonment (which until then was granted by way of clemency only) (BVerfGE 45, p. 187). In 1986, legislation was introduced (57a G.C.C.) setting the minimum to be served at 15 years. The constitutional court in 1992 (BVerfGNJW 1992, p. 2947) decided that the rule of law requires predictable periods of detention for life imprisonment. The court ruled that (with the exception of very dangerous offenders) life prisoners for average cases (of murder) should ordinarily be paroled after 15 years. For cases with aggravating circumstances, a standard of approximately 20 years was set. Thus, in practice the constitutional court converted life imprisonment into a fixed period of imprisonment, something critics, assuming that life imprisonment violated human rights, had demanded since the seventies (Jung 1992).

Another major change that affected prison admission occurred around 1980 with respect to fine collection. In the early 1980s, fine defaults (and substitute imprisonment) increased, mainly due to increasing rates of unemployment (Kerner and Kästner 1986). To reduce the additional burden put on the prison system, community service was introduced as an option for fine defaulters, with overall positive results (Albrecht and Schädler 1986). Currently, the conversion rate is six hours community service equal one day imprisonment.

Sentencing Practice and Sentencing Outcomes

Several long-term trends concerning sentencing practices stand out. The absolute number of offenders convicted and sentenced has been stable since the early 1970s (ranging between 600,000 and 700,000 per year; in 1991: 622,390). Diversion policies have cut off steadily increasing numbers of suspects. The use of prison sentences (suspended and immediate) has also been stable since the beginning of the 1970s, with a proportion of 16 to 18 percent of all sentences (in 1991: 16.2 percent). Sentences to immediate (that is, nonsuspended) imprisonment declined until the end of the 1980s, from 92,576 in 1967 to 40,270 in 1970 and varying between 30,000 and 40,000 per year in the 1970s and 1980s (in 1991: 32,359 or 5 percent of all criminal penalties). The number of suspended prison sentences increased until the end of the eighties (in 1991: 70 percent of all prison sentences or 11 percent of all criminal penalties).

The use of fines increased sharply at the end of the 1960s (as a consequence of giving fines priority over short-term imprisonment) and remains stable (82 to 84 percent of all sentences during the past two decades; in 1991: 83.8 percent).

Overall, while the number of sentenced prisoners decreased considerably in the long run (from 56,870 in 1963 to 34,398 on January 30, 1994, yielding a rate of sentenced prisoners of 55 per 100,000), the number of offenders placed under probation supervision increased (from 27,000 in 1963 to 150,000 at the beginning of the 1990s).

These changes lend support to some assumptions on the roles and functions of various punishments. Imprisonment constitutes physical and immediate control over restricted parts of the population. But facilities are limited and inelastic and inadequate for dealing with growing numbers of offenders. With expanded intermediate sanctions such as probation and parole, the role of imprisonment changed from provision of immediate physical control to use as a last resort, strengthening the deterrent impact of a type of sanction based on supervision and control outside the prison but nevertheless backed up by the threat of imprisonment.

While the use of imprisonment may be reduced to a relatively stable (and perhaps mere symbolic) level, the greater elasticity of probation and parole allows for a widened scope of judicial control over varying proportions of precarious populations. In the 1960s, the probation population was characterized by low risk (as measured by prior record) and a limited need for control (no prior record and a stable work were major preconditions for granting suspension of a prison sentence). However, since the mid-1970s the target group for probation has been a group that formerly had been sent to prison.

A consequence of this distribution of criminal penalties was a high average period of imprisonment compared with that in other European countries (approximately six months compared to an average of around two months, e.g., in the Netherlands), but a low rate of offenders receiving unconditional prison sentences and admitted to prisons. Thus, the prisoner rate at the beginning of the 1990s was around 60 per 100,000 in Germany. In the Netherlands and Sweden, the corresponding rates were well below 50 per 100,000. However, the rate of offenders who received sentences of immediate imprisonment was 73 per 100,000 in Germany and 113 in the Netherlands and 166 in Sweden.

Although long prison sentences may appear to be the result of recent criminal law reforms, prison sentences amounting to more than two years are rare. In 1991, of all prison sentences (immediate and suspended), 6,560, or 6 percent, exceeded two years (of these 56 were for life imprisonment). Among all criminal penalties in 1991, only 1 percent were prison sentences of two years or longer. Although judges could impose many longer sentences, they do not. Sentencing decisions tend toward the minimum authorized penalty, displaying not a normal but a J-type distribution within the range allowed for most offense categories.

However, there was no uniform development in sentencing practice over the past two decades for most traditional crimes (e.g., traffic offenses, property crimes, robbery, and assault). Prosecutors and courts tended to use diversion options and to favor fines and prison sentences near the minimum allowed. For simple theft, approximately nine out of 10 offenders were fined. A corresponding pattern characterizes assault cases and criminal damage. However, serious property offenses and drug offenses also result in considerable proportions of fines. In 1991, one out of four aggravated thefts was followed by a fine, and approximately half of drug offenders received fines.

For other offenses, sentencing practice changed at the end of the 1970s. This was true for violent sexual offenses, especially rape and child sexual abuse (Schöch 1992). The length of prison sentences for rape cases increased significantly, with prison sentences of more than five years doubling between 1978 and 1983 (up to 10 percent of all rape sentences from 5 percent). Sentences for drug offenses, especially drug trafficking, also became more severe. In a 1980 amendment of the law on illicit drugs, both minimum periods of imprisonment and maximums were raised substantially, and courts tended to impose prison sentences well above the minimum.

These changes in sentencing practice became evident between 1980 and 1984, when the prison population increased significantly because of increasing proportions of drug and violent offenders in the prison population and because of a growing number of admissions with long-term prison sentences.

A turnaround took place again around 1985, which may also be partially explained by demographic changes. In the second half of the 1980s, pretrial detention rose, with growing numbers of offenders of foreign nationality being placed in pretrial detention (they made up more than half of the pretrial detention population in the 1990s).

What Lies Ahead?

German criminal law provides for a simple system of penalties. Day fines and (suspended or immediate) imprisonment serve as the main penalties. Community service and probation are not available as penalties in their own right. The past decade saw vivid debates on whether other penalties should be added. Particular interest was voiced in the development of alternative penalties (community sanctions), and in strengthening the roles of restitution and victim-offender mediation. The issues discussed involved proposals to extend the range of prison sentences eligible for suspension from two to three years, to allow partial suspension of prison sentences, to transform suspended prison sentences into a criminal penalty of its own (comparable with probation and stressing the punitive impact of supervision, as well as the conditions), to introduce community service and revocation of the drivers' license as sole sanctions and, most important, to establish out-of-court restitution procedures as a major device for dealing in a principled way with all types of criminal offenders (Schöch 1992). Some of these proposals have been taken up in a formal draft brought into the Federal Parliament at the end of 1993 by the Social Democratic Party (Entwurf eines Gesetzes zur Reform des strafrecht-lichen Sanktionensystems, Bundestagsdrucksache 12/6141, 11.11.1993).

After German reunification, bias-motivated crime or hate crime became a prominent target of criminal policy. Since hate violence is committed to a con-siderable extent by groups of juveniles and young adults, the issue of how young adults should be treated in the criminal justice system came up again. However, a proposal offered by conservative political parties to make sentencing of young adults as if they were juveniles the exceptional case received little support in the legal professions, the parliament, or the public.

Major reforms of the sentencing process and the system of criminal penalties cannot be expected to take place in the near future (Schöch 1992, p. 11). Federal government reports in 1986 and 1992 concluded that there was no need to re-consider the system of sentencing and penalties, since the current state seemed to be satisfactory. Some minor changes will be effected by recent legislation that increases maximum penalties for assault (up to five years from three years in order to lift assault sentencing ranges to those found for simple theft) and legislation that requires that restitution and offender-victim mediation be taken into account in the sentencing decision and in the decision to suspend a prison sentence. A major meeting of the legal professions in Germany (Deutscher Juristentag) discussed in 1992 an in-depth study on criminal penalties that recommended introduction of additional community sanctions, as well as the out-of-court restitution procedure already mentioned (Schöch 1992). The debate showed that a majority in the legal professions do not favor such changes but adopt a pragmatic view and are not interested in complicating sentencing and the system of penalties.

France

French Prison Numbers Stable since 1988, but Populations Changing (August 1998)
Annie Kensey and Pierre Tournier

France's prison population is increasing, but more slowly than those in many other countries. The prison population has fluctuated widely but has been held in check by a series of amnesties and collective pardons. The January 1, 1998, population of 50,744, for example, was only 3 percent higher than the population 10 years earlier (49,328). A number of significant changes are disguised by that apparent stability. Average sentence lengths for convicted offenders have steadily increased for 25 years, while in recent years the numbers of people admitted to prison have declined. Other significant changes include shifts in offenses for which people are imprisoned (drugs, sex offenses, immigration offenses up; theft down) and in the proportions in prison of French nationals (down) and people of other nationalities (up).

Whether the French prison population is on the increase depends on the periods compared. Since 1988, largely as a result of pardons and amnesties, the population has been flat. Since 1975, however, it has doubled. The aim of this article is to identify the underlying trends over the past quarter century.

Between January 1975 and January 1988, the number of prison inmates rose from 26,032 to 50,744 in metropolitan France (see table 2.10). This represented an increase of almost 100 percent. These numbers are the total incarcerated population, including persons held in pretrial detention and persons sentenced to imprisonment.

Inmate Characteristics

The SEPT (Series Pénitentiares Temporelles) database was used in the analyses reported in this article. This base was created in 1981, using manual quarterly statistics reported by prison authorities, and updated regularly ever since. For practical reasons, the base includes only prisoners in metropolitan France.

Table 2.10. Prison Population, Metropolitan France, 1975–1998

Year	Number of Prisoners on January 1	Annual Percentage Change	Pardons, Amnesties, Etc.
1975	26,032	13.3	July 11, 1975, law on the additional reduction of sentence
1976	29,482	3.5	
1977	30,511	5.7	
1978	32,259	3.3	
1979	33,315	7.0	
1980	35,655	9.3	Collective pardon
1981	38,957	−22.1	Collective pardon; law of amnesty, August 4, 1981
1982	30,340	14.0	
1983	34,579	11.7	
1984	38,634	11.1	
1985	42,937	−0.7	July 9, 1984, law on remand came into force on January 1, 1985; collective pardon
1986	42,617	11.9	September 19, 1986, law on reduction in sentences
1987	47,694	3.4	
1988	49,328	−8.8	Collective pardon; law of amnesty, July 20, 1988
1989	44,981	−2.4	Collective pardon
1990	43,913	7.4	
1991	47,160	2.0	Collective pardon
1992	48,113	0.1	Collective pardon
1993	48,164	4.3	Collective pardon
1994	50,240	2.8	Collective pardon
1995	51,623	2.0	Collective pardon; law of amnesty
1996	52,658	−1.9	Collective pardon
1997	51,640	−1.7	Collective pardon
1998	50,744		Collective pardon

Source: Ministry of Justice, Series Pénitentiaires Temporelles (SEPT).

Before examining trends in prison use, it may be useful to compare French trends with those in other European countries (table 2.11) using 1986–1996 Council of Europe data. Prison populations are increasing over the whole of Europe, with the exceptions of Austria and Denmark. The rate of increase, however, varies considerably between countries. France, below average at 13 percent, comes in tenth position as of September 1, 1996, with 89.9 inmates per 100,000 inhabitants (overseas departments included).

Sentencing Trends

Prison population changes can be examined by looking at changes in admissions and lengths of stay. As used here, "admissions" refers to the number of imprisonments per year, not the number of individuals. The same individual can be counted more than once (either for different offenses during the same year or for different imprisonments for the same offense at different times during the proceedings).

Average length of stay is calculated by relating the average number of prison inmates during the year to the number of admissions. This rather unsophisticated method of calculation means that changes observed over two consecutive years are not significant. However, this method is extremely informative for demonstrating trends.

Table 2.11. Prison Population, 14 European Countries, 1986–1996

	Prison Population Sept. 1, 1986	Prison Population Sept. 1, 1996	Percentage Change 1986–1996	Incarceration Rate per 100,000 Inhabitants (1996)
Austria	7,778	6,778	−12.9	84.0
Belgium	6,193	7,656	23.6	75.6
Denmark	3,322	3,203	−3.6	61.0
England & Wales	46,581	55,537	19.2	106.8
France[1]	47,628	54,014	13.4	89.9
Greece	3,780	5,304	40.3	51.0
Ireland	1,853	2,182	17.8	62.3
Italy	43,685	48,545	11.1	85.0
Netherlands	4,906	11,578	136.0	75.2
Norway	2,021	2,290	13.3	52.4
Portugal	8,100	14,177	75.0	140.0
Spain[2]	25,059	40,157	60.2	122.4
Sweden	4,098	5,768	40.8	65.0
Switzerland	3,203	6,047	88.8	85.4

Notes:
1. Including overseas departments.
2. Spanish prison population as of September 1, 1995, and detention rate as of September 1, 1995.

Source: Council of Europe, Statistique Pénale Annuelle du Conseil de l'Europe.

To allow for amnesties following presidential elections, we break down the analyses in table 2.12 into four periods that correspond to Valéry Giscard d'Estaing's seven-year term of office (1974–1980), François Mitterrand's first seven-year term (1981–1987), his second seven-year term (1988–1994), and Jacques Chirac's first three years in office (1995–1997).

1974–1981   The 11,850 increase in the number of prisoners was primarily the result of an increase in the number of admissions; detention lengths remained fairly stable. In 1974, there were 72,500 admissions compared with 97,000 in 1980, an increase of a third in six years. If this trend had continued beyond 1980, in 1992 there would have been 50,000 more admissions than in 1980, for a total of 147,000. In fact, there were 88,586.

1981–1988   The increase in the number of prisoners slowed slightly in absolute terms (up 10,400), thanks, in part, to a great drop in 1981 following an amnesty and collective pardon. What is very different is the pattern: the increase during this period was mainly the result of longer average prison stays, the number of new admissions falling in 1981 and 1982 and fluctuating thereafter. During this period there were an average of 84,600 admissions per year, well below the 96,955 in 1980. This trend must be considered alongside the development of alternatives to short prison terms, especially supervision orders, and the introduction of community service orders in 1983. Although it is not possible to prove that these measures led to the drop in admissions, the data implicitly contradict the defeatist ideas of those who suggest that none of the measures introduced during the 1980s to reduce recourse to prison as a form of punishment had any effect. However, because lengths of stay increased steadily during this period, the drop in admissions was not sufficient to solve the prison population explosion.

1988–1994   During this period, the number of prisoners grew only a little (up 2,295 prisoners), thanks to annual collective pardons on July 14. Although average lengths of stay continued to lengthen, with a record high of 7.3 months in 1993, annual admissions declined slightly from the preceding period. These trends, which had been observed in France since 1981, are to be found in other European countries. During the 1980s, admissions decreased in Belgium, Germany, Greece, Italy, the Netherlands, and Portugal. At the same time, with the exception of Germany, prison populations increased due to longer detention times.

1995–1997   During this period, the prison population has fluctuated within a narrow range, from 50,744 to 52,658 (see table 2.10). This stability is partly the product of annual collective pardons and partly a product of a continuing decline in admissions. The 1997 figure of 75,738 is the lowest since 1989 and closer to the levels of the mid-1970s. The same trends of longer stays and fewer admissions that characterized the preceding two periods continued.

Table 2.12. Prison Admissions and
Length of Sentences, Metropolitan
France, 1974–1997 (in months)

Periods	Admissions	Length
1974–1980		
1974	72,491	4.4
1975	77,117	4.3
1976	74,308	4.8
1977	79,353	4.7
1978	83,711	4.7
1979	88,906	4.7
1980	96,955	4.6
Average	81,834	4.6
1981–1987		
1981	80,898	5.1
1982	74,427	5.2
1983	86,362	5.1
1984	89,295	5.5
1985	82,917	6.2
1986	87,906	6.2
1987	90,697	6.4
Average	84,643	5.7
1988–1994		
1988	83,517	6.8
1989	75,940	7.0
1990	78,442	7.0
1991	87,787	6.5
1992	88,586	6.5
1993	80,421	7.3
1994	85,761	7.1
Average	82,922	6.9
1995–1997		
1995	82,860	7.6
1996	79,938	7.8
1997	75,738	8.1
Average	79,512	7.8

Source: Ministry of Justice, Series Pénitentiaires Temporelles.

Longer Terms of Confinement

The length-of-stay indicator that was introduced in 1981 (annual admissions divided by January 1 population) and that has been used as a reference ever since does not take into account the legal status of the prisoners. The greater periods of time spent in prison may be explained by a number of different factors: (1) increases in length of legal proceedings (remand period, trial, sentencing, appeal), and heavier sentences because of changes in types of offenses or because of different punishments for the same offenses, (2) changes in the law or practices concerning individualization of sentences (e.g., remission/good time or release on parole/license granted less often). Although we lack sufficient data to study the process in all its complexity, certain observations may be made.

Over twenty-five years, the number of convicted prisoners increased by 132 percent. Both for the lesser criminal offenses (*correctionel*) and for serious crimes (*criminel*), the proportionate increase varies directly with length of sentence.

As table 2.13 shows, the rate of increase was very high for sentences for lesser criminal offenses ranging from three to five years (up 235 percent), and extremely high for sentences for lesser criminal offenses of five years and more (up 2,000 percent). These sentences are handed down mainly for drug trafficking offenses. There was also a sharp increase in the number of life sentences. On January 1, 1975, 33 percent of all convicted prisoners (4,345 prisoners) were serving sentences of three years or more. Twenty years later, 52 percent of all convicted prisoners (15,816 prisoners) were serving such sentences. These figures must be considered in the light of the changes in the types of offenses involved.

Table 2.13. Convicted Prisoners, Metropolitan France, by Sentence Length, 1975, 1995, 1998

	Jan. 1, 1975	Jan. 1, 1995	Jan. 1, 1998	Ratio 1998: 1975
All convicted prisoners	12,972	29,166	30,175	2.33
Sentences for lesser criminal offenses				
Under six months	2,896	3,876	3,516	1.21
Six months to under one year	1,997	4,097	4,097	2.05
One year to under three years	3,588	7,127	6,733	1.88
Three years to under five years	1,159	3,838	3,888	3.35
Five years and over	246	3,074	5,245	21.32
Sentences for serious criminal offenses				
Fixed sentences	2,755	5,658	6,149	2.23
Life	185	496	534	2.89

Source: Ministry of Justice, Series Pénitentiaires Temporelles.

Types of Offense

The data presented in table 2.14 show how the composition of the convicted prison population has changed since 1975 in terms of types of offenses committed. There has been a major shift from 1975, when 48.7 percent of prisoners had been convicted of theft, to 1998, when that percentage was reduced by two-thirds (to 16 percent) and drug and sexual offenses were the most common offenses.

In 1998, drug offenders (included in "other offenses" before 1988, counted separately since then by prison authorities) were the most common category of offenders (18.7 percent). Very few of those in prison were convicted of simple possession.

Two other types of offense contributed to the prison population explosion: rape and sexual offenses and breaches of immigration legislation. Were more offenses committed, were more offenses reported to the police, were the sentences handed down by the judges tougher? In order to answer these questions, we examine some figures concerning rape.

From 1978 to 1993, as table 2.15 shows, the number of rapes recorded by the police increased by 3.4 times. At the same time, the number of suspected offenders increased by 2.3 times. This lower rate of increase, despite the higher clearance rate, can be explained by a change in the relationship between the number of cases solved and the number of suspected offenders, which went from 1.27 to 0.75. This may be the result of a relative drop in the number of gang rapes (one offense, several suspected offenders) or an increase in the number of multiple

Table 2.14. Convicted Prisoners, Metropolitan France, by Principal Offense, Selected Years

	% as of January 1			
	1975	1985	1995	1998
All convicted prisoners	100.0	100.0	100.0	100.0
Drug-related crimes	in.	in.	20.9	18.7
Theft	48.7	37.2	20.4	16.0
Rape and sexual of- fenses	4.9	7.9	12.5	18.3
Intentional killing	9.1	11.0	10.0	10.1
Robbery	9.3	9.8	9.5	12.1
Assault	6.1	6.3	6.5	7.3
Breaches of immigration legislation	0.9	1.5	4.5	3.4
Fraud	3.2	2.8	2.4	2.2
Breaches of military reg- ulations	2.0	1.7	1.8	0.2
Worthless checks	1.6	1.9	0.8	0.5
Procuring	1.8	2.0	0.8	0.4
Others	10.6	15.5	7.9	9.0

Note: in. = no separate statistics, included in "others."

Source: Ministry of Justice, Series Pénitentiaires Temporelles.

Table 2.15. Rape Statistics, Metropolitan France, 1978–1993

Year	Recorded by the Police	Clear-Up Rate (%)	Number of Suspected Offenders	Convictions[1]	% of Prison Sentences of 10 Years and More
1978	1,631	79	1,711	343	13
no data available for 1979–83					
1984	2,859	81	2,600	563	17
1985	2,823	82	2,558	618	23
1986	2,937	82	2,179	619	22
1987	3,196	86	2,548	574	21
1988	3,776	86	3,068	624	29
1989	4,342	85	3,604	677	36
1990	4,582	85	3,617	729	35
1991	5,068	83	3,940	913	33
1992	5,355	88	4,000	892	35
1993	5,605	82	3,984		

Note: [1] whole of France.

Sources: Ministry of the Interior; Ministry of Justice.

offenses attributed to the same individual (one suspected offender, several offenses).

The substantial differences between the number of suspected offenders and the number of those convicted—which was relatively constant over the period considered—probably occurred because some suspects were eliminated during investigations or had their cases dismissed during trial or were charged with other offenses instead of rape. Having said this, there were 2.6 times as many convictions for rape in 1992 as in 1978, and the sentences were heavier; the proportion of convictions resulting in prison terms of 10 years and more rose from 13 percent to 35 percent.

The Question of Remand

The number of remand prisoners has increased steadily since 1974 and by January 1985 had comprised more than 51 percent of all prisoners, making a total of 22,000, as opposed to 12,000 in 1974 (see table 2.16). On January 1, 1985, the July 1984 law introducing the right for an accused person to have a lawyer was implemented, and at the same time the number of remand prisoners dropped, stabilizing at around 20,000, a level at which it has remained for nearly 15 years.

In a very large proportion of cases in which the accused has a lawyer, the accused is retained in custody before trial (about 90 percent). The presence of a lawyer is therefore not in itself a factor in the drop in the number of remand prisoners. More likely, the complications introduced by the requirement that a lawyer be present have led to fewer cases being brought, in particular under the

Table 2.16. Remand Prisoners, Metropolitan France, 1974–1998, Counts as of January 1, Admissions, and Duration (in months)

Periods	Population	Admission	Length
1974–1980			
1974	12,023	58,630	2.5
1975	12,889	65,143	2.4
1976	12,825	57,876	2.7
1977	13,065	60,183	2.7
1978	13,820	60,006	2.8
1979	14,167	63,404	2.8
1980	15,849	68,947	2.9
Average	13,520	62,027	2.7
1981–1987			
1981	17,313	64,478	3.0
1982	15,274	65,952	3.0
1983	17,643	72,541	3.1
1984	20,080	72,316	3.5
1985	22,060	66,332	3.9
1986	21,146	67,727	3.8
1987	21,411	65,181	3.8
Average	19,275	67,790	3.4
1988–1994			
1988	20,251	64,804	3.7
1989	19,526	64,027	3.7
1990	19,909	61,216	3.8
1991	19,047	66,034	3.5
1992	19,550	69,861	3.4
1993	20,101	62,098	3.9
1994	20,026	65,898	3.8
Average	19,773	64,848	3.7
1995–1998			
1995	22,159	62,833	4.1
1996	20,899	60,881	4.2
1997	21,366	56,588	4.4
1998	20,301	—	—
Average	21,181	60,101	4.2

Source: Ministry of Justice, Series Pénitentiaires Temporelles.

procedures in which the accused is brought to trial immediately without committal proceedings. As a result of the interaction of these two trends, there are currently fewer prisoners being held before trial, relatively speaking, than in 1974. On June 1, 1974, 44 percent of prisoners were pretrial detainees, compared with 40 percent in 1998.

The length of time prisoners spent in pretrial confinement went up considerably between 1974 and 1985 (from 2.5 months to 3.9 months), fluctuated for nearly 10 years, and recently has resumed its increase, to 4.4 months in 1997 (see table 2.16). A similar trend can be observed concerning the number of remand prisoners.

The situation in France concerning remand prisoners is often represented as being exceptional in comparison with the nation's European partners. But just how true is this? Using the SPACE (Statistique pénale annuelle du Conseil de l'Europe) database, it has been possible to calculate the rate of remand prisoners for 19 European countries as of September 1, 1993. With a rate of 33.7 per 100,000 inhabitants, France had a middling position. Nine countries had a higher rate of remand prisoners: several former communist countries, Lithuania (105 per 100,000), Romania (81), the Czech Republic (78), and Poland (38), and also Italy (48), Portugal (42), Spain (34), Belgium, and Luxembourg (35). However, there were fewer remand prisoners in Austria, Bulgaria, Germany, and Northern Ireland (31), Scotland (20), Sweden (14), Finland and Ireland (5), and Iceland (1).

Foreign Prisoners

An important phenomenon that cannot be ignored is the considerable increase in the number of foreign prisoners held in France over the last few years, rising from 18 percent of all prisoners in 1975 to 29 percent in 1995. The same thing can be seen in other European countries with comparable immigration patterns. The breakdown of foreign prisoners in terms of nationality has also changed considerably; the proportion of those coming from sub-Saharan Africa rose from 4 percent in 1975 to 16 percent in 1985.

It is important, however, to draw a distinction between those foreigners who are in prison for breaches of immigration regulations (administrative matters) and the others, who are held in criminal matters. This distinction is made possible by use of prison statistics available since September 1983. Though the increase from 1984 to 1995 in the number of foreign prisoners was much greater than for French nationals (48 percent compared with 29 percent), this is entirely due to arrests of foreigners without residence or work permits. Their number increased by 180 percent. For the other foreign prisoners, the increase (29 percent) was exactly the same as for French prisoners.

The question of illegal immigrants aside, it is possible to show that the way the criminal justice system functions is unfavorable toward foreigners. Table 2.17 shows the most common offenses and the proportion of unsuspended custodial sentences in 1991. Overall, 44 percent of foreign defendants received prison sentences, compared with only 17 percent of French nationals. For many offenses, foreign defendants' rate of imprisonment was twice as high as for French nationals:

Table 2.17. Unsuspended Prison Sentences, by Most Serious Offense and
Nationality, 1991

	French Nationals		Foreigners	
	All	%	All	%
All offenses	262,241	16.7	49,255	44.1
Illegal entry or residence of a foreigner	202	36.6	8,500	76.9
Robbery	4,369	57.3	1,176	63.5
Possession and acquisition of drugs	3,955	40.8	1,495	80.1
Burglary	13,046	36.7	1,780	48.5
Illegal use of drugs	3,687	23.3	795	55.8
Handling stolen goods	9,258	19.9	2,319	46.1
Theft	49,592	21.2	9,736	39.7
Assault with victim off work for ≤ 8 days aggravating circumstances	5,021	21.3	969	29.4
Criminal damage	5,333	12.8	761	23.7
Assault with victim off work for > 8 days aggravating circumstances	6,502	12.1	1,190	15.7
Obstructing a police officer	3,787	7.8	448	14.0
Issuing a worthless check	5,292	6.7	500	7.0
Drinking and driving	69,830	5.9	4,875	6.5
Abandoning one's family	4,190	5.4	327	6.4
Hit-and-run	5,519	4.1	571	5.6
Careless driving leading to injury	5,758	0.6	404	1.5

Source: Ministry of Justice.

entering and residing in France without papers, possession and acquisition of drugs, illegal use of drugs, handling stolen goods, theft, and criminal damage. It is hardly surprising that there are so many foreigners in the prison system.

70,000 Prisoners in the Year 2000?

In the newspaper *Témoignage chrétien* on March 18, 1994, the then Minister of Justice, M. Pierre Méhaignerie, declared that "in line with a statistical model whose predictions have been accurate since 1981, there should be 70,000 prisoners in France at the beginning of the century." What should we think of such an assertion?

Prison population projections have been calculated regularly since the beginning of the 1980s. Based on a very simple "model," they are calculated from a linear extrapolation of past trends, while allowing for seasonal adjustments (numbers on the first of each month). It is often difficult to get those for whom the calculations are intended to understand the difference between projections and predictions. If we imagine it is January 1995, for example, the technique used gives a good estimate of the number of prisoners on the first day of each month for 1995 or 1996—provided no "disruptive phenomena" occur that were not allowed for in the projection, such as an amnesty or a collective pardon, the scope and procedure of which can modify the prison population considerably. To illustrate this point, let us look at projections that were calculated in 1980. Depending on the different calculation modes, the projections forecast 40,400 to 45,000 prisoners in French prisons (including overseas departments) on January 1, 1982. The actual number was 31,500.

Though these projections may not be capable of predicting the future, they do show the numeric consequences of simple hypotheses: if the trend of the past few years continues, where are we heading? The word "if" is the operative word! It is also a good means to look at the current situation by putting the monthly statistics into perspective (allowing for seasonal adjustments), measuring the effects of new legislation and regulations, and so on. Above all, these calculations should encourage us to think about the means necessary to reverse troubling trends. In this way, all the factors already described that contribute to the prison population explosion make it necessary to look at the question of alternative sentences in a new light. The question of alternatives to short prison sentences remains topical, of course, but shouldn't the question be extended to finding alternatives to long prison sentences?

Netherlands

Sentencing and Punishment in the Netherlands (October 1994)
Peter J. P. Tak

Dutch penal policies have become harsher in some ways since 1980 and are likely to become harsher still. Prison sentences became longer and the number of prison cells nearly tripled, rising from 3,789 in 1980 to 10,059 in 1994, with an additional 1,800 to come on line early in 1996.

During the same period, however, the use of short-term imprisonment fell, use of a new prosecutorial diversion program grew rapidly, community service orders came into use, and an experimental intensive supervision program began in 1993.

Thus, the stereotype of the Netherlands as a country with exceedingly mild penal policies is—like most stereotypes—greatly oversimplified.

This article gives an overview of changes in Dutch sentencing policy since 1980, discussing the pressures for greater penal severity, sentencing trends, the development of community penalties, and the laws of sentencing.

Background

The Dutch criminal justice system has long been noted for its mildness. Although still mild in comparison with those in many other European countries (and more so compared with that in the United States), the penal climate has become harsher since the late 1970s. The incarceration rate of 24 per 100,000 population in 1980, for example, had grown to 61 per 100,000 by October 1994.

After three decades of low crime rates, a steep increase in crime between 1976 and 1984 caused serious and widely shared concern. The number of recorded crimes rose by around 60 percent, but public expenditure for law enforcement, the judiciary, and prison administration failed to keep pace. This resulted in a falling detection rate, a lower percentage of criminal cases dealt with by the courts, and insufficient prison capacity.

Parliament asked for a policy plan for crime prevention and for improvement of criminal law administration. In 1983, the Minister of Justice appointed the Roethof Committee, a seven-member panel that included a former minister of justice, a police commander, Amsterdam's chief prosecutor, the mayor of Hengelo, and several university professors. It was directed to assess the causes of the crime increase and the effectiveness of existing policies and to propose ways to improve crime prevention and control.

The Roethof Committee issued an interim report in 1984 (and a final one in 1986) (Roethof Committee 1984, 1986) and presented a set of recommendations, which were incorporated into the 1985 government policy plan "Society and Crime" (Ministry of Justice 1985). After five years' assessment, in 1990 a new plan, called "Law in Motion," was published (Ministry of Justice 1990a).

Both plans proposed to raise the level of criminal law enforcement and to intensify crime prevention by extending the statutory powers of the police to investigate organized crime, by improving the efficiency of the prosecution service, by increasing prison capacity, and by intensifying crime prevention programs. Numerous laws have since been enacted and measures taken to support the new policies.

Sentences, 1980–1992

As measured by the number of cases tried by courts (see table 2.18), criminality seems to have risen only slightly since 1980. However, the number of crimes recorded by the police increased greatly. The different trends for recorded crimes and court cases result from the introduction in 1983 of a prosecutorial diversion scheme.

The 1983 Financial Penalties Act authorized prosecutors to resolve criminal cases on the basis of an arrangement in which the suspect pays a sum of money

Table 2.18. Crimes Recorded by Police, Detected, and Tried by Courts

	1980	1985	1990	1992	% Detected in 1992
Total	705,600	1,093,700	1,133,800	1,268,500	19.2
Of which violent crimes	26,500	37,100	49,600	58,400	48.5
Property crimes	500,900	840,600	840,400	950,100	13.7
Against public order and destruction	84,800	117,500	142,900	154,600	16.6
Detected %	29	24	22	19	
Cases tried by courts	79,100	77,500	88,600	87,100	

Source: Dutch Central Bureau of Statistics.

to the treasury in order to avoid further prosecution and a public trial. (This resembles German "conditional dismissals" under §153a of the German Code of Criminal Procedure.) The prosecution service can use this power for any offense that carries a potential prison term of six years or less. Only one-third of criminal cases are tried by criminal courts. The remainder are settled out of court by the Prosecution Service.

Criminal cases tried by courts in 1993 differed significantly from those tried in 1980. Between those years, the number of convictions for sexual offenses and capital offenses each increased by 250 and the numbers of violent threats, drug offenses, and robberies by 400, 800, and 1,000, respectively. The number of prison sentences remained stable. This is a result partly of the increased use of the prosecutorial diversion scheme and partly of a decrease of 2,000 in the number of prison sentences for drunk driving.

Because courts are trying more severe offenses, the average prison term has increased considerably—by one month for drug offenses, by 16 months for murder and homicide, by 13 months for rape, and by eight months for violent theft.

Although the number of prison sentences imposed in 1991 does not differ much from that for 1980 (see table 2.19), the number of years of detention ordered differs considerably: 2,848 in 1980, 4,887 in 1985, 5,958 in 1990, and 6,442 in 1991.

Prison Reduction Policy

Penal policy in the 1980s was characterized by strong tendencies to reduce the use of short-term imprisonment and to expand the use of noncustodial sanctions.

THE 1983 FINANCIAL PENALTIES ACT   The aim of this legislation was to improve the enforcement of fines so that fines could better function as an alternative to short-term prison sentences.

Since 1983, the fine has been legally presumed to be the appropriate penalty. All offenses, including ones subject to life imprisonment, may be sentenced with a fine. The minimum fine for all offenses is five Dutch guilders (roughly three U.S. dollars). The maximum depends on the fine category into which a crime or infraction is placed. The 1983 Act created six categories with maxima of 500

Table 2.19. Prison Sentences, 1980–1991

Years	Total	One Month	One to Twelve Months	One to Three Years	Three to Six Years	Six Years or More
1980	15,309	8,944	5,602	646	175	—
1985	16,348	6,719	8,665	1,281	215	72
1990	15,182	4,946	8,772	1,437	394	144
1991	15,683	5,052	9,019	1,614	519	148

Source: Dutch Central Bureau of Statistics.

guilders, 5,000 guilders, 10,000 guilders, 25,000 guilders, 100,000 guilders, and 1 million guilders (category VI).

Category VI fines can be imposed on corporate bodies and on individuals under a few special criminal laws, such as the Economic Offenses Act and the Narcotic Drug Offenses Act.

COMMUNITY SANCTIONS   In 1989, following eight years of experimentation, a new principal penalty, "the performance of unpaid work for the general good," also known as the community service order ("CSO"), was introduced in the penal code.

CSOs function as a substitute for unconditional prison sentences of six months or less and can be imposed only with the consent of the offender and subject to a maximum of 240 hours. There is no minimum. A CSO of less than 120 hours must be carried out within six months; one for more than 120 hours must be met within 12 months.

The Prosecution Service supervises compliance with CSOs, with assistance from the probation service. If the work is not carried out properly (roughly 10 percent of all CSOs), the judge may, at the request of the prosecutor, replace the CSO with a prison sentence to be served in full or in part.

The number of CSOs imposed increased from 213 in 1981—when the experiment started—to 8,585 in 1992. The 1990 policy plan "Law in Motion," contemplates a further annual increase of 10 percent. Recent research indicates that CSOs in many cases have substituted not for short-term prison terms but for suspended sentences. However, it is unknown to what extent this was the case.

In 1993, new community-based sanctions, including an intensive day program and intensive supervision, have been introduced by way of experiments on a restricted scale.

EARLIER PAROLE RELEASE   Another target of penal policy in the 1980s was to reduce the effective term of imprisonment. Under a 1987 change in the parole legislation, prisoners serving a sentence up to one year must be released after serving six months plus one-third of the remaining term. Prisoners sentenced to more than one year must be released after serving two-thirds of the sentence. The prisoner's right to be released early can be restricted only in a few exceptional cases.

Sentencing Process

The Dutch judiciary is vested with wide discretionary power in choosing the type and severity of sanctions. The few statutory rules are general and do not limit judges' choices in individual cases. The court can fully individualize the sentence, giving full consideration to the crime, the situation, and the offender.

The penal code lists four principal penalties in order of severity—imprisonment, detention, community service, and fine. Maximum terms of imprisonment are specified and reflect the gravity of the worst possible case—for murder either a life sentence or imprisonment up to 20 years, 12 years for rape, six years for domestic burglary, and four years for theft. Few crimes are subject to life imprisonment, and for these there is an alternative of a fixed term up to 20 years.

The code does not prescribe life imprisonment or a maximum prison term in any circumstances or for any crime. The statutory minimum term of imprisonment is one day and is the same for all crimes, regardless of the generic seriousness of the offense.

The choice of sanction lies with the court but is subject to procedural requirements concerning the judge's reasoning. Section 359(6) of the Code of Criminal Procedure ("CCP") requires the court to give special reasons whenever a custodial sentence is ordered instead of a fine, which is by law preferred as the chief sentence.

Section 359(7) CCP requires a statement of reasons when the court imposes a more severe sentence than the Prosecution Service has requested. Furthermore, section 359(8) CCP requires reasons when the court denies the defendant's offer to perform a community service order.

The choice of sentence is in principle determined by the seriousness of the offense and the aims of sentencing. In theory, factors connected with the suspect's personality and criminal history are to be considered only in the case of recidivists. When the defendant has displayed indifference to sentences imposed after earlier convictions, this also may justify a sentence that would not be indicated on the basis of the seriousness of the offense.

The statutory aims of sentencing are retribution, special or general deterrence, reformation, protection of society, and reparation, and the court may choose among them in each individual case.

Although the choice of sanction lies with the court, subject only to statutory requirements concerning the judge's reasons for any deviation, Supreme Court case law offers guidance on matters to be considered in determining the severity of the sentence.

Various personal or isolated factors may be reasons to adjust the sentence upward or downward. An upward adjustment may be justified by the criminal past of the accused (Hoge Raad [Supreme Court] 19 June 1986, Nederlandse Jurisprudentie [Dutch Case Law] 1987, 61) or by the negative attitude of the accused during the examination in court. Examples are an accused who consequently denies having committed the crime (Hoge Raad 10 December 1984, Nederlandse Juris-prudentie 1985, 358) or an accused who wishes to evade a sentence by making several false statements (Hoge Raad 27 January 1987, Nederlandse Jurisprudentie 1987, 711); other factors may be the motives that compelled him to commit the offense, for instance jealousy and hate (Hoge Raad 15 April 1986, Nederlandse Jurisprudentie 1987, 25), the circumstance that the accused did not want to cooperate in a psychiatric evaluation (Court Amsterdam 19 December 1991, Nederlandse Jurisprudentie 1992, 142), or the fact that the accused fails to understand that his behavior was wrong (Hoge Raad 12 November 1985, Nederlandse Jurisprudentie 1986, 409).

A downward adjustment may be indicated by serious delay between the time the crime was committed and the trial, by the offender's voluntarily offering compensation for damages inflicted, by expression of regret by the accused, by lack of previous convictions, or by positive probation prospects.

The absence of mandatory rules for sentencing and sentencing guidelines may contribute to the present mild penal climate but may also result in great disparity in sentencing, as recent research has shown. A number of proposals have been developed to reduce disparity in sentencing. Some of them will likely lead to considerably higher sentences and a harsher penal climate.

Policy from 1993

Despite all efforts to reduce the number and the length of prison sentences, it has been clear since 1985 that a serious prison construction program had to be set to meet the need for prison capacity. The actual need for capacity has repeatedly proven higher than expected, mainly due to developments such as the internationalization of criminality, the rise of organized crime, and the improvement of law enforcement policies.

As a result of the prison construction program, prison capacity nearly tripled, from 3,789 prison cells in 1980 to 10,059 cells in 1994, and decisions were made to increase the number of prison cells to 11,818, to be available early in 1996. Nevertheless, a prison capacity shortage of 1,600 cells in 1998 is expected. To reduce the expected shortage, proposals will be developed to detain drug-addicted or disturbed prisoners in other than penal establishments, to improve the use of alternatives to imprisonment, to implement conditional release due to good behavior after the offender has served half of the sentence, and to begin experiments with use of electronic monitoring in the last phase of a long-term sentence.

Prisoners today are detained for more serious offenses than in the 1970s and 1980s. Furthermore, a large number of prisoners are foreigners, addicted to drugs, or suffering from psychiatric disturbances. Those prisoners are difficult to handle. This has had a negative impact on the prison regime.

Recently, a new prison memorandum concerning the prison regime was submitted to Parliament. The high level of aspiration, a full resocialization, that formed the backbone of previous prison regime memoranda has been reduced to a basic target: a safe and effective but humane detention. The central goal in the new prison regime is labor plus the statutorily guaranteed fresh air, visits, recreation, and sports. Additional vocational training is possible. A regime of restricted contacts with inmates is applied to a prisoner who is not participating in these activities. Sentencing became harsher in the Netherlands between 1980 and 1993; in the near future as well, implementation of sentences will become harsher. No one can deny that Dutch penal policy has changed considerably.

Prison Population Growing Faster in the Netherlands than in the
United States (June 1998)
Peter J. P. Tak and Anton M. van Kalmthout

The Dutch prison population is among the fastest growing in the world. The incarceration rate per 100,000 inhabitants grew 123 percent between 1985 and

1997, slightly more than the 116 percent increase in the U.S. rate for state and federal prisoners during the same period.

Dutch incarceration rates in absolute terms are much lower than those in the United States. The 1997 rate of 78 per 100,000 was about an eighth of the U.S. rate (prisons and jails combined) of 648 per 100,000 at mid-year 1997. Nonetheless, the relative increases were comparable.

The increase in Dutch imprisonment is the result partly of an increase in lengths of prison terms, partly of an increase in the likelihood of imprisonment given a conviction, and partly of government policy decisions to build more prisons. The first two causes are a reflection of rising crime rates and more punitive attitudes of judges and prosecutors. Prison expansion, of course, reflects changed attitudes but is also a response to sustained criticisms of a distinctive Dutch practice in the 1980s and 1990s of delaying execution of prison sentences until space became available to house the affected offenders. Convicted offenders were sentenced to prison but told that they should not appear at the prison until several or many months later.

Delayed execution of prison sentences was criticized by a series of official agencies and reports. A 1990 report from the Prosecution Service argued that delayed execution undermined the credibility of the criminal justice system (Ministry of Justice 1990b). The Committee on Reconsideration of the Instruments of Law Enforcement (Ministry of Justice 1996) and the State Audit Committee (1997) also criticized the practice and urged that it be ended.

In response to these criticisms, prison capacity has steadily expanded, and recently the Minister of Justice announced a two-track policy: continued expansion of prison capacity and substantial expansion in the availability and use of community penalties.

This article provides an overview of recent sentencing and crime trends, pressures to expand prison capacity, and plans to develop new community penalties. First, though, as necessary background, we provide a brief description of the organization of the Dutch prosecution and sentencing systems.

Dutch Prosecution and Sentencing

Only a small percentage of crimes recorded by the police are tried by a criminal court. While the number of recorded crimes increased by more than five times between 1970 and 1995, the number of cases tried in court only doubled.

One reason for this is that public expenditure for law enforcement has not kept pace with crime rates. The police must set priorities in detecting and investigating cases. This is illustrated by the sharply falling clearance rate—from 41 percent in 1970 to 18 percent in 1995.

A second reason that relatively few cases are tried by criminal courts is that, since the late 1960s, more and more cases have been settled out of court by the prosecution service. The Prosecution Service has been given adjudicatory powers that formerly were exclusively within the domain of the judiciary. Two settlement methods are used: nonprosecution and "transactions."

WAIVER OF PROSECUTION The right to prosecute is exclusively granted to the Prosecution Service. This does not mean that every crime brought to its notice is prosecuted. The prosecution may decide not to prosecute a case because of lack of evidence or because of technicalities (technical or procedural waiver). The prosecution may also decide not to prosecute because of policy considerations. The "expediency principle" laid down in Code of Criminal Procedure Section 167 authorizes the Prosecution Service to waive prosecution "for reasons of public interest."

Before the late 1960s, the discretionary power to waive prosecution was seldom exercised, but thereafter a remarkable change took place. Research into the effects of law enforcement and the limited resources of law enforcement agencies showed that it was impossible, undesirable, and in some circumstances counterproductive to prosecute all investigated offenses.

Since then, the discretionary power not to prosecute for policy reasons has been exercised more widely. The governing body, the Assembly of Prosecutors-General, issued national prosecution guidelines, and prosecutors are bound by these guidelines except under special circumstances. The proportion of unconditional waivers on policy grounds was high in the early 1980s: approximately 28 percent of cleared crimes were not prosecuted. The assumption was that prosecution should not be automatic but should serve a concrete social objective.

However, the government's 1985 criminal policy plan, "Society and Crime," concluded that such a high proportion of waivers could no longer be justified (Ministry of Justice 1985). The Prosecution Service has been instructed to reduce the number of unconditional waivers by making more frequent use of conditional waivers, reprimands, and transactions. As a result, unconditional policy waivers fell to around 4 percent of dispositions in 1996.

TRANSACTIONS Prosecutors have been authorized since 1983 to resolve criminal cases by means of "transactions," arrangements in which the suspect pays a sum of money to the treasury in order to avoid further prosecution and a public trial. The Prosecution Service can exercise this power for any offense carrying a potential prison term of six years or less. That restriction has limited effect since the overwhelming majority of crimes carry a statutory maximum of less than six years.

The broad power to resolve criminal cases by use of "transactions" has been strongly criticized. The most important criticisms are that the increased use of transactions introduced into Dutch practice something resembling plea bargaining, represented a fundamental breach of the theory of the separation of powers, weakened the legal protection of the accused, favored certain social groups, and entrusted the Prosecution Service with powers that should be reserved for the judiciary.

Despite these criticisms, transactions have been widely used. More than 30 percent of all prosecuted crimes are settled out of court with a transaction. This is in line with the 1990 criminal policy plan, "Criminal Law and Criminal Policy," which set as a target for 1995 that one-third of all crimes prosecuted be settled by use of a transaction (Ministry of Justice 1990b).

SENTENCING   The Dutch judiciary is vested with wide discretionary power over sentences. The few statutory rules are general and do not limit the court in choosing the type or severity of sanctions in individual cases. The statutory framework is broad. The minimum authorized term of imprisonment is one day and is the same for all crimes, regardless of the seriousness of the offense. Maximum terms of imprisonment are specified and reflect the gravity of the worst possible case. Few crimes are subject to life imprisonment, but fixed terms up to 20 years can be imposed, as also can be a fine.

Such broad discretion inevitably presents risks of unwarranted disparities. For certain groups of offenses, this risk has been reduced because the prosecution service has established guidelines concerning sentence recommendations by the prosecutor. Affected offenses include drunk driving, social security fraud, tax fraud, and drug crimes. In practice, courts give considerable weight to prosecutors' sentence recommendations.

More recently, a project for the development of national guidelines for sentencing was started within the Prosecution Service (Steenhuis 1997). In this project, 35 new guidelines are being formulated that may lead to reduced disparities in sentencing for the majority of crimes.

Crime Trends

Crime rates rose rapidly in Holland from 1976 to 1984. This was followed by a steady but gradual increase from 1985 to 1994. In 1995 and 1996, however, recorded crimes decreased by 3 and 6 percent, respectively. Within that overall decline, however, some forms of violent crime continued to increase. The number of rapes and crimes against life remained stable, but violent threats, serious bodily harm, and violent thefts increased.

Dispositions

Case disposition patterns changed significantly between 1975 and 1995. The clearance rate fell dramatically (from 33 percent in 1975 to 18 percent in 1995). The discretionary prosecutorial powers to waive cases or to settle criminal cases through a "transaction" were used extensively. Nonetheless, the number of cases tried by criminal courts substantially has increased in recent years, rising from 83,700 in 1990 to 102,000 in 1995. The seriousness of the cases tried by courts also changed considerably. Cases that prior to the introduction of the transaction policy were tried by criminal courts are now often resolved by the Prosecution Service. The result is that courts now deal with very serious cases that are not eligible for settlement through a transaction.

Sentencing Trends

Traditionally in Holland, a large percentage of prison sentences were suspended, but between 1990 and 1995 this began to change. From 1990 to 1995 the number of nonsuspended and partly suspended prison sentences increased from 14,633 to more than 25,000. The number of nonsuspended prison sentences showed a particularly strong increase. In 1990, the proportion of unsuspended to suspended prison sentences was 1:1.5; in 1995 this ratio was 1:0.8. In particular, fewer suspended prison sentences were imposed for drug crimes, violent crimes, and property crimes.

Tables 2.20 and 2.21, providing data on sentences imposed in 1985 and 1995, show the percentages of cases that resulted in nonsuspended prison sentences and the number of sentences imposed of various durations. During this period, the likelihood that a nonsuspended sentence would be imposed increased significantly for drug, violent, and property crime, and the number of years of detention ordered nearly doubled (up from 5,900 years in 1985 to 10,900 in 1995). Longer sentences become much more common; the number of sentences of a year or longer nearly tripled, rising from 2,383 in 1985 to 6,159 in 1995.

Why were so many more and much longer nonsuspended prison sentences imposed in 1995 than in 1985? There are at least five possible causes: (1) criminal law reforms by which the statutory maximum sentences were increased, (2) increased willingness of the public to report crimes, (3) changes in police detection and investigation policies and expansion of the police force, (4) changes in offense seriousness, volume, and type, and (5) more punitive sentencing policies. Research on the development of prison sentences between 1985 and 1995 and interviews with representatives of the police, the Prosecution Service, the judiciary, and lawyers disclosed two primary causes: increased offense seriousness and harsher sentences (Grapendaal, Groen, and van der Heide 1997). Criminality, particularly violent criminality, became more serious in the 1990s. Violent criminality leads to more severe sentences. In addition, half of the increase of the number of detention years ordered was the consequence of more severe sentences for violent crimes as judges and prosecutors became more punitive.

Table 2.22 shows the prison sentence duration for five types of offenses and average duration in 1985 and in 1995. Although the length of sentences for drug

Table 2.20. Percentage of Cases for Which a Nonsuspended Prison Sentence Has Been Imposed, by Type of Crime

Crime	1985	1995
Drug	22	34
Violent	16	21
Property	13	18
Sexual	18	17
Firearms	12	10
Public order	6	6
Traffic act	8	3
Economic	0	1

Source: Grapendaal, Groen, and van der Heide (1997).

Table 2.21. Number of Nonsuspended
Sentences, by Duration

Duration of Sentence	1985	1995
Less than 2 weeks	133	149
2 weeks to 1 month	285	352
1–3 months	881	1,362
3–6 months	1,111	1,615
6–9 months	538	357
9 months–1 year	439	947
1–2 years	1,018	2,361
2–4 years	673	2,002
More than 4 years	692	1,796

Source: Grapendaal, Groen, and van der Heide (1997).

and property offenses fell slightly, the average prison sentence for sexual offenses doubled and for violent offenses increased by two-thirds.

The Netherlands has lacked sufficient prison capacity since the early 1980s. Thousands of pretrial detention orders were not carried out, and many thousands of prison sentences were implemented only after a considerable delay. To alleviate these problems, a large prison construction program began in the early 1990s. Between 1994 and 1996, 14 new prisons were opened, and prison capacity was projected to reach 16,300 cells by 1999. In 15 years, prison capacity will have quadrupled. Recent estimates project a prison capacity shortage of almost 2,000 cells in 2002.

Community Penalties

Penal policy since the 1980s has been characterized by strong tendencies to reduce the use of short-term imprisonment and to expand the use of alternatives to imprisonment (Tak 1997). Various types of community sentences are increasingly used as a substitute for custodial sentences. The community service order has since

Table 2.22. Average Prison Sentence
for Crimes (in days)

Crime	1985	1995
Drug	401	375
Violent	280	471
Property	94	91
Sexual	250	501
Public order	78	161
Total average	133	197

Source: Grapendaal, Groen, and van der Heide (1997).

1981 become a very successful substitute, and in 1995 nearly 19,000 community service sentences were imposed.

TRAINING AND COMBINATION ORDERS New community sentences have recently been introduced, including "training orders" and "combination orders." A training order requires the offender to learn specific skills or to be confronted with the consequences of his criminal behavior for the victim. Training orders are imposed mainly on juvenile and young adult offenders. They may be imposed for as little as five meetings or as much as three months or longer for 40 hours a week. Long-term intensive training orders may be imposed as a separate sentence on adult offenders only. Training orders are usually imposed in combination with a community service order or as a condition attached to a suspended sentence.

Community sentences are by far the most important sentences for juvenile delinquents. In 1995, both the community service order and the training order were introduced in the new juvenile criminal law. A community sentence is now imposed in 60 percent of all juvenile criminal cases and can be imposed by a court as a substitute for both youth detention and fines. The maximum number of hours is 200. The Prosecution Service can attach a community service obligation of up to 40 hours as a condition to a conditional waiver of prosecution.

ELECTRONIC MONITORING Electronic monitoring is the latest new community sentence and should achieve a statutory basis in the near future. Electronic monitoring is a viable substitute for imprisonment or other forms of deprivation of liberty, according to the findings of recent experiments with electronic monitoring in four jurisdictions in the Netherlands (Spaan and Verwers 1997). Electronic monitoring was utilized either in lieu of the last phase of a prison sentence, thereby shortening the sentence, or in combination with a community sentence.

The combination of electronic monitoring and a community sentence can substitute for imprisonment for between six and 12 months. Candidates for electronic monitoring were proposed by the probation service. The court had to authorize persons to serve their sentences through electronic monitoring in combination with the community sentence or in the last phase of detention. During the experiments, courts seldom combined electronic monitoring with a community service order.

PENITENTIARY PROGRAMS A new Penitentiary Principles Act will soon come into force. It will introduce the so-called penitentiary programs. Those programs start before the date of early release and aim to achieve a smooth transition from prison to free society. Eligible prisoners will participate in compulsory programs of outside activities during the day, during which time they will be electronically monitored. Over time, restrictions will diminish, and electronic monitoring will cease.

FUTURE LAW REFORM The government seeks to have 30,000 community service orders ("CSOs") imposed per year by 2000. To reach that target, restrictions in the penal code on use of community service orders will be removed. One major restriction is a statutory requirement that the offender must consent at trial to the community service order. In recent years, nearly 13,000 short-term prison sentences have been imposed annually on offenders who do not appear for trial. That means that they are not eligible for community service orders in place of incarceration. The statutory requirement will be changed to allow the defendant to consent in writing. It is expected that two-thirds of short-term prison sentences can be replaced by community service orders.

Another restriction is that the court can impose a CSO only if it would otherwise have imposed a short prison term. The proposed statutory changes will authorize imposition of a CSO as a substitute for a fine. In case of noncompliance with a CSO ordered as a substitute for a fine, a fine default detention will take place. This seems likely to prove counterproductive, since community service sentences are supposed to replace confinement sentences and not to increase them through the default mechanism.

A number of other proposals have been made concerning training orders. One is to extend the number of hours for a training order or a combination order to 480 hours, because training orders last much longer than community service orders. Another is to make a training order a principal penalty on its own. Until now training orders have mainly been used as a condition for conditional waiver of prosecution, as a conditional suspension of pretrial detention, or as a condition attached to a suspended prison sentence. Finally, the prosecution service will be authorized to use transactions to impose a training order of 120 hours maximum.

It is expected that, in the year 2000, the number of community sentences for adults will reach 26,800 and for juveniles 6,000. There are, however, some problems. The main problem is the lack of an adequate number of places in regular projects for the implementation of community service orders. Consequently, probation and aftercare institutions are increasingly setting up self-governing group projects, in which work masters employed by these institutions are charged with the supervision of offenders serving community sentences. Group projects are being developed with large project providers such as landscape planning organizations (Wijn 1997).

Conclusion

Despite efforts in Holland to reduce the incarceration rate and the number of prison sentences by adopting various alternatives to imprisonment, and despite their success, the prison population has increased substantially over the past decade. It may no longer be possible to develop additional viable alternatives. The Dutch may have to accept that their imprisonment rate, long one of the lowest in Western Europe, may become one of the highest.

A new minister of justice, to be appointed in the summer of 1998, will have to develop new policies if further increases are to be avoided. This will be difficult in a country that is more and more confronted with increases in serious crimes, in particular violent crime and organized crime. In four years' time — the term of appointment of the new minister — we will see what happens. The former minister, who when taking office promised to reduce the prison rate, was unfortunately not able to keep her promise.

The Netherlands Adopts Numerical Prosecution Guidelines (June 1999)

Gerrit Schurer and Reinier van Loon

New prosecution guidelines for sentence recommendations to judges took effect in the Netherlands on April 1, 1999. The 35 guidelines developed to date deal with 125 offenses that together constitute 80 percent of sentenced cases. Study groups are now considering whether and how the guidelines should be extended to cover serious violent and environmental crimes. This article describes the guidelines, their rationale, their development, and planning for their extension.[1]

The structure of the proposed new prosecutorial sentencing guidelines is very simple (Steenhuis 1997). For each crime, a number of sentencing points is set; for example, bicycle theft, 10 points; burglary, 60 points; motor vehicle theft, 20 points; shoplifting, 4 points; destruction, 6 points; bodily harm, 7 points; threat, 8 points; insult, 10 points; open or overt use of violence, 15 points; import or export of hard drugs, 30 points; burglary in a factory, 42 points. In special circumstances, the number of points can be higher or lower; for example, the use of weapons or victim injury leads to extra points. An attempted crime warrants a reduction of points. Recidivism increases the score by half. Multiple recidivism doubles the points.

Finally, the points are converted into a sentence. Not all the points count equally for the sentence. A conversion system has been elaborated. Up to 180 points, every sentencing point counts. Between 181 to 540 points each point counts as half a point, and above 541 points each point counts a quarter of a point. Each point leads to a fine of 50 guilders or to one day of imprisonment.

The Prosecution Service

The Netherlands Public Prosecution Service ("PPS") is responsible for law enforcement. Its 450 members supervise the detection and investigation of crimes, represent the state at trials, and oversee the implementation of sentences and decrees imposed. The prosecution guidelines relate principally to the second of these tasks.

Following conviction, the public prosecutor proposes a specific sentence. Judges are not bound by this proposal but often use it as a starting point. In practice, the 450 public prosecutors, distributed across 19 districts and 5 administrative regions, often pursued very different policies. Numerous studies show that substantial differences, which can not be explained by reference to the characteristics of individual cases, can often be observed (Fiselier 1985). For decades, complaints have been made about lack of consistency in prosecutors' sentence recommendations (Grapendaal, Groen, and van der Heide 1997).

Prior Guidelines

In the 1970s, the prosecution service created and implemented so-called prosecution guidelines (Steenhuis 1986), but without great success. In practice it was, and remains, difficult to convince prosecutors that guidelines are not inconsistent with sound exercise of professional judgment and that more consistent sentence recommendations based on objective factors will make an improved justice system.

In practice, despite the implementation of the earlier guidelines, consistency in sentence and equal treatment of offenders did not increase. In addition to prosecutors' skepticism, there was a structural problem. The original guidelines were difficult to use. They were insufficiently concrete, sometimes inconsistent, and often difficult to interpret (Schurer and Vreeling 1995).

The guidelines' inadequacy was painfully revealed when, early in 1994, it was decided to present the guidelines in a question-and-answer format in a computerized system. The judge would answer a number of questions about objective factors, and a Decision Supporting System ("DSS") would indicate the appropriate point of departure under the guidelines.

Whether such a structured form of presentation would lead to greater uniformity in judgments was investigated in 1995. In a pilot program, some 35 prosecution guidelines were included.[2] The goal was to determine whether judges' sentences were in greater conformity when the guidelines were in use than before. They were. Before the pilot program, in comparable cases 35 percent were adjudged in conformity with the guidelines. During the pilot, this increased to 70 percent (Oelen 1997).

During development of the pilot program software, it was discovered that lack of consistency could not be attributed only to the judges. The existing prosecution guidelines were in many respects vague. Thus, a bicycle thief would face a penalty between 150 and 750 Dutch guilders (NLG), but under the guidelines the amount could be higher or lower. The national guideline did not indicate how amounts were to be chosen within the NLG 150–NLG 750 range. As a result, the 19 district prosecutors' offices had drawn up local guidelines, indicating relevant factors to be considered within that district. For bicycle theft in one district, a penalty of NLG 300 was deemed fitting, whereas 30 miles away in a second district and in an identical case, NLG 1200 was deemed fitting, and in another district 30 miles further on, two weeks in prison was the starting point.

Not only minor offenses were characterized by such large local differences. For instance, for a burglary of a house in one district, one month's imprisonment per burglary was the starting point. In another district, it was four months per burglary. As a result of the DSS pilot program, an unexpected conclusion was drawn: "Supporting the guidelines by a computerized system can increase consistency, but current guidelines do not contribute to achievement of equality under the law. The guidelines must offer concrete, nationally uniform, points of departure. They do not meet this requirement and must be rewritten before a DSS can be useful" (Schurer and Vreeling 1995).

As a result, the Public Prosecution Service initiated the Polaris Project in 1994 to formulate a new, coherent system of prosecution guidelines. A working group was established to do this.

The working group contained two study groups, one to formulate new guidelines and the other to test them. For more than a year, the first group collected all local and national guidelines, which were then analyzed, structured, and rewritten. The results were submitted to the testing group, which checked the revised guidelines for content, internal consistency, and compliance with applicable legal standards.

The Current Guidelines

The new guidelines establish a consistent approach. Because of the way they have been formulated, their provisions are clear to the judge at a glance. The most minor form of the offense is taken as a point of departure. By means of objective factors with standard effects on the amount and nature of the penalty, consistent standards are achieved. The guidelines form one coherent whole, which was accomplished by scaling the "seriousness" of the different offenses in relation to each other and consistently weighting the factors that influence the sentence recommendation.

The guidelines indicate a recommended type and amount of penalty for any particular case. Of course, in some cases there may be special factors that have not been taken into account. These may relate to the offense or to the defendant. In such cases, the guidelines may be deviated from. However, reasons must be given for such deviations.

A point system is used, which includes both "penalty points" and "sanction points." The penalty points are a measurement for the seriousness of the offense. The sanction points determine the amount of the indicated penalty.

The process starts with determination of the basic offense in its simplest form, without taking account of additional aggravating or mitigating circumstances. For that basic offense, a number of "basic penalty points" is awarded.

Later, on the basis of "judgment factors" that relate to ways the particular offense differs from the basic offense, the number of penalty points can be increased or decreased. Because, in some cases, literal calculation of all applicable penalty points would yield sentences more severe than on policy grounds appears appropriate, a weighting system has been devised to "discount" the total point scores when they become too high. This yields the number of sanction points.

After calculation of the sanction points, the indicated sanction can be determined, with one sanction point representing a fixed amount of money (50 NLG), imprisonment (possibly to be converted into community service) of certain duration, or another sanction. The guidelines award points for various factors related to the basic character of the current offense, to the presence of general aggravating factors, and to the nature of the defendant's criminal record and role. One penalty point calls for one day's imprisonment, subject to various presumptions about when other penalties may be substituted. For example, when the point score is equivalent to less than six months, the guidelines call for substitution of a non-incarcerative penalty, such as community service, unless there are indications that the convicted person is not suited for community service (e.g., drug addicts or people without a fixed address).

Here is an example of how sentence recommendations are calculated. The defendant was convicted of assault and battery. He was apprehended immediately after the offense, in which he beat a police officer with a baseball bat, inflicting serious bruises that needed medical attention. The defendant's prior criminal history consists of seven prior convictions for offenses of comparable severity.

First, the "basic" offense score is calculated. Table 2.23 shows the relevant factors and how they are weighted. The offense is worth 22 points, for the basic offense (7 points) and its aggravating characteristics that injury was inflicted (8 points) and that the baseball bat was used as a weapon (7 points). The point values are taken from the guidelines, which spell out various aggravating circumstances. Had the injuries been greater or had there been a more lethal weapon, the aggravating point values would have been greater.

Then the "offense-specific factors" are taken into account. These are general considerations that might affect many kinds of crimes, including such things as whether there was a dependent victim, whether there were elements of racial or ethnic animus, or whether the victim was a public servant. Only the last of these

Table 2.23. Calculation for a Sentence Recommendation for an Assault and Battery Offense

---

Offense

A policeman is beaten with a baseball bat and receives serious bruises that require medical attention. The perpetrator is caught "redhanded."

Basic factors

Defendant convicted of assault and battery	7 points
The extent of the injury, in this case requiring medical attention	8 points
Use of a weapon (baseball bat)	7 points
Subtotal	22 points

Offense-specific factors

Defendant operated on his own	no extra points
No relation of dependence between victim and defendant	no extra points
Victim is a public servant (25% extra points) 22 points × 25%	5.5 points
Victim not chosen randomly by defendant	no extra points
No discriminatory aspects	no extra points
No connection with a sporting event	no extra points
Victim did not provoke the defendant	no extra points
Subtotal	27.5 points

Legal factors

Is the suspect the principal or an accomplice?	
In this case, the principal	no reduction of points
Defendant has a criminal record for 7 similar offenses (100% extra points) 27.5 × 100%	27.5 points
TOTAL	55 points

Sentence

55 points equals a prison sentence of 55 days. This is less than 6 months, so the public prosecutor will request a community service sentence of 80 hours.

---

applies to the hypothetical case, and under the guidelines it operates to increase the basic factor score by 25 percent (plus 5.5 points, raising the total to 27.5).

Next, consideration is given to the offender's criminal record and role. In this case, because of the defendant's prior record, the guidelines call for doubling of his combined basic and offense specific score (thus, plus 27.5 points, raising the total to 55).

Finally, the sentence must be calculated. Because the 55-point total is less than 180, the prosecutor should propose a nonincarcerative penalty. Of course, he may recommend some other penalty if he believes good reasons exist for doing so, but those reasons must be given, and they are subject to review within the Prosecution Service.

Here is another example. Imagine someone is stopped for drunken driving. He refuses the breath analysis order, insults the police officer, confesses that he has stolen a bike four times, and admits he has been sentenced twice for bicycle theft. That leads to the following calculations: refusal of breath analysis, 10 points; insult to the police officer, 10 points; four times bicycle theft, 40 points; that he has been sentenced twice for bicycle theft doubles the points, yielding 100 points (10 + 10 + 40 + 40). Because this is equivalent to less than six months (180 points), the public prosecutor will request a community service order of 150 hours (Tak 2001).

Here is one more example. A burglar is arrested redhanded. He confesses to 29 house burglaries and 11 burglaries in factories. It is his first arrest. The number of points for 29 burglaries in houses (60 each) is 1,740 points. Eleven burglaries in factories (11 × 42 points) equals 462 points, yielding 2,202 points. After use of the conversion system mentioned earlier (between 181 and 540, points are discounted by half and above 540 by three-fourths), the adjusted total is 775 points, which means that the public prosecutor will request a prison sentence of 775 days (Tak 2001).

Future Plans

Planning is under way for extension of the guidelines to environmental crimes and to serious crimes of violence.

ENVIRONMENTAL CRIMES An environmental study group is working on guidelines for environmental offenses. These concern, for instance, the illegal discharge of oil, cutting down woods, or illegal lighting of fireworks.

VIOLENT OFFENSES: THE "FIRST-OFFER" SYSTEM The PPS is considering whether the most serious offenses can be dealt with under the guideline system. These offenses include assault resulting in death, murder, manslaughter, rape, involuntary manslaughter, and public violence resulting in death.

At present, various prosecutors' offices use the so-called first-offer system for these relatively serious crimes. A "first offer" is understood as a point of departure for thinking about determination of the penalty without taking into consideration all its particular details (such as, for instance, the perpetrator's characteristics or victim precipitation). A first offer is a rough indication of what may be demanded at the trial for a certain offense, but nationally there are substantial differences among the first offers. Thus, in one district a term of imprisonment of three years is the starting point for manslaughter, and in another district it is five years. This is the reason that the PPS is considering extension of guidelines to such serious crimes. Consideration of possible guidelines for use in the first-offer system began in November 1998, with recommendations on their feasibility due by the end of 1999.

Conclusions

The ultimate goal of the guidelines is to increase consistency in sentences. The DSS pilot program showed that computerized support of guidelines can strongly contribute to consistency of results, provided the guidelines supported are themselves sufficiently consistent and concrete.

The Public Prosecution Service, through its sentence recommendations, guides the decision, with the expectation that judges will take account of the recommendations. It is not simple to guide people, including judges, unless they themselves accept the legitimacy of the guidance. With the DSS in its present state, the Prosecution Service believes it can show judges the guidelines' legitimacy. Computerized access to the guidelines, by means of a question-and-answer game, makes them more accessible and intelligible. By means of so-called hyperlinks, the user can easily leaf through the texts of the electronic guideline collection. Because fixed judgment factors are used in each offense, the chances of interpretive differences are reduced drastically. By the DSS, every decision the judge must take in respect of the amount of penalty is made visible, and reasons must be given. So the user will be accountable for each step. Ultimate rejection of the DSS recommendations can also occur only in a reasoned way.

A second goal also plays a part in the harmonization of penalty determinations by judges under the prosecution guidelines. The system offers the possibility to adjust penalties downward or upward in a systematic way. Via the DSS system, the consequences of policy changes can be predicted in a simple way. Thus, one may wonder, for instance, about the consequences for the available prison capacity of the implementation of a certain guideline. There is great interest from the Ministry of Justice about the potential the DSS system offers for tying prosecution policy to imprisonment policy.

NOTES

1. The complete guidelines are set out in a manual published by the Public Prosecution Service, The Netherlands (1999).

2. The Giant-Soft company helps the Netherlands Public Prosecution Service develop the new guidelines and build a knowledge-based system to aid prosecutors in use of the new guidelines.

New Sanctions Proliferating in the Netherlands (December 1999)
  Anton M. van Kalmthout and Peter J. P. Tak

Only 18 months ago we wrote in *Overcrowded Times* that "the Dutch may have to accept that their imprisonment rate, for a long time one of the lowest in Western Europe, may become one of the highest." This prediction was based, among other things, on the 1984–98 quadrupling of prison capacity, from 4,000 to 16,000 cells. Projections by the Ministry of Justice suggested the need for even more construction. The justice budget for 1999 authorized additional funds for prison building, to address an anticipated "further increase of serious forms of crime." The projections for 1999 envisioned capacity of 13,744 places in regular facilities for adults, 1,749 places in juvenile detention centers, and 1,051 cells in forensic psychiatric institutions. Another 2,000 cells were expected to be needed by 2002.

It was generally unexpected, then, when, in October 1999, the Research and Documentation Centre of the Ministry of Justice estimated that the Netherlands would have excess capacity of more than 1,600 places in 1999 and of nearly 1,100 in 2000. The changed projections result partly from stable and declining crime rates and partly from the development and reformulation of various community penalties.

This article examines the reasons for the slowed rate of increase, notably reduced crime rates and cessation of a trend toward longer sentences, and describes other new initiatives aimed at shaping prison populations.

Crime Trends

Two factors explain the erroneous crime projections. First, they assumed that the crime increases of 1985–95 would continue undiminished. This has not happened for many types of crime. Especially for property crime, there has been a substantial decrease since 1994. In 1994, the Public Prosecution Service counted 126,200 registered property offenses. Four years later, there were only 85,800, a decrease of 32 percent. The reason for this is not clear. Possibly, extensive prevention programs started over the past decade targeted especially at property crime have begun to pay off. Victimization surveys also indicate a decrease in property crime. However, property crimes receive low priority in investigation and prosecution, and changes in official practice may have influenced the drop. Most property offenses in 1995 (about 89 percent) were not solved and did not result in prosecutions.

This property crime decrease is offset to some extent by increases in other offenses, although the crime rate is essentially stable. The number of crimes of violence and street vandalism reported by the Public Prosecution Service increased about 8 percent between 1994 and 1998, from 41,400 to 44,500, and traffic offenses likewise grew from 45,200 to 49,100.

Soft-drug offenses are an exception. These increased from 2,700 in 1994 to 5,200 in 1998, approximately 93 percent. The most plausible explanation is a less permissive and tolerant attitude by Dutch authorities toward coffee shops and drugs (including soft drugs). According to the governmental memorandum "Continuity and Change," published in 1995, possession of more than 30 grams of soft drugs and possession of any quantity of hard drugs are regarded as serious crimes and are being investigated and prosecuted more extensively than before. A similar policy change took place with respect to the import, export, production, sale, and transport of soft drugs.

The second reason prison population projections had to be adjusted is that a predicted increase in average prison sentence lengths failed to occur. Between 1985 and 1995, average time served increased approximately 50 percent, from 133 to 199 days. This was widely considered a more important cause of the increase in imprisonment than the increase in the number of unconditional prison sentences. As was pointed out by Junger-Tas in the October 1998 *Overcrowded Times*, this increased term was due largely to violence, sexual offenses, and crimes against public order.

Notwithstanding social pressure to raise sentence lengths for these crimes, it didn't happen. Lengths appear to have stabilized, and few inmates are serving sentences longer than two years. On December 31, 1997, 25 percent of prisoners were serving sentences of more than four years; in 1998 this fell to 23 percent. The percentage of persons serving two to four years imprisonment remained essentially the same in 1997: 17 percent, 1 percent lower than in 1996.

Table 2.24 shows Ministry of Justice projections of sanctions use in 1998–2003. The most striking projected shift is from regular prisons to specialized institutions: forensic-psychiatric institutions, institutions for illegal aliens, and institutions for juveniles.

Table 2.24. Forecast of Annual Average Capacity Need, Various Sanctions, 1998–2003

Sanction	1998	1999	2000	2001	2002	2003	1998–2003 increase
Halt-settlements	21,000	22,500	24,100	26,000	27,900	30,100	43%
Task-sanctions juveniles	10,800	11,600	12,500	13,400	14,500	15,700	45%
Judicial homes for juveniles	1,590	1,780	2,000	2,200	2,380	2,540	59%
Task-sanctions adults	16,800	17,800	18,900	19,800	20,600	21,300	27%
Prisons (excluding custody of illegal foreigners)	11,600	11,800	12,100	12,300	12,500	12,700	10%
Custody of illegal foreigners	1,120	1,210	1,300	1,390	1,480	1,570	40%
Institutions for compulsory psychiatric treatment	1,130	1,180	1,240	1,300	1,340	1,390	23%

Source: Steinmann et al. (1999).

Capacity needs in the regular adult prisons will increase only a little. The projection assumes that two developments will more or less balance each other out: expected increases in sentence lengths for some crimes and new sanctions programs aimed at front- and back-end diversion.

Increased Maximum Sentences

The most important changes in sentence maxima involve illegal possession of arms, breaches of intellectual property laws, organized crime, exploitation of prostitution, and violent crime. The maximum sentence for illegal possession of arms will be increased from nine months to four years and for illegal arms traffic from four to eight years. Following the European Piracy Regulation and the Treaty of the World Trade Organisation, maximum sentences for trafficking in forged proprietary brands will increase from one to four years. The increased maxima for organized crime are already in force. The maximum for participating in a criminal organization has gone up from five to six years, and the leaders of such an organization can be sentenced to up to eight years of imprisonment (up from six years).

A bill recently took effect that legalizes prostitution but imposes heavy sentences for exploitation of prostitution involving violence, abuse, or minors. The maximum sentence for these activities increased from one year to six. The customer of a prostitute who is a minor may be punished with a maximum of four years. Previously, the offender was not punishable when the prostitute was 16 or older.

No decisions have been made concerning possible increases in maxima for offenses of violence. In the face of continuing (if small) increases in violence, the Dutch Parliament and the Ministry of Justice seem unable to ignore populist calls for heavier sentences. This has led to an instruction to the Public Prosecution Service not to allow use of task-penalties (e.g., community service orders, training programs) for persons convicted of violent and sexual offenses. A bill has been prepared on increases of maxima for offenses of violence. The idea is to increase the maximum for abuse (at present still two years) and the sentence for offenses of violence committed while intoxicated on alcohol or drugs.

Prison Reduction Initiatives

Against these capacity increasing measures are a number of initiatives aimed at diverting offenders from imprisonment or decreasing the effective lengths of prison terms.

TASK PENALTIES   Task penalties, sometimes called community sanctions, consist of community service and training orders. A bill has been taken up in Parliament that aims at a considerable extension of the reach of community sanctions. Until now, community sanctions have been meant to replace prison terms up to six months. The bill would extend this to 12 months, and the maximum for a community sanction would be raised to 480 hours. This sanction could consist of a community service order (maximum 240 hours), a training course (maximum 480 hours), or a combined order (maximum 480 hours). The Public Prosecution Service would also be authorized to attach one of these sanctions or a combination of them to a decision to drop the case. As a condition to this "transaction," the maximum may not exceed 120 hours.

A novelty is the potential to combine the task penalty with an unconditional sentence up to six months. This means that imprisonment up to 18 months could be replaced in part by a noncustodial task penalty. Furthermore, a judge could replace six months of imprisonment in a 12-month term with a task penalty of 240 hours, while the remaining six months could be executed by means of electronic monitoring.

ELECTRONIC MONITORING   In 2000, electronic monitoring will be introduced as a front-door sanction in the entire country. This will require the convicted person to do activities aimed at reintegration and rehabilitation for at least 26 hours a week under the supervision and attendance of the probation service. The remaining time the offender will be under house arrest.

PENITENTIARY PROGRAMS   Electronic monitoring is an essential part of the so-called penitentiary programs. The new Penitentiary Principles Act and Penitentiary Measure, which came into force on January 1, 1999, introduced this back-door variant of community sanctions. Although discretionary parole release was replaced in 1986 with automatic nonconditional early release, a new form of conditional release has been created that is open to only a limited category of prisoners.

Penitentiary programs are discretionary programs that can be granted to motivated detainees when they have served at least half of a term of imprisonment of at least one year. A penitentiary program lasts at least six weeks and at most one year and precedes automatic unconditional release, which is granted after two-thirds of the nominal sentence. Just as in the front-door versions of community sanctions, the convicted person is under supervision of the probation service and is obligated to participate in activities aimed at reintegration and rehabilitation outside the prison for at least 26 hours per week. The remaining hours are served not in prison but at home, of which between 12 and 16 weeks are spent under house arrest. Approximately 10 percent of prisoners with terms of more than one year will be eligible.

Extension of the community sanctions and the introduction of electronic monitoring and penitentiary programs are likely to offset the need for more prison capacity required for increases in sentence maxima and more strict prosecution. There is, however, need for extra capacity for specific categories of offenders.

Special Populations

There is a serious shortage of spaces in forensic-psychiatric institutions. The number of offenders sentenced to undergo inpatient treatment in forensic-psychiatric institutions because of mental illness or disturbance has grown rapidly for years. Capacity could not keep pace because of the high costs and the lack of specialized forensic-psychiatric experts. The average length of treatment has grown from more than three years in the mid-1980s to more than five in 1998. The average time an offender sentenced to this measure must wait—in a remand center not equipped for treatment—is more than nine months. In the next few years, increases in prison capacity will largely address these shortages. A 23 percent increase is expected, from 1,130 places for adults (1998) to 1,390 (2003).

A projected rise of 59 percent for juveniles, from 1,590 in 1998 to 2,540 in 2003, can largely be attributed to a need for places in treatment centers. In 1998, available capacity was 940; by 2003, this will be 1,510. The remaining expected extension of 650 cells to 1,030 concerns juvenile prisons. The anticipated extension of the number of noncustodial task penalties for juveniles from 10,800 to 15,700 in 2003 cannot sufficiently compensate for the trend to more and longer custodial sanctions for juveniles. This is mainly a result of juveniles being involved in more serious forms of crime.

An experiment, "night detention," was started at the end of 1999 as a new form of detention, as an alternative for pretrial detention. Juveniles will be able to go to school during the day and stay in a penitentiary institution in the evening, at night, and during the weekend.

The rise in capacity for the detention of illegal aliens is remarkable. Detention of illegal aliens is an administrative measure but is executed in a secure institution. The conditions are identical to those for pretrial detention. The average length of stay is about 50 days, and the current capacity is 1,120 places. This means that 20 percent of the yearly prison population (7,500–8,000 persons) consists of illegal immigrants. Ten years ago there were several hundred. In 2003, because of the stricter maintenance and the sharpening of the Immigration Act, capacity will be augmented by another 500 places. About 33 percent of the total prison population will be made up of administratively detained foreigners.

The latest development, not yet incorporated in the prognoses, concerns a new custodial measure to be introduced in 2000: compulsory detention of persistent drug addicts who frequently commit less serious offenses but are considered serious public nuisances. In view of the pettiness of the committed offenses, they are usually punished with minor prison sentences. Therefore, it is not possible effectively to start treatment in a penitentiary setting. The new measure will authorize confinement of addicts in a special "penitentiary treatment center" for up to two years. During this period, detention will be used to get the addict to cooperate in a treatment program aimed at detoxification, normalization, and reintegration. Part of the treatment can be carried out outside the institution. Despite fierce criticism from independent scientific circles, the measure is likely to be introduced in 2000. It will involve 258 intramural and 92 extramural places. The first institution for this new category of detainees will open shortly in Rotterdam.

Dutch Penal Policies Changing Direction (October 1998)
Josine Junger-Tas

Beginning in 1975, after more than a century of decline, Dutch confinement rates turned upward and, except for a minor pause in 1987, have continued upward since. Widespread changes in public and officials' attitudes to crime and extensive prison building plans suggest that rates will continue to rise. Early in the post-1975 period, increased confinement rates resulted mostly from increased rates of prison admission. Between 1985 and 1995, however, only 41 percent of the increase was attributable to increased admissions, and 59 percent to increases in lengths of prison sentences. This article discusses long-term changes in imprisonment patterns in Holland, and the reasons for those changes. The emphasis is mostly on the period 1985–95.

Long-Term Decline: 1837–1975

The Netherlands has long been known for its mild sanctioning climate, and in particular for its low imprisonment rates. The penal climate has been changing since the 1980s, and it is interesting to examine some of the processes taking place.

Complete prison statistics are available since 1837, and the number of yearly entries into prisons has been recorded since 1900. Van Ruller and Beijers (1995) calculated confinement rates between 1837 and 1993, including all types of inmates—prisoners, detainees awaiting trial, mentally disturbed prisoners in special institutions, and juveniles in state institutions. There was a continuous reduction in the confinement rate from 1837 to 1975, as figure 2.15 shows, with some interruptions during two economic recessions and the two world wars.

Since 1975 the rates have increased steadily, with minor interruption in 1987. Van Ruller and Beijers expect rates to continue to rise for some time because of the considerable prison building program now under way in Holland. They suggest this will lead to a structural expansion in the number of prison sentences and make a rapid decrease in imprisonment rates highly unlikely.

A number of factors contributed to the downward trend in confinement between 1837 and 1975. While in the 1850s prison terms of five years were considered long, by the 1970s and 1980s six months was considered long. Just as people's sensitivity to pain and suffering has increased over time, it seems likely that the general public tended to perceive ever-shorter detention periods as harsh and as sufficient retribution (van Ruller and Beijers 1995). This then led to the reduction in prison terms, for example by the use of early release—first as a reward for good behavior and later as a legal entitlement—and to use of the suspended sentence.

There have been many efforts to reduce prison sentences since the nineteenth century. The first alternative to imprisonment, the fine, was introduced in Dutch penal law in 1886, initially only for petty crimes but later, in 1925, also for more serious offenses. The Financial Penalties Act, dating from 1983, allows judges to dispose of practically all offenses with a fine. The possibilities of early release were expanded in 1916, and suspended sentences (or probation) were adopted in 1916. The Criminal Procedural Code, introduced in 1926, offered considerable legal safeguards for defendants and helped to create the mild penal climate that was maintained until the 1980s.

For the past century, influence over disposition of criminal cases has been shifting from judges to prosecutors. Table 2.25 shows criminal dispositions in Amsterdam in 1880, 1910, and 1989. Of course, the comparison between these years is far from perfect, because prosecutorial diversion programs called "transactions"

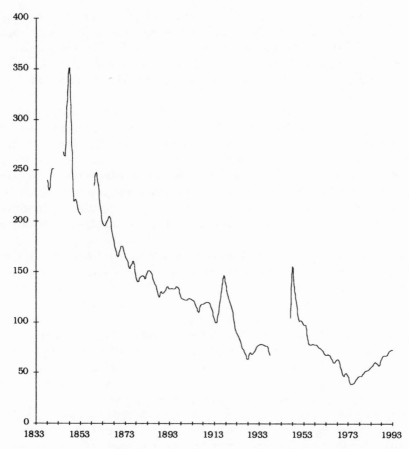

Figure 2.15. Average Daily Population in Institutions, per Year and per 100,000 Population Aged 15–64, Including Prisons, Jails (since 1846), Juvenile Institutions (since 1883), and Mental Institutions (since 1929). *Source*: van Ruller and Beijers (1995), p. 38.

Table 2.25. Dispositions by Prosecutors and Judges of Criminal Defendants in Amsterdam in Three Selected Years (by percentage)

Decision	1880 N = 963	1910 N = 606	1989 N = 9,942
Decision by prosecutor (transaction)	36%	39%	56%
Decision in court by a judge	63	55	38
Other (e.g., acquittal, joinders)	1	6	6
Total	100%	100%	100%

Source: van Ruller and Beijers (1995).

did not exist in 1880 and 1910. In a transaction, the prosecutor dismisses charges if the defendant agrees to pay a fine or otherwise make recompense for his activities. Table 2.25 shows the shift away from dealing with defendants in court toward out-of-court dealings by the prosecutor. In 1990, a transaction offer was allowed in cases of drunk driving, hit-and-run offenses, simple and aggravated theft, simple assault, and vandalism.

This extension of prosecutorial authority is continuing. For example, the 1995 juvenile justice law, which laid down the rules for imposing community sanctions, gives the prosecutor the power to offer a transaction to the defendant in the form of 40 hours of community service or a training order. The commission that introduced community service in adult penal practice in 1981 proposed the same possibility in the case of adults, but fierce opposition of judges prevented adoption. In a new bill on community sanctions (now called "task penalties"), the government has again submitted this proposal for adoption, in an effort to increase the use of alternatives.

A first consequence of changing sentencing patterns is the reduction in use of court-sanctioned fines, because of the enlarged power in this respect of the prosecutor. A second consequence is a reduction in the use of suspended prison sentences. This is probably caused by a combination of factors, such as increased sentencing powers of the prosecutors, an increase in use of community service orders, and an increase in imposition of unconditional prison sentences.

Even as recently as 1988, 87 percent of all minor infractions and 64 percent of all crimes were dealt with by the police and the prosecutor. Moreover, in contrast to developments in other countries, the limitations of prison capacity until that time did not lead to prison overcrowding or to double-celling. Instead, suspects were sent home to wait for a vacancy, a practice that raised increasing unrest and criticism. In the beginning of the 1980s, this practice helped to limit prison rates, but subsequently it led to a huge prison building program.

Longer Sentences: 1985–1995

Table 2.26 shows changes in types of sentences imposed between 1985 and 1995. Use of fines and suspended sentences fell, while use of unconditional prison sentences and community service orders grew. Because prosecutors' powers were en-

Table 2.26. Sentencing in 1985 and 1995 (by percentage)

Sentences[1]	1985 N = 82,712	1995 N = 98,901
Unconditional prison	24.5%	27.5%
Suspended sentences	29.5	13.5
Fines (unconditional)	65.0	46.5
Community service	11.5	14.0
Withdrawal of driver's license	10.5	9.0

Note: [1]Totals equal more than 100 percent because of sanction combinations.

Source: Grapendaal, Groen, and van der Heide (1997), p. 25.

larged in 1983, the workload of judges changed. For example, prosecution of traffic offenses, which once formed about half of the judges' workload, were considerably reduced between 1982 and 1990. Only the most serious offenses, those leading to serious injuries or death, are now dealt with in court. However, the kinds of cases that end up in court depend on a number of conditions, including changes in the crime picture, in prosecution policies, and in the public's views about the behaviors it wants to see more severely punished.

Figures 2.16 and 2.17 show changes in the number and length of prison sentences imposed between 1985 and 1995. The data clearly show that the rising imprisonment rates result both from an increase in the number of prison sentences and from an increase in the lengths of terms served.

Although the average lengths of prison terms seemed to stabilize in 1994 and 1995, the number of prison sentences continued to grow. The number of detention years (which is roughly the number of prison cells) nearly doubled during that period, from 5,861 years ordered in 1985 to 10,939 in 1995. Grapendaal, Groen, and van der Heide (1997) calculated that 41 percent of the increase in the number of detention years resulted from the increase in the number of prison sentences and 59 percent from increases in average prison terms. The increase of almost 100 percent in the number of detention years between 1982 and 1993 was caused largely by more prison sentences handed down for five crime types: robbery and extortion, aggravated theft, drug trafficking, crimes against life, and rape (Berghuis 1994).

Of course, the increase varies by offense type. For sex offenses, there was no increase in the number of prison sentences, but more cells were needed because of increases in the lengths of sentences. Half of the increase in detention years between 1985 and 1995 was due to convictions for violent offenses, mainly robberies, for which the number of prison sentences doubled. The trend is opposite to that for property and drug offenses, where the number of prison sentences increased but sentence lengths decreased. Since prison sentences for property offenses are usually short, these offenders do not occupy much prison space. Traffic offenses are slowly disappearing from court: only the most serious are dealt with by a judge. Most prison capacity is needed for property, drug, and violent offenders. These patterns are illustrated in table 2.27.

The largest increases in unconditional prison sentences were for violent, drug, and property offenses. These offenses account for 87 percent of all occupied cells.

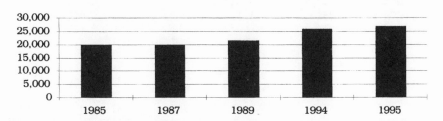

Figure 2.16. Number of Unconditional Prison Sentences, 1985–1995. *Source*: Grapendaal, Groen, and van der Heide (1997), p. 27.

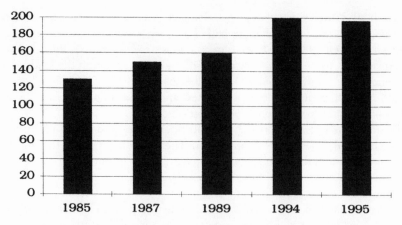

Figure 2.17. Average Length in Days of Unconditional Prison Sentences. *Source*: Grapendaal, Groen, and van der Heide (1997), p. 27.

However, the average term for property offenses is less than three months and scarcely increased between 1985 and 1995. As a consequence, property offenses account for only 30 percent of occupied cells.

By contrast, violent offenses—mainly robberies—account for half of the increased cell occupation: the number of prison sentences for these offenses has doubled in ten years, and the average term served has increased by almost 70 percent.

Both phenomena—more prison sentences and longer prison terms—explain the Dutch prison crisis: the number of prison sentences has increased by 34 percent, and average time served increased by 47 percent.

Table 2.27. Prison Sentences and Sentence Lengths, by Offense Category, 1985–1995

	Percentage of Unconditional Prison Sentences			Average Time Served (in days)		
All offenses	1985 N = 20,119	1995 N = 26,935	Change 34%	1985 133	1995 197	Change 48%
Violence	13%	17%	68%	280	471	68%
Sex offenses	2	2	19	250	501	101
Drugs	8	11	79	401	375	−7
Property	49	57	57	94	91	−3
Public order	6	5	1	78	161	108
Firearms	2	2	35	47	88	87
Traffic	18	4	−70	24	33	38
Other	1	2	244	42	176	325

Source: Grapendaal, Groen, and van der Heide (1997), p. 25.

Juvenile Sentencing

Juvenile justice trends are similar to those in the adult system. The previous practice among police and prosecutors of simply dropping charges in the case of petty offenses has become less common. The police increasingly will drop the case only if compensation is paid to the victim and reparative work is done. Similarly, prosecutors nearly always impose a transaction in the form of a fine, compensation, or community sanction as a condition for no further processing.

There are some essential differences in sentencing patterns between adults and juveniles, as figure 2.18 shows. The largest difference concerns the use of community sanctions. In 1994, they constituted about 60 percent of all sanctions imposed on juveniles, but only 16 percent in adult criminal cases. One-third of all adult sanctions consist at least in part of unconditional prison sentences, while only 10 percent of juvenile sentences include confinement.

Between 1985 and 1995, the number of juveniles sentenced to confinement changed little. Every year, about 6,000 juveniles appeared before the juvenile judges, and about one-fifth were deprived of their liberty. Juvenile penal law in exceptional cases allows for transfer of 16- to 18-year-old juveniles into adult court; of these, some 5 to 6 percent were sent to prison. In 1985 17.7 percent, and in 1995 19 percent, of 12- to 18-year-old juveniles who appeared before judges were sent to juvenile hall, a slight increase. However, the proportion of suspended sentences increased from 17.3 in 1985 to 31.3 percent in 1995, because no legislation on alternative sanctions had been enacted and these sanctions could be imposed only as a condition of probation.

Juvenile judges dealt with relatively more violent offenses (robberies) in 1995 (24 percent) than in 1985 (14 percent), which suggests changes in juvenile delinquency like those in adult criminal behavior.

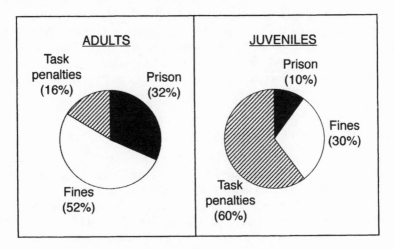

Figure 2.18. Main Dispositions in Adult and Juvenile Cases, 1994. *Source*: Netherlands Parliament, document no. 24,807, pp. 10–11.

The situation is changing quickly. In September 1995, a new juvenile justice law introducing longer sentences was adopted. Periods of confinement in state institutions doubled from six to 12 months for juveniles ages 12–16. For juveniles aged 16 to 18, confinement periods quadrupled from six months to two years, while the transfer of juveniles ages 16–18 to adult court was made considerably easier. Four and one-half percent of prison inmates in 1996 were ages 14–19; most were under 18 when they committed their offenses. The average number of days served in juvenile detention facilities increased from 56 in 1991 to 80 in 1996, and in treatment institutions from 394 to 424 days. About 58 percent of juveniles were institutionalized because of violent offenses and 36.5 because of property offenses (Directie Justitiële Inrichtingen 1997).

Community Sentences

Sixty percent of all juveniles sentenced in 1996 received alternative sanctions. By 1998, that proportion had increased to about 70 percent. In 1983, juvenile judges imposed 298 community service orders and six training orders. In 1995, there were roughly 3,000 community service orders and 1,500 training orders. Juvenile judges were willing to experiment with training orders, although this was something entirely new in juvenile justice. Training orders may vary from six meetings to a three-month program and are still imposed mainly on juveniles. Because of some positive evaluations (van der Laan and Essers 1990), the more intrusive training orders, which combine training with intensive supervision, were extended to young adults.

As for adults, in 1983 judges imposed about 1,700 community service orders, and in 1995, about 14,400; in 1,400 cases the sentence was a training order. Community service orders are imposed mainly for theft, assault and battery, vandalism, and social security fraud. Research showed that these sanctions are a substitute for short prison sentences in only half of the eligible cases; in the other half they are substitutes for a fine or a suspended sentence (Spaan 1995). Suspects charged with sexual or firearms offenses are generally ineligible, as are drug addicts, repeat offenders, and offenders without a fixed address. Over the years successful completion is achieved in 85 percent (adults) to 89 percent (juveniles) of cases.

Background of the Changes in Sentencing

Among the factors that might explain the increased imprisonment rate and the expansion of the prison system are legislative changes, increasing tendencies to report offenses to the police, chain effects in the criminal justice system, changes in the volume, nature, and seriousness of crime, and changes in the attitudes and behavior of the judiciary (Grapendaal, Groen, and van der Heide 1997). Others argue that fundamental social changes in Dutch society since the 1980s have led to increased punitiveness and repression (van Ruller and Beijers 1995).

First, in Holland, as elsewhere, new behaviors have been made criminal, including computer crimes, commercial surrogate motherhood, the trade in illegal immigrants, and environmental crimes. Maximum penalties for some crimes, including child pornography, fraud of legal documents, discrimination, and environmental pollution, have been raised. However, the aim of these changes was less to increase imprisonment than to facilitate investigations by prosecutors and police. For example, telephone tapping, infiltration, entering on premises, and pretrial detention are not permitted unless the crime is serious and punishable by a heavy penalty. So raising maximum penalties facilitated investigative processes. Moreover, considering that maximum penalties are hardly ever imposed, these changes probably had no significant effect on increased prison use (Grapendaal, Groen, and van der Heide 1997).

Second, it might be questioned whether an increased tendency to report offenses to the police affected imprisonment rates. Between 1982 and 1992, the reporting rate increased from 30 percent to 37 percent (Kester and Junger-Tas 1994). However, the highest reporting percentages are for motor vehicle theft and burglary (75 percent) and are related to insurance companies' requirements that losses be reported to the police.

Reporting rates for violent and sexual offenses have increased, thanks to a heightened sensitivity and social awareness of violence and of sex offenses (Kester and Junger-Tas 1994). However, serious crimes have always been reported, and the increase, while real, is not so sizable as to have significant influence on sentencing. As Grapendaal, Groen, and van der Heide (1997) observe, only 11 percent of all crimes known to the police are referred to the prosecutor, and only 12 percent of all cases dealt with in court (by prosecutor and judge) result in an unconditional prison sentence. In 1995, roughly 225,000 penal cases were dealt with, of which 27,000 resulted in deprivation of liberty.

A third possibility is that changes in police capacity and efficiency increased the number of people eligible for prison. Indeed, the police have shifted their attention from petty offending to more serious crimes such as burglary, simple robbery, armed robbery, rape, and assault. However, this has not resulted in significantly higher clearance rates for such offenses. A rising police budget has not had much effect either, mainly because the increase went into computer equipment and police cars, rather than into manpower.

Fourth, most people believe that the nature, volume, and seriousness of criminal offenses have changed. More specifically, they believe that, compared with the period 1945–1980, many more new and different offenses are committed and that these are of a considerably more serious nature than those committed in earlier years. With respect to the nature of the crime, the only really "new" offense is the trade in refugees, and this is a relatively rare offense. However, acquisitive crime by drug addicts, although generally of a nonserious nature, causes considerable trouble, irritation, and fear among residents of some big-city neighborhoods.

Considerable media attention and public pressures helped create perceptions of a crime wave. Of great concern has been the rise in armed robberies of banks, gasoline stations, and post offices and sometimes even of private dwellings. Also of concern is the relatively high juvenile crime rate of some minority groups—notably Moroccan and Antillean boys—who tend to threaten their victims or use violence.

But, apart from changes in the nature of crime, what worries people more than anything else is the increase in violence. Again, it is difficult to disentangle changes in crime rates and patterns from what appears in police data, and perceived increases may be largely the result of heightened sensitivities to violence, more reporting, and more police investigation. Victim surveys and self-report surveys suggest that there is a real increase in violent behavior, although police figures probably overstate the extent of the increase (Junger-Tas 1996).

There has, however, been no significant increase in the volume of criminal incidents since 1985. Both police data and the biannual Dutch victim surveys (Kester and Junger-Tas 1994) show that. The annual increases shown by both data sources were about 1 percent per year, but taking into account population increase, reporting and recording changes, and a greater tendency to report offenses to the police, the actual amounted to about 0.5 percent.

Harsher Penalties

The punishment severity increase can be seen by comparing 1985 and 1995 data on crime rates and prison sentences. Though crime rates increased by 10 percent in those 10 years, the number of unconditional prison sentences was a third higher in 1995, the average sentence length was nearly half again longer, and the number of detention years ordered nearly doubled (Grapendaal, Groen, and van der Heide 1997).

The inescapable conclusion is that the major factor explaining the rise in prison sentences is the tendency to impose more severe sentences. Analogous to the conversion of the welfare state since the 1980s into what is called a "market economy," diminishing the responsibility of the state to its citizens and heavily emphasizing individual responsibility, causes of criminal behavior are seen not as lying in the criminal's social background, life situation, and the circumstances of the offense but as located in the moral fault of the actor, resulting in acts of free will for which he is fully responsible.

Others have observed that the Dutch criminal justice system and the Ministry of Justice have long been operated by a liberal and tolerant elite of experts, legislators, and high-ranking civil servants. They were not plagued by the media, which were usually quite discreet and not much interested in criminal matters (van Ruller and Beijers 1995). However, this situation has changed dramatically as the number of victims of petty offenses increased. Moreover, crime became a highly topical and marketable subject in the media. Crime coverage is extreme and often not in proportion to what happens in reality. Pressures on the government, Parliament, and the judiciary for tougher laws and harsher penalties increased.

Although there have been some legislative changes, including the new juvenile justice law and higher maximum penalties for a number of crimes, their influence on sentencing is limited. The important influence on sentencing comes from the prosecutors who decide on the proceedings, including pretrial detention, and propose the sentences. They determine to a large extent the bounds within which the options of the judge are restricted. Interviews with prosecutors indicate they see themselves as real crime fighters. They consider the tendency to tougher sentences both justifiable and inevitable and declare that "as criminality has become more serious, they honor society's claims for harsher punishment" (Grapendaal, Groen, and van der Heide 1997, p. 54).

Harsher penalties are meted out for offenses that used to be punished in more lenient ways. For example, in 1980 the average prison term served for rape was 250 days, while in 1993 it was nearly 600 (Berghuis 1994). Purse snatching is now defined as theft with violence instead of as simple theft, incurring stiffer penalties than before (Kester and Junger-Tas 1994). The district court in Gröningen recently doubled the average term for burglary in private houses and in businesses. In Amsterdam, public-order offenses and pickpocketing are punished increasingly severely because of concern that the frequency of these offenses could threaten the tourist appeal of Amsterdam. Two other court districts experienced exceptionally high numbers of shoplifting cases with violence; it appears that private security officers provoked the violence, leading to charges of theft with violence, a more serious offense. Finally, introducing appeal, instead of leading to milder sentences as was usually the case, now frequently leads to even more severe sentences (Grapendaal, Groen, and van der Heide 1997).

The results of all this are rapidly rising incarceration rates, a trebling of prison capacity since the 1980s, and, by the end of the 1990s, expectations of a fourfold increase in capacity.

Switzerland

Sentencing in Switzerland in 2000 (December 1999)
   Martin Killias, Marcelo F. Aebi, André Kuhn, and Simone Rônez

Swiss sentencing laws and practices have long been influenced by diverse legal traditions, including the French Code Civil and German legislation. In criminal law, Switzerland has a typical continental system, with one unified criminal code at the federal level and 26 autonomous procedural systems at the cantonal level. Despite that formal diversity, the cantonal systems have many common features, such as the inquisitorial system, limited discretion of police and prosecutors, and protection of fundamental procedural rights of defendants as guaranteed by the European Convention of Human Rights.

The definitions of offenses are contained in the Swiss Criminal Code and a few major federal laws, such as the Narcotics Act and the Road Traffic Act. Sentences are imposed, as elsewhere in Europe, by the same bench of judges who found the defendant guilty. The panels consist usually of three to five judges, with a senior judge in the chair. They, by simple majority, decide guilt and sentence. Typically, the sentence is meted out immediately after the verdict and at the same hearing.

For most offenses, judges have wide sentencing discretion. In most cases, imprisonment of several years or a few days or even a fine are available options. Custodial sentences can be suspended if they do not exceed 18 months and the defendant's record does not warrant an immediate custodial sentence. In practice, sentences often are set either at 18 months in order to make suspension possible or just longer than that in order to sidestep the question whether the offender's record would permit suspension (Kuhn 1993, pp. 113–17).

There are no sentencing guidelines. There are, however, a few general rules in the criminal code concerning aggravating and mitigating factors and a few more general principles. In practice judges are required to explain why they chose a particular type of punishment and why they imposed a particular sentence. In recent years, these requirements have been substantially increased by the Federal Supreme Court of Switzerland (Nay 1994). Although the supreme court does not review sentences as such, it watches over the conformity of sentences imposed by lower courts (and the reasons given) in light of criminal code criteria and what the court considers appropriate interpretation of these principles. In the lower courts and for mass offenses—such as minor thefts, drunken driving, and drug offenses—sentencing conventions have developed on an informal basis. They are seldom quoted in opinions.

Inmates are eligible for parole after having served two-thirds of their sentence, but not less than three months (Criminal Code sec. 38). Given the overcrowding of correctional institutions, about 80 percent of inmates are nowadays granted parole (Languin et al. 1994, p. 83).

Prevailing Sentencing Patterns

Short custodial sentences are widely used. In 1995, 72 percent of incarcerations involved sentences of less than three months (Office fédéral de la statistique ["OFS"] 1997, pp. 9, 18). Switzerland resembles the Netherlands and the Scandinavian countries, but a few qualifications are necessary.

First, the high prevalence of short sentences may be the result not, as in the Netherlands, of a general pattern in sentencing but of frequent use of short sentences in road traffic offenses—such as drunken driving, which made up 38.5 percent of all immediate custodial sentences in 1995 (OFS 1997, p. 22). For more serious crimes, sentences tend to be long by European standards.

Second, for minor offenses (assaults, thefts, and most drug offenses), the probability of being sentenced to an unsuspended custodial sentence is consistent with general European practices (see table 2.28). This is also true of the proportion of sentences of less than one year and the average lengths of sentences.

Although the probability of incarceration is considerably lower in Europe than in the United States, American sentences in 1995–96 were roughly twice as long as those in Switzerland for many offenses. However, American data pertain to aggravated assault, whereas the European data include common assaults, which means that differences for that offense may be overstated.

Compared with other European countries, sentences in Switzerland tend to be about average for homicide, but shorter for robbery, rape, and drug trafficking (see table 2.29, part. C). The proportion of sentences for less than one year is about average (table 2.29, part. B), however, the probability of receiving an immediate custodial sentence is lower than in most other countries (table 2.29, part. A).

Table 2.28. Unsuspended Custodial Sentences in Europe (1995) and in the United States (1996)

	Persons Sentenced to an Unsuspended Sentence (per 100 convicted)			Length of Unsuspended Sentences: Percentage under 1 year and Average in Months (in parentheses)					
	Assaults	Theft	Drugs	Assaults		Theft		Drugs	
England/Wales	27	20	17	65%	(15)	79%	(9)	43%	(28)
France	20	32	45	82	(7)	85	(6)	50	(18)
Germany	6	8	18	56	—	66	—	33	—
Sweden	28	10	21	83	(5)	89	(5)	66	(16)
Switzerland	17	34	37	68	(15)	76	(5)	44	(17)
Europe (mean)	26	27	37	68	(21)	71	(15)	48	(28)
United States	72	63	73	—	(43)	—	(22)	—	(32)

Sources: Council of Europe (1999), tables 3.B.3.3., 3.B.3.7, 3.B.3.10, 3.B.4.3, 3.B.4.6, 3.B.4.8; Brown and Langan (1999), tables 3 to 6.

The likeliest explanation for these patterns is that those receiving unsuspended custodial sentences, on average, have committed more serious offenses or have longer records, or both. The relatively mild average sentences for drug trafficking may result from the widespread practice among drug addicts of earning their living through small-scale deals, which means that those convicted are often low-scale user-dealers. If more serious drug trafficking (involving larger quantities) is considered, the average sentence length (37 months) is more in line with what is usual in other countries.

Compared with American practice in 1996, the probability of unsuspended custodial sentences is low in Switzerland, and the length of those sentences is roughly half as long. In light of the more complete data available here, it is doubtful whether American and European sentences are as similar as was suggested by Lynch (1993).

Wide use of short prison sentences has led to a comparatively high prevalence of imprisonment in the general population. According to a survey on the cohort born in 1955, 6.5 percent of male Swiss who live in Switzerland had experienced incarceration at least once by age 33, and 24 percent had been convicted at least once between age 18 and 33 (Killias and Aeschbacher 1988). This is similar to the incarceration prevalence rate in England and Wales (Harvey and Pease 1987), although convictions (among males) are considerably more prevalent there (30 percent by age 28).

Changes in Sentencing Patterns during the Past Decade

Sentencing patterns may change over time. Figure 2.19 shows average custodial sentences between 1984 and 1997 for intentional homicide (including attempts), rape, robbery, and theft. Overall, sentencing patterns remained stable. Nevertheless, sentence lengths for rape fluctuated most widely, rising by 54 percent between

Table 2.29. Unsuspended Custodial Sentences in Europe (1995) and in the United States (1996)

	A. Persons Sentenced to an Unsuspended Sentence (per 100 convicted)			
	Homicide	Robbery	Rape	Drug Trafficking
England/Wales	85	63	87	44
France	95	65	93	59
Germany	89	39	59	—
Sweden	96	60	93	—
Switzerland	93	55	69	39
Europe (mean)	92	70	78	53
United States	95	88	79	73

	B. Persons Sentenced to an Unsuspended Term of Less than 1 Year (per 100 receiving an unsuspended sentence)			
	Homicide	Robbery	Rape	Drug Trafficking
England/Wales	2	23	1	37
France	1	58	2	39
Germany	2	11	2	—
Sweden	0	25	8	—
Switzerland	1	22	6	33
Europe (mean)	2	22	14	38
United States	—	—	—	—

	C. Average Length of Unsuspended Sentences (in months)			
	Homicide	Robbery	Rape	Drug Trafficking
England/Wales	68	38	78	31
France	128	21	110	22
Germany	—	—	—	—
Sweden	76	23	30	—
Switzerland	98	28	44	26
Europe (mean)	99	41	62	33
United States	244	88	98	38

Sources: Council of Europe (1999), tables 3.B.3.3, 3.B.3.7, 3.B.3.10, 3.B.3.11, 3.B.4.3, 3.B.4.6, 3.B.4.8, 3.B.4.9; Brown and Langan (1999), tables 7 to 10.

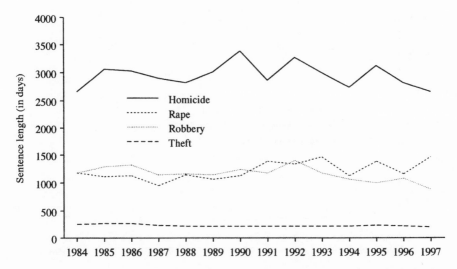

Figure 2.19. Average Length (in days), Unsuspended Custodial Sentences, Switzerland, 1984–1997. *Source*: Unpublished data from the Office fédéral de la statistique.

1987 and 1997 and by 26 percent since 1984. For theft, sentence length decreased by 21 percent from 1984 to 1997. For robbery the decrease was 36 percent between 1992 and 1997 and 24 percent since 1984. For homicide, sentence lengths fluctuate within a 10–15 percent range.

As figure 2.20 shows, the same overall stability characterizes sentencing in drug cases, although sentences became less severe after 1994. The decrease was small for serious drug trafficking (down 13 percent after 1994 and 7 percent since 1984), but more substantial for user-dealers (minus 51 percent, not shown). The picture of overall stability illustrates the power of unwritten sentencing standards. Even in the absence of sentencing guidelines, judges look at their and their colleagues' former sentences in similar cases. The prevailing practice of entrusting a bench rather than a single judge with sentencing decisions may facilitate the flow of information concerning the "usual" sentence length in similar cases.

Two qualifications to the preceding comments about stability in sentencing are warranted. First, substantial numbers of offenders convicted of any of the offenses considered here have been simultaneously convicted (and thus sentenced) for other offenses. It is not likely, however, that offense combinations have changed in a way that would invalidate the generalizations offered here. Second, a stable trend in length of custodial sentences might mask shifts in the frequency of such sentences compared with other sentencing options. As the following section demonstrates, custodial sentences have indeed decreased since 1989, but the prevailing trend has been remarkably stable.

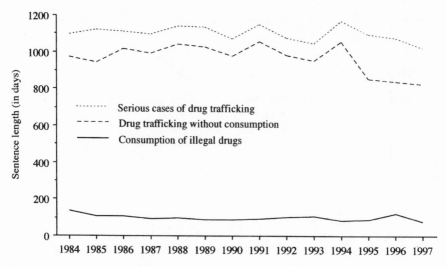

Figure 2.20. Average Length (in days), Unsuspended Custodial Sentences, Switzerland, 1984–1997. *Source:* Unpublished data from the Office fédéral de la statistique.

Trends in Prison Populations

The incarceration rate in Switzerland was comparatively low for many years, even by Western European standards. From 42 per 100,000 in 1972, it rose to 73 in 1988 (Killias 1991, p. 383), to 81 in 1995, and to 88 in 1997 (Council of Europe 1999, table 4.B.1). In 1983, Switzerland ranked 7th among 18 countries in incarceration rate (Council of Europe 1990, 1992), while in 1997 it ranked 19 among 34 countries (Council of Europe 1999, table 4.B.1). Thus, Switzerland's prison population (in absolute numbers and per 100,000 population) has increased at about the same pace as that in the rest of Europe.

Not unlike the Netherlands, France, and the Scandinavian countries, Switzerland once had much higher prison populations—around 150 per 100,000 population in the early 1940s and more than 120 per 100,000 in the 1920s (Killias 1991, pp. 369, 378). It is not obvious why use of imprisonment declined so greatly after World War II. Perhaps the Swiss Criminal Code, which took effect in 1942 and replaced the codes of the then 25 cantons, reshaped sentencing policies, and reduced the length of custodial sentences. But, given the absence of data on prison populations between 1942 and the 1970s, this explanation is speculative at best. Unemployment, which was a major problem in those times and which, after 50 years of virtually no unemployment, has recently reached more than 5 percent of the labor force, can almost certainly be ruled out as an explanatory variable. For one thing, the recent increase in prison populations preceded the new employment crisis. Second, labor market fluctuations have always correlated more with pretrial detention than with imprisonment as a penal sanction (Killias and Grandjean 1986), a pattern that has been noted in other European countries (Melossi

1995). This time, it is imprisonment, rather than pretrial detention, that has increased dramatically.

Increasing prison populations have led to overcrowding in many institutions. Despite signs of overcrowding in the early 1980s (OFS 1985), major building did not start until the late 1980s. In the early 1990s, crowding reduced the space available for pretrial confinement and constrained police from making arrests, even in more serious cases. This phenomenon has been most pronounced in Zurich in connection with the internationally known "needle park" and the high prevalence of nonresident drug dealers.

Figure 2.21 shows overall trends in prison admissions, prison populations, and average time served from 1982 to 1997, in each case using data from 1982 as a base (1982 = 100) and showing changes in proportion to that base.

Average time served and overall population numbers have increased much more than has the number of prison admissions. Admissions increased between 1982 and 1989, followed by a substantial decrease. Time served, however, steadily increased, from an average of 74 days in 1982 to 172 in 1997.

One might suppose that judges are today sentencing offenders to longer prison terms. The data presented in figures 2.19 and 2.20, however, do not suggest such an explanation. Average sentence lengths have been stable or decreased, except for rape, where, given the low numbers involved, the longer sentences may have increased the absolute number of inmates by less than 2 percent.

From 1984 to 1992, the most plausible explanation for increasing prison population is the growth in convictions of large-scale drug dealers. More recently, however, the story may be different. After 1990, the number of unsuspended cus-

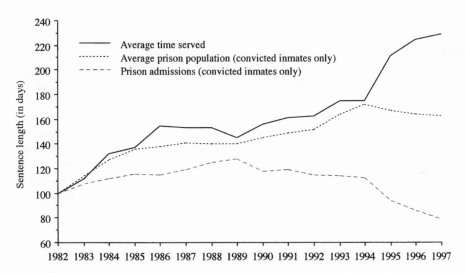

Figure 2.21. Percent Changes, Prison Populations, Prison Admissions, and Time Served, Switzerland, 1982–1997 (1982 = 100). *Source:* Unpublished data from the Office fédéral de la statistique.

todial sentences for serious offenses remained stable, with some qualifications: prison sentences increased 91 percent for homicide, 26 percent for rape, and 48 percent for drug trafficking but decreased for robbery (down 20 percent) and theft (down 2 percent). Taking the changes in sentence length into account (figures 2.19 and 2.20), the use of imprisonment has decreased for these offenses by 6 percent since 1990. In 1997, Swiss courts imposed, all in all, 4,335 years of custody for these offenses, compared to 4,616 in 1990. Therefore, the increase (by 13 percent) in Switzerland's convicted prison population between 1990 and 1997 cannot be attributed to more or longer sentences for serious offenses (homicide, robbery, rape, drug trafficking). Since the number of prison admissions decreased during the same period by 33 percent, the reason cannot be increased use of imprisonment for other offenses. However, it is possible that the length of custodial sentences for other offenses of medium or lower seriousness, such as road traffic offenses (including drunken driving), which involve large numbers of offenders, has increased.

Of course, the increasing use of community service in place of short prison terms (see later discussion) and, concomitantly, lower admission rates automatically increases the average length of the remaining custodial sentences. This statistical effect, however, can account for the increase in sentence length only to the extent that the population of convicted prisoners remains stable (which was the case after 1994). During the whole period under consideration (1990 to 1997, or 1984 to 1997), however, the "stock" of convicted inmates has increased substantially (up 13 percent since 1990, and up 63 percent since 1984), whereas the number of admissions decreased by 33 percent since 1990 and by 21 percent since 1984.

Current Policy Initiatives

In a few years, Switzerland may have a new criminal code. A draft currently being debated in Parliament includes proposals for instituting a minimum prison sentence duration of six months (instead of three days under current legislation), granting authority to judges to suspend sentences up to 36 (instead of 18) months, and introducing new sanctions, such as day fines and community service orders. This agenda is largely inspired by German reforms of the early 1970s. Community service orders have been introduced as an alternative to execution of short custodial sentences in most of Switzerland's 26 cantons. Offenders sentenced to relatively short sentences may, in the cantons that adopted this system on an experimental basis, perform four hours of community work for each day they would otherwise have served in prison.

Evaluations of this program have shown its feasibility (Fichter 1994; von Witzleben 1994), and that recidivism rates are lower among those randomly assigned to community service than among those sentenced to prison (Killias, Aebi, and Ribeaud 2000). The increasing popularity of community service contributed substantially to the reduction in prison admissions after 1991 (OFS 1997, p. 19).

Sanctions and prisons in Switzerland have changed dramatically since 1980, but the changes "just happened" — unplanned, uncoordinated, and unanticipated.

Other than plans to build new and enlarge existing prisons, no policy has yet been designed to address problems of prison overcrowding. The only option seriously debated has been the abolition of short prison sentences, but this has stemmed more from traditional hostility to such sentences among German and Swiss criminal law teachers than from concern with finding responses to the current crisis.

Any serious effort to reduce the prison population must address the issue of shortening long sentences, particularly in the area of drug offenses. Amendment of the Narcotics Act in 1975, which introduced harsher penalties for drug trafficking, was a major cause of the crowding crisis during the early 1990s (Kuhn 1987).

Recent trends in sentences imposed for drug trafficking seem to suggest, however, that judges have started to reduce sentence lengths in this area, along with a new drug policy which includes prescription of methadone and heroin to addicts (Killias 1999). This shift in informal sentencing practices may have contributed more than any other measure to stabilizing Switzerland's prison population in recent years.

Japan

Prison Population in Japan Stable for 30 Years (February 1999)
Koichi Hamai

Compared with other industrialized nations, Japan commits remarkably few of its convicted criminals to prison. Its imprisonment rate per 100,000 persons was only 39.7 in 1997, compared with approximately 645 in the United States. The Japanese prison population on the last day of 1997 (40,389) was a little more than a third of the 112,973 in the U.S. federal correctional institutions alone. The Japanese incarceration rate is a half to a fourth of the 60–120 per 100,000 that characterizes most Western industrialized countries.

Except for a brief period of social unrest after the Second World War, Japanese prisons have not experienced severe overcrowding. The average daily population of convicted prisoners in 1996 was 39,522, around 80 percent of the total capacity for convicted prisoners, while the average daily population of unconvicted prisoners awaiting trial was 8,503, just over 50 percent of the total capacity for unconvicted prisoners.

Figure 2.22 shows the average daily populations of Japanese prisons for total, convicted, and remand prisoners (pretrial detainees) from 1946 to 1997. After a period of long-term decline from the early 1950s to the early 1970s, the total confined population has fluctuated between 50,000 and 60,000 inmates for a quarter century. Resembling the population figures, the incarceration rate reached a peak in 1951 and fell steadily through the mid-1970s and has since fluctuated between 30 and 40 per 100,000, with a slight fall in the early 1990s.

Figure 2.23 shows annual prison admissions for the period 1946–1997. The pattern resembles those in figure 2.22, albeit with a steady but modest increase during the period 1974–85 followed by a significant drop in the late 1980s before a new, lower equilibrium was reached in 1991.

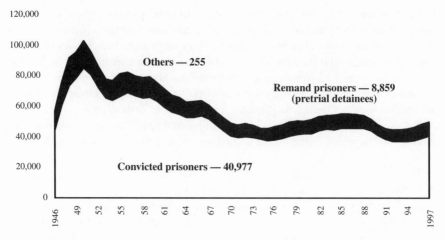

Figure 2.22. Trend in Average Daily Population, 1946–1997. *Source*: Annual Report of Statistics on Corrections.

Prison receptions reached their peak during the postwar period: 70,727 in 1948. Since then, they have generally decreased, although there was another, smaller peak of 32,060 in 1984. Receptions declined after 1985 and reached a record low of 20,864 in 1992; since then they have gradually increased to 22,667 in 1997.

As figure 2.23 also shows, and as is also true in many countries, including the United States, prison admissions have been rising more for women than for men. The proportion of female prisoners continuously increased until 1985 after recording its lowest level of 1.8 percent of all prisoners in 1974. It held stable at the 4 percent mark until 1992 and since then has resumed its long-term increase.

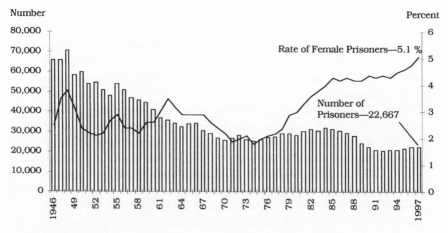

Figure 2.23. Trends in Number of Newly Admitted Prisoners, 1946–1997. *Source*: Annual Report of Statistics on Corrections.

There are several reasons why the Japanese prisons remain free from the over-crowding that some other Western nations have faced. One, as noted, is that annual admissions to prison in the early 1990s were less than half those of the 1940s, and rates of admission have fluctuated between stability and decline for thirty years. A second, necessarily related to the first, is that the incidence of violent crime has declined dramatically in recent decades.

Crime Rate

The incidence of crime is low in Japan. The number of penal code offenses reported by the police, which amounted to levels above 1.6 million in 1948 and 1949, decreased after that period before increasing again to a peak of more than 1.9 million in 1970 (mainly due to increases in the number of traffic [professional negligence] offenses). Since 1993, the number has been around the 2.4 million level and reached its peak in 1996.

Since 1946, excluding traffic (professional negligence) offenses, larceny has accounted for 70–89 percent of total penal code offenses. Fraud, embezzlement, bodily injury, assault, and extortion have been other main offenses.

Figures 2.24, 2.25, and 2.26 show trends in absolute numbers of reported crimes for the period 1946 to 1994. With the exceptions of larceny and fraud, the inci-dence of all serious crimes was significantly lower in the late 1990s than in earlier periods. The crime rate decreases are, of course, even greater because Japan's population has grown considerably in the 50 years since 1946.

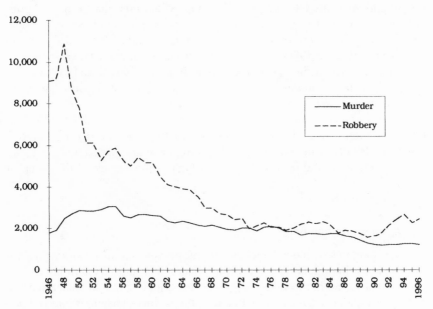

Figure 2.24. Trends in the Number of Reported Serious Crimes

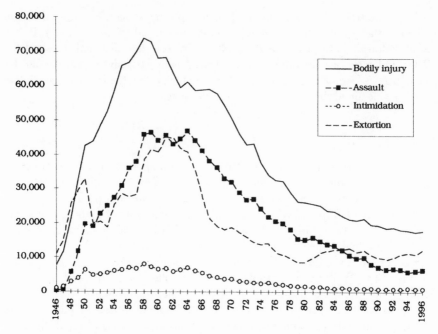

Figure 2.25. Trends in the Number of Reported Violent Crimes

Figure 2.24 shows murder and robbery trends. The number of robberies peaked in 1950 and generally fell through 1990, since when there has been an upturn. The number of murders peaked in the late 1950s and has gradually fallen since.

Figure 2.25 shows trends in assault with injury, assault by threat, and extortion. All peaked in the late 1950s or early 1960s and have generally fallen since.

Figure 2.26, which shows data for larceny and fraud, reveals different patterns. Levels of reported fraud have been relatively stable since 1970, while larceny has rapidly increased. When comparing the reported major crime rate per 100,000 inhabitants in Japan and four other countries, namely the United States, England and Wales, Germany, and France, from 1986 to 1995, we find that Japan has the lowest rate. Japan's crime rate was steady during the entire period, unlike those in the other countries, and is only one-fifth as high as the average of the other four countries.

Few Offenders Are Imprisoned

Japan has long placed less reliance on imprisonment as a means of dealing with crime and criminals than have the United States and other Western nations.

The Japanese authorities often suspend prosecution, apply financial penalties, or impose suspended sentences (with and without work obligations), according to the seriousness of the offense. Consequently, only a small proportion of offenders are imprisoned.

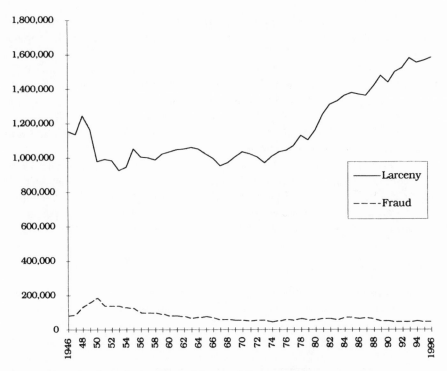

Figure 2.26. Trends in the Number of Reported Property Crimes

The majority of offenders are either diverted from the criminal justice system or placed under treatment in the community. In this regard, public prosecutors play an important role, acting under the principle of discretionary prosecution. The present Code of Criminal Procedure offers general guidelines but leaves case-by-case decision making to the prosecutors' discretion. Article 248 reads: "If after considering the character, age, and situation of the offender, the gravity of the offense, the circumstances under which the offense was committed, and the conditions subsequent to the offense, prosecution is deemed unnecessary, prosecution need not be instituted." The public prosecutors are empowered to discontinue a case in light of such positive factors as apparent repentance, state of progress in compensation to the victim, and so on.

Also, at the stage of trial, the judiciary always considers the possibility of suspended sentences. The judge is authorized to suspend a sentence to prison under "extenuating circumstances." Article 25 of the Penal Code limits leniency to persons who would have been sentenced to prison for no more than three years or, if previously imprisoned, have faced imprisonment again within five years after satisfaction of the previous prison sentence. In practice, "extenuating circumstances" include such things as the following: the defendant has no, or a minimal, criminal record or is young enough to change attitudes and lifestyle; the victim excuses the offender; the victim and the defendant have agreed to terms for restitution; the offense was accidental, not deliberate. In addition, the idea that "we hate crimes not criminals; condemn the offense but not its perpetrator" has taken deep root in Japanese society and is widely accepted among the general public.

Thus, by international standards, the imprisonment rate in Japan is remarkably low; it is even lower than would be expected from the low incidence of crime. For example, in 1996, 2,061,526 suspects were processed by the public prosecutors' offices. Of these, only 98,508 (4.7 percent)[1] were put to formal trial, while 1,023,891 were dealt with under summary proceedings that resulted in a fine, and 641,805 received suspended prosecutions.

In 1995, approximately 59,000 offenders were sentenced to imprisonment with a determinate term, and, since 61.6 percent were granted suspension of their sentences, 22,724, or about 1 percent, of those received by the public prosecutors' offices were actually imprisoned. By contrast, in the United States, 71 percent of all convicted felons were sentenced to a period of confinement in 1994.[2]

Length of Sentences

Japanese prisons receive only that small number of offenders whom it is deemed necessary and reasonable to separate from the larger society. However, these of-

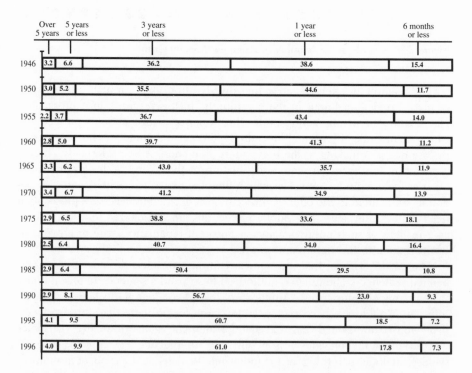

Figure 2.27. Percentage of Newly Admitted Prisoners, by Length of Sentence, 1946–1996. *Note:* "Over 5 Years" includes life imprisonment. *Source:* Annual Report of Statistics on Corrections.

fenders receive relatively short-term sentences. Further, indeterminate sentences are not adopted in Japan except for a small portion of juveniles. Figure 2.27 shows the percentage of prison reception by length of sentence between 1946 and 1996. In 1996, approximately 75 percent of newly admitted prisoners were sentenced to three years or less, and only 0.16 percent were sentenced to life.

Thus, the average length of imprisonment served by Japanese prisoners, including lifers, is less than 20 months. Table 2.30 shows, by offense type, lengths of sentences imposed by Japanese courts in 1995. Recall, however, that all sentences for three years or less are eligible for suspension and that only slightly less than two-thirds of sentences were suspended.

Parole and Recidivism

Prisoners can be released early on parole or on expiration of the full sentence. Correctional programs place special emphasis on parole as a way of ensuring a smooth reintegration into society. The penal code provides only two requirements for parole eligibility: that the prisoner have served one-third of a determinate sentence or 10 years of a life sentence and that he demonstrate evidence of rehabilitation. In practice, a classification committee in each institution meets at least once a month before the eligibility dates for parole to decide whether to submit an application for parole to the parole board. The most important criterion in evaluating suitability for parole is a low probability of recidivism. In 1996, among the 22,182 prisoners released, 12,316, or 57.6 percent, were released on parole.

Of prisoners released in 1991, some 55 percent never returned to prison. This may not seem too impressive unless one bears in mind that convicted prisoners are carefully selected hardcore offenders. I therefore contend that Japanese prisons function to rehabilitate offenders. Prisons in Japan receive a very small proportion of offenders processed by public prosecutors. The public prosecutors select only the least promising individuals for the correctional institutions: those who were previously incarcerated, members of criminal syndicates, and those who otherwise possess "advanced criminal tendencies."

Conclusion

Many factors work to limit the use of incarceration as a penal sanction in Japan. Among those factors, the decisions of public prosecutors and sentencing judges, as discussed, are the most visible manifestation of a criminal justice system that diverts a substantial proportion of offenders from the prisons. Most offenders are filtered out through the criminal justice process and diverted into community disposal. As Johnson (1996) pointed out, this policy is an emanation of a culture that pushes both offenders and nonoffenders toward the restoration of harmony. As Haley (1989) summarizes, "the vast majority of those accused of criminal offenses confess, display repentance, negotiate for their victims' pardon and submit to the mercy of the authorities. In return, they are treated with extraordinary leniency."

Table 2.30. Number of the Convicted Sentenced to Death or Imprisonment by Courts of First Instance, by Offense and Term of Imprisonment, 1995

Offense	Total	Death	Life	Imprisonment with or without Work					
				Over 10 Years	10 Years or Less	5 Years or Less	3 Years or Less	Less than 1 Year	Less than 6 Months
Total	59,145	11	37	136	737	2,047	41,747	9,035	5,395
Penal code offenses	32,925	11	37	128	615	1,522	24,530	5,859	223
Homicide	635	—	8	92	250	103	181	1	—
Robbery	800	11	29	26	195	319	220	—	—
Robbery resulting in death, bodily injury	*322*	*11*	*29*	*18*	*114*	*146*	*4*	—	—
Rape in the course of robbery	*41*	—	—	*7*	*28*	*6*	—	—	—
Bodily injury	2,954	—	—	1	32	129	1,830	922	40
Bodily injury resulting in death	*268*	—	—	*1*	*31*	*109*	*127*	—	—
Extortion	1,775	—	—	—	2	27	1,672	73	1
Larceny	13,567	—	—	—	20	531	10,876	2,130	10
Fraud	3,092	—	—	—	15	113	2,631	333	—
Rape	534	—	—	2	43	128	361	—	—
Arson	344	—	—	7	34	87	216	—	—
Gambling lottery	521	—	—	—	—	—	373	145	3
Violent acts	396	—	—	—	—	3	223	161	9
Professional negligence	4,587	—	—	—	—	1	3,337	1,198	51
Others	3,720	—	—	—	24	81	2,610	896	109
Special law offenses	26,220	—	—	8	122	525	17,217	3,176	5,172
Election Law	649	—	—	—	—	—	389	255	5
Firearms and swords	475	—	—	2	43	160	221	36	13
Stimulant drugs	12,776	—	—	6	52	295	12,193	229	1
Narcotic drugs	169	—	—	—	11	20	127	11	—
Horse Race Law	145	—	—	—	—	—	100	43	2
Immigration control	3,340	—	—	—	—	—	3,074	264	2
Road traffic violations	6,294	—	—	—	—	—	43	1,278	4,973
Others	2,372	—	—	—	16	50	1,070	1,060	176

Notes: For some offenses (robbery, bodily injury) the main entry is the total, and the indented subcategories in **bold italic** figures are included within the total. Thus, columns total when main entries are added.

"Others" of special law offenses include violations of the Law for the Punishment of Crimes of Tax Stamps, the Law Concerning Unlawful Seizure of Aircrafts and Other Related Crimes, the Law for the Punishment of Crimes Relating to the Environmental Pollution which Adversely Affects the Health of Persons, the Law Concerning Punishments of Acts Endangering Air Navigation, and the Law for the Punishment of Compulsion and Other Related Acts Committed by those having taken Hostages.

Source: Annual Report of Judicial Statistics.

This characteristic of the Japanese criminal justice system, in which more than 90 percent of indicted people plead guilty, enables all the factors discussed to perform at their best: keeping the crime rate increase at a minimum level, sending fewer offenders to the court and to the prisons, allowing judges to pass less severe sentences, allowing the authorities to release more prisoners on parole, and making the trial shorter. Thus, Japan has since 1970 enjoyed a low imprisonment rate of fewer than 40 per 100,000 population.

In 1996, a public opinion poll on the function of prisons was undertaken by the Research and Training Institute of the Ministry of Justice (1997). The outcome was incorporated in the 1997 issue of the White Paper on Crime in an article entitled "The Perception of the People toward Crime and Treatment of Offenders." According to the survey results, 36.8 percent of the general population and 53 percent of those from prisoners' families regarded prison as helpful for resocializing offenders, while 12.6 percent of the former and 9.5 percent of the latter did not. The 1996 prison surveys also show that more than 80 percent of prisoners thought they had gained something positive from their imprisonment. It can be realistically claimed that the prison system in Japan has the confidence of both the public and the inmates.

NOTES

Many figures and tables in this paper were originally created for the White Paper on Crime (1997) and modified by the author.

This article is based on a paper presented at the 12th International Congress on Criminology in Seoul, Korea, August 24–29, 1998, by Koichi Hamai.

1. This is a statistical figure based on charged offenses and therefore is larger than the actual number of persons.

2. Criminal Sentencing Statistics by Bureau of Justice Statistics of the U.S. Department of Justice (2,226,119 people were arrested for Index offenses, and 521,970 offenders were admitted to prisons or jails.)

THREE

Penal Developments in English-Speaking Countries

England, Canada, Australia, and New Zealand share language, history, and the common law with the United States but share social democratic traditions and etatist political cultures with Europe. Familiarity and easy intercourse with the United States have meant that American ideas have particular influence. Deeper commitment to social welfare values and the notion that the legal system should be somewhat insulated from political influence has buffered the influence of populist punitivism. As a result, and perhaps suspiciously tidily, penal politics, policies, and trends in the English-speaking countries fall between those in Europe and the United States.

The case is clear in punishment trends. Among Western countries, and for this purpose excluding the newly democratic and independent countries of Eastern Europe, the American imprisonment rate in 2000 of 700 per 100,000 residents was highest, and incomparably higher than other nations'. The next highest were about 160 per 100,000: England, New Zealand, and Portugal. Australia's rate has increased rapidly in recent years after a period of long-term stability at around 110 per 100,000. Only Canada has exhibited relative stability for most of the past 20 years.

By contrast, there is no overall European pattern. In Holland and Portugal, rates steadily increased in the 1980s and 1990s. In Finland, they fell. In France and Italy, they gyrated. In Germany and most of Scandinavia, they fluctuated within a narrow range. At the end of the twentieth century, rate increases were the most common pattern, but this was neither universal nor, in most countries, clearly a long-term trend.

The case is also clear in penal politics. Crime first appeared as a notable issue in American politics in the Johnson-Goldwater presidential election of 1964. By 1972, it had become a central and deeply ideological issue that ostensibly distinguished Republicans from Democrats, conservatives from liberals. In broad stereo-type, Republicans and conservatives worried about public safety and crime on the streets, cared about victims, believed that most crime is primarily the product of personal irresponsibility, and called for harsher penalties to deter and incapacitate criminals. Democrats and liberals ostensibly worried about social injustice, cared about offenders, believed that most crime is primarily the product of economic and social disadvantage, and called for better social programs generally and more rehabilitative programs in the criminal justice system.

Both stereotypes are simplistic and overstated. The important point is that the Republican-conservative stereotype played vastly more successfully with the elec-torate, and by the 1980s candidates typically competed to be toughest and penal policy followed suit. Few elected politicians could risk opposing harsh proposals, no matter how draconic or misconceived, and few did. By the early 1990s, a stalemate occurred when President Bill Clinton and most mainstream Democrats adopted the policy of not letting Republicans get to their right on crime issues. That ended the toughness bidding contests but also left American crime policy at an impasse of remarkable severity and illiberality.

Crime did not become a central issue in partisan and ideological politics in the other English-speaking countries until the late 1980s and 1990s. Until then, social welfare values left crime policy primarily in the hands of officials and ra-tionalistic policy elites. Since then, U.S.-style right-left crime politics have caught on in England and Australia, and England now suffers its own impasse in which the Labour government has given into populist politics, resolved not to let the Tories get to its right, and allowed the prison population to rise rapidly to un-precedented heights. Arie Freiberg's several articles in this volume tell of the adop-tion in the 1990s by the conservative governments of most Australian states of new laws patterned on U.S. models — truth-in-sentencing, mandatory minimums, and sexual psychopath laws — and of their effects on the prisons. Articles by Andrew Ashworth and Rod Morgan chart the English path. England has most fully adopted the populist politics of American crime control. This is shown by adoption of three- and even two-strikes laws and by the Labour government's proposal of a wide range of new symbolic policies including cutbacks in rights to trial by jury and abrogation of the double jeopardy rule.

However, and it is an important however, conservative policymakers in other English-speaking countries have pulled their punches where U.S. policy makers have not. Their countries' imprisonment rates remain a fifth to a sixth the U.S. rate. Their mandatory sentencing laws cover few offenses, are narrowly drawn, and typically require sentences of a few years. In the United States such laws cover many offenses, are broadly drawn (California's "any felony" three-strikes law is the classic example), and often require sentences measured in decades or of life with-out possibility of parole. Australia and England also both adopted the boot camp, a politically popular innovation for young offenders known from its outset to be misconceived. In both places, the form of boot camp established was much less harsh than the typical U.S. boot camp, and in both cases the program was soon abandoned.

Australia

Sentencing and Punishment in Australia in the 1990s
(February 1995)
Arie Freiberg

Unevenly, but seemingly inexorably, Australia is being swept up in the international movement to "get tough" on crime in the hope that such policies will restore communal peace and harmony. Prison populations, which were steady or declining, have begun to grow in a number of jurisdictions. •

Predominant concerns about sentencing have fundamentally changed in 20 years. In the 1970s, prison conditions, development of community-based penalties, and reduction in sentencing disparities were the major goals of sentencing reform. In the mid-1990s these problems — though certainly not "solved" — have been displaced by calls for tougher penalties, incapacitative sentencing, and vindication of the interests of victims.

Responsibility for sentencing in Australia is divided among six state governments, two self-governing territories, and the federal government. Federations inevitably tend to diversity, and Australia is no exception. Recognizable similarities in policy and legislation most commonly emerge from "the temper of the times," sometimes from conscious emulation, and rarely from concerted action. It is very difficult to do justice to the changes in all the jurisdictions and to describe each of their histories and legislation in minute detail. Rather, I have tried to capture the general flavor of the changes and to speculate on their likely impact.

In sentencing, as in so many other areas of social policy, the only constant is change. Following the election of politically conservative governments in New South Wales in 1988, Victoria in 1992, and Western Australia and South Australia in 1993 and the reelection of a conservative government in the Northern Territory in 1994, the political complexion of the country has changed dramatically.

Background

Sentencing reform in Australia in the late 1960s and early 1970s reflected the times. Disillusionment with the prison led to the development of a wider range of community-based sanctions. These were primarily community work, suspension of sentence, and forms of periodic detention. Though imprisonment rates increased slowly across Australia in the 1970s, they declined in the early 1980s, possibly as a result of the proliferation of alternatives to custody, including increased use of parole (Walker 1994, p. 22).

Federal Government

The first systematic review of sentencing took place in South Australia (South Australia, Criminal Law and Penal Methods Reform Committee [Mitchell Committee] 1973) but did not bear fruit until 1988, when it appeared in a greatly attenuated form in the *Criminal Procedure (Sentencing) Act* 1988 ("SA"). More influential in sentencing policy, although not in practice, was a comprehensive inquiry into sentencing undertaken by the Australian Law Reform Commission (Australian Law Reform Commission 1988). Although the federal government plays only a small part in the administration of criminal justice in Australia, the eight-year inquiry helped shape the sentencing debate. It identified a long list of problems: "lack of sentencing policy; lack of guidance as to criteria for determining sentence; lack of guidance in relation to the procedure for determining sentence; unsatisfactory penalty structure and lack of satisfactory rules as to sanction choice; lack of sentencing information; early conditional release; excessive use of imprisonment as a sanction; under utilization of noncustodial options; unwarranted disparity; [and poor] public perceptions of the sentencing process" (Zdenkowski 1994, p. 192).

The commission's final report, delivered in 1988, precipitated a number of changes to federal legislation, not all of which were in accordance with its recommendations. The changes, however, are relatively minor—concerning parole release and eligibility and some specification of factors courts should consider in sentencing—and do not constitute an integrated package. They failed to remedy the problems the commission identified, have made federal sentencing law unduly complicated and opaque, and have generated further calls for change.

New South Wales

No lengthy inquiries preceded New South Wales's sentencing reform. In 1989, responding to "law and order" concerns, Parliament abolished remissions (good time) in the name of "truth in sentencing." Together with a direction that the nonparole period must be two-thirds of the sentence imposed, and in the absence of a binding legislative direction to the courts to reduce sentence lengths to compensate for the abolition of remissions, the result was a rapid increase of 47 percent in prison population, from 4,369 in 1988–89 to 6,117 in October of 1993. Truth in sentencing in New South Wales came to mean longer sentences, rather than a sentencing system in which the time served by offenders more closely reflected the sentence imposed by the courts.

Victoria

The background to sentencing reform in Victoria has been set out in a previous article (Freiberg 1993). The reforms outlined briefly there, and in more detail elsewhere (Freiberg 1994), have partially influenced the development of sentencing legislation in other jurisdictions. The *Sentencing Act 1991* (Vic) provided for abolition of remission but—unlike its New South Wales predecessor—directed judges thereafter to reduce sentence lengths to adjust for absence of remission. Judges by and large complied, and the prison population held steady.

Queensland

In 1992, four years after an extensive examination of the prison system, Queensland comprehensively recast its sentencing legislation by enacting a new *Penalties and Sentences Act*. Adopting a similar structure to the *Sentencing Act* 1991 (Vic), it consolidates the sentencing powers of the court in one act. It provides for a range of identified "intermediate" orders, including probation orders, community service orders, and a new order, the intensive correction order. The intensive correction order is modeled on a similar Victorian sanction that filled a perceived gap between imprisonment and community service. This order is intended to replace short terms of imprisonment (up to one year) with intensive community service work, counseling, and possibly residence in community residential facilities for treatment for periods of up to a week. In Victoria, this order has had little impact, primarily because the resources required to support its rehabilitative component have not been provided. Though drawing its clientele from the potential prison population, thus fulfilling its role as a diversionary device, the intensive nature of the supervision and the onerousness of its community work provisions have resulted in a relatively high failure rate (30–40 percent).

Both the Queensland and the Victorian acts codify the general common law sentencing principles, identified as imposition of just punishment, deterrence, rehabilitation, denunciation, and protection of the community. No priorities among principles are established.

Queensland's legislation differed in one significant way from the Victorian legislation. It contained a provision allowing for indefinite sentences to be imposed on violent offenders. This concept was imported into Victorian law in 1993 by the newly elected conservative government and, together with other measures to deal with serious violent and sexual offenders, marked a turnaround in Victorian sentencing policy.

Northern Territory

Victoria's influence is also noticeable in a major piece of sentencing legislation that was put before the Parliament of the Northern Territory prior to an election in June 1994 that saw a conservative government returned to office. The *Sentencing Bill*, part of a law, order, and public safety campaign, combined the form and structure of the Victorian and the Queensland statutes with even "tougher" innovations, including fixed nonparole periods for sex offenders (70 percent of the term of imprisonment), the abolition of remissions with no compensatory changes in sentence length, and the introduction of indefinite sentences for violent offenders. The bill did not pass but is expected to be reintroduced with even more stringent measures, such as mandatory imprisonment for repeat offenders.

Prison Populations

Australia's prison population is low relative to that of the United States. In April 1994 the average imprisonment rate was 86.2 per 100,000 of the total population, or 114 per 100,000 of the adult population (17 years of age and over). These average figures, however, mask great variations among the states (see table 3.1).

These variations can be attributed to a number of factors. The Northern Territory and Western Australia have larger Aboriginal populations, which, in turn, have a very high imprisonment rate. In the Northern Territory, the imprisonment rate is 1,431 per 100,000 of the Aboriginal population. The Territory's population is also more masculine and more youthful than those in other jurisdictions (Walker 1994, p. 23). In Western Australia, approximately 35 percent of prisoners are Aboriginal, although Aborigines make up only 2.7 percent of the general population. Another important factor is the rate of imprisonment for fine default. Although fine defaulters represent only a small percentage of prisoners in custody at any one time, in some jurisdictions they make up a large proportion of prison receptions. In 1993, fine defaulters made up 41 percent of total prisoners received in prison in South Australia, 40 percent in Western Australia and Tasmania, 28 percent in New South Wales, 26 percent in the Northern Territory, 18 percent in Queensland, and only 7 percent in Victoria.

The variations, however, cannot be attributed to differences in crime rates or to different offense profiles. Victoria's historically low imprisonment rate relative to those in other Australian states and, indeed, in the rest of the world can be attributed to a number of features of its sentencing policy: an extensive range of noncustodial options that are well supported by the courts; a successful suspended sentence option, particularly for first offenders; the reluctance of the courts to impose imprisonment in default of fines and for breach of intermediate sanctions; limited use of short terms of imprisonment, resulting in low prison reception rates; and restrained use of very long or indefinite sentences of imprisonment.

Overall, in Australia, imprisonment is used sparingly. In Victoria, for example, in 1993, in the higher courts that deal with only 5 percent of criminal cases, sentences of imprisonment constituted only half the sentences imposed, with suspended sentences of imprisonment, introduced in 1986, accounting for nearly 30 percent of sentences. Intermediate sanctions make up 10 percent of sentences and lower-order sanctions, such as bonds and fines, another 10 percent. In the magistrates' courts, which sentence 90 percent of all offenders, more than 50 percent

Table 3.1. Australian Prison Populations, April 1994

Jurisdiction	Daily Average Population	Rate per 100,000 Adult Population	Rate per 100,000 Total Population
Northern Territory	484	414.9	286.1
Western Australia	2,062	163.4	121.7
New South Wales	6,354	138.5	105.0
South Australia	1,268	112.4	86.5
Queensland	2,406	101.0	75.6
Victoria	2,431	71.3	54.3
Tasmania	245	69.5	51.8

Source: Australian Institute of Criminology (1994).

of offenses are dealt with through lower-order sanctions, such as fines and bonds, with imprisonment accounting for around 13 percent of sentences. Here, as in the higher courts, the suspended sentence has occupied an important sentencing space, diverting offenders not only from imprisonment but also from intermediate sanctions such as the community-based order.

Until recently, in Victoria, the general judicial and political ethos was that imprisonment was a necessary and expensive evil, the use of which was to be a very last resort. However, that ethos has withered in the face of increasing public fear of crime, a fear that is paradoxically rising as the general crime rate falls.

Recent Changes in Sentencing Policy

Sentencing policy in Australia has historically been governed by the concept of proportionality. However, proportionality, or just deserts, is conceived of as setting the general outer limits of punishment, rather than determining the exact type and precise quantity of the sanction. The policy has been affirmed on numerous occasions by the High Court of Australia as a primary sentencing consideration, and the recently introduced statutory codifications of principles in Victoria, Queensland and, most recently, in Western Australia ("A sentence imposed on an offender shall be commensurate with the seriousness of the offence") are regarded as merely legislative recognition of what was decided by the High Court.

Principles of proportionality have also found their way into new juvenile justice legislation, previously dominated by considerations of welfare. Thus, Queensland's *Juvenile Justice Act* 1992 requires that there be a "fitting proportion between sentence and offence" and contains an ordered sanctioning hierarchy to assist in calibrating offenses and penalties.

However, these developments are counterbalanced by other measures. In some jurisdictions, for limited classes of offenses, courts are required to have regard primarily to "the protection of the community" as the principal purpose of sentencing and may, in order to achieve that purpose, impose a sentence *longer* than that which is proportionate to the gravity of the offense. Proportion gives way to prophylaxis.

Preventive sentences are not unknown in Australia. Habitual-offender provisions existed in the statute books of most jurisdictions but fell into desuetude in recent decades. Their revival or transformation into "dangerous" or "violent" offender laws is now a feature of most sentencing regimes, including juvenile justice statutes (see *Crime [Serious and Repeat] Offenders Sentencing Act* 1992 [WA]). Based on past crimes or predictions of future offending, or their combination, these laws have, as yet, been little used. However, they represent a significant, symbolic, and temptingly expandable inroad into the hitherto sacrosanct concept of proportionality. As courts are increasingly induced, or coerced, to use preventive sentences, warehoused offenders will make up a greater proportion of the stock of prisoners. Although baseball is but a minor sport in Australia, the notion of "three strikes and you're out" is becoming a familiar refrain in conservative circles.

A process of conflating the concepts of proportion and prevention is under way. Longer sentences are more deserved, it is sometimes said, because previous scales of punishment were unduly lenient and are manifestly inadequate for modern notions of desert that more closely reflect the punitiveness of the populace, rather than the theorizing of criminologists, sentencing commissions, or, indeed, the judiciary. Longer sentences are also more incapacitative, and possibly deterrent. Hence, such sentences are sought for a wider range of offenses.

The pressure to increase sentence length is manifested in moves to increase statutory maximum penalties, court-imposed sentences, and the actual time served by prisoners. Increasing statutory maxima have long been the first response to crises in criminal justice, and this has indeed occurred in a number of jurisdictions. In particular, penalties for sex offenses and offenses against children have been increased in response to pressures by victims' lobbies and some women's groups. In Victoria, in particular, the courts have responded by significantly increasing the length of sentences imposed on such offenders. This may also have the unintended (or perhaps intended) effect of raising sentences across the board in order to maintain some semblance of internal consistency in the judicial sentencing scale.

Another technique by which sentence length can be increased is by requiring courts to cumulate sentences for multiple offending. Principles of totality, proportionality, and rehabilitation are made subservient to the notion that each offense must be justly, proportionately, and manifestly punished. In part, this development is an outgrowth of the victims' movement, sections of which regard concurrent sentences as a denial of justice to individual victims.

Longer sentences can also be brought about by the abolition of remissions. As noted, New South Wales and Victoria did so some years ago, Queensland and South Australia have recently followed suit, and the Northern Territory is likely soon to do so, usually without adjustment of the sentence imposed by the courts.

In my 1993 *Overcrowded Times* article (Freiberg 1993), I indicated that the Victorian prison population had remained stable after remission was abolished. This occurred in part because Section 10 of the *Sentencing Act 1991* (Vic) directed judges to reduce sentences to take account of the absence of remission and thereby to provide that offenders' actual time in prison would not be increased compared with time served by comparable offenders during the period when remission was available. Since that time, however, the situation has deteriorated markedly.

A decision by the Supreme Court of Victoria in 1994, subsequently upheld by the High Court of Australia, threw the operation of Section 10 of the *Sentencing Act* 1991 (Vic) into doubt. Its effect was that Section 10 was only applicable to offenses whose maximum penalty had not changed. Because the *Sentencing Act* 1991 (Vic) has altered most maxima as part of a major rationalization of the penalty structure, Section 10 was effectively rendered nugatory. As a result of this decision, and also of pressure from government, victims' groups, and the media for longer sentences, the Victorian prison population increased from around 2,200 in early 1993 to approximately 2,500 in mid-1994. Victoria's experience now resembles that of New South Wales.

The response of government to increasing prison populations in Australia is to build new prisons, preferably private ones. In 1989, there were no private prisons in Australia. In 1994, Queensland had two, and New South Wales two. Within two years, Victoria will have three private facilities housing over half the total (and growing) prison population. Other states are actively considering this option. In a short time, Australia will probably have the highest proportion of private prisoners in the world. The modern discourse is about prison management and fiscal responsibility, not about penal philosophy. Apparently, reduction in prison use is no longer a major political aim. Prison populations can be larger, so long as the prisons are cheaper and more efficient.

The trend away from a focus on just disposition of individual cases and toward a focus on efficient management and economy is also evident in other aspects of court administration. In Victoria, guilty pleas, particularly early pleas, are encouraged by legislation that permits courts to discount sentences on account of such conduct.

In New South Wales, plea bargaining has now been formalized by the introduction of "sentence indication hearings" that permit accused persons to appear before a judge, even before entering a plea, to obtain an indication of the sentence that they would be likely to receive if they plead guilty. The accused person is able to change his or her mind as to the plea and to opt for a trial.

Future Directions

New South Wales is Australia's most populous state and goes to the polls in March 1995. In January 1994, the government instituted an inquiry into sentencing reform that produced an issues paper later that year (see New South Wales, Attorney-General's Department, *Sentencing Review* 1994). The government's stated aim was to finetune, rather than dramatically overhaul, its sentencing legislation and to strengthen its commitment to truth in sentencing legislation.

Reflecting developments elsewhere in Australia, the reform agenda included the consolidation of legislation; codification of sentencing principles; rationalization of sanctions; introduction of a sanction hierarchy; strengthening of habitual-criminal legislation; the desirability of an American-style sentencing grid to provide consistency in sentences of imprisonment; the need for a Sentencing Policy Advisory Council; strengthening of the power of the Court of Criminal Appeal to issue sentencing guideline judgments; and recognition of the need for minimum sentences and for a wider range of intermediate sanctions, in particular, an intensive correction order.

Queensland, also facing an election within the next year or so, sees all political parties vying for the "tougher-than-thou" crown. Proposed revisions to its criminal code contain many increases in maximum penalties, with many carrying life imprisonment. Plans are afoot to build a superjail to hold intractable prisoners, and the state is adding another 500 cells to the prison system to cope with overcrowding and to cater to expected increases resulting from longer sentences and the abolition of remissions.

Even in advance of implementation of these policies, prison numbers increased by approximately 200 in two months, to 2,627 in June 1994.

Conclusion

Sentencing reform in Australia over the past five years reflects sharply disparate policies. On the one hand there has been the move to consolidate, articulate, and rationalize sentencing laws. The modern Australian sentencing statute contains statements of principle and some guidance to sentencers and stipulates the range of sanctions, how they are to be used, and what should happen in the event of breach. Sentencing policies should provide a rational maximum penalty structure, an internally consistent penalty scale, and a coherent set of relationships between the forms of sanctions. Many of the statutes recently introduced contain these elements.

On the other hand, the inherently political character of sentencing policymaking engenders ad hocery and irrationality. Harshness replaces hope, retribution displaces rehabilitation, and prevention erodes proportionality. The constituency of legislators and judges is changing. The state of prisons is of less concern than the state of the victim's health. The victim impact statement comes to carry more weight than the presentence report. The delicate sentencing balance among the interests of the offender, the state, and the victim is shifting away from the first two and toward the third. In sum, the greater sensitivity to the rights and interests of victims and the protection of the community in general is being reflected in more severe sentences.

Sentencing reform builds on the economics of fear. The most recent reforms represent a poverty of the political and criminological imagination. They confirm the observation that in Australia, at least, "rates of imprisonment tend to increase during periods of conservative government and tend to reduce during periods of Labor governments" (Walker 1994, p. 26).

As these negative policies fail to "control" crime, as they have failed to do wherever they have been tried, the calls for harsher penalties will likely increase, resulting in the imposition of even more punitive and ineffective sentences. The perverse result of these policies will be a cycle of repression in which crime will increase, rather than decrease. Then, a new round of sentencing reform may again begin, searching again for ways to empty the overcrowded prisons and deal with offenders in more humane and positive ways.

Prison Populations Up, Sentencing Policy Harsher in Australia
(February 1998)
  Arie Freiberg

Australian prisons and jails in September 1997 held 17,667 prisoners, an increase of 6,170, or 54 percent, over 1986 figures. The imprisonment rate increased by 29 percent, from 92.9 per 100,000 of the adult population to 120 per 100,000 adults.

Although this increase is not as spectacular as those that have occurred in the United Kingdom and in the United States, it is, nonetheless a predictable outcome of the globalization of the punitive polices currently in vogue in those jurisdictions. As a net importer of penal culture, Australia has lagged behind both the United

States and the United Kingdom only in the timing and scope of its penal policy, but not in its direction.

Incarceration Rates

Figure 3.1,, which shows imprisonment rates for the period 1983–1997 for all the Australian states and territories, reveals a complex picture of regional variation.

Between 1986 and 1997, the New South Wales imprisonment rate jumped from 95 per 100,000 adults to 132.2 (39 percent); most of the increase occurred between 1988 and 1992 following the abolition of good time and a restructuring of the method by which prison sentences are imposed by the courts (see Freiberg

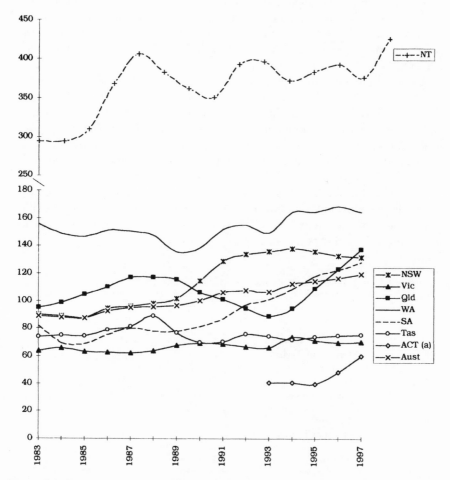

Figure 3.1. Imprisonment Rates, 1983–1997 (prisoners per 100,000 adults). *Note*: The ACT rate included ACT sentenced prisoners held in NSW prisons. Comparable data for the ACT were available only on a financial-year basis and for 1992–1993. *Source*: Steering Committee (1998).

1997). Steadier but more consistent increases occurred in South Australia, from 75.4 per 100,000 adults in 1986 to 128.5 in 1997 (70.4 percent), and in Queensland, from 110.3 per 100,000 adults to 137.6 (24.7 percent), although in the latter state the rate dipped to 89 per 100,000 adults in 1993, making the increase 54.6 percent in a period of four years.

Jurisdictions with historically high imprisonment rates, namely Western Australia and the Northern Territory, remain so, with increases of 8.9 percent and 16 percent, respectively, while those with historically low rates, Victoria and Tasmania, showed small increases or decreases: a 12.4 percent increase in Victoria and a 4.5 percent decrease in Tasmania.

Between 1986 and 1996, the nature of Australian prison populations changed (Australian Bureau of Statistics 1997). The average age of prisoners rose from 29.9 years to 31.8 years, the proportion of prisoners age 25 years or less decreased from 36.5 percent to 28.6 percent, and the proportion of female prisoners rose from 4.8 percent to 5.3 percent. Sex offenses increased from 9.1 percent of offenses by most serious offense category to 13.6 percent, as did assaults, from 5.9 percent to 12 percent. Property offenses, however, declined.

Table 3.2 presents Australian prison populations as of September 1997 and the rates per 100,000 of the adult population for the year 1996–97. The reasons for these variations are complex. The number of indigenous persons in a jurisdiction and the indigenous imprisonment rate are certainly contributing factors. According to the Australian Bureau of Statistics (1997), the average rate of indigenous imprisonment in Australia was 1,576 per 100,000 adult indigenous population. Aboriginal offenders make up 70 percent of the Northern Territory prison population, 33 percent of the Western Australian prison population, and 26.6 percent of the Queensland population, but only 4.6 percent of the Victorian prison population. Crime rates also vary across jurisdictions, but these differences are not sufficient to account for the differences in imprisonment rates. Nor, would it seem, do the

Table 3.2. Australian Prison Populations, 1997

Jurisdiction	Daily Average Population	Rate per 100,000 Adults
New South Wales	6,385	132.2
Victoria	2,643	70.6
Queensland	3,987	137.6
South Australia	1,480	128.5
Western Australia	2,244	165.0
Tasmania	267	75.6
Northern Territory	629	427.7
ACT	112	60.6
Australia	17,667	120.0

Notes: ACT = Australian Capital Territory; rate based on average daily prisoner numbers 1996–97; daily average population as of September 1997.

Source: Australian Bureau of Statistics (1997).

differences in sentencing legislation or the sentencing options available to the courts.

Sentencing Legislation

Since 1991, five states or territories have comprehensively overhauled their sentencing statutes: *Sentencing Act 1991* (Victoria); *Penalties and Sentences Act 1992* (Queensland); *Sentencing Act 1995* (Northern Territory); *Sentencing Act 1995* (Western Australia); and *Sentencing Act 1997* (Tasmania). South Australia has recently embarked on the process once again, after significant reforms in 1988 (*Criminal Law Sentencing Act 1988*) (SA), while New South Wales is considering new legislation following a comprehensive report from its Law Reform Commission (1996).

Much of this legislation is in the nature of consolidation, rather than codification. Though the statutory underpinnings of sentencing law have become better defined, the underlying dynamic is that of the common law: judges and their discretion remain at the center of the process. In this respect, none of the changes has been as radical as those in the United States. No jurisdiction has countenanced the introduction of numerical sentencing guidelines, although they have been much discussed. Guideline judgments are possible under the Western Australian legislation, but courts have been reluctant to make them.

The statutory enunciation of the purposes of sentencing has occurred in Victoria, Queensland, and the Northern Territory, but, for the general run of cases, the legislation declares that no one purpose is paramount. Nor have the courts resolved the dilemmas of conflicting purposes, and the common law remains unclear. In the main, proportionality remains the bedrock principle, reaffirmed a number of times by the High Court of Australia.

Sex Offender Legislation

However, the enunciation of the aims has encouraged some legislatures to seize on one purpose, that of the "protection of the community," to justify special measures against various classes of offenders, such as the violent or dangerous and especially the sex offender. These measures, which include indefinite sentences, cumulative sentences, and increased maximum penalties, are becoming increasingly popular with politicians, although the courts remain skeptical, if not antipathetic. An attempt by the New South Wales ("NSW") government to legislate to allow the imprisonment of a single dangerous offender following civil proceedings, without the need for charges to be laid, was struck down by the High Court (see *Community Protection Act 1994* [NSW] and *Kable* [1996] 138 A.L.R. 577). The legislation was enacted just prior to his release from a long term of imprisonment after fears had been raised about his potential for future violence.

Queensland introduced provisions for indefinite sentences for serious violent or sex offenders in 1992, but to date no such sentences have been imposed. Victoria emulated these provisions in 1993, and to date only three offenders have been subjected to them. Though the laws are highly symbolic, their practical effect has been extremely limited, and they cannot be said to have contributed to the rising rates of imprisonment.

Mandatory Penalties

Measures with greater potential for increasing imprisonment rates are those that remove the discretion of the courts, in particular those that seem to draw their inspiration from American-style "three-strikes" legislation. In New South Wales, the recent *Crimes Amendment (Mandatory Life Sentences) Act 1996* (NSW) provides for mandatory life sentences in certain cases of murder and trafficking in commercial quantities of heroin or cocaine. More powerful, and objectionable, however, are mandatory provisions recently introduced in the Northern Territory ("NT") and in Western Australia ("WA"), both under conservative governments that already boast the highest imprisonment rates in Australia.

In the former jurisdiction, amendments to the *Sentencing Act 1995* (NT) and the *Juvenile Justice Act 1983* (NT) introduced in 1996 what effectively amounted to "one-strike" legislation (Flynn 1997). The legislation requires a court to impose a mandatory minimum term for persons convicted of a range of property offenses: 14 days for adult first offenders, 90 days for an adult with one prior property conviction, and 12 months for an adult with two or more prior property convictions. A juvenile (15–17 years old) with one or more prior property convictions must be sentenced to 28 days in a detention center. In March 1997, the Northern Territory government allocated $A3 million for 140 new prisons (Flynn 1997).

In Western Australia, 10 days after the *Sentencing Act 1995* (WA) came into force, the *Criminal Code Amendment Act (No 2) 1996* (WA) introduced provisions that require the courts to impose a mandatory 12-month prison sentence on a person classified as a repeat offender. This legislation, which was designed to deal with a spate of "home invasions," is directed at offenders with at least one prior conviction for burglary and is expected to increase the number of juveniles and adults in the prison system, particularly indigenous offenders (Morgan 1996). It follows earlier legislation to the same effect, the *Crimes (Serious and Repeat Offenders) Sentencing Act 1992* (WA), which Harding and his colleagues have condemned as a failure (Harding 1995).

Alternative Sanctions

Other American-style innovations, such as boot camps, have been tried in Western Australia and failed (Atkinson 1995; Newman 1996). Intensive supervision orders, home detention, and electronic monitoring are in various stages of development around the country but capture little of the sentencing market. Intermediate sanctions such as bonds, fines, probation, and community service still form the bulk of noncustodial sanctions and are extensively used in the lower courts. According to recent figures, Australian prisons held 24 percent of all offenders under some form of penal order and absorbed 89 percent of recurrent expenditures, whereas community supervision sanctions accounted for 73 percent of penal orders and took 10 percent of recurrent expenditures (Steering Committee 1998, p. 409).

One sanction that has seen a revival in recent years is the suspended sentence.

In Victoria, since it was introduced in 1985, the suspended sentence has captured nearly one-third of the sentencing market in the higher courts and about 5–6 percent in the lower courts. It has been estimated that about half of those cases represent diversion from imprisonment, although the net diversion, after breach, may be less (Tait 1995). Similar provisions have now been introduced in Western Australia, the Northern Territory, and Tasmania and have been recommended for introduction in New South Wales, but it remains to be seen whether after the implementation of these sentences they can duplicate their success in Victoria or will follow the more punitive ethos that appears to permeate those jurisdictions.

Conclusion

Although the Australian states' legislation has become increasingly similar, the persistent differences in imprisonment rates among them have remained. The recent wave of sentencing legislation has created converging frameworks, but ever more diverging practices. Thus, Queensland, which enacted a sentencing Act very similar to Victoria's, has seen a massive rise in the number of prisoners, while Victoria's rise has been quite uneven. And, although Western Australia and the Northern Territory also have legislated in similar fashion, they will continue to see rates of imprisonment far higher than those elsewhere in Australia. Sentencing law and sentencing practice appear to be coupled only loosely.

Although conclusive data are not available, it appears that sentence lengths are slowly increasing, in particular in relation to those offenses over which there have been recent moral panics: sex offenses generally, sexual abuse of children, drunken driving, culpable driving causing death, domestic violence, and drugs. Sentencing has become more bifurcated: fewer but more serious offenders are being imprisoned for longer periods of time.

In all but one Australian jurisdiction, conservative governments are in power. The post-Keynsian world of neoliberalism, with its emphasis on economic and political individualism, its dismantling of welfare institutions, and its promotion of the market and managerialism, has produced a changed penal ethos, away from interventionism and rehabilitation and toward individual responsibility and retribution (O'Malley 1994).

Law and order and community protection are the watchwords of penal policy, and it is to these intangible, though perceptible, factors, rather than to the formal structures of the criminal law or sentencing statutes, to which one must look to explain the steadily increasing overcrowding of Australian prisons (see Young and Brown 1993, p. 38).

Understanding Rising Prison Populations in Australia
(October 1999)
  Arie Freiberg

For the first time in more than a decade, Australian press reports are dominated by stories of overcrowded prisons, riots, disturbances, and emergency measures to deal with facilities stretched beyond their design capacities. Prisoners are reported to be sleeping on floors and portable beds. In Western Australia, prisoners are being housed in steel shipping containers fitted out as maximum security cells. Increased rates of violence, suicides, and self-mutilation are being reported. In New South Wales and Victoria, prisons that have been closed as being too old and unsuitable are being recommissioned. New prison projects, both public and private, are announced in response to burgeoning prison populations that are the product of more than a decade of government initiatives designed to produce this result.

In other words, the trends noted in previous reports in *Overcrowded Times* (Freiberg 1995, 1998) have continued unabated and, if anything, have been accentuated. While crime rates show no signs of the downward trends reported in the United States, their fluctuations, which vary across jurisdictions, bear little relationship to changes in imprisonment rates.

Table 3.3 shows the changes that have occurred in Australian prison populations over the past three years. Overall, the number of prisoners has increased by 14 percent and the incarceration rate by 18 percent (to 141 per 100,000) during that period.

These official data, which are available to March 1999, do not fully reflect some of the rapid changes taking place in some states. Later, nonofficial reports place the New South Wales prison population at around 7,300 and the Victorian numbers as topping 3,000. Only one state, South Australia, has shown a decline in numbers.

Driving Prison Numbers Higher

There is no one single factor that can be singled out as being primarily responsible for the steady but significant increase in Australian prison numbers. Although the

Table 3.3. Australian Prison Populations, 1997–1999

Jurisdiction	Daily Average Population 1997	Rate per 100,000 Adults 1997	Daily Average Population March 1999 (% change)		Rate per 100,000 Adults March 1999 (% change)	
New South Wales	6,385	132	6,900	(8%)	144	(9%)
Victoria	2,643	71	2,840	(7%)	79	(11%)
Queensland	3,987	138	5,164	(30%)	197	(43%)
South Australia	1,480	128	1,379	(−7%)	121	(−5%)
Western Australia	2,244	165	2,851	(27%)	209	(27%)
Tasmania	267	76	317	(19%)	89	(17%)
Northern Territory	629	428	640	(2%)	476	(11%)
ACT	112	61	121	(8%)	52	(−15%)
Australia	17,667	120	20,122	(14%)	141	(18%)

Note: ACT = Australian Capital Territory.

Source: Australian Bureau of Statistics, Corrective Services (June 1999).

level of crime differs between states, as does the mix of offenses, there is no evidence of increases concomitant with the increases in the prison populations. The Australian Bureau of Statistics data for nine major crime categories show that between 1997 and 1998, the Australian crime rate increased from 6,719 per 100,000 of the adult population in 1997 to 6,965 in 1998, an increase of 3.7 percent. Population growth has also been small. Levels of violent crime, which make up only a small proportion of overall crime rates, have increased marginally in a number of jurisdictions, but not sufficiently to explain the changes in incarceration rates. Rather, the explanation is to be found in the courts' reaction to legislative signals and calls for "tougher" penalties and sentences. Popular pressure, through newspaper coverage, talk-back radio (the "shock jocks"), and opinion polls, remains unabated.

Signals in the former category include increased statutory maximum penalties, statutory changes in the aims of sentencing to favor incapacitative sentences, the introduction of indefinite, mandatory, and minimum sentences (Bayes 1999; Hogg 1999), a requirement that some sentences be cumulative rather than concurrent, and an emphasis on the rights and interests of victims of crime in the sentencing process.

But it is not the "headline" statutory changes, that is, those that appear the "toughest" or most egregious, that have most affected prison numbers. Very few indefinite sentences have been imposed in those jurisdictions in which they are available. Judges remain averse to sentences that fundamentally breach proportionality principles. Mandatory and minimum sentences are rare. Even in the Northern Territory, which has made the most extensive use of them and which has the highest imprisonment rate in Australia, their overall impact appears to be surprisingly marginal, with prison numbers increasing by only 2 percent over the past three years. This may be because most such sentences are short, so that while the number of receptions has increased, daily average numbers in custody are not substantially affected.

Rather, prison populations appear to be driven by a combination of small, subtle, but ultimately important responses. This was the finding of a preliminary report of the Queensland Criminal Justice Commission (1990a), which examined the increase in that state's prison population (30 percent over the past three years and 116 percent over the past six years). The factors identified can be applied variously across Australia, but not all factors apply equally in all jurisdictions and some not at all.

One contributing factor is the increase in the total proportion of persons sentenced by courts who receive a prison sentence, especially in the higher courts. In New South Wales ("NSW"), for example, the proportion of persons sentenced to prison by these courts increased from 50.7 in 1993–94 to 62.6 in 1997–98 (NSW Bureau of Crime Statistics and Research 1999). The increased use of imprisonment is reflected in the growth in the number of admissions, with Queensland showing an annual average growth rate of 14 percent since 1993. Short-term sentences (less than one year) have increased and represent 80 percent of admissions in Queensland, compared with 65 percent in 1993. Victoria also reports an increase in the number of sentences of less than six months. These trends may reflect a loss of confidence in community sentences and may also emphasize the short, sharp, symbolic shock of the prison sentence to the community. Young offenders are less likely to receive leniency in sentencing. In Victoria, traditionally one of the least punitive jurisdictions, there has been a large increase in the number of young offenders ordered to serve custodial sentences: more than 200 more than the previous year. This has resulted in increased pressure on juvenile justice facilities and in calls for new detention centers.

In New South Wales, average sentence lengths (for minimum, nonparole periods) in respect of sentences imposed by the higher courts increased by 11 percent between 1993 and 1998 (from 26.3 months to 29.2 months). Similar trends are emerging in Victoria in relation to a range of offenses to which the public are particularly sensitive: culpable driving, sex offenses, aggravated burglaries, incest, and the like. Offenses related to substance abuse feature prominently in public discourse with ambivalent responses by policymakers. Australian politicians, the public, and the courts vacillate between harm minimization and law enforcement approaches. Two states, New South Wales and South Australia, are experimenting with drug courts.

Even where nominal sentence lengths have not increased, abolition of remissions (good time) in most jurisdictions without concomitant decreases in sentence lengths has resulted in increased duration of custody. Nervous or sensitive parole or early-release boards are setting more stringent criteria for release and are more ready to revoke parole. Similarly, community corrections authorities, aware of the public impact of offenses committed by offenders under sentence, appear more willing to revoke offenders' parole for conduct that might previously have been ignored or dealt with administratively. Courts that deal with those breaches are less likely to return offenders to the community if that would be seen to diminish the community's confidence in community-based orders. In Queensland, the numbers imprisoned for "enforcement of orders" doubled between 1992–93 and 1997–98.

Decreasing government and communal tolerance of offenses committed on bail has led in some jurisdictions to tightening of bail conditions and a growth in the number of unsentenced prisoners held in custody. Remand in custody rates per 100,000 of adult population vary between 12.7 in Victoria to 80.3 in the Northern Territory, with an Australian average of 22.7 (Australian Bureau of Statistics 1999). Imprisonment for fine default also varies widely between jurisdictions, with Queensland holding an average of 247 offenders in March 1999 compared with Victoria's five.

Sentencing Policies

The wave of legislative sentencing reform designed to get tough on crime that commenced in the late 1980s appears to have run its course. Governmental action is now focused on dealing with the crises in the prisons, managing the introduction of private-sector provision of correctional services, and forecasting and paying for correctional populations.

As noted, courts' responses have been relatively subtle and incremental. However, some courts have recognized the symbolic dimensions of the potential loss of confidence in their role and have attempted to take a proactive role in winning back the ground lost to activist sentencing parliaments. The New South Wales Court of Criminal Appeal, under its recently installed Chief Justice Jim Spigelman, has introduced guideline judgments, a move that he has described as a "significant development . . . with respect to the exercise of discretion by sentencing judges" (Spigelman 1999). To date, guidelines have been handed down in respect of two offenses, culpable driving (*Jurisic* [1998] 45 NSWLR 209) and armed robbery (*Henry* [1999] NSWCCA 111), both of which signaled upward movements in the tariff.

In a recent address to judges, the chief justice argued that guidelines were necessary to deal with two major problems that had been identified but not properly addressed by the courts: inconsistency and systemic excessive leniency. Thus, in *Jurisic*, it was the court of criminal appeal's view that primary sentencing courts had not responded to parliamentary and appellate court signals for a sharp upward movement in sentences. In addition, differently constituted courts of appeal had been inconsistent in their judgments, thereby failing to provide clear leadership to courts further down the hierarchy.

The chief justice also acknowledged that one of the purposes of such judgments was to reinforce public confidence in the administration of justice. The perceived decline in public confidence in the courts in New South Wales required a curial response. The judgments, which received wide media coverage, contained a large element of public education: they were not only statements about appropriate levels of sentences but also a reaffirmation that courts were responsive to public concerns.

In reaction to *Jurisic*, the New South Wales Parliament legislated a new provision (*Criminal Procedure Act* 1986 [NSW], s.26[2]), which allows the attorney general to apply to the court of criminal appeal to give a guideline judgment in respect of a specified indictable offense or a category of indictable offenses. The court, however, is not obliged to lay one down, even if requested to do so.

The New South Wales experience can be contrasted with that of Western Australia, where the appellate court had legislative power to make guideline judgments but had not done so. The government passed legislation in 1998 to introduce a "sentencing matrix," in effect the beginning of a numerical guidelines regime. It is intended to make the sentencing process clearer, more consistent, and more understandable to the public and, ultimately, to give Parliament more control over sentences imposed by the courts. Courts are to be made more "accountable" to Parliament through a system of information gathering, publication of benchmark sentences, and legislative prescription of "presumed" sentences, deviation from which will create an automatic right of appeal (Morgan and Murray 1999). The chief justice, on behalf of supreme and district court judges, formally condemned the introduction of matrix sentences through his annual report, which was tabled in Parliament. Constitutional challenges to the right of Parliament to order imposition of minimum or mandatory penalties have failed.

The dialogue between courts and parliaments continues in Australia. No state has yet introduced legislatively binding numerical guidelines, and judicial guidelines are not formally binding. Judicial discretion still remains at the core of Australian sentencing.

The Broader Picture

Professor Anthony Bottoms, of Cambridge University, recently argued that increasing social insecurity provides one explanation for the increasing penal severity expressed in more and longer sentences and in increases in imprisonment rates. As social and economic certainties erode, particularly for the older members of the community, they seek solace in tougher laws (Bottoms 1995, p. 47; see also Freiberg and Ross 1999). Politicians are adept at tapping into these fears and argue that legislative "get-tough" responses to the often inarticulate concerns of the electorate are examples of "democracy at work" (Beckett 1997b, p. 8).

In their study of public support for punitive policies such as the "three-strikes" laws in California, Tyler and Boeckmann (1997) found that such initiatives were part of a wider move to support the removal of discretionary authority from the courts, signaling a repudiation of legal authority more generally. General confidence in legal and political authority seems to be waning, leading to greater support for nonlegal means of dealing with crime or for reducing the role and scope of courts' discretion. Support for three-strikes laws was not related to judgments about the future dangerousness of offenders as much as to moral cohesion. In other words, the instrumental effects of sentencing policy, that is, reducing the rate of crime or the chances of being victimized, were less important than judgments about social conditions: concern over the decline of social institutions such as the family, the lack of a moral and social consensus, the decline of social ties, and a discomfort with growing social and ethnic diversity. Their study suggests that declining moral cohesion leads to more punitive attitudes because people who are skeptical of the courts, of politics, and of society in general are also skeptical of the ability of social, welfare, and penal agencies to rehabilitate, integrate, or remoralize offenders.

Until recently, political imperatives have not been regarded as being part of the judicial decision-making process. But, as has been seen with the introduction of guideline judgments in New South Wales, courts feel responsible to, or see the need to be partly responsive to, public sentiment. The introduction of "matrix" sentences in Western Australia marks a new phase of overt and direct political control of judicial sentencing.

If there is an historical cycle (Tonry 1999b), Australia (increasing incarceration rates, increasing or steady crime rates) probably lags the United States (increasing incarceration rates, declining crime rates). If the American psyche eventually comes to terms with being a prosperous, low-unemployment, and low(er)-crime society, its punitive incarcerative binge may subside and imprisonment rates fall. As the United States carries Australia in its economic and cultural wake, growing prosperity and an increasing sense of personal and social security may relieve the pressure on courts and governments to deal firmly with offenders. In the interim, however, Australian times are becoming ever more overcrowded.

Canada

Reforming Sentencing and Parole in Canada (August 1999)
Julian V. Roberts

Three years have elapsed since Canada's Parliament passed the first sentencing reform bill in this country's history. We are now in position to draw some conclusions about the success of the statutory reforms of 1996. This brief article reviews developments in penal policy with respect to adult offenders.

A number of commissions of inquiry have examined sentencing and parole in recent years. Two in particular made a number of suggestions to reform sentencing, including the creation of a permanent sentencing commission and the adoption of sentencing guidelines. The federal government took considerable time in responding to the reports of these commissions before introducing its own reform proposals which became law in September 1996 (see Roberts and Cole 1999 for a review). The government rejected the notion of sentencing guidelines—even voluntary guidelines—and opted instead for a far more modest reform package.

Bill C-41 wrought two principal changes: a statement of the purposes and principles of sentencing was placed in the criminal code, and a new sanction, the conditional prison sentence, was created, with the explicit intention of reducing the number of sentenced admissions to custody.

Purpose and Principles

American sentencing guideline systems pay scant attention to the purposes that underlie sentencing. Most simply cite the most familiar purposes and then proceed to the mechanics of the sentencing grid. Canada, however, has witnessed a lively debate about the nature of punishment and the sentencing purposes that should be pursued by judges. The 1987 Canadian Sentencing Commission report produced a lengthy and thoughtful statement of purpose that was rejected by the government (Canadian Sentencing Commission 1987).

Instead, the government created its own statement, which has echoes of previous formulations, and placed this statement in the criminal code. According to section 718, the fundamental purpose of sentencing is to "contribute, along with crime prevention initiatives, to respect for the law and the maintenance of a just, peaceful and safe society *by imposing just sanctions*" (emphasis added). Section 718.1 contains a clear affirmation of proportionality in sentencing: "A sentence *must be proportionate* to the gravity of the offense and the degree of responsibility of the offender" (emphasis added; see the appendix to this article for the complete statement and Roberts and von Hirsch [1999] for further discussion).

While utilitarian considerations are present, taken as a whole, the statement is oriented towards desert-based sentencing. Note, however, that the list of utilitarian sentencing objectives includes a restorative justice element along with the more traditional punishment-oriented objectives such as deterrence and incapacitation.

Has the statement of purpose and principle affected sentencing patterns in trial courts? This is difficult to answer with confidence, because the scantiness of sentencing statistics in Canada prevents researchers from establishing whether sentences have become more uniform or whether sentencers have become more parsimonious in the use of incarceration. The statement has been cited in case law that has developed since 1996, which suggests that the judiciary may be following Parliament's direction. The statement has been cited frequently with reference to the second principal reform: the new conditional sentence of imprisonment.

The statement also contains a number of secondary sentencing principles. One, in section 718.2(e), is a clear admonition to judges considering the use of custody as a sanction: "all available sanctions other than imprisonment that are reasonable in the circumstances should be considered for all offenders, with particular attention to the circumstances of aboriginal offenders." Further, under section 718.2(d), "an offender should not be deprived of liberty, if less restrictive sanctions may be appropriate in the circumstances." These expressions of restraint in the use of incarceration are one way in which it was hoped that the sentencing reforms would reduce Canada's relatively high rate of incarceration.

Conditional Sentence of Imprisonment

Conditional sentencing in some form is an option in most common law jurisdictions. For example, in England and Wales it is called a suspended term of imprisonment. The concept is that a determinate sentence of custody is imposed, but its execution is immediately suspended. If the offender successfully completes the supervised sentence in the community, imprisonment is avoided.

The Canadian conditional sentence follows these general lines but contains features that stretch the credibility of conditional sentencing to the breaking point. According to section 742, if the offender was convicted of an offense that does not carry a minimum penalty and the judge has imposed a sentence of custody, is satisfied that serving the sentence in the community would not endanger the community, and is satisfied that the conditional sentence would be consistent with the purpose and principles of sentencing, the sentence of imprisonment can be served by the offender at home.

Reading this clause in conjunction with the provision that all alternatives to imprisonment should be used makes the paradox of the conditional sentence apparent: having determined that only incarceration will accomplish the goals of sentencing, a judge then decides whether the offender should be imprisoned. This paradoxical reasoning has generated considerable outcry from members of the public, politicians, victims' rights groups, and prosecutors. Much of this criticism was sparked by media accounts of serious crimes of violence for which the offender received a conditional sentence of imprisonment to be served in the community.

Critics have called for repeal of the conditional sentence or passage of amendments that would restrict its use to offenders convicted of nonviolent crimes. To date the government has rejected these demands. We now await the reaction of the Canadian Supreme Court, which heard six conditional sentence appeals in May 1999 and which will hand down what will in all probability be a guideline judgment later this year. (For further information, see Cole [1999].)

Has the conditional sentence had its stated effect of reducing the use of incarceration? Correctional admission statistics, which, unlike sentencing statistics, are published on an annual basis, suggest that introduction of the new sanction has had no discernible impact on the incarceration rate. The incarceration rate two years *after* creation of the new sentence was unchanged from the year before the sentence was introduced. Over this period, approximately 25,000 conditional sentences were imposed (Reed and Roberts 1999).

If the number of cases involving incarceration did not decline, where did the conditional sentences go? The answer appears to be that judges are using the new conditional term of imprisonment as a replacement not for terms of custody but for terms of probation. It has become an intermediate sanction for cases that prior to the reform would have received probation. The situation may change after the supreme court ruling later in 1999, but for the present the statistical pattern suggests that Canada has provided another example of the phenomenon known as "widening the net."

Penal Populism

Sentencing and parole reform was not restricted to the 1996 bill. Parliament also adopted a number of other changes, without ensuring that they were consistent with the 1996 reforms. The rather incoherent approach to sentencing and parole reform is apparent from three other legislative developments, two of which have become law, the other of which has a final parliamentary hurdle to overcome. All three reveal the influence of what may be termed "penal populism," which will be familiar to sentencing scholars in other jurisdictions.

MANDATORY MINIMUM TERMS   In 1996, the federal government passed legislation relating to firearms. One provision created mandatory minimum penalties of four years' imprisonment for offenders convicted of a number of offenses if these involved the use of a gun. The government could hardly claim that it was unaware of the research literature showing the restricted utility of mandatory sentences: a 1994 research report published by the federal department of justice showed that the existing mandatory penalties had had little impact and were often circumvented by the exercise of prosecutorial discretion. The findings of this report are consistent with the research on mandatory penalties in other jurisdictions, yet obviously had no influence on politicians or policy makers.

The effect of the new law was rapidly brought home. In one case, an offender was sentenced to a two-year community sentence for shooting her husband to death. Commentators were quick to point out that, had the crime been committed a week later, the court would have had no choice but to sentence the woman to at least four years in prison.

The passage of the mandatory minima probably had more to do with political factors or penal populism than anything else. The government was under attack from the political right for requiring all gun owners to register their weapons. The mandatory sentences demonstrated that the government was prepared to get tough with individuals who used guns for criminal purposes.

PAROLE ELIGIBILITY FOR LIFE PRISONERS   Penal populism also lay behind reform of the parole system. In Canada, first-degree murder carries a mandatory sentence of life imprisonment, with no prospect of parole until the inmate has served 25 years in prison. However, according to section 745.6, these life prisoners may apply for a jury review of their parole eligibility after having served 15 years. The jury hears evidence from the applicant about his progress in prison and about his plans for life after release on parole. It has the power to decide whether the inmate can make an earlier application for parole, as early as 15 rather than 25 years. Jurors to date have shown some considerable degree of sympathy for these life prisoners. Fully 80 percent of applications have resulted in reductions in the number of years the applicant has to serve.

Analysis of these jury decisions showed that jurors were responding reasonably and were able to distinguish cases according to their degree of merit. However, this provision began to attract hostile reaction, which intensified when Canada's most notorious inmate (convicted of a number of killings in the 1970s) made an application. The jury rejected his application after about ten minutes' deliberation, and he was required to serve his sentence on to the 25-year mark. Nevertheless, the government felt forced to act and passed legislation that tightened the rules that regulate applications. For example, under the previous arrangements, the jury was required to come to a simple majority decision. As a result of the reforms, a unanimous decision is now required. This move to unanimity is likely to reduce significantly the number of successful applications, as a single juror will be able to block a reduction in the number of years that an inmate must serve.

MULTIPLE MURDER: LIFE WITHOUT PAROLE   The last illustration provides the clearest illustration of penal populism at work. It relates to offenders convicted of multiple murders. At present, an offender convicted of two counts of murder will be sentenced to concurrent life terms, which means that he will be eligible for parole after 25 years. The effect of the new bill will be to make these life terms consecutive, which would seem a physical impossibility to all except the private member of Parliament who introduced the bill.

If the bill becomes law (and there is every likelihood that it will), an offender convicted of two counts of murder will have to serve 25 years for each count before becoming eligible for parole — 50 years without parole, in short. Since the median age of lifers on admission to prison in Canada is 39, consecutive life sentences will in all probability mean imprisonment without the prospect of parole. There has been no serious discussion of life without parole in Canada to date; this bill introduces the concept by the back door.

The bill was mildly opposed by government members of Parliament, including the minister of justice. However, when the bill came to a vote, the prospect of taking a stand and voting in public (and on live television) *against* such a populist bill proved too much for the government members, almost all of whom (including the justice minister herself) suddenly found that they had pressing business elsewhere. The "consecutive life" bill passed by a resounding margin and headed for the upper chamber of Canada's bicameral Parliament. The Senate will review the bill in late 1999.

Where does all this leave sentencing reform in Canada? Clearly, the 1996 reform statute has yet to have an important impact. Canada has struggled to reduce the use of incarceration, using a statement of purpose and a new sanction, but has yet to effect a change in sentencing practices at the trial court level. It cannot be said that the reforms have failed, because no explicit policy goals were identified. When he introduced the 1996 reforms in Parliament, the then minister of justice was coy about the goals of the bill, talking about "moving sentencing into the twenty-first century," rather than anything that can be empirically tested, such as reductions in the use of custody.

Perhaps the most disconcerting aspect of the Canadian reforms is that Parliament approved a statutory statement of sentencing purpose in 1996 and then blithely passed a number of additional laws that violate provisions of that statement. Mandatory minima violate the principle of restraint, while consecutive life sentences violate section 718.2(c), which states that "where consecutive sentences are imposed, the combined sentence should not be unduly long." Most people would consider 50 years an unduly long sentence.

The conditional sentence may yet reduce the number of admissions to custody, but in all probability it will take some time, and much will depend on the reaction of the supreme court in response to the six pending appeals. As for the statement of purpose, before its effects can be determined, the government will have to put in place a research plan capable of determining whether sentencing patterns have become more uniform or more proportionate. To date, the government has displayed little enthusiasm for evaluating its own reform. In short, the reforms have been relatively modest, at least by American standards, and for that reason will probably have modest effects.

APPENDIX A
Statement of the Purpose and Principles of Sentencing

718. The fundamental purpose of sentencing is to contribute, along with crime prevention initiatives, to respect for the law and the maintenance of a just, peaceful and safe society by imposing just sanctions that have one or more of the following objectives:

 (a) to denounce unlawful conduct
 (b) to deter the offender and other persons from committing offenses
 (c) to separate offenders from society, where necessary
 (d) to assist in rehabilitating offenders
 (e) to provide reparations for harm done to victims or the community
 (f) to promote a sense of responsibility in offenders, and acknowledgment of the harm done to victims and to the community.

Fundamental Principle

718.1. A sentence must be proportionate to the gravity of the offense and the degree of responsibility of the offender.

Other Sentencing Principles

718.2. A court that imposes a sentence shall also take into consideration the following principles:

(a) a sentence should be increased or reduced to account for any relevant aggravating or mitigating circumstances relating to the offense or the offender, and, without limiting the generality of the foregoing,
   (i) evidence that the offense was motivated by bias, prejudice or hate based on race, national or ethnic origin, language, color, religion, sex, age, mental or physical disability, sexual orientation or any other similar factor,
   (ii) evidence that the offender, in committing the offense, abused the offender's spouse or child,
   (iii) evidence that the offender, in committing the offense, abused a position of trust or authority in relation to the victim, or
   (iv) evidence that the offense was committed for the benefit of, at the direction of or in association with a criminal organization, shall be deemed aggravating circumstances;
(b) a sentence should be similar to sentences imposed on similar offenders for similar offenses committed in similar circumstances;
(c) where consecutive sentences are imposed, the combined sentence should not be unduly long or harsh;
(d) an offender should not be deprived of liberty, if less restrictive sanctions may be appropriate in the circumstances; and
(e) all available sanctions other than imprisonment that are reasonable in the circumstances should be considered for all offenders, with particular attention to the circumstances of aboriginal offenders.

Imprisonment Rates in Canada: One Law, 10 Outcomes
(August 1998)
Jane B. Sprott and Anthony N. Doob

Canada provides an interesting case study to examine variation in imprisonment rates because, unlike the United States, the criminal law in Canada is solely federal. The criminal law is the same across the country, but it is administered provincially. Consequently, a rather "pure" measure of imprisonment can be obtained, since the governing laws are the same across all provinces and crime and imprisonment reporting systems are relatively uniform across the country. Although Canada has both provincial and federal prisons, the decision on where an offender is imprisoned is made according to a simple administrative rule: "short" sentences (under two years) are served in provincial prisons, while "longer" sentences (two years or more) are served in federal penitentiaries. With the identical criminal law administered by 10 different political jurisdictions, we can examine whether the variation in imprisonment rates across Canada's 10 provinces makes any more sense than does variation across other jurisdictions that do not have a uniform criminal law.[1]

Two findings from our analysis stand out. First, notwithstanding a single criminal law and an identical distribution of function between provincial and federal prisons, Canadian provinces vary greatly in their use of imprisonment, whether considered relative to population, crime patterns, or prosecution patterns. Second, length of sentence has much more influence on total prison population size than do admission numbers, and an effort to reduce population might focus on sentence length, not admissions.

Studies of imprisonment rates generally fall into one of two categories. First, there have been studies that compare rates of imprisonment in different jurisdictions (e.g., across countries). As Young and Brown (1993) point out, these suffer from a number of problems including problems of defining how "imprisonment" is to be measured. Furthermore, it is sometimes difficult to know whether differences across countries are the result of different laws or different practices. A second approach has been to examine changes in imprisonment rates within a single jurisdiction over time. We have, in effect, chosen the first approach: looking in detail at one year (1994–1995) across provinces. Our reason is simple: we were interested in how the law is administered within one country subject to the same criminal legislation.

In an effort to understand Canada's "policy" of imprisonment, we examine, in this article, only those people sentenced to prison who are "actually in" the institution. This, more clearly than other measures of imprisonment, can be seen as a measure of the use of imprisonment as punishment for crimes committed. A large group that it excludes, however, are those held in custody while awaiting trial. We are not suggesting that such a group is not important. It clearly is, in part because in Canada individuals detained in custody awaiting trial are more likely to be sentenced to prison than are those granted bail (Friedland 1965; Koza and Doob 1975; Commission on Systemic Racism in the Ontario Criminal Justice System 1995). However, we decided to focus on sentenced admissions and counts because they are directly reflective of sentencing decisions, rather than decisions made before sentencing.

Athough sentenced admissions are a function of sentencing decisions, sentenced prison *counts* are a reflection not only of sentencing decisions but also of release decisions, most notably various forms of conditional release. By focusing on those who are "actually in" (rather than "on register") serving their sentences, we exclude a nontrivial number of people who are on other forms of release— temporary absence passes, for example. These complexities should be kept in mind when interpreting the data that follow and should be kept in mind when comparing our estimate of the overall rate of imprisonment (98 per 100,000) with another often cited rate (roughly 130 per 100,000), which includes *all* those who are registered as being in prison for whatever reason.

There is, furthermore, no clear consensus on how "rates" of imprisonment should be calculated. We have already described our decisions in calculating the numerators: we took admissions (1994/95) and counts (1995) of those admitted to prison or actually in prison as a result of a court imposed sentence.[2] For the denominator we primarily used each province's total population, though we also looked at rates where "reported crimes" or "adults charged" were the denominators.

Variation in Admissions Rates

Table 3.4 shows total admissions to Canadian prisons in 1994–95 per 1,000 persons overall and separately for provincial and federal prisons. On all measures there is enormous province-to-province variation in the rate of admissions. The extreme provinces for admissions for short (provincial) sentences are in the same region—Canada's prairies (Manitoba, Saskatchewan, and Alberta). There are, per capita, more than two and a half times as many people admitted to prison for short sentences in provincial prisons in Alberta as are admitted in Manitoba.

Turning to federal penitentiaries (longer sentences that exceed two years), Nova Scotia's admission rate is about 2.8 times that of neighboring New Brunswick. The consistency that one does find is with Canada's provinces that have the largest populations—Quebec, Ontario, and British Columbia. These provinces have relatively low rates of admission to provincial institutions (short sentences) and, with the exception of Quebec, rather low rates of admission to federal institutions (long sentences) (see table 3.4).

Since there are about 25 times as many admissions for short sentences in Canada as for long sentences, overall admissions parallel admissions for short sentences to provincial prisons. There is no relationship across provinces between the rate of admission to prisons for short sentences and the rate of admission for long sentences (Rho = .05).[3]

Table 3.4. Rates of Admission (per 1,000 total population in each province) to Provincial and Federal Institutions, 1994–1995

Canada and the 10 Provinces	Rate of Admission (overall) to Prison per 1,000 Total Population (1994–1995)	Rate of Admission to Prison for Short (provincial) Sentences per 1,000 Total Population (1994–1995)	Rate of Admission to Prison for Long (federal) Sentences per 1,000 Total Population (1994–1995)
Canada	4.20	4.03	.16
Newfoundland	4.92	4.75	.16
Prince Edward Island	6.16	5.96	.19
Nova Scotia	3.35	2.93	.42
New Brunswick	4.98	4.83	.15
Quebec	3.73	3.55	.18
Ontario	3.66	3.55	.11
Manitoba	2.88	2.68	.20
Saskatchewan	6.82	6.62	.19
Alberta	7.54	7.28	.26
British Columbia	3.50	3.39	.11

Sources: Canadian Centre for Justice Statistics; Correctional Services Canada.

Correlation of Prison Admissions with Prison Counts

Prison "counts" are governed not solely by prison admissions but also by length of sentence. Looking across the 10 provinces, the rank order correlation between the overall admissions rates and total (federal and provincial) prison counts is almost zero (Rho = .10). However, when the independent effect of short (provincial) and long (federal) admissions on prison counts is examined, it is the long (federal) admissions that are driving the overall prison counts in the provinces (Rho = .08 for short [provincial] admissions on combined counts and Rho = .78 for long [federal] admissions on combined counts). In other words, even though 25 times as many short sentences are being served in Canada as long sentences, the long sentences explain the overall variation in prison population across the 10 provinces.

However, when looking across the 10 provinces, the rate of admission to provincial institutions does correlate with the rate of provincial counts (Rho = .61), just as the rate of admission to federal institutions correlates with the rate of federal counts for that province (Rho = .59). Thus there is *some* support for the logic that the more people you put in a prison system, the more will be there on a given day.

Given that there is no appreciable relationship between the rate of *overall* admissions to prisons and penitentiaries and the *overall* custodial count, it is not surprising that there is quite a different pattern across provinces in the rate of imprisonment (counts), as shown in table 3.5. Looking at the total rate of imprisonment (those "actually in" provincial and federal institutions) in the first column of data in table 3.5, a rather clear pattern emerges: the three largest provinces (Quebec, Ontario, and British Columbia) incarcerate their residents at rates that

Table 3.5. Prison (sentenced "actual in" count) Population from Each Province, 1995 (per 1,000 total population from each province)

Canada and the 10 Provinces	Rate "in" Prisons (total) per 1,000 Total Population (1994)	Rate "in" Prison Serving Short (provincial) Sentences per 1,000 Total Population (1994)	Rate "in" Prison Serving Long (federal) Sentences per 1,000 Total Population (1994)
Canada	.98	.49	.49
Newfoundland	1.43	.61	.82
Prince Edward Island	1.27	.62	.65
Nova Scotia	1.52	.40	1.12
New Brunswick	1.22	.50	.72
Quebec	.88	.32	.56
Ontario	.76	.42	.33
Manitoba	1.43	.62	.81
Saskatchewan	1.93	1.06	.87
Alberta	1.29	.82	.47
British Columbia	.81	.51	.30

Sources: Canadian Centre for Justice Statistics; Correctional Services Canada.

are considerably lower than those of any Atlantic (Newfoundland, Nova Scotia, New Brunswick, and Prince Edward Island) or Prairie (Manitoba, Saskatchewan, and Alberta) province. However, this regional regularity obscures a rather interesting finding: provinces with similar overall incarceration rates (e.g., Quebec, Ontario, and British Columbia) have dramatically different proportions of short and long sentences. Quebec, for example, has about 36 percent of its prison population in provincial prisons (serving short sentences), whereas Ontario and British Columbia have 55 percent and 63 percent, respectively, of their prisoners in provincial institutions (serving short sentences). Thus, although all the provinces are guided by one law, and although there are some similar overall prison populations across the provinces, there are, in fact, dramatically different proportions of people serving short and long sentences.

Comparing the other provinces, Nova Scotia has 26 percent of its prisoners serving short sentences (in provincial prisons), compared with Alberta, with a relatively similar overall imprisonment rate, which has 64 percent of its prisoners serving short sentences. It could be argued that four of the provinces (Newfoundland, Prince Edward Island, New Brunswick, and Manitoba) have patterns of prison counts that look somewhat similar to one another. Another two (Ontario and British Columbia) are similar to each other, but different from the previous group. The other four provinces (Nova Scotia, Quebec, Saskatchewan, and Alberta), in terms of their patterns of prison (short sentences) and penitentiary (long sentences) counts, constitute four quite distinct penal societies. Not surprisingly, the rank order correlation between the rate of provincial and federal imprisonment (counts) is quite low (Rho = .13).

The Effect of Overall Crime Rates on Prison Counts

Factors other than admissions—crime rates, for example—may contribute to the overall prison population. Thus, it makes sense to see what effect crime rates have on prison counts, since differences in counts may disappear when expressed in terms of rates per 1,000 people charged or per 1,000 reported incidents. As shown in table 3.6, this is not the case.

The pattern is not dramatically different from the pattern that emerged (table 3.5) when prison counts are expressed in terms of the overall population. However, using these indexes, Quebec looks more like Alberta and Manitoba than like Ontario or British Columbia. More important, the differences do not disappear when either 1994 charges or incidents are used as the denominator. Because it could be argued that using a crime rate from one year (charges or incidents) is not sufficient to understand how crime rates relate to imprisonment counts, we also calculated the average charge and incident rates over the previous five years (1990–94) for the provinces and then used them as denominators. In the last two columns of table 3.6, we present these data. Although there are some changes in rates per 1,000 charges or incidents when using an average over five years instead of only 1994 crime rates, the differences still persist: using crimes or people charged as the denominator does not make the provincial variation disappear.[4]

Table 3.6. Prison (sentenced "actual in" count) Population from Each Province per 1,000 Criminal Charges or Incidents (for 1994 and averaged over 1990–1994)

Canada and the 10 Provinces	Number "in" Federal and Provincial Prisons per 1,000 People Charged ("all incidents") 1994	Number "in" Federal and Provincial Prisons per 1,000 Reported Criminal ("all") Incidents (1994)	Number "in" Federal and Provincial Prisons per 1,000 People Charged ("all Incidents"); averaged over 1990–1994	Number "in" Federal and Provincial Prisons per 1,000 Reported Criminal ("all") Incidents (averaged over 1990–1994)
Canada	49.80	9.81	41.55	8.98
Newfoundland	86.58	22.78	62.84	18.45
Prince Edward Island	76.58	15.96	40.66	11.78
Nova Scotia	77.62	16.88	52.72	13.97
New Brunswick	71.18	15.63	58.65	14.02
Quebec	52.54	11.46	53.22	11.04
Ontario	41.18	8.06	29.41	7.32
Manitoba	56.85	11.42	55.62	11.59
Saskatchewan	63.34	15.49	50.51	14.11
Alberta	51.85	12.27	45.17	9.92
British Columbia	38.80	5.28	41.50	5.10

Sources: Canadian Centre for Justice Statistics; Correctional Services Canada.

Conclusion

From our analyses, it becomes clear that aggregate Canadian data obscure enormous provincial variation in sentenced admissions and prison counts. In addition, it also becomes clear that, as Landreville (1995) concluded on the basis of Quebec data, it is the longer sentences that contribute significantly to the prison population. This should not be seen as an argument against the use of intermediate sanctions instead of short sentences. But it does suggest that, although such a strategy may well reduce sentenced prison admissions, its effect on prison counts will be marginal. International experience supports the conclusion that reducing prison admissions does not produce an appreciable decrease in prison counts. In Germany, in the late 1960s, a change in the law reduced prison admissions from about 136,000 to 42,000 (a reduction of admissions by about 70 percent). This dramatic drop in admissions did, obviously, have an impact on prison counts — but it was by no means as dramatic. Prison counts appear to have been reduced by no more than about a third (Weigend 1997).

The lessons are clear: prison counts are multiply determined. A single "simple" change will not have a dramatic impact on the overall size of a prison population. If a government is serious about conserving scarce criminal justice resources and using these resources in a manner that most effectively addresses legitimate concerns about public security, it might focus first on mechanisms to reduce the number of long sentences or the proportion of time that those serving long sentences are in a prison setting.

NOTES

This paper is adapted from J. B. Sprott and A. N. Doob, "Understanding Provincial Variation in Incarceration Rates," *Canadian Journal of Criminology* (1998) 40:305–22.

1. We report data only on the 10 provinces in Canada and leave out the two (soon to be three) territories. The two territories have small populations and a different relationship with the federal government compared with the provinces. The territories are also culturally quite different from the provinces, with very high proportions of aboriginal people, many of whom live in small and remote communities. As in the United States, aboriginal people are overrepresented in prison populations. The two territories have, compared with the provinces, very high rates of prison admissions and counts.

2. Most of the data we present are from the Canadian Centre for Justice Statistics annual publication series *Adult Correctional Services in Canada*. The "crime statistics" that we use are similarly published annually in the series *Canadian Crime Statistics*. Only one set of data is not generally available: the province in which current federally housed (penitentiary) prisoners were sentenced. We asked Correctional Services Canada for this information for 1994–95. Such information was readily available for 12,221 of the 14,274 prisoners who were their guests on March 31, 1995. We attributed the "province of sentencing" of the others in proportion to the province of sentencing of those for whom this information was known. We do not expect that this creates a serious distortion, but, obviously, we cannot be certain of this.

3. We use the rank order correlation (Rho) as a convenient and easily interpretable descriptive measure of the degree of association of two scores, since a correlation of +/−

1.0 would indicate a perfect ordering across provinces of the two measures. Since we have used the total population of provinces, it does not make sense to talk about the statistical significance of the relationships. If one were to treat these data as a sample (e.g., of all possible years), one would need a correlation of about .55 to be significant at the .05 level 1-tail.

4. Nor does the provincial variation disappear when using the number of homicide incidents/charges, violent incidents/charges, criminal code (nontraffic) incidents/charges, drug incidents/charges, or criminal code traffic incidents/charges as the denominator.

England/Wales

New Sentencing Laws Take Effect in England (October 1992)
Andrew Ashworth

Prison overcrowding has been a dominant feature of the English criminal justice system for the past 25 years. It is not merely that there have been insufficient prison places for each prisoner to have an individual cell so that in 1991, with a prison population of over 45,000, some 13,000 were held either two or three to a cell. There has also been a growing acceptance that some offenders are sent to prison unnecessarily, and others for unnecessarily long. Even before riots at Strangeways Prison in Manchester and in other prisons in April 1990 brought the world's attention to English prison problems, strategies aimed at reduced prison use were announced by the government in its 1990 White Paper, *Crime, Justice and Protecting the Public* (Home Office 1990). These strategies were incorporated in the Criminal Justice Act 1991, most of which came into force on October 1, 1992.

The Policy

The official aim is to move towards a twin-track policy of sentencing—dealing severely with people who commit serious offenses involving violence, sex, or drugs and lowering the level of penal response to those who commit less serious offenses. Offenders sentenced to four years' imprisonment or longer will be eligible for parole: if they are not paroled, they will be released conditionally after serving three-quarters of the sentence, with a liability to serve any unexpired portion if they reoffend before the end of the full term. Offenders serving less than four years' imprisonment will benefit from automatic conditional release after serving one-half. However, a major element in the strategy is its "lower track"—that a higher proportion of offenders should be "punished in the community," instead of being sent to prison. To help induce courts to use community sanctions, the Act introduces a new, tougher form of sentence called the "combination order" (a mixture of probation and community service), and probation orders themselves are made more rigorous by the adoption of new "National Standards" for their content and enforcement.

The Sentencing Framework

The Criminal Justice Act 1991 introduces a new sentencing framework, which can perhaps best be visualized as the pyramid shown in figure 3.2.

In all but the most serious group of cases, courts are expected to start at the base of the pyramid and work up. If the features of the case do not indicate that the offender should be given an absolute or conditional discharge, the penalty is likely to be a fine. Around 40 percent of "indictable offenses" (roughly equivalent to American felonies) now result in a fine. That figure once was closer to 60 percent, and government policy is to persuade courts to impose fines more often. Magistrates' courts, which deal with less serious crimes, are required to adopt a form of day-fine system called "unit fines," aimed at achieving a fairer relation between the amount to be paid and the financial resources of the offender.

Section 6(1) of the Act is designed to ensure that a court moves up from a fine to a community sentence only if it is satisfied that the offense is sufficiently serious to warrant this. Once the court crosses this threshold, it may choose between a probation order, a community service order, and a combination order. In making this choice and in deciding the length of the order, it must not only choose the one most suitable to the needs of the offender but also ensure that the "restrictions on liberty" involved are "commensurate with the seriousness of the offense."

The final step up the pyramid, from a community sentence to prison, should be taken only if the court is satisfied that the offense is "so serious that only a custodial sentence can be justified" (section 1(2)). If the court is of that opinion, the length of the prison sentence must be "commensurate with the seriousness of the offence" (section 2(2)). These provisions rule out disproportionately long sentences based on individual deterrence or general deterrence. However, there is a limited exception for incapacitative sentences. A court may impose a prison sentence for a sexual or violent offense if it believes that only such a sentence would be adequate to protect the public from serious harm from the offender; such a sentence may be longer than would be proportionate to the seriousness of the offense committed.

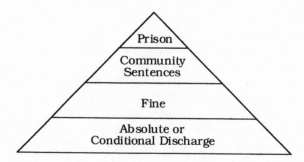

Figure 3.2. Hierarchy of Sanctions

The Common Law of Sentencing

The 1991 Act does not introduce a complete new code of sentencing laws. Instead, it superimposes a framework on the existing common law of sentencing, developed by the Court of Appeal over the past 80 years. The White Paper of 1990 envisaged a partnership between the legislature and the courts, in which the Court of Appeal through its judgments would give guidance that put "the flesh" on the "bones" established by Parliament. During the 1980s the Court of Appeal handed down about a dozen "guideline judgments," each of which includes some sentencing standards for a major offense such as drug trafficking, rape, causing death by reckless driving, and child abuse. The government expressed the "hope" that the Court would continue to fulfill this function in relation to the 1991 Act.

The practical impact of the Court of Appeal will probably be twofold. First, it will continue to develop a kind of "tariff" for the more serious types of offense, using appellate judgments to decide what sentence levels are proportionate or disproportionate. Second, it may give an authoritative interpretation of the key concept of "seriousness of offense," which determines virtually every step up the pyramid of sanctions. The practical frequency of problems at the "in/out" borderline mean that the Court must give guidance on how to evaluate thefts, burglaries, and deceptions if the 1991 Act is to achieve even a modest success. In the past, the Court has shown far more confidence in its judgments on very serious crimes. Its jurisprudence on the more mundane crimes that are the daily fare of most judges and magistrates remains underdeveloped.

Repeat and Multiple Offenders

One unusual and controversial feature of the 1991 Act is its approach to prior record and to multiple offenses, both of which tend to occur in a majority of Crown Court cases. Section 29(1) states that an offense "shall not be regarded as more serious . . . by reason of any previous convictions of the offender." While section 28 allows courts to take account of a good previous record as a mitigating factor, section 29 means that the seriousness of the current offense establishes a kind of "ceiling" beyond which the sentence may not go. The policy behind this is to restrain courts from imposing severe sentences on repeat small-time offenders — and, in fact, to remove many petty thieves and property offenders from prison. The same policy underlies the provision that, when a court is deciding whether an offense is so serious that only a custodial sentence can be justified and the offender stands convicted of several offenses, the court may take account only of two of them in deciding whether the case is serious enough. Even if the offender is being sentenced for 20 or 120 check frauds, the "two-offense rule" restricts the court to aggregating any two of the offenses in order to gauge the seriousness of the case.

The policy behind this is to keep small-time criminals out of prison, but many sentencers find the provisions artificial and unacceptable. Some judicial circumvention is always a possibility, and it remains to be seen whether the essence of the new policy will survive.

The Likely Impact of the 1991 Act

Will the effect of introducing the new Act in October 1992 be to reduce, or even to control, the English prison population? The British government itself seemed unclear about this when the 1990 White Paper was issued, but its latest estimate is that the prison population will decline by 3,500, or around 10 percent, by 1995. Many hope that they are right: a concerted effort has been put into the development of community sanctions, and in the 1980s there were successes in reducing the use of custody for juveniles and young adults.

Unfortunately, at least five sources of difficulty appear. First, the Act abolishes remission (good time) and alters the provisions for early release: this will result in offenders staying longer in prison unless the courts voluntarily reduce their sentencing levels in the middle range of current sentences, from one to four years. No move in this direction has yet been announced. Second, between 1985 and 1990 the number of prisoners serving sentences of four years or longer doubled, and under the "twin-track" strategy this is set to continue. Third, if more offenders are given more demanding community sanctions, they may well violate them in larger numbers and thus enter prison by that route. Fourth, much will depend on how the Court of Appeal, under the new lord chief justice, Lord Taylor, approaches its task: the Court should give an early and positive lead to other judges.

This leads us to the fifth question, which may or may not prove to be a difficulty. Many judges and magistrates seem skeptical about the new Act. Wholesale change in one's working practices is rarely welcome to anyone, and the obscurity of some language in the new Act hardly encourages a sympathetic response. But the Act does leave a considerable degree of discretion to the courts. Will they use this to neutralize the spirit of the legislation? Or will they use it to advance the primary aim of proportionality in sentencing and to move toward greater use of community sentences? The new English statute leaves far more power in the hands of the judiciary than do sentencing reforms in most other jurisdictions. Criminological research might suggest that judges will alter their approach as little as possible, co-opting the new Act into established working practices. Whether they will confound their critics and show that the judiciary can participate in the process of reform remains to be seen.

English Penal Policies and Prisons: Going for Broke
(December 1996)
  Rod Morgan

On the last occasion that I surveyed the state of English prisons (Morgan 1997), I adopted a pessimistic, some would argue overly pessimistic, tone. I described how the prison population for England and Wales had fallen from an all-time high of just over 50,000 in 1988–89 to around 43,000 at the beginning of 1993 but was then back to 48,000 and rising. I reported that a Home Office prison population projection of 57,000 for the year 2000 was in swift order revised downward to 50,400 and then sharply upward to 55,700 and that reluctance to predict the future had set in. I feared the worst in the light of Home Secretary Michael Howard's frequently intoned assertion that "prison works." In the event, things turned out much worse than I envisaged.

As I write (November 1996), the prison population stands at 57,633 — a staggering increase of one-third over three years — and there is no sign of any slackening in the upward trend. No one any longer places much reliance on population projections. And with good reason. In the run-up to the general election that must take place before May 1997, the Conservative government is intent on rushing through additional legislation — there have been no fewer than 33 criminal justice statutes introduced since the Conservatives came to office in 1979 — which, if passed in its present form, will add a new sharp twist to the upward prison population spiral. What is going on?

In a scenario familiar to American readers, the Conservative government and the opposition Labour party are engaged in competitive "out-toughing" of each other's "law-and-order" policies. Every passing exigency is responded to with immediate, often ill-thought-out legislation, thereby demonstrating the government's virility and commitment to act against the latest well-publicized menace. Owners of dangerous dogs, road construction protesters, crossbow wielders, marauding football supporters, and rave partygoers — all have been given their statutory due. The latest candidates are the owners of handguns — in the wake of the Dunblane school massacre — and combat knives — following the recent murder by stabbing of a London headmaster by a triad-inspired youth. The government proposes to ban more types of handguns than the official inquiry into the Dunblane incident recommended, and the Labour party has gone further: they will ban ownership of all handguns and wish now to add combat knives. Moreover, the Labour party has seriously proposed that lengthy periods of imprisonment be available for breach of "community safety orders" made on the testimony of police or local government officers against persons engaging in "chronic antisocial behavior" — nuisance, noise, and so on — not necessarily criminal or for which there may be insufficient evidence to bring a prosecution (von Hirsch et al. 1995). The political parties are struggling for the "law-and-order" high ground, which all the psephological evidence suggests is important for anxious middle-income voters.

Most important for the future size of the prison population is the Crime (Sentences) Bill introduced by the government this autumn, passage of which is now a pre-election priority. The key elements in the bill were set out in a policy paper, *Protecting the Public*, published earlier this year (Home Office 1996). England looks set to import most of the current North American sentencing fashions, in spite of the dire warnings from across the Atlantic organized by leading British penal pressure groups (see Elliott Currie's speech to the National Association for the Care and Rehabilitation of Offenders 1996). The government has taken up the notion of statutory minimum sentences, a notion largely foreign to the English sentencing tradition and vehemently opposed by the English judiciary. "Three strikes and you're out" has in one area been reduced to "two strikes and you're out," and the idea of "truth in sentencing" — here called "honesty in sentencing" — has also been adopted. Mandatory three-year sentences are proposed for adult burglars on their third conviction and mandatory seven-year sentences on third conviction for hard drug dealers. Life sentences are to become mandatory for offenders convicted of second serious violent or sexual crimes. Parole, and the existing automatic early release system at the halfway point for offenders serving sentences of less than four years, is to be abolished. Instead, prisoners are to be able to earn up to 15 percent off their sentences for positive participation in recently introduced prison work incentive schemes. Defendants are also to be given a 20 percent discount on mandatory sentences as a reward for "timely" guilty pleas.

The government predicts that there will be an increase in the prison population but that it will be modest and will take several years to accrue — an additional 10,800 prisoners by 2011–2012 (Home Office 1996, para. 13.8). This view is based on the assumptions that sentencers, when imposing nonmandatory terms of imprisonment, will scale down sentence lengths in recognition of the abolition of early release; that mandatory sentences will have a significant deterrent effect, thereby reducing the need for prison places; and that the overall sentencing pattern will be little affected.

These naïve assumptions are far removed from the more realistic assessment supported by extensive research and promulgated by the government as recently as 1990, namely that the doctrine of individual deterrence had much "immediate appeal" but was an "unrealistic" basis on which to ground sentencing arrangements (Home Office 1990, para. 2.8). The new assumptions are also belied by the current steep rise in the prison population. This rise is explicable only in terms of a change in the sentencing climate, a response to the prevailing tough political rhetoric of "prison works" and in *anticipation* of the legislation. The Prison Service is battening down the hatches for a rough ride: there is talk of a prison population of 75,000. With 111 prisoners per 100,000 population, the English prison population is already the highest in Western Europe with the exception of Portugal. A rise of the sort now being contemplated would push the United Kingdom in the direction of the former Warsaw Pact nations of Eastern Europe.

A combination of penal populism, a retreat from rehabilitative ambition into the "austere" prison regimes advocated by Mr. Howard, and the need to provide additional prison places rapidly without, in the short term at least, incurring a huge increase in government expenditure has also given a fillip to the privatized management of prisons, a movement that Britain, alone in Western Europe, has so far joined. Four years ago, for the first time in almost half a century, system crowding had been eliminated, and prison managers were optimistic about the prospect of putting it behind them. Overcrowding is back with a vengeance. Today there are approximately 5,000 more prisoners (9 percent) than there are prison places. Housing prisoners three to a cell in cells designed for one or two, a practice outlawed three years ago, is happening again. In order rapidly to expand the system, Mr. Howard has announced that he intends to enlist the services of the private sector on a considerable scale.

Four of 135 prisons in England and Wales are now privately managed. Six more are planned. However, when introducing his crime bill to the House of Commons in late October, Mr. Howard announced that he now proposed that there be 12 additional prisons built and managed privately, all of them substantially larger, at 900 places, than has previously been thought wise in Britain. There seems little room for speculation, pessimistic or otherwise: the government is preparing for a system of more than 70,000 places and there is little doubt they will need them.

If the extent of imprisonment in England is expanding rapidly, so also is its depth. In the wake of two serious breaches of security at maximum security prisons, in September 1994 and January 1995, the government instituted an independent review of security, headed by a retired general, Sir John Learmont, which was published in October 1995 (Home Office 1995). It is doubtful whether most of Learmont's recommendations, which were not greeted with critical acclaim, will be implemented. But enough of the spirit or letter of his proposals has already been adopted to represent a significant increase in the security quotient of the system. Home leave for prisoners generally has been cut back; visiting arrangements have been tightened; the highest-security prisoners are now subject to such harsh restrictions that litigation is pending; prison and prisoner searching has been increased, which, given the number of staff involved, has led to a cutback in prisoner programs; there is random compulsory drug testing throughout the system; and prisoners are now subject to an earned-privileges scheme the basic regime for which is very basic indeed. Low-security prisons now have all the perimeter and other security paraphernalia that a few years ago was reserved for high-security prisons.

The British—for developments are little better in Scotland and in Northern Ireland—are returning to old punitive obsessions. Desperate politicians are trying to come to terms with the worst repercussions of the free-market forces that they have unleashed. And yet, strangely, they continue to look to the United States for guidance.

English Believe Sentences Soft and Crime Rising
(February 1998)
Michael Hough and Julian V. Roberts

Members of the general public in England (as in the United States) believe that crime is rising when it is not, that punishments are softer than they are, and that sentencing is too lenient, according to recently released results from the 1996 British Crime Survey. As in the United States, there is evidence that such beliefs are predicated on lack of knowledge, or mistaken beliefs, concerning crime and punishment.

Everyone agrees that public opinion has a part to play in the formulation of criminal justice policy. Precisely how responsive policy should be to public opinion is a contentious issue. For most of the postwar period in England, there was political consensus that opinion was something to be *managed*, rather than responded to. More recently, however, politicians have been much more responsive to public opinion. There has been a great deal of political rhetoric around the slogan "prison works," and this has almost certainly had its effect on the sentencing climate. With no significant increase in the number of convicted offenders and no significant changes in legislation, the prison population has increased by 50 percent in five years.

One surprising feature of these developments has been the almost total absence of any firm evidence about the relationship between public attitudes toward sentencing and public knowledge of sentencing. There have been plenty of polls that document public frustration with overlenient sentences—but these have rarely paused to ask if people's opinions were grounded in accurate knowledge. The 1996 British Crime Survey ("BCS") set out to fill this gap.

The British Crime Survey is a large national survey that asks people about crimes they have experienced in the past year and about various other crime-related topics. In the 1996 BCS, people were asked about their knowledge of crime and punishment and about their attitudes toward sentencers and sentencing. Each sweep of the BCS since 1984 has also asked victims how they would like "their" offender to be punished.

The British Crime Survey has been an important source of information about attitudes to punishment in England and Wales since it was set up in 1982. This report presents findings mainly from the most recent sweep, carried out in 1996. One part of the interview was devoted specifically to sentencing issues. Roughly half the sample were asked a series of questions covering their knowledge of crime and sentencing, their assessments of sentencers and sentences, the sentence they thought should be imposed in a specific case of burglary, and their views on the best ways to tackle crime.

Those identified by the survey as victims have been asked since 1984 what punishment they thought their offender should get; results for victims of burglary and car theft are included here.

Knowledge of Crime and Sentencing

The 1996 BCS found widespread ignorance among the public in England and Wales about crime and criminal justice statistics. Misperceptions were systematic rather than random, in that majorities overestimated the gravity of crime problems and underestimated the severity of the criminal justice system.

Between 1993 and 1995, the national recorded crime rate fell by 8 percent. People were asked what they thought the trend had been. Figure 3.3 shows that the majority were wrong. People were also asked what proportion of crime was violent. The right answer, depending on definitions, was between 6 percent and 20 percent. Again, as figure 3.4 shows, most people were substantially wide of the mark.

People were asked to say what proportion of convicted rapists, burglars, and muggers get prison sentences. The right answers for 1995 were 97 percent for rapists, 61 percent for burglars, and 60–80 percent for muggers. Figure 3.5 shows that majorities made substantial underestimates. Thus, roughly six out of 10 people thought that prison sentences were handed out to fewer than 60 percent of rapists, fewer than a third of burglars, and fewer than 45 percent of muggers.

Other findings about public misperceptions include a tendency to underestimate the proportion of the population with criminal records; lack of awareness among large minorities of the upward trend in the use of imprisonment; ignorance about the clearance rate; and widespread ignorance of sentences available to the court.

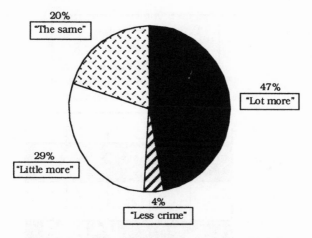

Question: "Would you say that there is more [recorded] crime, less crime, or about the same amount since two years ago?"

Figure 3.3. Changes in Recorded Crime

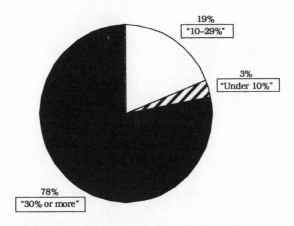

Question: "Of every 100 crimes recorded by the police, what number do you think involve violence or the threat of violence?"

Figure 3.4. How Much Crime Is Violent?

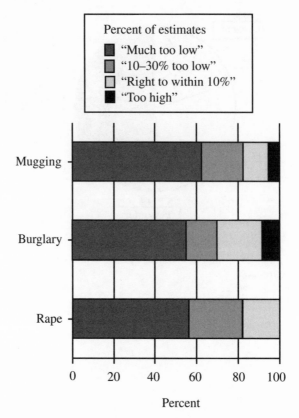

Figure 3.5. Knowledge of Sentencing Practice, Estimates of Courts' Use of Custody

Assessments of Sentencers and Sentences

The survey shows that the public in England and Wales take a jaundiced view of sentencers and sentencing. Four-fifths of people think that sentences are too lenient, half saying that they are much too lenient (see figure 3.6). Eighty-two percent of the sample thought that judges were out of touch with the public; the figure for magistrates was 63 percent (see figure 3.7). Judges were thought to be doing the worst job among criminal justice professionals, as figure 3.8 shows. Multivariate analysis strongly suggests that, at least in part, ignorance about crime and sentencing practice fuels public dissatisfaction. Those who were most dissatisfied were most likely to overestimate the growth in crime and the degree to which crime is violent, to underestimate the courts' use of imprisonment, and to underestimate the clearance rate.

Those who were most likely to underestimate the courts' use of imprisonment had lower educational attainment than others, were likely to be above average age, and were more likely to read tabloid newspapers. Women were more likely than men to underestimate the proportion of convicted rapists sent to prison, and owner-

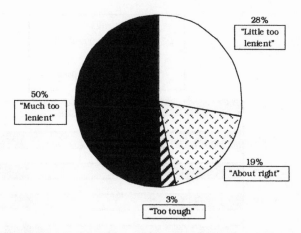

Question: "In general, would you say that sentences handed down by the courts are too tough, about right, or too lenient?"

Figure 3.6. Are Sentences Tough Enough?

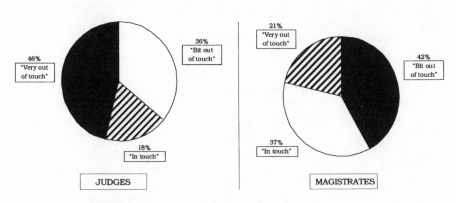

Question: "Do you think that [judges/magistrates] are generally in touch or out of touch with what ordinary people think?"

Figure 3.7. Are Sentencers in Touch?

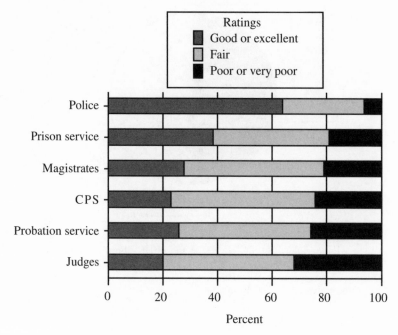

Question: "We would like to know how good a job you
think each of these groups of people are doing? How
good a job are the [police, etc.] doing? Would that be an
excellent, good, fair, poor, or very poor job?"

Figure 3.8. "How Good a Job Are They Doing?": Sentencers and Other Justice Agencies

occupiers more likely than others to underestimate the use of imprisonment for
burglars.

When people were asked about a real case of burglary, their sentencing prescriptions were, on balance, well in line with current sentencing practice. They
were told that the burglary was committed by someone with previous convictions
in daytime and involved the theft of a video and television set from the home of
an elderly man who was out at the time. Fifty-four percent wanted a prison sentence, with sentence lengths averaging less than the two years that the actual
burglar got. The remainder of the sample proposed community service orders (26
percent), a fine (21 percent), a suspended sentence (18 percent), electronic tagging
(11 percent), or probation (9 percent). A large minority (44 percent) suggested
restitution, either by itself or in combination with imprisonment or another penalty. Those who had been victims of crime were no more punitive than others;
this held true for victims of burglary as well as for victims of other types of crime.
The survey included an experiment to see whether people's preference for imprisonment was a function of their ignorance of the alternatives. While most of
the sample selected their preferred sentences from a "menu" on a showcard, a

subsample were denied this, having to make "top of the head" choices instead. This group was much less inclined to select community penalties and restitution, and more inclined to select imprisonment—67 percent against 54 percent. The finding underscores how sentencing preferences are shaped by the level of information available to respondents.

The Best Ways of Tackling Crime

Most of the sample thought that many diverse factors underlie current levels of crime. They believed that sentencing levels were an important determinant of crime trends. However, the most popular strategy for reducing crime, selected by 36 percent of the sample, was to increase family discipline, and the next most popular, selected by 25 percent, was to reduce unemployment. One in five opted for tougher sentences, and one in 10 for more police.

Attitudes toward greater use of imprisonment were at least ambivalent, with a widespread belief that imprisonment can stimulate, as well as prevent, further crime. Far more people expressed a preference for tougher community penalties (56 percent) than for building new prisons (18 percent) as a means of tackling prison overcrowding.

Victims' Sentencing Preferences

The BCS shows that there was a marked increase over the period from 1984 to 1996 in victims' preference for tough sentencing, at least in relation to two types of crime: burglary and car theft (see figure 3.9). There was no evidence to suggest that this trend was a function simply of increasing severity of the average crime of this sort. Nor was there any evidence that the experience of victimization fuels a desire for tougher penalties. Victims' preferences did not seem, on balance, to be substantially out of line with current sentencing practice.

Policy Implications

The 1996 BCS suggests that there is a crisis of confidence in sentencers that needs tackling with some urgency. People think that sentencers are out of touch and that their sentences are far too soft.

A criminal justice policy of "playing to the gallery" and toughening up sentences would probably be counterproductive. The BCS suggests an ingrained belief in lenient sentences whatever the reality—the same way that people assume prices are rising, regardless of the actual rate of inflation. The most likely reason for this is that information about sentencing comes largely from the media, and media news values militate against balanced coverage. Erratic court sentences make news, and sensible ones do not. As a result, large segments of the population are exposed to a steady stream of unrepresentative stories about sentencing incompetence.

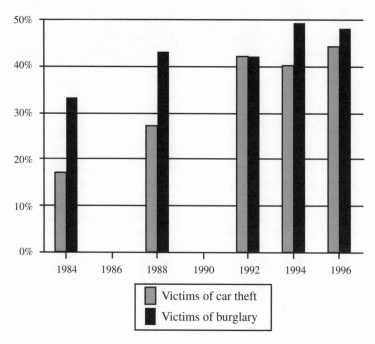

Figure 3.9. Victims' Preferred Sentence (percentage favoring imprisonment)

Correcting public misperception about sentencing trends in England and Wales should promote greater public confidence in judges and magistrates. And, since the judiciary occupy such a critical place in the criminal justice system, increasing confidence in the courts should promote confidence in the administration of justice.

The most challenging demands are in identifying effective ways to interrupt the processes that feed public cynicism. To date, very limited use has been made of the communication techniques of the late twentieth century in letting the public know about current sentencing practice. A successful strategy for tackling public misperceptions will almost certainly have to resort to these techniques. It will have to identify key audiences, such as opinion leaders, victims, potential offenders, and people at risk of offending, and convey appropriately to each audience an accurate portrayal of current sentencing practice.

Methodology

The 1996 BCS had a nationally representative core sample of 16,348 respondents age 16 or over. Social and Community Planning Research conducted the interviews, which took place between January and April 1996. The sample was drawn from the small users Postcode Address File. The response rate for the 1996 survey was 83 percent.

NOTE

The full report *Attitudes to Punishment: Findings from the British Crime Survey*, Home Office Research Study no. 179, by Michael Hough and Julian Roberts, is available from the Home Office RSD, Room 201, 50 Queen Anne's Gate, London SW1H 9AT, (tel.) 44 171 273 2084.

Imprisonment in England and Wales: Flood Tide, but on the
Turn? (October 1998)
Rod Morgan

Since my last foray in *Overcrowded Times* (in this volume, p. 242), the biggest surge in the prison population in English penal history has continued unabated. But the prison population may now have peaked, and the question is whether it is set to decline. The critical factors in the equation are the settling in of a Labour government elected with an overwhelming majority in May 1997; the new government's growing confidence that it can make subtle changes of policy direction without jeopardizing new-found public confidence in Labour's capacity to deliver "law and order"; the fiscal unsustainability of sentencers' increasing reliance on imprisonment; and the widespread conviction that imprisonment is a less than cost-effective method for combating major types of crime, particularly prolific property-related offending by persons addicted to drugs. Prison numbers will henceforward be managed. But the government's approach will be hardheaded. It is doubtful that the English prison population will in the medium term decline more than marginally.

During the period 1990–1993, the English prison population stabilized at around 45,000, having risen above 50,000 in the late 1980s. The conjunction of extensive prison riots in 1990, followed by a major inquiry (Woolf Report 1991), and legislation, the Criminal Justice Act 1991, premised on the parsimonious use of imprisonment proportionate to desert, created a sentencing climate in which the threshold for custody was set high. But this cautionary climate was short-lived, largely for political reasons. The Criminal Justice Act 1991 ("1991 CJA") was poorly drafted and early unraveled. In spite of winning the 1993 general election the Conservative party lost confidence and, increasingly vulnerable to Labour challenges about "law and order," a contest began between the government and the opposition as to who could out-tough the other (see Downes and Morgan 1997). The home secretary announced, contrary to everything that had been said in Home Office policy statements in the runup to the 1991 CJA, that "prison works." He said he did not flinch from providing prison places for many more prisoners. The courts responded with alacrity, interpreting the new legislation in a manner far from that intended. Since the end of 1992, when the prison population fell to a seasonal low of 40,600, the number of people in prison had by September 1998 risen to 66,500, an increase of well over 50 percent. During the years 1992–1996, the proportion of offenders sentenced to imprisonment in the higher courts rose from 44 to 60 percent, and in the lower courts from 6 to 10 percent. In the higher courts the average length of sentence also rose, from 21 to 23.4 months.

The courts' willingness to respond to ministerial rhetoric surprised Home Office planners (Home Office 1998, para. 3) and overwhelmed the prison service. In 1991–1992, the number of prison places at last exceeded prisoners. There seemed a real prospect that system overcrowding, which had blighted the service since the end of World War II, might be a thing of the past. The prison service gained confidence. It had room in which to maneuver and to implement the reformist agenda set out in the Woolf Report. Yet, by 1994, in spite of the largest prison building program since the middle of the nineteenth century, system overcrowding had returned. Between 1990 and 1996, 21 new prisons were opened, which, together with additions at existing prisons, provided 18,785 more places. A further 17,000 prison places are planned by 2011–2012. The new prisons include temporary ready-to-use accommodation erected alongside existing cell blocks and a prison ship, the Weare, towed across the Atlantic, moored in a southern harbor, and now in use for 400 prisoners. System overcrowding today stands at 108 percent, which means that some prisons are now between 30 and 60 percent overcrowded.

The reason that some institutions are disproportionately crowded goes beyond the marginal disjunctions that in any system lie between the geographical distributions of court committals and prison places. The Conservative government determined that prisons should also be "austere," thereby better to deter. Thus, when, in 1994–1995, two escapes from high-security units embarrassed the prison service, the home secretary responded — although the prisoners were speedily recaptured and the breaches were against the trend of an improving prison system security record — by accepting the recommendations of an inquiry report (Learmont Report 1995) that the "depth" of imprisonment be greatly increased. Home leaves were cut back, visiting procedures were tightened, prisoners' possession of personal property restricted, and prison perimeters strengthened. It is notable, therefore, that while some closed prisons are bursting at the seams, the dwindling number of open establishments remain underoccupied. Moreover, the heightened security quotient of most prisons has cost money and staff to such an extent that prisoner programs have been cut back. The vigorously independent chief inspector of prisons has complained that the combination of overcrowding and reduced resources is threatening much of the progress made in the aftermath of the Woolf Report and that the prison service is in danger once again of being locked into a downward spiral not of its own making (Her Majesty's Chief Inspector of Prisons 1998, p. 4).

Yet, sotto voce, there are signs that Jack Straw, Labour's home secretary, is intent on managing the prison population, probably at its present level. While in opposition, the Labour party did not contest the major provisions of the Crime Sentences Act 1997 ("CSA"), several of which, according to the government's own estimates, would significantly have increased the prison population (Home Office 1996, chap. 13). But in government, Labour has not implemented those particular CSA measures — the abolition of discretionary parole for determinate sentence prisoners and presumptive sentences for repeat burglars — that would most have increased imprisonment. Straw has implemented those CSA provisions that sound tough—presumptive life sentences for second-time serious violent or sexual offenders and presumptive minimum seven-year sentences for repeat trafficking offenses in class A drugs—but do not significantly differ from existing sentencing practice.

It is in this context that two recent publications become significant. First, the latest Home Office (1998) estimates for the prison population provide, for the first time, projections for different policy scenarios, one of which assumes that custody rates and sentence lengths do not rise further but remain at 1997 levels. This "low scenario" generates a prison population to 2005—the likely lifetime of a reelected Labour government?—that does not exceed the present population level and that, if fulfilled, would mean that the government, on the basis of construction already in the pipeline, could see an end to system crowding and cut back the planned building program. What is clear is that if subtle changes in government rhetoric fail to influence sentencers' reliance on custody, Mr. Straw means to manage prison numbers executively. The government has announced that it will use electronically monitored home detention curfew orders (introduced by the 1991 CJA and piloted in selected areas since) for the early release of short- and medium-term prisoners—that is, those serving sentences of three months to four years. The new system will mean that such prisoners could, depending on their length of sentence, be released two weeks to two months early. For the period that their sentence would otherwise continue, they will be electronically tagged and compelled to abide by a curfew for at least nine hours a day. Breach of this provision will result in their reimprisonment. There will be no automatic entitlement to early release—it will depend on a so-called risk assessment by the prison service. Nevertheless, the Home Office estimates that the measure will reduce the average daily prison population by 3,000 (*Hansard*, June 15, 1998, col. 13), and, it goes without saying, the measure could be used more liberally. The parole board, for example, could be encouraged to become more liberal when considering early release for prisoners serving four years or more had it the tough-sounding backup of electronic tagging.

Hardheadedness runs through the second notable publication recently to appear, the review by the Labour-dominated House of Commons Home Affairs Committee on Alternatives to Imprisonment (Home Affairs Committee 1998). The tone of the report is striking. A good deal of attention is given to the arguments that Britain does not, as is frequently asserted, rely disproportionately on imprisonment relative to its neighbors in Western Europe; some offenders not currently sentenced to imprisonment arguably should be; noncustodial sentences generally have no better record for preventing recidivism than imprisonment; indeed, if proper methodological allowances were made—many offenses committed by offenders subject to noncustodial penalties go undetected—then imprisonment might be judged a more effective defense against recidivism than the alternatives. The committee unequivocally sets its face against the proposition, which some persons who gave testimony advanced, that the English prison population should be substantially larger than it is. But the committee accepted that imprisonment was the proper disposition for dangerous and persistent offenders and, though it recommended that alternatives be used for other offenders, it insisted that these alternatives had to be made more effective. The committee was critical of much recent noncustodial practice. The committee was, for example, "astonished" at the general absence of assessment of the effectiveness of community sanctions and "alarmed" at the low level of compliance by local probation services with the national standards for supervision and enforcement of orders laid down by the Home Office.

The committee was persuaded by evidence that community programs based on what are now referred to as "what works?" principles (broadly, cognitive-behavioral approaches that are proportionate to the level of risk posed, that require the active participation of the offender, that are skills oriented and employment focused) offer a more cost-effective response to much offending than does imprisonment, and this is in line with the government's thinking as represented by the Crime and Disorder Act 1998, which will be implemented this autumn. The government's oft-repeated slogan is "tough on crime, tough on the causes of crime," and both sides of the equation are prominent in the Act. The government is pressing ahead, for example, with measures (new detention and training orders) that will almost certainly mean that many more prolific young juvenile offenders, including 10- and 11-year olds, will be locked up, albeit in institutions no longer to be run by the prison service. Moreover, a reprimand and final warning system is to replace police cautions, with much stricter rules for their use. However, the introduction of drug treatment and testing orders ("DTTOs"), which may be residential or nonresidential and which will involve regular drug-testing requirements, signals official recognition that simply punishing, often by way of imprisonment, prolific property offenders whose activities are driven by the need to buy drugs on which they are dependent is an unproductive ritual with which everyone concerned—including the police and the public at large—is becoming increasingly impatient. Britain is suffering an opiates epidemic that is arguably not best tackled by suppressing with a blunderbuss a whole range of illegal substances that are now widely used and among which, the evidence suggests (Parker et al. 1998), young people are able better to discriminate than are their parents and political leaders.

The hard question concerns the degree to which the government is willing and able to back the new community-based initiatives with resources. The Crime and Disorder Act, for example, also places an obligation on local authorities to establish crime prevention agency partnerships and to prepare local crime and disorder strategies. But the government has so far asserted that these efforts must be paid for out of savings achieved. To be widely available to the courts, DTTOs will require a major injection of funds to set up the community-based drug treatment centers and trained staff that are currently conspicuous by their absence. Reigning in the portion of the "law-and-order" budget currently devoted to imprisonment is almost certainly a precondition for this to happen. But the government will make these changes only to the extent that it is able to carry with it a public as much angry at as afraid of being the victims of commonplace property offenses. Marginal change, rather than radical shift, is the most likely prospect.

English Sentencing: From Enlightenment to Darkness in a
Decade (October 1999)
  Andrew Ashworth

At the beginning of the 1990s there were distinct signs of enlightenment in official English sentencing policy. The Criminal Justice Act of 1991 introduced a new sentencing framework that provided a clearer rationale for sentencing, aimed to reduce prison sentences for nonserious offenses, promoted the wider use of community sanctions, and tried to place greater emphasis on fair financial penalties. As we head for the end of the 1990s, the forces of darkness are gaining the upper hand: the increasingly repressive prison policies of the former Conservative government have not been discontinued by the Labour government, which, despite its large parliamentary majority and its huge lead in the opinion polls, has maintained the rhetoric of punitiveness. In this brief survey of English sentencing at the end of the 1990s, five developments can be singled out for discussion.

The Prison Population

After the 1991 Act came into force, the prison population dwindled to its lowest for several years, dipping to 40,000 in February 1993. Since then it rose sharply and steadily through the end of 1998, fueled by politicians' statements that "prison works" and by considerable support from the media. In five years it increased by more than 50 percent: even though total custodial rates are lower than those in the United States, the magnitude of this increase is remarkable. In 1999, the prison population appears to have stabilized at around 65,000.

Of course there are various problems in reading too much into statistics on the overall use of imprisonment, but it is worth emphasizing two points here. First, the sharp increase is reflected in the numbers of sentenced prisoners: it cannot be put down to rises in the use of pretrial detention. Second, the sharp increase cannot be put down to a rise in the crime rate. On the contrary, each of the years from 1993 to 1997 saw a drop in the recorded crime rate, although crimes of violence increased during that period. There was also a fall in the number of people being convicted in the courts.

Imprisonment Rates

The change over the 1990s is seen most clearly by examining the proportionate use of imprisonment by the courts for "indictable offenses," a category that includes all serious crimes and some others (e.g., all thefts, irrespective of the value of the property taken). In the first three years, the imprisonment rate for men age 21 and over was steady at 18 percent; by 1996 and 1997, it had reached 26 percent. For women age 21 and over, the imprisonment rate more than doubled, from 6 to 13 percent.

These figures should be seen as part of a general "ratcheting up" of the sentencing tariff. Thus, the use of community sanctions also increased over the same period, from 16 to 24 percent for men and from 21 to 31 percent for women. It is the lesser penalties, notably the fine, that are being used much less frequently.

The Arrival of Mandatory Sentences

Although England and Wales have had a mandatory penalty of life imprisonment for murder for many years, the wider use of mandatory sentences seen in so many other countries had been avoided. But almost the last throw of the Conservative government in 1997 was to introduce some mandatories, and it did so without protest from the then Labour opposition. The Crime (Sentences) Act 1997 contains three relevant provisions. Section 2 of the Act provides a mandatory sentence of life imprisonment for a second serious sexual or violent offense, unless the court finds "exceptional circumstances" for not imposing that sentence. The Court of Appeal has considered this escape clause on several occasions already, and it is clear that it will be interpreted narrowly: for example, in *Kelly* [1999] Crim.L.R. 240 the Court held that the lengthy period between the two convictions (18 years) did not constitute "exceptional circumstances," nor did the fact that the offender was not regarded as a danger to the public or that the first offense was committed when he was young.

Section 3 of the Act provides for a prescribed minimum sentence of seven years for a third offense of trafficking in hard drugs. Little has been heard of this provision in practice, since most such offenders receive long sentences, anyway. Of greater relevance is section 4 of the Act, which provides for a prescribed minimum sentence of three years for a third offense of burglary of a dwelling. This is not a mandatory sentence as such, since the court need not impose the prescribed sentence if it would be "unjust in all the circumstances" to do so—a relatively wide escape clause. Section 4 is not yet in force, but the Labour government has decided to bring it into force at the end of 1999—not for any explicit penal policy reasons, but evidently for political purposes. It remains to be seen how much it will impinge on the practice of the courts: many repeat burglars already receive sentences in excess of three years, and where the court thinks that a lower sentence would be appropriate it will surely not be difficult to find that three years would be "unjust in all the circumstances." This provision is therefore a much-diluted version of the mandatory penalty in section 2.

Expanding Sentencing Guidelines

Sentencing guidelines in England mean something entirely different from the American conception. Since the late 1970s the Court of Appeal has been formulating guideline judgments on various types of crime, expanding the amount of guidance available to judges in the lower courts. These guideline judgments are not joined together in any overall scheme and do not look like U.S. guideline systems. They look like ordinary appellate judgments, except that they have a wider reach, dealing not just with the facts of the case but also with many other manifestations of that type of crime. They are generally respected by sentencers, because they are well grounded in judicial practice and appear in a narrative form, rather than as a numerical table.

In the second half of the 1990s, the Court of Appeal, under the leadership of Lord Bingham as lord chief justice, has considerably increased the number of guideline judgments. Although many crimes are still not covered, an increasing number are. Thus, to take six recent examples, the Court has laid down guidelines for the sentencing of cannabis offenses in *Ronchetti* [1998] Crim.L.R. 227, amphetamine offenses in *Wijs* [1998] Crim.L.R. 587, offenses involving guns in *Avis* [1998] Crim.L.R. 428, offenses involving explosives in *Martin* [1999] Crim.L.R. 91, and offenses of indecent assault in *Wellman* [1999] Crim.L.R. 343, and it tried once again to give guidance on the sentencing of burglary of a dwelling in *Brewster* [1998] 1 Cr.App.R (S) 181.

Not a Sentencing Commission

In terms of policy-making in the field of sentencing, a recent innovation is the creation by a 1998 statute of a Sentencing Advisory Panel. Now, just as English sentencing guidelines are a world apart from U.S. sentencing guidelines, so the new panel should not be confused with the kind of sentencing commission that operates in the United States. The panel has limited powers, but they are still new powers and have aroused considerable interest. The purpose of the panel is to make proposals to the Court of Appeal for sentencing guidelines for a particular type of offense: the panel will draft some guidelines, together with an explanatory text, but it will be for the Court of Appeal to decide whether to act on the recommendation. There are three routes by which types of offense may arise for consideration by the panel: the Court of Appeal can refer a crime to the panel, the home secretary can make a reference (various offenses against the environment, including pollution, have already been referred), and the panel can make its own decision to work on a particular crime (it is currently working on offenses of possession of knives and other offensive weapons). The panel members include judges, magistrates, a former prison governor, a probation officer, academics, and three laypersons.

The proof of the pudding will be in the eating: how often will the Court of Appeal follow the panel's proposals? What if the panel makes proposals that are not in accordance with government policy? How will the panel's proposals be received by the popular press? Doubts of these kinds abound, but the creation of the panel is an attempt to preserve the essentials of a system based on judicial guidance while offering a new, and more broad-based, channel of advice to the lord chief justice. Whether the panel will be a force of enlightenment or will fail to penetrate the growing darkness remains to be seen.

Ireland

Sentencing and Punishment in Ireland (October 1997)
Ian O'Donnell

Sentencing and punishment in Ireland may appear in many people's eyes para-doxical. While having one of the lowest crime rates in Europe, Ireland has over-crowded prisons, plans to double prison capacity, and has the highest rate of ad-missions to prison of any European country. Yet, despite the high admissions rate, Ireland has one of the lowest imprisonment rates in Europe—half that of England and less than a tenth that of the United States. And, while political attention for the first time in many years has shifted toward toughness, the government has also announced initiatives that point toward balanced and humane policies.

It is difficult to come to any clear conclusions about the operation of the Irish penal system because official data are sparse, sometimes irrelevant, and usually out of date. Academic critique is also rare, partly due to lack of materials and problems of access but also because there is not one department of criminology in Ireland, and there are no full-time academic positions in the discipline.

Trawling through the published data reveals a complicated and fascinating picture. For example, in terms of absolute numbers, the prison population of Ireland is the smallest of any Western European country—it stood at 2,032 in 1995. This equates to a rate of 60 per 100,000 population, 10 times lower than the United States and a little more than half the rate for England and Wales. In 1995, the only European country with a lower rate (58) was Switzerland. Over the period 1987–95, the prison population in Ireland rose by 5 percent, at a time when most countries were experiencing much more substantial surges (e.g., the Netherlands, 106 percent; Spain, 70 percent; Germany, 32 percent).

However, the low average daily population conceals a high rate of receptions into custody: in other words, a low prison "stock" hides a high prisoner turnover. Indeed, in his recent book *Mountjoy Prisoners*, Paul O'Mahony showed that with a committal rate (including pretrial detention) of 328 per 100,000 population, Ireland resorted to imprisonment more frequently than any other country in the Council of Europe.

The first reason that such huge throughput generates such a small average daily population is that the Irish prison population is made up of many short-sentence prisoners. Half of all committals to prison under sentence are for less than six months, and only one in four is for more than a year.

A further contributory factor is that many of those committed to prison before trial are soon afterward released on bail—fewer than 10 percent of the prison population is made up of those awaiting trial or sentence. Additionally, about one in three of all committals are fine defaulters, who serve very short sentences. Like those held briefly on remand, they contribute little to stock, while significantly elevating throughput.

Finally, the Irish prison system suffers from an acute lack of space, and to ease overcrowding there is a haphazard system of temporary release. For example, it is not uncommon for an offender who receives several months' imprisonment to be released within days and to serve out the remainder of the sentence, unsupervised, in the community. At any given time, there are some 500 prisoners on such temporary release.

All prisoners released in this way are subject to certain conditions, such as keeping the peace and being on good behavior. They may also be required to report to a police station at specified times or to report back to prison at stated intervals so that their release license may be renewed. If they comply with these conditions, they are considered to have served out their sentence as soon as the term imposed by the court has expired. Many do not comply and so become "unlawfully at large." There are about 1,400 prisoners in this situation at present.

There are further peculiarities. Of the 31 countries in a Council of Europe survey carried out in 1995, Ireland had the highest proportion of prisoners under 21 years of age (25 percent). By 1996, this had risen to 33 percent. It had the lowest proportion of women prisoners (1.8 percent).

The demand for prison accommodation and the extensive use of custody by the courts could perhaps be understood if they reflected a high underlying level of serious crime. However, the rate of recorded crime in Ireland is extremely low and largely an urban phenomenon. In 1995, there were 57 crimes recorded per 1,000 population in Dublin, four times higher than in the rest of the country (where it stood at 14 per 1,000). In some parts of rural Ireland, the rate was staggeringly low—for example, eight per 1,000 population in County Mayo and 12 in County Clare.

The low crime rate makes the high incarceration rate more startling. If imprisonment rates were expressed per 1,000 recorded crimes rather than per head of population, the Irish situation would diverge still further from that in the rest of Europe.

Although prison populations are driven by sentencing practices, we know virtually nothing about the nature of sentencing in Ireland. Sentencing policy is not set out in legislation, there are no statutory criteria that might aid judges, nor are there clear judicial guidelines.

There have been some recent calls for clarity, consistency, and greater transparency in sentencing. The Law Reform Commission (1996) recommended that punishment should be proportionate to offense seriousness and should not be unduly influenced by considerations of deterrence, incapacitation, or rehabilitation. It also proposed the adoption of nonstatutory guidelines that would set out potential aggravating and mitigating factors in an attempt to help structure judicial discretion.

At present, the main sanctions available to the courts are imprisonment, probation, community service, and fines. It is not unusual for a custodial sentence to be deferred or suspended in part or in full. Although the suspended sentence has no statutory basis in Irish law, it is considered a valid and useful penalty by the courts, despite some confusion about how it might operate.

For example, in 1990 a 10-year prison sentence was suspended on condition that the offender keep the peace and be on good behavior for 10 years. It was not clear what would happen in the event that this condition was breached after, say, six years. The reality, however, is that it would be unlikely for such a breach to come to the notice of the courts as there is no formal mechanism for notifying the courts of noncompliance.

The rationale for the partly suspended sentence is even less clear. It may involve having the offender serve a fixed period of the sentence in custody, with the remainder suspended. Or it may involve having the judge review the sentence after a certain portion of it has been served. If the offender has behaved well in custody or sought treatment for his offending behavior, the judge may decide at the review to suspend the remainder.

Until very recently, politicians were not much excited by crime and punishment and seemed happy to allow a poorly understood system to muddle along without much support. However, things have changed dramatically over the past two or three years. A number of unsolved gangland killings sickened and frightened the public. It was widely perceived that the police were powerless to deal with the small number of individuals who were believed to control organized crime and the drugs trade in Dublin.

Frustration grew along with increasing media coverage of the key figures and their lavish lifestyles. Their identities were widely known, and they were referred to by nicknames such as "The General," "The Penguin," "The Boxer," and "The Monk." Despite this celebrity, they seemed to act with impunity.

Public concern escalated with the killing of a police officer on June 7, 1996. Detective Garda Jerry McCabe was shot dead by a renegade IRA unit during the attempted robbery of a post office van in Adare, County Limerick. Two weeks later (June 25, 1996), the award-winning investigative journalist Veronica Guerin was brutally murdered as she sat in her car at traffic lights in Dublin. Her newspaper exposés of key gangland figures in Dublin had led to a previous attempt on her life, and it is thought that her killing was ordered by one of these figures to prevent further revelations.

This killing was a defining moment in the debate about crime in Ireland and was the catalyst for a hardening in public and political attitudes. Crime control became a national priority, and it was almost as if a state of national emergency had been declared. The Irish Parliament, the Dáil, was recalled for a special debate on crime. During the general election campaign that took place in 1997, law and order were key issues, and public concern was at an all-time high. Politicians engaged in a frenzied bidding war, promising more police, more prisons, and less tolerance.

A number of dramatic changes followed, including an amendment to the constitution to widen the grounds on which courts could refuse bail, demands for an immediate review of the consequences for suspects of remaining silent in the face of police questioning, calls for mandatory minimum sentences for offenses involving drugs, and a commitment by the government almost to double prison capacity. The prevailing political mood—seemingly reckless as to the economic and social costs—holds out ever more severe and repressive policies as the solutions to crime.

There are few independent voices calling out for a more balanced approach. The Irish Penal Reform Trust ("IPRT") was founded in 1994, and the author has recently been appointed as its first director. The IPRT is dedicated to raising the level of the debate, ensuring that political discussions are evidence based, and encouraging policymakers to adopt a restorative view of justice. These activities are carried out in parallel with campaigns for humane treatment of prisoners and attempts to counter current enthusiasm for prison building.

The outlook is not entirely grim. The seeds of a dispassionate and reasoned analysis of the extent of crime and approaches to its management are contained within the discussion paper *Tackling Crime*, which was published in May 1997 by the Department of Justice (Department of Justice 1997). This worthy document is an attempt to devise a criminal justice strategy based on sound principles. It expresses a commitment to basic research and places a firm emphasis on consultation, coordination, and review. It is the first attempt since the foundation of the modern Irish state to piece together a coherent strategy on crime and punishment.

The department outlines 12 goals, each accompanied by an indication of how it might best be realized. The first goal is concerned with the provision of information about crime. This is to be achieved through the stimulation of quality research at universities and other institutions. It is acknowledged that policymaking and public understanding are hindered by a lack of comprehensive and up-to-date statistical data. This vacuum must be filled if real progress is to be made.

Other goals include nurturing multiagency approaches to crime, regularly reviewing and updating the criminal law, and ensuring that the police, courts, and prisons operate effectively and provide value for money. Dealing with drug-related offending (including alcohol abuse) is seen as a key priority. These are all important aspirations.

Ireland has a low crime rate and is a small country where, at a fundamental level, charity and forgiveness are still important values. It is widely recognized that Irish prisons hold some of the most disadvantaged and desperate of its citizens and reflect, to some extent at least, societal failure. In other words, it is possible that public support could be cultivated for a progressive penal policy based on reintegration and social inclusion, some elements of which are contained in the department of justice's strategy.

As an overall package, *Tackling Crime* is a much-needed attempt to impose coherence on a system that is at present oriented almost exclusively toward punishment. It places a welcome emphasis on prison as a sanction of last resort and offers strong support for alternative sanctions, especially community penalties, which are at present poorly developed. It is to be hoped that the progressive ideas in this document do not wither in the current harsh climate.

NOTE

Despite the absence of academic criminologists from Ireland and limitations on data and information about the justice system, a number of impressive books have appeared over the past several years, most notably Paul O'Mahony's trio: *Crime and Punishment in Ireland* (1993), *Criminal Chaos* (1996), and *Mountjoy Prisoners: A Sociological and Criminological Profile* (1997); Tom O'Malley's *Sexual Offences: Law, Policy and Punishment* (1996); and John Brewer, Bill Lockhart, and Paula Rodgers's *Crime in Ireland 1945–95* (1997). Before 1990, virtually nothing about Ireland had been published in the fields of criminology or penology.

References

Albrecht, Hans-Jörg. 1994. *Strafzumessung bei schwerer Kriminalität. Eine vergleichende theoretische und empirische Untersuchung zur Herstellung und Darstellung des Strafmasses*. Berlin: Duncker & Humblot.

———. 2001. "Post-Adjudication Dispositions in Comparative Perspective." In *Sentencing and Sanctions in Western Countries*, edited by Michael Tonry and Richard S. Frase. New York: Oxford University Press.

Albrecht, H.-J., and W. Schädler. 1986. Community Service, Gemeinnützige Arbeit, Dienstverlening, Travail d'Intêret General. "A New Option in Punishing Offenders in Europe." Freiburg: Max-Planck-Institut.

Alschuler, Albert W. 1978. "Sentencing Reform and Prosecutorial Power." *University of Pennsylvania Law Review* 126:550–77.

American Bar Association. 1994. *Standards for Criminal Justice: Sentencing*, 3d ed. Chicago: American Bar Association Press.

American Law Institute. 1962. *Model Penal Code (Proposed Official Draft)*. Philadelphia: American Law Institute.

Anttila, Inkeri. 1986. "Trends in Criminal Law." In *Criminal Law in Action: An Overview of Current Issues in Western Societies*, edited by Jan van Dijk, C. Haffmans, and P. Rüter. Arnhem: Gouda Quint.

Ashworth, Andrew. 2001. "The Decline of English Sentencing and Other Stories." In *Sentencing and Sanctions in Western Countries*, edited by Michael Tonry and Richard S. Frase. New York: Oxford University Press.

Atkinson, L. 1995. "Boot Camps and Justice: A Contradiction in Terms?" *Trends and Issues in Crime and Criminal Justice*, no. 46. Canberra: Australian Institute of Criminology.

Australian Bureau of Statistics. 1997. *Prisoners in Australia, 1996*. Canberra.

———. 1999. *Corrective Services, Australia*. Canberra.

Australian Institute of Criminology. 1994. *Australian Prison Trends*. Canberra ACT: Australian Institute of Criminology.

Australian Law Reform Commission. 1988. *Report No. 44: Sentencing*. Canberra: Australian Law Reform Commission.

Bayes, Helen. 1999. "Punishment Is Blind: Mandatory Sentencing of Children in Western Australia and the Northern Territory." *University of New South Wales Law Journal Forum* 5:14–16.

Beckett, Katherine. 1997a. *Making Crime Pay: Law and Order in Contemporary American Politics*. New York: Oxford University Press.

————. 1997b. "Political Preoccupation with Crime Leads, Not Follows, Public Opinion." *Overcrowded Times* 8(5):1, 8–11.

Berghuis, A. C. 1994. "Punitiviteitsfeiten." In *Hoe Punitief is Nederland?*, edited by M. Moerings. Arnhem: Gouda Quint.

Biles, David. 1995. "Prisoners in Asia and the Pacific." *Overcrowded Times* 6(6):5–6.

Blumstein, Alfred. 1993a. "Racial Disproportionality of U.S. Prison Populations Revisited." *University of Colorado Law Review* 64:743–60.

————. 1993b. "Making Rationality Relevant: The American Society of Criminology 1992 Presidential Address." *Criminology* 31:1–16.

Boswell, John. 1980. *Christianity, Social Tolerance, and Homosexuality*. Chicago: University of Chicago Press.

Bottoms, Anthony. 1995. "The Philosophy and Politics of Punishment and Sentencing." In *The Politics of Sentencing Reform*, edited by Chris Clarkson and Rod Morgan. Oxford: Oxford University Press.

Brewer, John, Bill Lockhart, and Paula Rodgers. 1997. *Crime in Ireland 1945–95*. Oxford: Clarendon Press.

Brown, J. M., and P. A. Langan. 1999. *Felony Sentences in the United States—1996*. Washington, D.C.: Bureau of Justice Statistics.

Bureau of Justice Statistics. 1994. *Prisoners in 1993*. Washington, D.C.: U.S. Department of Justice.

————. 1997. *Census of Federal and State Correctional Facilities, 1995*. Washington, D.C.: U.S. Department of Justice.

————. 1997a. *Correctional Populations in the United States, 1995*. Washington, D.C.: U.S. Department of Justice.

————. 1997b. *Criminal Victimization, 1973–95*. Washington, D.C.: U.S. Department of Justice.

————. 1997c. *Prisoners in 1996*. Washington, D.C.: U.S. Department of Justice.

————. 1997d. *Lifetime Likelihood of Going to State or Federal Prison*. Special Report NCJ-160092. Washington, D.C.: U.S. Department of Justice, Office of Justice Programs.

————. 1998a. *Prison and Jail Inmates at Midyear 1997*. Washington, D.C.: U.S. Department of Justice.

————. 1998b. *Prisoners in 1997*. BJS Bulletin NCJ 170014. Washington, D.C.: U.S. Department of Justice, Office of Justice Programs.

————. 1999a. *Prison and Jail Inmates at Midyear 1998*. Washington, D.C.: U.S. Department of Justice, Bureau of Justice Statistics.

————. 1999b. *Prisoners in 1998*. Washington, D.C.: U.S. Department of Justice, Bureau of Justice Statistics.

————. Various Years. *Correctional Populations in the United States*. Washington, D.C.: U.S. Department of Justice, Bureau of Justice Statistics.

Bureau of Labor Statistics. 1990. *Employment and Earnings* (January). Washington, D.C.: U.S. Bureau of Labor Statistics.

————. 1995. *Employment and Earnings* (January). Washington, D.C.: U.S. Bureau of Labor Statistics.

Canadian Centre for Justice Statistics, Statistics Canada. 1995. *Canadian Crime Statistics, 1994*. Ottawa: Statistics Canada.

————. 1996. *Adult Correctional Services in Canada, 1994–95*. Ottawa: Statistics Canada.

Canadian Sentencing Commission. 1987. *Sentencing Reform: A Canadian Approach*. Ottawa: Canadian Government Publishing Centre.

Caplow, Theodore, and Jonathan Simon. 1999. "Understanding Prison Policy and Population Trends." In *Prisons*, edited by Michael Tonry and Joan Petersilia. Vol. 26 of *Crime and Justice: A Review of Research*, edited by Michael Tonry. Chicago: University of Chicago Press.

Cohn, Steven Barkan, and William Halteman. 1991. "Punitive Attitudes toward Criminals: Racial Consensus or Racial Conflict?" *Social Problems* 38:287–96.

Cole, D. P. 1999. "Conditional Sentencing: Recent Developments." In *Making Sense of Sentencing*, edited by J. V. Roberts and D. P. Cole. Toronto: University of Toronto Press.

Commission on Systemic Racism in the Ontario Criminal Justice System. 1995. *Report of the Commission on Systemic Racism in the Ontario Criminal Justice System*. Toronto: Queen's Printer for Ontario.

Council of Europe. 1990. *Bulletin d'information pénologique*, no. 15 (September). Strasbourg: Council of Europe.

———. 1992. *Bulletin d'information pénologique*, no. 17 (December). Strasbourg: Council of Europe.

———. 1999. *European Sourcebook of Crime and Criminal Justice Statistics*. Strasbourg: Council of Europe.

Cullen, Francis T., Gregory A. Clark, and John F. Wozniak. 1985. "Explaining the Get-Tough Movement: Can the Public Be Blamed?" *Federal Probation* 45(2):16–24.

Cullen, Francis T., Sandra Evans Skovron, Joseph E. Scott, and Velmer S. Burton, Jr. 1990. "Public Support for Correctional Treatment." *Criminal Justice and Behavior* 17(1): 2–18.

Currie, E. 1996. *Is America Really Winning the War on Crime and Should Britain Follow Its Example?* London: National Association for Care and Resettlement of Offenders.

Death Penalty Information Center. 2000. Available online at www.deathpenaltyinfo.org/index.html. (Click on "Information Topics" and "General.")

Department of Justice. 1997. *Tackling Crime Discussion Document*. Dublin: Stationery Office.

Directie Justitiële Inrichtingen. 1997. *Feiten in Cijfers* (Facts in Numbers). Den Haag: Ministerie van Justitie.

Doob, Anthony, and Voula Marinos. 1995. "Reconceptualizing Punishment: Understanding the Limitations on the Use of Intermediate Punishments." *University of Chicago Law School Roundtable* 2:413–33.

Downes, David, and Rod Morgan. 1997. "Dumping the 'Hostages to Fortune'? The Politics of Law and Order in Post-War Britain." In *The Oxford Handbook of Criminology*, edited by M. Maguire, R. Morgan, and R. Reiner, 2d ed. (rev.). Oxford: Clarendon.

Durham, A. M. 1994. *Crisis and Reform: Current Issues in American Punishment*. Boston: Little Brown.

Edsall, Thomas, and Mary Edsall. 1991. *Chain Reaction: The Impact of Race, Rights, and Taxes on American Politics*. New York: Norton.

Federal Bureau of Investigation. 1997 [and various years]. *Crime in the United States—1996* [and various years]. Washington, D.C.: U.S. Government Printing Office.

Fichter, J. 1994. "First Experiences with Community Service in the Canton of Vaud." In *Réforme des sanctions pénales*, edited by S. Bauhofer and P. H. Bolle. Chur and Zurich, Switzerland: Rüegger.

Fiselier, J. P. S. 1985. "Regionale verscheidenheid in de strafrechtspleging." *Delikt en Delinkwent* 15: 204–21.

Flynn, M. 1997. "One Strike and You're Out." *Alternative Law Journal* 22:72–76.

Frankel, Marvin E. 1973. *Criminal Sentences: Law without Order*. New York: Hill & Wang.

Frase, Richard S. 1993. "Implementing Commission-Based Sentencing Guidelines: The Lessons of the First Ten Years in Minnesota." *Cornell Journal of Law and Public Policy* 2:279–337.

———. 2000. "Is Guided Discretion Sufficient? Overview of State Sentencing Guidelines." *St. Louis University Law Journal* 44:425–46.

Freiberg, A. 1993. "Sentencing Reform in Victoria." *Overcrowded Times* 4(4):7–9.

———. 1994. "Sentencing Reform in Victoria: A Case Study." In *The Politics of Sentencing Reform*, edited by C. Clarkson and R. Morgan. Oxford: Oxford University Press.

———. 1995. "Sentencing and Punishment in Australia" *Overcrowded Times* 6(1):1, 11–15.

———. 1997. "Sentencing and Punishment in Australia in the 1990s." In *Sentencing Reform in Overcrowded Times*, edited by Michael Tonry and Kathleen Hatlestad. New York: Oxford University Press.

———. 1998. "Prison Populations Up, Sentencing Policy Harsher in Australia." *Overcrowded Times* 9(1):1, 9–11.

———. 2001. "Three Strikes and You're Out—It's Not Cricket." In *Sentencing and Sanctions in Western Countries*, edited by Michael Tonry and Richard S. Frase. New York: Oxford University Press.

Freiberg, Arie, and Stuart Ross. 1999. *Sentencing Reform and Penal Change: The Victorian Experience*. Sydney: Federation Press.

Friedland, Martin L. 1965. *Detention before Trial: A Study of Criminal Cases Tried in the Toronto Magistrates' Courts*. Toronto: University of Toronto Press.

Garland, David. 2000. "The Culture of High Crime Societies: Some Preconditions of Recent 'Law and Order' Policies." *British Journal of Criminology* 40:347–75.

———, ed. 2001. *Mass Imprisonment in the United States: Social Causes and Consequences*. London: Sage.

Gebelein, Richard S. 1996. "SENTAC Changing Delaware Sentencing." *Overcrowded Times* 7(4):1, 9–11.

Gilliard, Darrell K., and Allen J. Beck. 1997. *Prison and Jail Inmates at Midyear 1996*. Washington, D.C.: U.S. Department of Justice, Bureau of Justice Statistics.

Gilmore, Grant. 1974. *The Death of Contract*. Columbus: Ohio State University Press.

Gorta, A. 1997. "Truth in Sentencing in New South Wales." In *Sentencing Reform in Overcrowded Times: A Comparative Perspective*, edited by Michael Tonry and Kathleen Hatlestad. New York: Oxford University Press.

Grapendaal, M., P. P. Groen, and W. van der Heide. 1997. "Duration and Volume. Development of the Non-suspended Custodial Sentence between 1985 and 1995; Facts and Statements." Research and Documentation Centre Report. The Hague: Ministry of Justice.

Greve, Vagn. 1995. "European Criminal Policy. Towards Universal Laws?" In *Towards Universal Laws—Trends in National, European and International Lawmaking*, edited by Nils Jareborg. Uppsala: Iustus.

Gurr, Ted Robert. 1981. "Historical Trends in Violent Crimes: A Critical Review of the Evidence." In *Crime and Justice: An Annual Review of Research*, vol. 3, edited by Michael Tonry and Norval Morris. Chicago: University of Chicago Press.

———. 1989. "Historical Trends in Violent Crime: England, Western Europe, and the United States." In *Violence in America: The History of Crime*, vol. 1, edited by T. R. Gurr. Newbury Park, Calif.: Sage.

Hagan, John. 1994. *Crime and Disrepute*. Thousand Oaks, Calif.: Pine Forge.

Haley, J. O. 1989. "Confession, Repentance, and Absolution." In *Mediation and Criminal Justice*, edited by Martin Wright and Burt Galaway. Newbury Park, Calif.: Sage.

Hamai, Koichi. 1999. "Prison Population in Japan Stable for Thirty Years." *Overcrowded Times* 10(1):1, 14–19.

Harding, R., ed. 1995. *Repeat Juvenile Offenders: The Failure of Selective Incapacitation in Western Australia*, 2d ed. Perth: University of Western Australia, Crime Research Centre.

Harvey, L., and K. Pease. 1987. "The Lifetime Prevalence of Custodial Sentences." *British Journal of Criminology* 27:311–15.

Her Majesty's Chief Inspector of Prisons. 1998. *Annual Report 1996–97*. London: H. M. Stationery Office.

Hogg, Russell. 1999. "Mandatory Sentencing Laws and the Symbolic Politics of Law and Order." *University of New South Wales Law Journal Forum* 5:3–5.

Home Affairs Committee. 1998. *Alternatives to Prison Sentences*. House of Commons, Session 1997–98. London: H.M. Stationery Office.

Home Office. 1990. *Crime, Justice and Protecting the Public: The Government's Proposals for Legislation*, Cm. 965. London: H.M. Stationery Office.

———. 1995. *Review of Prison Service Security in England and Wales and the Escape from Parkhurst Prison on Tuesday 3rd January 1995*, Cm. 3020. London: H. M. Stationery Office.

———. 1996. *Protecting the Public: The Government's Strategy on Crime in England and Wales*, Cm. 3190. London: H. M. Stationery Office.

———. 1998. *Revised Projections of Long-term Trends in the Prison Population to 2005*. Research and Statistics Directorate. London: Home Office.

Hough, Mike, and Julian Roberts. 1998. "English Believe Sentences Soft and Crime Rising." *Overcrowded Times* 9(1):1, 12–15.

Hunt, Kim. 1998. "Sentencing Commissions as Centers for Policy Analysis and Research." *Law and Policy* 20:465–89.

Irwin, John, and James Austin. 1994. *It's about Time: America's Imprisonment Binge*. Belmont, Calif.: Wadsworth.

Jareborg, Nils. 1995. "The Swedish Sentencing Reform." In *The Politics of Sentencing Reform*, edited by Chris Clarkson and Rod Morgan. Oxford: Clarendon.

Johnson, E. H. 1996. *Japanese Corrections: Managing Convicted Offenders in an Orderly Society*. Carbondale: Southern Illinois University Press.

Joutsen, Matti. 1989. *The Criminal Justice System of Finland: A General Introduction*. Helsinki: Finnish Ministry of Justice.

Jung, H. 1992. *Sanktionensysteme und Menschenrechte*. Bern et al.: Haupt.

Junger-Tas, J. 1996. "Youth and Violence in Europe." *Studies on Crime and Crime Prevention* 5:31–58.

———. 1998. "Dutch Penal Policies Changing Direction." *Overcrowded Times* 9(5):1, 14–20.

Justis-og politidepartement. 1998. St meld nr 27. (1997–98) "Om kriminalomsorgen" (On the Probation and Prison Service). Tilr°ading fra Justis-og politidepartementet av 23. april 1998, godkjent. Oslo, Norway, Ministry of Justice.

Kaiser, G. 1990. *Befinden sich die kriminalrechtlichen Maßregeln in der Krise?* München.

Kensey, Annie, and Pierre Tournier. 1998. "French Prison Numbers Stable Since 1988, But Populations Changing." *Overcrowded Times* 9(4):1, 10–16.

Kerner, H. J., and O. Kästner. 1986. *Gemeinnützige Arbeit in der Strafrechtspflege*. Bonn.

Kester, J. G. C., and J. Junger-Tas. 1994. *Criminaliteit en Strafrechtelijke Reactie—Ontwikkelingen en Samen-hangen*. Arnhem: Gouda Quint.

Killias, M. 1991. *Introduction to Criminology*. Berne: Stämpfli.

———. 1999. "Fighting Evils or Preventing Harm: Switzerland's Drug Policy as a Test of Situational Crime Prevention Policies?" In *The Changing Face of Crime and Criminal*

Policy in Europe, edited by Roger Hood and Nestor E. Courakis. Oxford: University of Oxford, Centre for Criminological Research.

Killias, M., M. F. Aebi, and D. Ribeaud. 2000. "Does Community Service Rehabilitate Better Than Short-term Imprisonment? Results of a Controlled Experiment." *Howard Journal of Criminal Justice* 39(1):40–57.

Killias, M., and R. Aeschbacher. 1988. "How Many Swiss Have Experienced Incarceration?" *Bulletin de criminologie* 14:3–14.

Killias, M., and C. Grandjean. 1986. "Unemployment and the Incarceration Rate: The Case of Switzerland between 1890 and 1941." *Déviance et société* 10(4):309–22.

Koza, Pamela, and Anthony N. Doob. 1975. "The Relationship of Pretrial Custody to the Outcome of a Trial." *Criminal Law Quarterly* 17:391–400.

Kuhn, André. 1987. "The Origins of Prison Overcrowding in Switzerland." *Déviance et société* 11:365–79.

———. 1993. *Punitiveness, Crime Policies, and Prison Overcrowding: Or How to Reduce Prison Populations.* Berne, Switzerland, and Stuttgart, Germany: Haupt.

———. 1997. "Prison Populations in Western Europe." In *Sentencing Reform in Overcrowded Times—A Comparative Perspective,* edited by Michael Tonry and Kathleen Hatlestad. New York: Oxford University Press.

———. 1998. "Sanctions and their Severity." In *Crime and Criminal Justice Systems in Europe and North America 1990–1994,* edited by K. Kangasunta, M. Joutsen, and N. Ollus. Helsinki: European Institute for Crime Prevention and Control (HEUNI).

Kuhn, Thomas. 1996. *The Structure of Scientific Revolutions,* 3d ed. Chicago: University of Chicago Press.

Kurki, Leena. 1999. "Incorporating Restorative and Community Justice into American Sentencing and Corrections." Washington, D.C.: National Institute of Justice.

———. 2000. "Restorative and Community Justice in the United States." In *Crime and Justice: A Review of Research,* vol. 27, edited by Michael Tonry. Chicago: University of Chicago Press.

———. 2001. "International Standards and Limits on Sentencing and Punishment." In *Sentencing and Sanctions in Western Countries,* edited by Michael Tonry and Richard S. Frase. New York: Oxford University Press.

Lambropoulou, E. 1993. "Umwandlung der Freiheitsstrafe als kriminalpolitisches Modell? Zur Diskrepanz von Verurteilungen und Inhaftierungen in Griechenland." *Monatsschrift für Kriminologie und Strafrechtsreform* 76(2):91–100.

Landreville, Pierre. 1995. "Prison Overpopulation and Strategies for Decarceration." *Canadian Journal of Criminology* 37:39–60.

Lane, Roger. 1992. "Urban Police and Crime in Nineteenth-Century America." In *Modern Policing,* edited by Michael Tonry and Norval Morris. Vol. 15 of *Crime and Justice: A Review of Research,* edited by Michael Tonry. Chicago: University of Chicago Press.

———. 1999. "Murder in America: A Historian's Perspective." In *Crime and Justice: A Review of Research,* vol. 25, edited by Michael Tonry. Chicago: University of Chicago Press.

Languin, N., C. Lucco-Denereaz, C. N. Robert, and R. Roth. 1994. *La Libération conditionnelle: risque ou chance? La pratique en 1990 dans les cantons romands.* Bâle: Helbing & Lichtenhahn.

Lappi-Seppälä, Tapio. 1994. "Alternative Penal Sanctions." In *Finnish National Reports to the Fourteenth Congress of the International Academy of Comparative Law,* edited by A. Suviranta. Helsinki: Finnish Lawyer's Publishing.

———. 1998a. *Regulating the Prison Population. Experiences from a Long-Term Policy in*

Finland. Research Communications 38/1998. Helsinki: National Research Institute of Legal Policy.

———. 1998*b*. *Official Statistics of Finland. Criminal Cases Tried by the Courts.* Series XXIII B.

———. 2001. "Sentencing and Punishment in Finland." In *Sentencing and Sanctions in Western Countries,* edited by Michael Tonry and Richard S. Frase. New York: Oxford University Press.

Larsson, Paul. 1993. "Norwegian Penal Policy in the 80's." *Chroniques* 8.

Law Reform Commission, Republic of Ireland. 1996. *Report on Sentencing.* Dublin: Law Reform Commission.

Law Reform Commission, New South Wales. 1996. *Sentencing.* Report 79. Sydney: New South Wales, Law Reform Commission

Learmont Report. 1995. *Review of Prison Service Security in England and Wales and the Escape from Parkhurst Prison on Tuesday 3rd January 1995,* Cm 3020. London: H.M. Stationery Office.

Lopes Rocha, M. A. 1987. "Évaluation critique du Code Pénal portugais." *Annales Internationales de Criminologie.*

Lynch, J. 1993. "A Cross-National Comparison of the Length of Custodial Sentences for Serious Crimes." *Justice Quarterly* 10:639–60.

Lynn, L. E. 1978. *Knowledge and Policy: The Uncertain Connections.* Washington, D.C.: National Academy of Sciences.

Maguire, Kathleen, and Ann L. Pastore, eds. 1997. *Sourcebook of Criminal Justice Statistics—1996.* Washington, D.C.: U.S. Government Printing Office.

———. 1998. *Sourcebook of Criminal Justice Statistics—1997.* Washington, D.C.: U.S. Government Printing Office.

———. 1999. *Sourcebook of Criminal Justice Statistics—1998.* Washington, D.C.: U.S. Government Printing Office.

———. 2000. *Sourcebook of Criminal Justice Statistics [Online],* table 6.36. Available at http://www.albany.edu/sourcebook [2000].

Marvell, Thomas B. 1995. "Sentencing Guidelines and Prison Population Growth." *Journal of Criminal Law and Criminology* 85:696–707.

Mauer, Marc. 1994. *Americans behind Bars: The International Use of Incarceration.* Washington, D.C.: Sentencing Project.

Mayhew, Pat, and Jan van Dijk. 1997*a. Criminal Victimisation in Eleven Industrialized Countries: Key Findings from the 1996 International Crime Victims Survey.* The Hague: Dutch Ministry of Justice.

———. 1997*b. Criminal Victimisation in the Industrialised World.* The Hague: Dutch Ministry of Justice.

McGarrell, Edmund, and Marla Sandys. 1996. "The Misperception of Public Opinion toward Capital Punishment." *American Behavioral Scientist* 39(4):500–13.

Melossi, D. 1995. "The Effects of Economic Circumstances on the Criminal Justice System." In *Crime and Economy.* Strasbourg: Council of Europe.

Ministerie van Justitie. 1996. *In Proper Proportion—Policy Intentions with Regard to Law Enforcement and Safety.* The Hague: Ministry of Justice.

Ministry of Justice. 1985. *Society and Crime: A Policy Plan for the Netherlands.* [Introduction and main chapters in English.] The Hague: Ministry of Justice.

———. 1990*a. Law in Motion.* The Hague: Ministry of Justice.

———. 1990*b. Strafrecht met beleid.* [Criminal Law and Criminal Policy, Policy Plan 1990–1995.] The Hague: Ministry of Justice.

————. 1995. *Report of the Committee on the Reconsideration of the Instruments for Law Enforcement.* The Hague: Ministry of Justice.

————. 1995a. "Continuity and Change." Governmental Memorandum. The Hague: Ministry of Justice.

————. 1996. *Een juiste verhouding.* [In Good Balance.] The Hague: Ministry of Justice.

————. 1999. Press releases. The Hague: Ministry of Justice.

Ministry of Justice, Dutch National Agency for Correctional Institutions. 1999. *Facts in Figures.* The Hague: Ministry of Justice.

Morgan, N. 1996. "Non-Custodial Sentences Under WA's New Sentencing Laws: Business as Usual or a New Utopia?" *University of Western Australia Law Review* 26(2):364–88.

Morgan, Neil, and Belinda Murray. 1999. "What's in a Name? Guideline Judgments in Australia." *Criminal Law Journal* 23:90–107.

Morgan, Rod. 1997. "Punitive Policies and Politics Crowding English Prisons." In *Sentencing Reform in Overcrowded Times,* edited by Michael Tonry and Kathleen Hatlestad. New York: Oxford University Press.

————. 1998. "Imprisonment in England and Wales: Flood Tide, But on the Turn?" *Overcrowded Times* 9(5):1, 3–5.

————. 2001. "International Standards and Controls on Sentencing and Incarceration Use." In *Sentencing and Sanctions in Western Countries,* edited by Michael Tonry and Richard S. Frase. New York: Oxford University Press.

Morris, Norval, and Michael Tonry. 1990. *Between Prison and Probation—Intermediate Punishments in a Rational Sentencing System.* New York: Oxford University Press.

Musto, David. 1987. *The American Disease: Origins of Narcotic Control,* second edition. New York: Oxford University Press.

Nagel, Ilene H., and Stephen J. Schulhofer. 1992. "A Tale of Three Cities: An Empirical Study of Charging and Bargaining Practices under the Federal Sentencing Guidelines." *Southern California Law Review* 66:501–66.

National Statistical Office. 1990–1998. *Criminal Statistics.* Rijswijk/Heerlen: National Statistical Office.

Nay, G. 1994. "Recent Developments in the Jurisprudence of the Federal Supreme Court's Criminal Law Branch." *Swiss Criminal Law Review* 112:170–93.

Newman, K. 1996. *Report of His Honour Kingsley Newman into the Kurli Murri Work Camp, Laverton, Western Australia and the Management of Young Offenders.* Perth.

New South Wales Attorney-General's Department. 1994. *Sentencing Review.* Sydney: Government of New South Wales.

NSW Bureau of Crime Statistics and Research. 1999. *Key Trends in Crime and Justice in NSW 1998.* Sydney, New South Wales.

Oelen, U. H. 1997. "Experiences of Users with the Decision Supporting System." Gröningen: University of Gröningen, Department of Law (unpublished manuscript).

OFS (Swiss Bureau of Statistics). 1985. *Swiss Prisons: "No Vacancies!"* Berne: OFS.

————. 1994a. Statistics of Corrections 1993. Berne (unpublished).

————. 1994b. *Drugs and Criminal Law in Switzerland.* Berne: OFS.

————. 1994c. *On the National Origin of Prison Inmates.* Berne: OFS.

————. 1997. *Statistics of Corrections 1996.* Berne: OFS.

Oikeustilastollinen vuosikirja. 1992–93. *Yearbook of Justice Statistics.* Helsinki: Statistics Finland.

Olaussen, Leif Petter. 1995. "Voldskriminalitetens utvikling" (Developments in Violent Crimes). *Nordisk tidsskrift for kriminalvidenskab* 2.

O'Mahony, Paul. 1993. *Crime and Punishment in Ireland.* Dublin: Round Hall Press.

————. 1996. *Criminal Chaos: Seven Crises in Irish Criminal Justice*. Dublin: Round Hall Sweet & Maxwell.

————. 1997. *Mountjoy Prisoners: A Sociological and Criminological Profile*. Dublin: Stationery Office.

O'Malley, P. 1994. "Neo-Liberal Crime Control — Political Agendas and the Future of Crime Prevention in Australia." In *The Australian Criminal Justice System — The Mid 1990s*, edited by D. Chappell and P. Wilson. Sydney: Butterworths.

O'Malley, Tom. 1996. *Sexual Offences: Law, Policy and Punishment*. Dublin: Round Hall Sweet & Maxwell.

Organisation for Economic Cooperation and Development. 1991. *Employment Outlook*. Paris: Organisation for Economic Cooperation and Development (OECD).

————. 1992. *Employment Outlook*. Paris: OECD.

————. 1993. *Employment Outlook*. Paris: OECD.

————. 1994a. *Employment Outlook*. Paris: OECD.

————. 1994b. *New Orientations for Social Policy*. Paris: OECD.

————. 1994c. *The OECD Jobs Study: Evidence and Explanation*. Paris: OECD.

Packer, Herbert L. 1968. *The Limits of the Criminal Sanction*. Palo Alto, Calif.: Stanford University Press.

Parker, H., J. Aldridge, and F. Measham. 1998. *Illegal Leisure: The Normalization of Adolescent Recreational Drug Use*. London: Routledge.

Pfeiffer, Christian. 1996. "Crisis in American Criminal Policy? Questions and Comments. A Letter to Mrs J. Reno, Attorney General of the United States of America." *European Journal of Criminal Policy and Research* 4(2):119–39.

Public Prosecution Service, the Netherlands. 1998. *Annual Report*. The Hague: Public Prosecution Service.

————. 1999. *Kader strafvorderingsrichtlijnen. Polaris Richtlijnen voor strafvordering*. Conceptversie januari 1998. The Hague: Public Prosecution Service.

Queensland Criminal Justice Commission. 1999a. *Prisoner Numbers in Queensland, Preliminary Report*. Unpublished.

————. 1999b. *Criminal Justice System Monitor*.

Reed, M., and J. V. Roberts. 1999. "Adult Correctional Services in Canada." *Juristat* 19(4).

Reitz, Kevin R. 1997. "Sentencing Guideline Systems and Sentence Appeals: A Comparison of Federal and State Experiences." *Northwestern Law Review* 91:1441–1506.

————. 2001. "The Disassembly and Reassembly of U.S. Sentencing Practices." In *Sentencing and Sanctions in Western Countries*, edited by Michael Tonry and Richard S. Frase. New York: Oxford University Press.

Research and Training Institute of the Ministry of Justice. 1997. "White Paper on Crime 1997." Tokyo, Japan: Ministry of Justice, Research and Training Institute.

Roberts, Julian V. 1992. "Public Opinion, Crime, and Criminal Justice." In *Crime and Justice: A Review of Research*, vol. 16, edited by Michael Tonry. Chicago: University of Chicago Press.

Roberts, J. V., and D. P. Cole. 1999. *Making Sense of Sentencing*. Toronto: University of Toronto Press.

Roberts, Julian, and Loretta Stalans. 1997. *Public Opinion, Crime, and Criminal Justice*. Boulder, Colo.: Westview.

Roberts, J. V., and A. von Hirsch. 1999. "Legislating the Purposes and Principles of Sentencing." In *Making Sense of Sentencing*, edited by J. V. Roberts and D. P. Cole. Toronto: University of Toronto Press.

Roethof Committee. 1984. *Interim rapport van de Commissie kleine criminaliteit*. Staatsuitgeverij 's-Gravenhage (in Dutch).

————. 1986. *Eindrapport Commissie kleine criminaliteit.* Staatsuitgeverij 's-Gravenhage (in Dutch).

Sasson, Theodore. 1995. *Crime Talk: How Citizens Construct a Social Problem.* New York: Aldine de Gruyter.

Schöch, H. 1992. *Empfehlen sich Änderungen und Erg"nzungen bei den strafrechtlichen Sanktionen ohne Freiheit-sentzug?* Gutachten C zum 59. *Deutschen Juristentag,* Hannover 1992. München: Beck.

Schurer, G., and H. J. Vreeling. 1995. Evaluation Polaris Team. "The Guidelines Looked at Critically." Unpublished paper. Leeuwarden: Netherlands Public Prosecution Service.

Scott, Robert E., and William J. Stuntz. 1992. "Plea Bargaining as Contract." *Yale Law Journal* 101:1909–68.

Smith, Michael E., and Walter Dickey. 1999. "Reforming Sentencing and Corrections for Just Punishment and Public Safety." Washington, D.C.: National Institute of Justice.

South Australia Criminal Law and Penal Methods Reform Committee (Mitchell Committee). 1973. *First Report: Sentencing and Corrections.* Adelaide: Government Printer.

Spaan, E. C. 1995. *Werken of Zitten—De toepassing van werkstraffen en korte vrijheidsstraffen in 1992.* Arnhem: Gouda Quint.

Spaan, E., and C. Verwers. 1997. "Electronisch toezicht in Nederland." [Electronic Monitoring in the Netherlands.] Serie Onderzoek en Beleid, no. 164. The Hague: Ministry of Justice, Research and Documentation Center.

Sparks, Richard, Anthony Bottoms, and Will Hay. 1996. *Prisons and the Problem of Order.* Oxford: Clarendon.

Spigelman, Jim. 1999. *Sentencing Guideline Judgments.* Unpublished paper, New South Wales Court of Criminal Appeal, June 24.

State Audit Committee. 1997. *Heenzending en tenuitvoerlegging van straffen, Hansard 1997–1998, no. 25630.* The Hague: Ministry of Justice, Research and Documentation Center.

Steenhuis, D. W. 1986. "Policy Formulation by the Public Prosecution Service for Custodial Sentences." *Custodial Sentence.* Arnhem: Gouda Quint.

————. 1997. "Nieuwe richtlijnen stap naar rechtsgelijkheid." [New Prosecutorial Sentencing Guidelines in the Fight Against Sentencing Disparity.] *Opportuun* 4(3):3–6.

Steering Committee for the Review of Commonwealth/State Service Provision. 1998. *Report on Government Services,* vol. 1. Canberra.

Steinmann, P. L. M., F. F. van Tulder, and W. van der Heide. 1999. *Prognose van de Sanctiecapaciteit 1999–2003.* WODC no. 181. The Hague: Ministry of Justice.

Stith, Kate, and José A. Cabranes. 1998. *Fear of Judging: Sentencing Guidelines in the Federal Courts.* Chicago: University of Chicago Press.

Tait, D. 1995. "The Invisible Sanction: Suspended Sentences in Victoria 1985–1991." *Australian and New Zealand Journal of Criminology* 28:143–161.

Tak, Peter J. P. 1997. "Sentencing and Punishment in the Netherlands," and "Netherlands Successfully Implements Community Service Orders." In *Sentencing Reform in Overcrowded Times,* edited by Michael Tonry and Kathleen Hatlestad. New York: Oxford.

————. 2001. "Sentencing and Punishment in the Netherlands." In *Sentencing and Sanctions in Western Countries,* edited by Michael Tonry and Richard S. Frase. New York: Oxford University Press.

Tonry, Michael. 1993. "The Success of Judge Frankel's Sentencing Commission." *University of Colorado Law Review* 64:713–22.

————. 1995. *Malign Neglect—Race, Crime, and Punishment in America.* New York: Oxford University Press.

————. 1996. *Sentencing Matters.* New York: Oxford University Press.

————. 1998. "Intermediate Sanctions in Sentencing Guidelines." In *Crime and Justice: A Review of Research*, vol. 23, edited by Michael Tonry. Chicago: University of Chicago Press.

————. 1999a. "Reconsidering Indeterminate and Structured Sentencing." Washington, D.C.: National Institute of Justice.

————. 1999b. "Why Are U.S. Incarceration Rates So High?" *Crime and Delinquency* 45(4):419–37.

————. 1999c. "Rethinking Unthinkable Punishment Policies in America." *UCLA Law Review* 46:1751–91.

————. 1999d. "Parochialism in U.S. Sentencing Policy." *Crime and Delinquency* 45(1): 48–65.

————, ed. 1997. *Ethnicity, Crime, and Immigration—Comparative and Cross-national Perspectives*, vol. 21 of *Crime and Justice: A Review of Research*, edited by Michael Tonry. Chicago: University of Chicago Press.

Törnudd, Patrik. 1993. *Fifteen Years of Decreasing Prisoner Rates in Finland*. Research Communication 8/1993. Helsinki: National Research Institute of Legal Policy.

————. 1996. *Facts, Values and Visions. Essays in Criminology and Crime Policy*. Research reports 138/1996. Helsinki: National Research Institute of Legal Policy.

————. 1997. "Sentencing and Punishment in Finland." In *Sentencing Reform in Overcrowded Times: A Comparative Perspective*, edited by M. Tonry and K. Hatlestad. New York: Oxford University Press.

Träskman, Per-Ole. 1997. " 'Corpus juris'—Ett frestande eller ett främmande förslag till en enhetlig europeiska rättsfär?" *Nordisk Tidsskrift for Kriminal-videnskab* 1997:262–77.

Tubex, H., and S. Snacken. 1995. "L'évolution des longues peines: Aperçu international et analyse des causes." *Déviance et Société* 19(2):103–26.

Tyler, Tom R. 1990. *Why People Obey the Law: Procedural Justice, Legitimacy, and Compliance*. New Haven, Conn.: Yale University Press.

Tyler, Tom R., and Robert J. Boeckmann. 1997. "Three Strikes and You Are Out, But Why? The Psychology of Public Support for Punishing Rule Breakers." *Law and Society Review* 31(2):237–65.

van der Laan, P. H., and A. A. M. Essers. 1990. *De Kwartaalcursus en Recidive—Een onderzoek naar de effecten van het experiment Kwartaalcursus*. Arnhem: Gouda Quint.

van Ruller, S., and W. M. E. H. Beijers. 1995. "Trends in Detentie—Twee eeuwen gevangenisstatistiek." Justitiële Verkenningen 21(6):35–53.

von Hirsch, A., A. Ashworth, A. Wasik, A. Smith, R. Morgan, and J. Gardner. 1995. "Overtaking on the Right"? *New Law Journal*, October 13.

von Hirsch, Andrew, Anthony Bottoms, Elisabeth Burney, and Per-Olof Wikström. 1999. *Criminal Deterrence and Sentence Severity*. Oxford, England: Hart.

von Witzleben, T. 1994. "Intermediate Findings of the Evaluation of the Community Service Pilot Project in the Canton of Berne." In *Réforme des sanctions pénales*, edited by S. Bauhofer and P. H. Bolle. Chur and Zurich, Switzerland: Rüegger.

Wacquant, Löic. 2001. "Deadly Symbiosis: When Ghetto and Prison Meet and Merge." *Punishment and Society* 3:95–133.

Walker, J. 1994. "Trends in Crime and Justice." In *The Australian Criminal Justice System: The Mid 1990s*, edited by D. Chappell and P. Wilson. Sydney: Butterworths.

Walker, Samuel. 1998. *Popular Justice: A History of American Criminal Justice*, rev. ed. New York: Oxford University Press.

Weigend, Thomas. 1997. "Germany Reduces Use of Prison Sentences." In *Sentencing Reform in Overcrowded Times*, edited by Michael Tonry and Kathleen Hatlestad. New York: Oxford.

————. 2001. "Sentencing Policy in Germany." In *Sentencing and Sanctions in Western Countries*, edited by Michael Tonry and Richard S. Frase. New York: Oxford University Press.

Wijn, N. 1997. *Taakstraffen, stand van zaken, praktijk en resultaten*. [Community Sentences, Present State of Affairs, Practices, and Results.] The Hague: Ministry of Justice.

Wilson, James Q., and Richard Herrnstein. 1985. *Crime and Human Nature*. New York: Simon & Schuster.

Windlesham, Lord. 1998. *Politics, Punishment, and Populism*. New York: Oxford University Press.

Wisconsin Governor's Task Force on Sentencing and Corrections. 1996. "Final Report." *Overcrowded Times* 7(6):5–17.

Woolf Report. 1991. *Prison Disturbances April 1990: Report of an Inquiry by the Rt. Hon. Lord Woolf (Parts I and II) and His Honour Judge Stephen Tumin (Part II)*, Cm. 1456. London: H.M. Stationery Office.

Wright, Ronald F. 1998. "Flexibility in North Carolina Structured Sentencing, 1995–1997." *Overcrowded Times* 9(6):1, 11–15.

Young, W., and M. Brown. 1993. "Cross-national Comparisons of Imprisonment." In *Crime and Justice: A Review of Research*, vol. 17, edited by Michael Tonry. Chicago: University of Chicago Press.

Zdenkowski, G. 1994. "Contemporary Sentencing Issues." In *The Australian Criminal Justice System: The Mid 1990s*, edited by D. Chappell and P. Wilson. Sydney: Butterworths.

Zimring, Franklin E., and Gordin Hawkins. 1993. *The Scale of Imprisonment*. Chicago: University of Chicago Press.

————. 1997. *Crime Is Not the Problem: Lethal Violence in America*. New York: Oxford University Press.

Zimring, Franklin E., Gordon Hawkins, and Sam Kamin. 2000. *Punishment and Democracy: Three Strikes and You're Out in California*. New York: Oxford University Press.

Acknowledgments

All of the articles in this collection, except for the general and chapter introductions, were orginally published in the journal *Overcrowded Times* in the issues listed below.

Marcelo F. Aebi: "Sentencing in Switzerland in 2000" (December 1999)

Hans-Jörg Albrecht: "Sentencing and Punishment in Germany" (February 1995)

Andrew Ashworth: "New Sentencing Laws Take Effect in England" (October 1992); "English Sentencing: From Enlightenment to Darkness in a Decade" (October 1999)

Katherine Beckett: "Political Preoccupation with Crime Leads, Not Follows, Public Opinion" (October 1997); "The Penal System as Labor Market Institution: Jobs and Jails, 1980–1995" (December 1997)

Anthony N. Doob: "Imprisonment Rates in Canada: One Law, 10 Outcomes" (August 1998)

Arie Freiberg: "Sentencing and Punishment in Australia in the 1990s" (February 1995); "Prison Populations Up, Sentencing Policy Harsher in Australia" (February 1998); "Understanding Rising Prison Populations in Australia" (October 1999)

Koichi Hamai: "Prison Population in Japan Stable for 30 Years" (February 1999)

Michael Hough: "English Believe Sentences Soft and Crime Rising" (February 1998)

Nils Jareborg: "Sentencing Law, Policy, and Patterns in Sweden" (October 1999)

Josine Junger-Tas: "Dutch Penal Policies Changing Direction" (October 1998)

Cynthia Kempinen: "Pennsylvania Revises Sentencing Guidelines" (August 1997)

Annie Kensey: "French Prison Numbers Stable since 1988, but Populations Changing" (August 1998)

Martin Killias: "Sentencing in Switzerland in 2000" (December 1999)

André Kuhn: "Incarceration Rates across the World" (April 1999); "Sentencing in Switzerland in 2000" (December 1999)

Britta Kyvsgaard: "Penal Sanctions and the Use of Imprisonment in Denmark" (December 1998)

Tapio Lappi-Seppälä: "Recent Trends in Finnish Sentencing Policy" (October 1999)

Paul Larsson: "Norway Prison Use Up Slightly, Community Penalties Lots" (February 1999)

Robin L. Lubitz: "Sentencing Changes in North Carolina" (June 1996)

Rod Morgan: "English Penal Policies and Prisons: Going for Broke" (December 1996); "Imprisonment in England and Wales: Flood Tide, but on the Turn?" (October 1998)

Ian O'Donnell: "Sentencing and Punishment in Ireland" (October 1997)

Fritz Rauschenberg: "Ohio Guidelines Take Effect" (August 1997)

Kevin R. Reitz: "The Status of Sentencing Guideline Reforms in the United States" (December 1999)

Julian V. Roberts: "English Believe Sentences Soft and Crime Rising" (February 1998); "Reforming Sentencing and Parole in Canada" (August 1999)

Simone Rônez: "Sentencing in Switzerland in 2000" (December 1999)

Gerrit Schurer: "The Netherlands Adopts Numerical Prosecution Guidelines" (June 1999)

Jane B. Sprott: "Imprisonment Rates in Canada: One Law, 10 Outcomes" (August 1998)

Peter J. P. Tak: "Sentencing and Punishment in the Netherlands" (October 1994);

"Prison Population Growing Faster in the Netherlands than in the United States" (June 1998); "New Sanctions Proliferating in the Netherlands" (December 1999)

Michael Tonry: "Why Are U.S. Incarceration Rates So High" (June 1999); "U.S. Sentencing Systems Fragmenting" (August 1999)

Patrik Törnudd: "Sentencing and Punishment in Finland" (December 1994)

Pierre Tournier: "French Prison Numbers Stable since 1988, but Populations Changing" (August 1998)

Anton M. van Kalmthout: "Prison Population Growing Faster in the Netherlands than in the United States" (June 1998); "New Sanctions Proliferating in the Netherlands" (December 1999)

Reinier van Loon: "The Netherlands Adopts Numerical Prosecution Guidelines" (June 1999)

Richard D. Van Wagenen: "Washington State Sentencing Changes, 1994–1997" (December 1997)

Bruce Western: "The Penal System as Labor Market Institution: Jobs and Jails, 1980–1995" (December 1997)

Ronald F. Wright: "North Carolina Prepares for Guidelines Sentencing" (February 1994); "Flexibility in North Carolina Structured Sentencing, 1995–1997" (December 1998)